SEIZE
THE
TIME

SEIZE
THE
TIME

The Story of the
Black Panther Party and
Huey P. Newton

BOBBY
SEALE

Random House  New York

Library of Congress Catalog Card Number: 74–115816

Manufactured in the United States of America

9 8 7 6 5 4 3 2

CONTENTS

THE PARTY GROWS, ELDRIDGE JOINS

PICKING UP THE GUN

THE SHIT COMES DOWN: "FREE HUEY!"

SEIZE THE TIME

FOREWORD

■ There are a lot of misconceptions about the Black Panther Party. I wanted to write this book so people could have better insight into the inner workings of the Party, so that people would have a more true understanding of the Black Panther Party—what it really does, the kind of people who are in it, their everyday lives, the things that have happened to the Party.

Many things about us that appear in the mass media are distortions. In addition, the demagogic politicians have lied about the Party and have lied about who the real enemy is. But here are the facts—a picture of what the Black Panther Party really is and how it operates. This book shows the chronological development of our Party and how it grew out of the social evils of an unjust, oppressive system. It also shows that repression is a natural product of this wealthy, technological society, owned and controlled by a small minority of the people.

Marx and Lenin would probably turn over in their graves if they could see lumpen proletarian Afro-Americans putting together the ideology of the Black Panther Party. Both Marx and Lenin used to say that the lumpen proletariat wouldn't do anything for the revolution. But today, in a modern, highly technological society, with its CIA, FBI, electronic surveillance, and cops armed and equipped for overkill, here are black Americans *demanding* our constitutional rights, and *demanding* that our basic desires and needs be fulfilled, thus becoming the vanguard of a revolution, despite all attempts to totally wipe us out.

We're not the vanguard because we wanted to be, but because it was given to us through the blood and death of our members, and because nearly 100 of us are political prisoners at present. So I see this book as the work of our leader and Minister of Defense, Huey P. Newton, and of Alprentice "Bunchy" Carter, Bobby Hutton, John Huggins, Fred Hampton, Mark Clark, and all of our brothers who have been murdered; and of political prisoners like Erica Huggins, Langdon Williams, Rory Hithe, the Panther 21 in New York, and the Panther 14 in Connecticut; of political exiles like Eldridge and Kathleen Cleaver; and all the dedicated Black Panther Party members functioning throughout the country.

The life and existence of the Black Panther Party, the ideology of the Party in motion, is a biography of oppressed America, black and white, that no news report, TV documentary, book, or magazine has yet expressed. To do so, the media would let the people know what's *really* going on, how things have happened, and how we're struggling for our freedom. So before the power structure, through its pigs, attempts to murder any more of us, or take more political prisoners in its age-old attempt to keep us "niggers," as they like to say, "in our place," I have put together the true story of the Black Panther Party.

I dedicate this book to my wife, Artie, to Erica, the widow of John Huggins, to my son, Malik Nkrumah Stagolee Seale, and his brother. One of my son's names derives from the lumpen proletarian politically unaware brothers in the streets. Stagolee fought his brothers and sisters, and he shouldn't have. The Stagolees of today should take on the messages of Malcolm X as Huey Newton did, to oppose this racist, capitalist oppression our people and other peoples are subjected to.

Malik must not fight his brothers. One is named after revolutionaries of our times, and me, who loves both of them. Power to the youth; all power to the people, and power to the latest born in the Black Panther Party, little Huey Bunchy (Li'l) Bobby John Eric Eldridge Seale, whose mother is Rose Mary. Brothers and sisters will struggle together in unity from generation to generation for liberation and freedom with the love of we fathers and mothers who brought our young ones into the world.

We dedicate this book to all the youth of America, from Huey, the Central Committee, and all the dedicated members of the Black Panther Party.

Bobby Seale
Chairman, Black Panther Party
led by the Minister of Defense,
Huey P. Newton

San Francisco County Jail
1969–1970

Huey P. Newton, Minister of Defense of the Black Panther Party, the baddest motherfucker ever to set foot in history. Huey P. Newton, the brother, black man, a nigger, the descendant of slaves, who stood up in the heart of the ghetto, at night, in alleys, confronted by racist pigs with guns and said: "My name is Huey P. Newton. I'm the Minister of Defense of the Black Panther Party. I'm standing on my constitutional rights. I'm not going to allow you to brutalize me. I'm going to stop you from brutalizing my people. You got your gun, pig, I got mine. If you shoot at me, I'm shooting back."

GROWING UP: BEFORE THE PARTY

WHO I AM

■ When Malcolm X was killed in 1965, I ran down the street. I went to my mother's house, and I got six loose red bricks from the garden. I got to the corner, and broke the motherfuckers in half. I wanted to have the most shots that I could have, this very same day Malcolm was killed. Every time I saw a paddy roll by in a car, I picked up one of the half-bricks, and threw it at the motherfuckers. I threw about half the bricks, and then I cried like a baby. I was righteously crying. I was pissed off and mad. Every paddy I'd see, whop! I'd throw a brick, and it would hit the cars, and zoom! They're driving down the street, and I'm throwing bricks for a motherfucker. I thought that was all I could do. I was ready to die that day.

Kenny Freeman and the rest of the cultural nationalists came down there to get me, and I told them to leave me alone. I said, "Get away. You niggers are crazy." I got mad, and I busted a window in the house. I put my fist through a window. I told them all, "Fuck it, I'll make my own self into a motherfucking Malcolm X, and if they want to kill me, they'll have to kill me." That was a big change with me. They never understood that.

Eldridge says Malcolm X had an impact on everybody like that, and Malcolm X had that impact on me.

. . .

When my wife Artie had a baby boy, I said, "The nigger's name is Malik Nkrumah Stagolee Seale."

"I don't want him named that!" Artie said.

I had read all that book history about Stagolee, that black folkloric history, because I was hung up on that stuff at the time, so I said, "Malik Nkrumah *Stagolee* Seale!"

"Why Stagolee?" Artie asked.

"Because Stagolee was a bad nigger off the block and didn't take shit from nobody. All you had to do was organize him, like Malcolm X, make him politically conscious. All we have to do is organize a state, like Nkrumah attempted to do."

Nkrumah was a bad motherfucker and Malcolm X was a bad nigger. Huey P. Newton showed me the nigger on the block was ten motherfuckers when politically educated, and if you got him organized. I said, "Stagolee, put Stagolee on his name," because Stagolee was an unorganized nigger, to me, like a brother on the block. I related to Huey P. Newton because Huey was fighting niggers on the block. Huey was a nigger that came along and he incorporated Malcolm X, he incorporated Stagolee, he incorporated Nkrumah, all of them.

"The nigger out of prison *knows,*" Huey used to say. "The nigger out of prison has seen the man naked and cold, and the nigger out of prison, if he's got himself together, will come out just like Malcolm X came out of prison. You never have to worry about him. He'll go with you." That's what Huey related to, and I said, "Malik for Malcolm,* Nkrumah Stagolee Seale."

I was born in Dallas, Texas, October 22, 1936. I grew up with a brother, a sister, and a cousin who lived with us named Alvin Turner. He was the son of my mother's identical twin. Off and on, I learned things like everybody else learned things. I'm no different from other people growing up and living and learning. I was raised up like the average

---

* Malcolm's Muslim name was El Hajj Malik Shabazz.

black man, like a brother in the black community. A lot of things affected me in a way that caused me to see things. Huey was most significant, but a lot of things in the past affected me before Huey molded my attitude—unjust things that happened.

The farthest back I can remember is when I was unjustly whopped by my father—I can never forget that. My father and mother were having an argument. I was supposed to be washing some shirt in the back yard of a house we had in San Antonio. I was the oldest of three children, and was about six years old. I remember very vividly that I was playing in the back, and how my father told me to get the wash basin, put some water in it, and wash his shirt. I tried to wash his shirt, but then I guess I started playing. He was arguing with my mother, and it had something to do with that shirt. My father came outside and was mad at me because I hadn't finished the shirt; he took his belt off and really beat me. He went back inside the house and argued again with my mother. I was crying. When he came back and beat me again, my mother came out and stopped him and snatched the strap away, but he got it back from her and argued with her. Then he pushed her and beat me again. He told me to wash that shirt. I never forgot that beating. I never have, because it was an unjust beating. The argument he was having with my mother was directly related to him taking it out on me, and it wasn't right.

My father was a carpenter in Port Arthur, Texas. My mother had left him a couple of times, and one time when they got back together he built a house up from the ground. My father was a master carpenter. That's where I learned my carpentry work. I learned drafting in school, but I knew basic building structure from being around my father. He taught it to me and my brother off and on while we were growing up.

I grew up just like any other brother. We didn't always have money. During the war we had a little money, but after my father built the house he went to San Antonio, and then we were back in poverty again. It was still wartime and there was some money around, but I remember that whenever my mother and father rented a house, they would rent half out to some other people, a whole family.

I think the first time I really began to oppose things that I saw was when we were at Cordonices Village, the government housing project in Berkeley. People were living in poverty and semi-poverty. We lived in very crowded conditions with my mother's twin sister and her son. The place was always dirty. My mother always tried to save money, but the money was used up every time my father was laid off. (He wasn't able to get in the union at that time. Later, he and three other guys were the only black cats in the carpenter's union in all of California.)

We lived in poverty mostly because of my father's eighth-grade education. His father used to be rough on him. My father was a lot rougher on me in certain periods of my life, just like his father was rough on him. His father used to beat him, and one day my father left and wouldn't work for his father any more. I pulled the same thing. One day I stopped and I wouldn't work for my father any more because he wouldn't pay me. At that time I didn't know what the word *exploitation* meant, but that's exactly what it was, and I rejected it and opposed it.

My mother never really had any money. When I was thirteen, I used to make money on my own, hauling groceries and cutting lawns. It wasn't always profitable, but sometimes I could make a dollar or two here and there, me and a couple of brothers I used to run around with. I ran around with a couple of gangs in my younger days, when I was fourteen, fifteen, and sixteen.

Another cousin, who was already grown during World War II, came to stay with us in Port Arthur, Texas, and that's when I first really learned about sex.

Through a knothole I saw my cousin making love with his wife. My sister and brother and me were all together in this little closet. There was no inner wall section to the inside of the closet, and we just happened to be in there playing one day, while he was making love with his wife. He was in the army, and he was getting ready to go to war. We saw them through the hole. That was my first understanding of sex. We called sex "peeping," because we were peeping through a hole. My mother didn't know what was going on, but she said, "What are y'all peeping at in there?" That's where we got the term from. During the war, when my cousin got home on leave, we knew he and his wife were going to be peeping.

By the time I turned sixteen, I was more opposed to society and the injustices and bad things in it, but I wasn't very articulate about it. In learning history, I picked up on things that had been done wrong—and I began to find out about the American Indian, how rotten he'd been treated, when I met Steve Brumfield. He was about a month younger than I am and he's dead now. He killed himself, they say. We were opposed to the white man for taking the land away from the Indians, and we identified with the Indians because our parents had Indian in them. We didn't know about Africa yet.

It was very easy for me to identify with Africa when I got to Merritt College. I had gotten rid of the stereotyped notion of American Indians when I was sixteen years old, so when the Afro-American Association started talking about identifying, it was easy for me to grasp it and get rid of the Tarzan notion of Africa.

Before I went to college, when I was in the service, I wasn't aware of civil rights; I'd been hearing about civil rights through the papers but not focusing in on it that much. I was personally more concerned then with getting some kind of education. I'd go to the library and read a lot, but at the same time, I was trying to get some clothes, and I bought a set of encyclopedias. I had also begun to play drums. I'd gotten myself a $600 set of drums, which I was also making payments on. I made a mistake in overloading myself, and I got behind three payments on the drums.

I'd bought the drums in Oakland, and they sent a collection agency out after I had missed two payments. At the time, in 1958, I was at Ellsworth Air Force Base, in South Dakota, and they went all the way up there to collect. Colonel King, the commanding officer of the squadron, happened to be related to the people who owned the collection agency, and he was threatening to put me in jail if I didn't pay my bills. I had run around the base for four months trying to get one of the staff sergeants to co-sign for me, to get an allotment that would be automatically taken out of my pay, so I could pay off the bill. I wanted to keep my drums because I was engrossed in being a righteous jazz drummer. It was an outlet, because you couldn't go anywhere, except for the few times we got to go to one of the faraway cities to find a woman or a girl friend. In the afternoon, I would go with these other cats who were musicians and we had a righteous group. We practiced and rehearsed, went to a movie or the service club, got a hamburger, came back, and went to bed.

One day Colonel King called me in his office and told me for about the fifth time that he was going to put me in jail if I didn't pay my bill. By that time I was run down and I wanted my drums, so I told him, "Colonel King, I'm trying to get the stuff paid off now. I'm doing everything I know how." He told me to get my ass out of the office and pay the damn bills off.

That night I went downtown and played a gig, and I got my $15. Another cat came around with a pint of whiskey, and I was so pissed off and depressed about the whole situation that I got kind of high. I was supposed to be back at the base by 12:00 but when I got there it was 12:30 and the sergeant was waiting. He said he was going to have to report me, and then he left. That pissed me off, and depressed me more.

One of the cats came in and got me to repair something —I was a sheet-metal mechanic—and then he came back again, with another piece which I couldn't repair because I didn't have the right kind of extrusions. I tried to fuck around and modify it. He was in such a hurry, he came back in cussing at me.

I said, "Motherfucker, don't be cussing at me. Get your motherfucking ass out of here." I was mad and pissed off, and I didn't want anybody messing with me, so he left. Then I got a call on the bitch box and the guy said, "Hey, Seale, what do you mean you're not going to repair this part for this guy over here." The cat had gone all the way over to the dispatch office a block away. I said, "I told the mother-fucker I couldn't repair the thing because I couldn't find the right kind of extrusion. I'm trying to modify the damn thing, and he's just going to have to wait, and stop rushing me, and not be coming over here cussing me."

"Who in the hell do you think you're cussing," the dis-patcher said. "You'll get court-martialed for this boy, you know that?"

I said, "Fuck you, sons-of-bitches," and I just ripped the bitch box out of the wall. Then the phone rang. And I grabbed the phone and just ripped the phone out of the wall. I walked outside into the little office and I saw my tool box, which reminded me that these motherfuckers were trying to charge me for some tools that some punk had stolen out of my box, and I threw the tool box across the room. Then I took the table and turned it over, and I went back into the office and turned over one of the desks.

My partner Rabbit came in, saw what was happening, and knocked me out. He actually knocked me out. He was a partner and he was really trying to help me. He saw I was pissed off and he knocked me out, got me into a truck, and took me to the barracks. When I came to, I walked all around the barracks drinking wine and I wound up in another barracks passed out.

The next morning, Rabbit came in, woke me up, and told me Colonel King wanted to see me. I had already made up my mind that I was going to jail. So when I went in the office, I didn't even salute the bastard, and I thought to myself, "He thinks he's a white god or something."

"You ain't paid those bills yet, huh?" he said, and I just looked at him. "Well, you better pay them goddam bills." He picked up this little steel model plane from his desk and was waving that thing in my face and talking about putting me in jail. When he said he'd put my ass in jail, I blew up and grabbed that model plane. The sergeant walked up behind me, jacked me up, got his arm around my neck, pulled me back, and threw me off balance. Another one came up and got my right arm, and they dragged me outside and pushed me up against the wall. I said, "Let me alone, and tell Colonel King to let me alone. If you're going to take the drums, take the drums. You don't have to put me in jail. He's trying to get the money for them just because he's working with the monkeys downtown."

At that point, they just stepped back and let me go. The sergeant said, "You'd better go on in there and tell him that. But you better be cool." I went back and sat down in a chair and I was just looking at him. I was a distance away from him. He was looking up at me and was writing something up on me, I could see that.

"This bastard," I said to myself. "Now why in the hell should I sit here and let him mess over me." The sergeant and the other cat had seen me sitting down and had gone in the back, so I just got up and walked right on out of the office.

I went over to the barracks and I said to myself, "I might as well leave this motherfucker. There's no reason for staying here. I ain't ever been AWOL but they can call it whatever they want to call it. I've been in this damn thing here three years and four months and I'm getting fucked over again. Later for them." So I proceeded to put on my civilian clothes. The next thing I knew, they had twenty-eight policemen over there grabbing me and handcuffing me.

I cussed Colonel King out for what he was. I cussed him all the way down the streets. I had a whole big crowd of cats jiving and watching me cuss him out while they were taking me down in front of the barracks and all the way back across the lawn in front of the squadron headquarters. They put me in a truck and I was still cussing him. I cussed him all the way across. Then I blotted them all out, I just forgot about them. And they put me in jail.

I wouldn't talk to any of them, I wouldn't say anything to anybody. So they said they were going to send me to a psychiatrist. They thought I was crazy. They fooled around for two and a half months and court-martialed me.

King told me he was giving me my discharge, a bad conduct discharge, and he said to me, "You're not going to be able to get a job when you get out of here, Seale."

"What the hell makes you think there were any jobs out there before I come here?" I said, and I laughed at him.

"Well," he said, "you've got five minutes to get off this base."

"What are you going to do with the other four minutes and fifty-nine seconds?" I said, " 'cause it won't take me any time to get away from here."

Because the colonel pulled that work thing on me, I decided not to let it impress me. I worked in every major aircraft plant and aircraft corporation, even those with government contracts. I was a top-flight sheet-metal mechanic. They would fire me after two months, when they found out about the bad conduct discharge. Places would hire me right away because they needed me, but two months or so later they'd find out.

I worked at Kaiser Aerospace Electronics near Oakland for six months. They ran my papers through and came back and said that I'd lied on my discharge. "If I'd told you the truth, I wouldn't have had a job," I said. "Anyway, I'm doing your work. If you want to fire me, fire me. If you don't want to fire me, forget it and I'll do the work." They needed somebody on the night shift out there and I knew the whole operation so the engineer decided to quash it and he left me alone. This was on the Gemini missile project. I was doing non-destructive testing. It involves testing for microscopic cracks in metals by a complicated chemical and magnetic process. It's a neat trade to learn and I learned it clean. I quit that job fifteen months later, because the war was going on and I felt I was aiding the government's operation.

I wanted to go to Africa by that time. I was out with the government then and I had become very hip. When I was working at night, I was going to Merritt College in the day. When I was working in the day, I was going to Merritt at night. When jobs got scarce in 1959–1960 because of the steel strike, I did some drafting work. I could read a blueprint sideways, any kind of precision blueprint.

I wanted to be an engineer when I went to college, but I got shifted right away since I became interested in American Black History and trying to solve some of the problems. During the court-martial they asked me what I thought about the civil rights movement. I hadn't known the significance of their question, but I was stupid and I had read something about the communists and I said, "Well, the communists are leading it, ain't they?" It's funny the way people learn things, and things affect a person.

All of 1959 and half of 1960 I was in Los Angeles. In 1960, I worked as a comedian off and on when I first went to Merritt College. I dropped out for one semester, but I went back in January of 1961 and I met Huey in September of 1962. That year I worked as a comedian in two or three clubs around Oakland and at private parties. I think a comedians know a hell of a lot. They know a lot of things that are oppressive and wrong.

I think that when I met Huey P. Newton, the experience of things I'd seen in the black community—killings that I'd witnessed, black people killing each other—and my own experience, just living, trying to make it, trying to do things, came to the surface. It came to the surface when I met Huey Newton at Merritt College. The last eight years I've been in the struggle in one form or another.

I MEET HUEY

■ Brother Huey P. Newton put the Black Panther Party into motion. Brother Huey is the Minister of Defense and leader of the Black Panther Party. He is presently a political prisoner, but he is still the philosophical theoretician, the practicioner, the head director, and top official spokesman for the Black Panther Party. It is impossible to talk about the Black Panther Party without first talking about Huey P. Newton, because brother Huey put it all into motion. We sometimes talk about "the genius of Huey P. Newton."

I met Huey P. Newton in the early Sixties, during the Cuban blockade when there were numerous street rallies going on around Merritt Junior College in West Oakland. One particular day there was a lot of discussion about black people and the blockade against Cuba. People were out in front of the college, in the streets, grouped up in bunches of 200, 250, what have you. Huey was holding down a crowd of about 250 people and I was one of the participants. After he held the conversation down to what in those days they called "shooting everybody down"—that means rapping off information and throwing facts—people would ask Huey a question or refer to something he said. They tried to shoot Huey down by citing some passage in a book concerning the subject matter being discussed, and before they knew it, Huey whipped out a copy of *Black Bourgeoisie* by E. Franklin Frazier and showed him what page, what paragraph, and corrected the person.

I guess I had the idea that I was supposed to ask questions in college, so I walked over to Huey and asked the brother, weren't all these civil rights laws the NAACP was trying to get for us doing us some good? And he shot me down too, just like he shot a whole lot of other people

down. He said, it's all a waste of money, black people don't
have anything in this country that is for them. He went on
to say that the laws already on the books weren't even
serving them in the first place, and what's the use of making
more laws when what was needed was to enforce the present
laws? So all the money that the people were giving to
Martin Luther King and the rest who were supposed to put
these laws on the books for black people, was a waste of the
black people's money. I was ready to accept that when he
started citing many more facts to back up his point of view.

Huey always brings out basic, practical things; that's the
way he talks to you, that's the way he explains things to
you. He gets to a point where you can't get around, so you
have to face things.

That's the kind of atmosphere I met Huey in. And all the
conflicts of this meeting, all this blowing that was going on
in the streets that day during the Cuban crisis, all of that
was involved with his association with the Afro-American
Association. A lot of arguments came down. A lot of people
were discussing with three or four cats in the Afro-American Association, which was developing the first black nationalist philosophy on the West Coast.

They got me caught up. They made me feel that I had to
help out, be a part and do something, to help out some way.
One or two days later I went around looking for Huey at the
school, and I went to the library. I found Huey in the
library, and I asked him where the meetings were. He gave
me an address and told me that there were book discussions.
And then he told me the name of the book they were
discussing at the time, which was *Black Bourgeoisie*.

Huey was a large influence on the whole campus. I got to
know where Huey was on campus. I wasn't a running partner of Huey's then, but I was catching him on the streets.
We would all wig out behind brother Huey, and I guess
everybody respected Huey's mind and also Huey's guts. He
had something about him, that he didn't drive over people,
but he would never let anyone drive over him. Especially in

a violent and rowdy fashion because—I didn't know it at the time but I learned later—Huey had a kind of hidden reputation on the block with the brothers.

There were cats all over East and West Oakland who had reputations for being bad, and they were known throughout the community for being bad. Huey didn't have this kind of reputation. The bad cats terrorized the community—and Huey terrorized the bad cats. You heard a lot of stories about Huey. Like one night at a party, Huey accidentally stepped on some brother's shoes, and Huey stepped back and he said, "Excuse me, brother." The brother—he was bad, one of those bad dudes—he said, "Motherfucker, 'scuse me, don't reshine my shoes." Huey knew his brothers very well. When the dude slid back to the side and dropped his arm slightly to the right, hanging behind his right thigh, Huey saw this. He knew this was the time to fire. Next thing you knew, Huey fired on him and decked him, and all the other bad dudes at the party who were this decked dude's friends or partners wanted to know who this cat thinks he is. And so they jumped up and said that Huey needs his ass kicked, and Huey told them, "I'll fight all of you one at a time or all of you at the same time and you won't wait outside for me, I'll be waiting outside for you." And then he walked outside and waited and dared them to come outside.

And this is something I think Huey understood too, that he would shock them because he was as bad as the noted dudes in the area. He shocked them because he had nerve enough to fight all of them. They would come outside and think they could get around him, or start sneaking around him to try and deck him, and the next thing you knew, Huey would come out with a fourteen- or fifteen-inch machete and he'd be righteously trying to whip heads and cut up some ass, and he would have niggers running everywhere.

Huey also used to get into fights with his partners who rode in his car with him. About the time he was coming out of high school and was around sixteen-and-a-half or seventeen years old, he had a car called the Gray Roach.

Huey always hit a corner, his car speeding down the road. Once he turned the corner, and a block up there was a railroad crossing with a little red light swinging, signaling that a train was coming. There was also a big building right on the corner that you couldn't see around. Huey started speeding up. He didn't know exactly where that train was, but he knew it was around that building somewhere. The next thing you knew, Huey had driven straight over that railroad crossing, and all the dudes in the car were cussing him out. He tried to tell them he couldn't die. He said he didn't believe he could die and, "Why die a thousand times, when you can only die once?"

Then Huey stopped the car, and he and his partners got out to fight. Afterwards, they all got back in the car. He kept driving and his partners would kept driving with him. I don't think Huey was trying to kill anybody. They were his partners; they rode with him and they liked the cat. They fought, but they kept riding with him. They would say he was crazy when he did things like that, but they thought his mind was out of sight. Most important, Huey would defend his partners—or whoever was with him.

The brother was too much in his day, and all the cats knew it. I know some pimps and hustlers and righteous gangsters on the block who knew and respected Huey. Some of them were dudes Huey used to fight. He had gotten into some tight situations with some of them, and they knew that he'd vamp on them if they got wrong.

One time, Huey walked into a liquor store to get some wine. You know how some brothers will be standing on the corner by the liquor store? He came back out and somebody said, "Hey nigger, give me some of that wine." Huey said, "Brother, you can have some of my wine, but don't be asking me like that, like you're going to take my wine." The dude launched to fire on Huey, so Huey stepped back and broke the bottle over his head. All the dudes were standing on the corner just looking at this one dude Huey had fired on.

This led to one of the baddest fights that ever happened

in West Oakland. Huey and a real bad dude named Mackelvain fought out there for half an hour. First Huey downed Mackelvain. Then Mackelvain downed Huey. It was a standoffish thing because all of Huey's boys stood off and sat back, and all of Mackelvain's boys did the same. I don't think Mackelvain's boys wanted to mess with Huey's boys, so they got on the fences and on the cars, and watched these two black men, both brothers off the block, thunder it out there in the street.

They fought all across the street until they could hardly raise their hands to throw a lick. At one point, they were so tired that Huey would come up and get a couple of licks on Mackelvain and down him, then Mackelvain would get up and down Huey. Huey thought he had downed him finally, then walked away. He'd been drinking a lot of wine before the fight, so he got down on one knee in the middle of the street, and started throwing up all his wine. The next thing he knew, he was seeing stars. He found out later that he'd been kicked in the head. Mackelvain had gotten up without Huey noticing him. Huey felt himself rolling over the pavement, but he got up and came back at Mackelvain and downed him again.

Eventually somebody called the pigs. That's the only thing that broke it up. The brothers saw a pig car coming down the street flashing its red light, and everybody split. Huey swore all up and down that the next time he saw Mackelvain he'd kill him, and Mackelvain swore that he was going to kill Huey.

About three years later, Huey was walking down Seventh Street in Oakland with a friend of his who had seen that fight. Huey's friend, Buddy, recognized Mackelvain as they approached him, but Huey didn't. Mackelvain had gotten a lot bigger. He'd been to the joint, and had been throwin' iron up there.

Buddy looked at Huey and said, "You know who this is, man?" Huey said he didn't. Then Buddy looked at Mackelvain and asked him, "You know who this is here with me?" "Naw," said Mackelvain. Then Buddy said, "Man, you dudes don't know each other?" They each shook their heads, so Buddy said, "You niggers had one of the baddest fights that ever was fought in West Oakland." They looked at each other and Mackelvain said, "That's Newton, man? Damn." So Buddy said, "Y'all ready to bury the hatchet now?" Somehow or other they agreed to bury the hatchet and forget it and drink some wine together.

When Huey was running around and living every day on the block with some of the toughest brothers, he was just as tough as the rest of them were. He'd fight it out with them and he survived in that environment.

He was at school one day, and somebody said something about some chick he was going with, some white boy, and Huey walked up to him, and said, "I don't want to hear anything more about my relations with this girl." The white boy opened his mouth again, and Huey said, "I said that I don't want you to say any more or make any statements about my relations with this particular girl." The white boy opened his mouth again, and Huey decked him. Laid him out on the basketball court on the campus there.

And that's when I liked the brother. He was a brother to you, to articulate things, explain things, and he could detect whether you were honest or dishonest, to some extent, or whether you were bullshitting or jiving. He's got some kind of intuition that he can detect this stuff about certain kinds of people. I could see Huey and say, man, loan me a dollar, and he'd let me hold a dollar, and he could see me and say, man, let me hold a couple of dollars—it was that kind of thing.

I would run into him in a café or something, and he might be sitting down blowing about something, anything from law to black nationalist philosophy, how we were interrelated to this system, the decadence of it, and he would be blowing facts. He wouldn't just be cleaning up the walls. And if you knew Huey and liked Huey, you would be pro-Huey when it came to an argument, because you would know Huey was going to come up with some righteous facts, some righteous philosophical point of view to make you see what was going on.

This is the way I saw him, and this is the way I've always thought of the cat. He's the kind of a cat you always respect. He's a kindhearted person. You can't use his kindness, but he'll give it away. So you look at him and say, what kind of cat is this? This brother here is something else.

HUEY BREAKS WITH THE CULTURAL NATIONALISTS

■ Among all the brothers, Huey was always respected for his insight. I've had a chance to meet a lot of the brothers he was partners with, and they always respected his ability, his perspective, and that he could explain things, how the system works against them. He could always give a valid reason why they were so right, why they were so right in whatever they did to try to survive.

When Huey went to college, he never took over eight or nine units a semester, and he'd always make it a point to make A's or very good grades, but he didn't get the grades just because he was looking for a grade in college.

Huey had a thing about going to school. It was an entertainment to his mind. But he explained the A's. A counselor told him when he got out of high school with D's—they more or less just rushed him through high school—that he wasn't supposed to be college material. His counselor told him, and he rejected the whole concept of these cats in these schools, these counselors, telling him that he wasn't college material. So, I saw it as him entertaining his mind, as he says, and trying to grasp something. And at the same time rejecting some white counselor, more than likely a racist, telling him that he couldn't do college. He always took six or seven units and he always would go and get outside reading material. He would go forth to prove, give validity by researching the references that any particular author

might have made, and some particular materials they might
have made, and some particular materials they might be
using in the school. So in the classroom he was very up to
date on things that were true and things that were false in
any subject matter, and he could see whether the facts were
valid.

Intertwined with all these facts, of course, was the direct
relation he had to black people, living in the confines of the
decadent system. Black people surviving, black people
knowing themselves, and Black History. Huey took an experimental sociology course. I guess he'd been at Merritt a
few years then. This experimental sociology course: he was
running down to me about how the course was for those in
it to deal with some specific problem in society, and he
swung the whole class to the need for Black History in the
schools. Huey P. Newton was one of the key people in the
first Black History course that was developed at Merritt
College, along with many of the other people in the experimental sociology course. I remember him telling me about
it, and I was enthused about it, because I had been doing
quite a bit of Black History study myself.

So come next semester there was a *Negro* History course.
I went and enrolled in the course and got Huey one day and
asked him to come to the class, because the class was all
jammed up. The cat that was teaching it didn't know what
he was doing. He really wasn't teaching Black History; he
was teaching American history and reiterating slavery and
the period of slavery, and the old traditional way they relate
to black people in slavery. Huey come in the class one day,
which was taught by Rodney Carlisle, a white instructor.
Huey, as always, shot Carlisle down for his reference to
Basil Davis and information concerning Africa, and Black
Mother, and African slave trade. Set him down on the point
of the piracy that initiated the slave trade. Huey gave inspi-
ration to a lot of brothers and sisters to do a lot of in-depth
study and realize the need to have knowledge of themselves
as black people.

.   .   .

About three years before this took place, I got into the Afro-American Association, and about two months later, Huey got out. I was wondering, why did Huey get out of the Afro-American Association? His partners, John Thomas and Richard Thorn, cats he knew around that time and ran with a lot, were college students. These dudes weren't dudes off the block. They also got out of the Afro-American Association. Huey began to explain how Donald Warden was using the Afro-American Association as a means to deceive black people. That Donald Warden was very up to date on a lot of historical facts, and used these facts to make black people see his program as being right. But Huey had finally seen through Donald Warden's program and had seen through Donald Warden.

One day in San Francisco—Fillmore Street—some white gang a couple of stories up began to hang out the window, hollering cuss words and bull crap. Some of them came downstairs. They got to acting like they were gonna jump on somebody. Huey and another brother were there throwing hands and knocking cats on their ass while Donald Warden wouldn't help defend the principle. That's one thing about Huey, he stands on principles. Black nationalist philosophy at this time was interrelated with his principles. Somebody was gonna try to jump on the brothers on the street corner where the Afro-American Association was holding a rally. Huey just went on and got out there and started throwing hands. And that's when he begin to find Donald Warden out, I think. From there, he begin to explain how Donald Warden was exploiting the old church thing, preacher-type attitude and concept, to bring the people around, and start talking about "buy black business." This was the real split in terms of the black nationalist philosophy at this time. Huey saw that more cooperative, socialistic-type things were necessary for black people to use, to oppose the system. He would explain many times that if a black businessman is charging you the same prices or higher, even higher prices than exploiting white businessmen, then he himself ain't nothing but an exploiter. So why should black people go for this kind of system? And he's always dealt with it in this fashion.

Coming on up the ladder, there were some long periods of time I didn't see Huey. Then one day I saw Huey and he was talking about a case he just beat. He defended himself in court and had beaten a petty theft case, and he was running it down how he got Olsen. Olsen was the dean of Merritt College. Dean Olsen had got up on the stand and testified to the fact that he had called the police in to have Huey P. Newton arrested, and had the police bring Huey to his office because some paddy boy over in the store had accused Huey of stealing a book. Huey explained to me that Olsen had asked him if those were his books. Huey said, "Yes, this is my property." Right in front of the face of this cop. And Olsen said, "Well, I'll just keep these books." And Huey said, "No, you won't keep those books. That's my property and I'll keep them myself. You called me in the office for something. I don't know what you want me for, but I'll keep my property." And Huey snatched the books back out of his hand and said, "If you want to arrest me, you'll have to arrest me, but I'm not going to stand here talking." And he walked right on out of the office.

So the same thing came up on the stand, and Huey asked Olsen on the stand, "Dean Olsen, why didn't you have me placed under arrest if you thought I had stolen the books?" (Huey was rapping, you know, if you ever catch him in court during a law procedure, he raps just like he's a right-eous lawyer.) Dean Olsen said, "Well, at that time, I just didn't know my rights as to whether or not I had the right to arrest you." Huey P. Newton looked at the jury, looked back at Dean Olsen, and looked back at the jury, and said, "Mr. Olsen, you're a dean at a college; have a Ph.D. in edu-cation. Here I am a student in the college, learning my rights, and you've got a Ph.D., and you tell me you didn't know your *rights?*" Huey went on to explain the impact he made on the jury with that point, and how they cut him loose. He became very, very famous, very well known, very notorious against anybody who'd done him wrong around the college. Well-liked cat, well-liked brother. Very friendly with people. And Huey had very human qualities about himself.

There's another thing about Huey. I remember one time, there were some black nationalists, cultural nationalists, on the campus who used to project all this cultural nationalism.* They were so engrossed in this cultural nationalism, they just *hated* white people simply for the color of their skin. This is where Huey and I got this thing about cultural nationalists. Huey had opened the door for a sister to go through. You know how a man opens the door for a woman? There happened to be a white girl, coming right behind the sister, and so the white girl walked in. So one of the cultural nationalists ran up to him and said, "How come you opened the door for that white girl?" And Huey turned around and looked at him. He said, "Look man, I'm a human being and I'm not a fool. I opened the door for the sister. There happened to be a white girl behind her. The white girl's not attacking me. She's not brutalizing me. So there's nothing wrong with me keeping the door open for her to pass through, too." And the cultural nationalists just went out of their minds, exaggerating the shit. That's just one point to show Huey's humanism toward all other human beings; this is the way he is.

When I look back at some of the things that Huey was thinking at that time, and a lot of the things that Huey understood then, I know that I didn't understand them at the time; but I followed Huey because he clarified these things to me.

* Cultural nationalists and Black Panthers are in conflict in many areas. Basically, cultural nationalism sees the white man as the oppressor and makes no distinction between racist whites and non-racist whites, as the Panthers do. The cultural nationalists say that a black man cannot be an enemy of the black people, while the Panthers believe that black capitalists are exploiters and oppressors. Although the Black Panther Party believes in black nationalism and black culture, it does not believe that either can lead to black liberation or the overthrow of the capitalist system.—Ed.

THE SOUL STUDENTS ADVISORY COUNCIL

■ I had been running with some cultural nationalists for around two or three years, the so-called West Coast underground RAM (Revolutionary Action Movement). I got very frustrated with those cats. I didn't think they were going to do anything, and I became very discouraged about being able to work with them. They had a lot of paranoid hang-ups and they began to accuse me of things. They had so many bull crap suspicions, I couldn't deal with them.

I broke loose from those cats. I got mad at them one night and busted down their door. All the niggers hid behind their damn beds. At that point, I couldn't deal with them anymore because they wouldn't defend themselves, even against one little old me. There were four or five of them in the pad, but they ran hiding. I just didn't respect them anymore. I was thinking to myself, "Later for these dudes. I'm going to find myself a righteous partner to righteously run with."

I really hadn't seen Huey for over a year now. One night I was just sitting on the street in front of James Oliver's house, about half a block up the street from Merritt College, and Huey came by. I didn't know who it was at first. I was sitting there in the car, drinking a beer or something, and Huey flashed a little flashlight through the window. I think he recognized my car. I had seen him walking down the street a couple of times, but I think he knew I had that car. I said, "What's happening, man?" I said to myself, now *this* is who I ought to be running with. I had wanted Huey to be a part of the same cultural nationalist group I'd been running with, and these dudes didn't want Huey to be a part of the organization. At first I couldn't figure out why, but I remember I had asked Huey to come up to the pad, and after he left, silly-ass Kenneth Freeman sat up and said some bull crap about "Huey P. Newton comes from a bourgie family."

Huey P. Newton was raised up righteously on the block, and of course, Kenny Freeman was the one who came from the bourgie family. He was also saying, "The dude's high, man." I said, "Well, what's the difference, he gets a little loaded off of something, and I drink whiskey." As I think about it, I don't think Kenny Freeman liked us field niggers too much. I don't think he dug us at all. Because he knew Huey was the type of dude who didn't take no shit, and I figure he had a little egotistical bourgie-ass fear about Huey kicking motherfuckers' asses and the way Huey articulates things.

Huey came walking up that night with that flashlight and I said this is who I need to be running with, old brother Huey. This brother can righteously run it down, and don't take no shit from nobody. This brother will stand with you, and this is the way I felt about the brother, knowing him for those years that I'd been knowing him, about four or five years by then.

I started talking to the brother about the struggle, and I think he must have recognized that I was well frustrated with those cultural nationalists I'd been running with, the so-called underground RAM.

One day I went over to his house and asked him if he had read Fanon. I'd read *Wretched of the Earth* six times. I knew Fanon was right and I knew he was running it down —but how do you put ideas like his over? Huey was laying up in bed, thinking, plotting on the man. I knew what he was doing. He used to tell me how he was plotting to make himself some money on the man. He was always involved with day-to-day survival like the average brother on the block.

He said no, he hadn't read Fanon. So I brought Fanon over one day. That brother got to reading Fanon, and man, let me tell you, when Huey got ahold of Fanon, and read Fanon (I had been always running down about how we need this organization, that organization, but never anything concrete), Huey'd be thinking. Hard. We would sit down with *Wretched of the Earth* and talk, go over another section or chapter of Fanon, and Huey would explain it in depth. It was the first time I ever had anybody who could show a clear-cut perception of what was said in one sentence, a paragraph, or chapter, and not have to read it again. He knew it already. He'd get on the streets. We'd be walking down the street and get in some discussion with somebody, and throughout the process of this discussion and argument, Huey would be citing facts, citing that material, and giving perception to it. At that time he was giving the same basic concepts as he's giving now, but now he's in a wider and broader area, because he's had a lot of experience in leadership in the Black Panther Party. His development now is at the head of the revolutionary struggle. But he always had this vast ability to do things along with a proper perspective, and he could run it down and get things going.

Huey was one for implementing things, and I guess this is where the Black Panther Party really started. Because once Huey got hung on that, he started explaining how we had to get something going. Before the Black Panther Party came the Soul Students Advisory Council. Some of the other cultural nationalists in the college and a couple that I'd broken up with and got tired of messing with—they were jiving to me, and are still jiving—some of them came around. They were talking about starting some organization, a school campus organization. Well, Huey and I got interested in the thing, and a couple of other cats, Virtual Murrell and Alex Papillion. We started talking about organizing what we named a little while later, Soul Students Advisory Council. We structured the thing in such a way where we really practiced ultrademocracy among ourselves; at the same time, Huey wanted to make the thing very meaningful, so the so-called central group of the Soul Students Advisory Council consisted of Virtual Murrell, Alex

Papillion, Bobby Seale, Huey P. Newton, Isaac Moore, and a couple of jive cultural nationalists around there.

Huey and I decided we were going to try and make the thing work: to develop a college campus group, and to help develop leadership; to go to the black community and serve the black community in a revolutionary fashion. I was with Huey all the way. So Soul Students was moving along, and meanwhile, Huey and I and Alex Papillion and Virtual Murrell put out a lot of hard, hard, hard work getting a few things off the ground. The draft of black men was a big thing on the college campuses; of course, just the draft itself became a high controversy. But we had just begun talking about the draft of black men. We organized one of the biggest rallies ever held at Merritt College, where five or six hundred black people attended, and ran it down. From there, Huey, Virtual, Alex, and myself were known as the leaders of the Soul Students Advisory Council.

Huey and I and Weasel, one of the brothers on the campus, were all sitting in the car one night. We decided we wanted to buy some records by T-Bone Walker, Lightnin' Hopkins, and Howlin' Wolf, these downhome brothers. I suggested that we go up to the Cal campus because up around there they have more LP's of T-Bone Walker, Howlin' Wolf, and all the brothers, than they have in the regular black record shop.

We started walking down the street on Telegraph toward the Forum, a restaurant up there. We were about a block from the Forum, when the brothers asked me to recite one of them poems I always liked. One of them was named, "Burn, Baby, Burn." The other was "Uncle Sammy Call Me Fulla Lucifer." I was walking down the street reciting "Burn, Baby, Burn," all the way down till we got to the next block, and then Huey and Weasel asked me to recite that other poem, "Uncle Sammy Call Me Fulla Lucifer."

So I got to reciting that poem. I said two or three words and when we got in front of the Forum, across the street,

one of the brothers, Weasel, got over and picked a chair up.
(It's kind of a sidewalk restaurant.) He said, "Here, Bobby,
stand on this." So we set the chair up by the curb there, and
I got on the chair and hollered, "Uncle Sammy Call Me
Fulla Lucifer." When I said that, I went on to recite the rest
of the poem. Then someone said, "Do it again. Run it down
again, man." So I got to the part of the poem where it said,
"You school my naive heart to sing red-white-and-blue-
stars-and-stripes songs." Some uniformed pig cop walked
up. He stood around ten or twelve feet away. I said, "You
school my naive heart to sing red-white-and-blue-stars-
and-stripes songs and to pledge eternal allegiance to all
things blue, true, blue-eyed blond, blond-haired, white
chalk white skin with U.S.A. tattooed all over."

Man, when I said that, this cop walks up and says,
"You're under arrest." I got down off the chair, said, "What
are you talking about, 'You're under arrest?' Under arrest
for what? What reason do you have for saying I'm under
arrest?" And he says, "You're blocking the sidewalk." And
I say, "What do you mean I'm blocking the sidewalk? I'm
standing over here." I noticed Huey, standing to my left.
Next thing I know, some people started grabbing on me.
"You under arrest, you under arrest." I started snatching
away from them, man. Next thing I know, Huey was battling up there, and three paddies had me down, tied down
onto the ground. One of the paddies that had hold of me,
Huey knocked him in the head a couple of times, and a
couple of other brothers stomped on the paddies. I got loose.
A big fight was going on. But boy, they say Huey whipped
up some motherfuckers up there. They say Huey was throwing hands.

That's why I say Huey or his partners, he always went
down with them. It's just one of them things. He just relates
to any brothers he's with. He doesn't let anybody mess over
his partners, or whoever he's running with. That's the way
he is. That's the way he is with his people, against this racist
decadent system. That's the way he gets with any human

being who tries to hurt him or his friends. And his people and his family. That was a big thing.

Huey and I got busted that night. I fooled around and got busted a block away from the thing. Since we were the leaders of the Soul Students Advisory Council at the time, and Huey and I had to have a lawyer, Virtual Murrell went to the SSAC treasury, got $50, and gave us $25 a piece to secure ourselves lawyers after we got bailed out. It took us three days to get Huey bailed out of jail. He was on probation and at first his probation officer put a hold on him, but later cut the hold loose.

Three weeks after Huey was bailed out, some brother got busted right in front of our car. Huey was getting ready to vamp on the pigs because he knew the brother wasn't doing a thing. He was a citizen, just standing around observing, about ten or twelve feet away from our car, and the cops went up to him and wanted to bust him for nothing. Huey said, "We've got some money in the SSAC treasury. We're going to bail this brother out."

Me and Alex Papillion held Huey back. More pigs came up and they made me and Alex line up against the wall, and drew pistols on us. Then they arrested the brother who had just been standing around. So we went and bailed the brother out. We were going to use the SSAC to begin learning how to serve our community. "The brother got busted on a bullshit tip for no reason. Bail the brother out," we said.

WE HIT THE STREETS

■ A short while later we had a meeting of the SSAC involving about 200 people who were very concerned about where the SSAC was going. The cultural nationalists had spread it around all over the campus that we were doing the Council wrong. They accused us of stealing money from the treasury. In fact money wasn't stolen. It was being used for bail and to secure lawyers for me and Huey.

The cultural nationalists also accused us of accepting money from a white man. We got the money from Bob Scheer, a former *Ramparts* editor who was running for Congress. Scheer had come up and asked us for support, and we said we didn't feel it was necessary to support anybody in the political arena because we didn't think they could voice our opinions adequately. We asked Scheer for $100, which he gave us. There weren't any strings attached to the money. We just said, "We need $100 to help get things off the ground here at Merritt College."

We felt we knew what we wanted to do, because Huey had already run it down to the central group of the SSAC that we had to arm ourselves. This was way before we organized the Black Panther Party, maybe eleven months before. Huey had run it down, to Douglas Allen, to Isaac Moore, to Kenny Freeman, and to Ernest Allen, that what we needed to do was to involve the black community. Huey understood the meaning of what Fanon was saying about organizing the lumpen proletariat first, because Fanon explicitly pointed out that if you didn't organize the lumpen proletariat, if the organization didn't relate to the lumpen proletariat and give a base for organizing the brother who's pimping, the brother who's hustling, the unemployed, the downtrodden, the brother who's robbing banks, who's not politically conscious—that's what lumpen proletariat means —that if you didn't relate to these cats, the power structure would organize these cats against you.

Huey said to all these cats on the central committee of the SSAC that we are going to have to show the brothers on the block that we have an organization that represents the community and we're going to have to show it in a real strong fashion.

So Huey suggested to the central group that we bring these brothers off the block, openly armed, on to the campus and bring the press down. We could reach the community (because the press would be hungry for it) and show them, on Malcolm X's birthday, May 19, that Malcolm X had advocated armed self-defense against the racist power structure and show the racist white power structure that we intend to use the guns to defend our people. All these cultural nationalists, these underground RAM bastards, all of them, were scared and rejected it. And I even have to say that Virtual Murrell wasn't too hot on it. Even Alex Papillion wasn't too hot on it. The only people hanging on to it were Huey P. Newton leading it and me—following Huey P. Newton because I dug brother Huey, because I felt I knew what the hell he was talking about, because at this time, he was explaining to me that you implement through practice, not just through a bunch of words, what Fanon was talking about.

Huey was running down that the law says that every man has the right to arm himself, by the Second Amendment of the jive-ass Constitution of the United States. He says that we are going to exhaust that, because in the end, the man will say that we don't have a Second Amendment of the Constitution. That's very important to understand. So when Huey said, "Let's exhaust it now," he meant relate specifically to what Malcolm X was thinking, don't relate to the personality of Malcolm so much, and relate more to what Malcolm X was saying to do. This is what Huey was trying to implement within the confines of the Soul Students, quite a while before the Black Panther Party got started. All these cats rejected it. Douglas Allen, the rest of them, they were scared. They were shook. Huey defined them as a bunch of scared cowards.

This is when we really, really, began to pick our bone with these cultural nationalist cats in the SSAC. They accused us of stealing money, and then rejected this idea about the guns and arming the people. They started accusing us, and they were trying to act bad on the campus like they were bad dudes off the block. You get these cultural nationalists that think they're bad, think they're badder than anybody else. So Huey says, "If they think they're bad, we're going to get our shit."

I had a 9mm pistol, and Huey called up his boys—the pimps, thugs off the block (people always call them thugs) —and he called up his nephew, who, like the brothers on the block, just liked to fight. They don't like to do much of anything but fight, and they liked Huey and they respected Huey's ideas, so we stacked a whole session there, that whole last day session. That was the day Huey and I resigned from the SSAC, with the brothers off the block, and Huey said, "Come on up here. These niggers think they're bad. We're going to show them if they're bad." We came off in there, and we had guns and sweaters and shit. Buddy Boy was there with a couple of his boys, and one of Huey's nephews, with his nine or ten brothers off the block and some more of his cousins. We were going to kick ass that day. But the cultural nationalists sloughed it off and got pissed off and scared because they knew we meant business.

Huey was in the back room and I was up there, standing around ten or twelve feet from Isaac Moore. Isaac Moore started talking about telling me to sit down. I told him, "You come over here and make me sit down," because I knew I had a 9mm for his ass. Isaac Moore was supposed to know a little bit of karate, but if he got acting bad I was going to prove to the nigger that karate don't judo chop buckshots and pistol bullets.

Huey was in the back room and he asked Kenny Freeman to come out of the corner, and Kenny Freeman backed his ass up, sat down, and kept quiet, because, you know, Huey P. Newton was a motherfucker. He doesn't like anybody to fuck over his friends. Huey has a thing—he gives. He's true, he's fair, and he likes to give, but he won't let nobody fuck over that. And that's what Kenny Freeman was trying to do, fuck over the fact that Huey will give things out. Huey never lets anybody mess over anything that he's ready to give to the people, or give to anyone—that is his fairness, his trueness. Kenny Freeman couldn't understand that Huey was ready to give, and Huey's dedication was to the people.

They talked all that shit about us stealing money and swayed the jive college intellectuals to think that we were stealing money. We told the fuckers we weren't stealing money, that we took the money and bailed out one brother, and Virtual Murrell said, "I took $50, and gave $25 to Huey P. Newton and $25 to Bobby to secure themselves a lawyer for that shit that happened up on Telegraph." The cultural nationalists have their minds so fucked up in the system and in pawn to the system that they couldn't believe it. They didn't want to believe it. They wanted to be treacherous and chickenshit, like the power structure, with their minds in pawn to the system. That's how they have a tendency to project themselves.

So Huey and I jumped up, and we said, "Well, fuck it. We resign. We're going to the black community and we intend to organize in the black community and organize an organization to lead the black liberation struggle." Huey ran all that down to them. "We don't have time for you," he said. "You're jiving in these colleges. You're hiding behind the ivory-walled towers in the college, and you're shucking and you're jiving." This was the real break with the SSAC that Huey established.

So we left and said, "Later for the punks," jive motherfuckers at the college. We just went to the streets, where we should have been in the first place—those four or five years that preceded this showed us that—and Huey, the brother off the block, had never really left the streets at all.

When we decided to go to the streets, it was all based basically on one thing: that Huey P. Newton was ready to go to the streets. Before Huey decided to leave college, he had wanted to implement things there, and educate those on the college level to the necessity of bringing the brothers off the block to the college level, and relating those college skills to the streets. This was Huey's objective, because he saw the necessity of this happening. But at the same time, Huey also realized that if the college boys didn't want to come on the streets, later for them. And that's how it happened, the college boys—the cultural nationalists, all the bullshit, jiving dudes who articulate bullshit all the time and don't ever want to get into the real practice of revolutionary struggle, the black liberation struggle in this country —Huey'd say, "Well, later for them. We'll go to the streets." And I'd say, "Huey, I'm with you, brother. Let's go on and do it." So, we went on out into the streets, and that was it.

All the passages that Fanon has covered, Huey covered. We used to underline them. I wish I had the books right now with the passages we underlined: everything that Fanon said about violence and the spontaneity of violence, how spontaneous violence educates those who are in a position with skills to lead the people to what needs to be done. Fanon ran the cultural nationalists down *cold*. He talked about them like they were *dogs*. This is why many of the cultural nationalists have really, in fact, thrown Fanon's book to the side. Malcolm X talked about organization and doing things, and righteously going out there and doing it. The cultural nationalists, on the other hand, wanted to sit down and articulate bullshit, while Huey P. Newton wanted to go out and implement stuff.

This is very important. This is the difference, the line of demarcation, in fact, between the revolutionaries and those who are jiving in the confines of the ivory walls, the ivory towers of the college. Huey and I began to talk about a lot of things. We really began to get very intense in how this thing was going to go and how we thought it should go. We had been rejected by people at San Francisco State, Merritt College, and on the Berkeley campus, because we talked and emphasized the necessity of arming the people with guns. The cultural nationalists and many of the leading white liberals, they look at it like, "You can't pick up guns. It's impossible to pick up guns." This is what they want to emphasize. This is what you could infer from all their rhetoric. But Huey said, "No, you must pick up guns, because guns are key."

USING THE POVERTY PROGRAM

■ In June 1966, the summer before the Black Panther Party was actually organized, I took a job at the North Oakland Neighborhood Anti-Poverty Center, as a foreman in the summer youth work program. The job paid $660 or $670 a month. I had previously worked in a poverty program and had been fired because I was teaching the youth Black History and teaching them not to be sucked in by the $1.35 an hour that they were given. I tried to get them not to think in Uncle Tomish ways but always to think in ways related to black people in the black community surviving and black people in the black community unifying. Through working in the poverty programs I was able to meet a lot of the young cats who would later become lumpen proletarians.

The same summer, Huey was a community organizer, so Huey and I were together quite often. Huey knew quite a few of the older cats in the community. Because of his articulateness, he was always welcomed by the brothers in the community who were generally referred to as hoods and criminals.

This summer work program provided jobs for about 100—twenty-five girls and seventy-five boys. They worked in the community cutting lawns, cutting hedges, digging up grounds, etc. They were supposed to do repairs on fences and steps and things like that, but the equipment wasn't available. There were four such programs, so only 400 kids were employed by the poverty program in Oakland.

My objective in the program was to teach Black American History if I could, and teach them also some degree of responsibility; not teach them responsibility in old Establishment terms, but in terms of their own people living in the community. In the poverty program the young brothers many times would try to be slick and think they were pimps,

or think they could out-gamble or out-talk or out-rap anybody. Some of them would fool around and carry knives,
and I'd have to hip them about the knife-carrying. In working with the poverty program, I never wanted to use the
authoritarian-type old school tactics which I had rejected,
and I knew these young brothers rejected. They drank wine,
shot dice, and things like that. I knew there was a way to
reach these brothers because I wasn't too much different
from them. I knew how to drink wine, how to shoot dice,
play cards, and chase women.

Sometimes I caught cats playing cards and I'd have to
make them stop. I'd say, "You cats can't play cards, man,
because you've got a job to do." But generally I refused to
be authoritarian. I did a lot of things that weren't conven-
tional. I tried to make the brothers understand that they had
a right to set a price on their labor. I knew that in the future
they probably would be workers, especially if we ever
change this system. If I had ten cats on a job, I would say,
"All right, you've got six hours of work today. You get one
hour for lunch. Now if all you cats get together and do this
job you can do it in four hours. I know you can do it easily
in four hours." Then I'd say, "I'll let you off for the next two
hours, and I'll see to it that you still get your pay for the
entire six hours." The administrators up there probably
didn't know what I was doing but I was trying to make the
young cats respect their labor. At the same time, I was
trying to make them respect responsibility, and to go ahead
and do things.

This is related a lot to my past. When I was younger,
about thirteen or fourteen years old, my mother would say,
"Make up the bed and clean your room." My brother and I
would loll around for half an hour or forty-five minutes,
trying to sneak outside and trying to get out of it. Then one
day, I figured it out and I said, "Hell, we could have cleaned
up the room in ten or fifteen minutes, made the bed up, and
been gone." I was using this discovery I had made as a kid
to show these brothers that with the labor they produce, if

they really get on it and get down to it, they could really do the job.

Every once in a while, I'd catch a lazy cat. When I'd catch one, I'd go to where he was working and go right to work, and we'd work real, real hard, and really start getting things cleaned up. Instead of trying to dock the pay or fire the lazy cat, I'd get all the other brothers together, and by me working too, I'd try to show them. Then the rest of the brothers would be falling behind me and they would ridicule the lazy cat. This was a means by which a lot of the cats could begin to see that they could get things done. Mr. Allen, the director of the poverty program, came from the old school, very strict and very hard. He wanted to do right, but his ideas and his notions related to old, conservative people. In essence, they say, "Do what the system says to do and you'll be all right." But that isn't the truth at all. Sometimes Mr. Allen would find things out and he would dock a cat's pay. The young brothers really try to be slick. They try to run jive games and they don't realize that all the people aren't foolish.

The very first day, I got all the cats in the room and the first thing I did was run down a little Black History to them. I kind of stimulated their interest a little and I recited "Burn, Baby, Burn" by Marvin Jackman. The poem was a catchy little thing, but a lot of cats were never able to explain that poem in terms of the political, social, and economic repression of black people. The poem's meaning is that the soul of a black man must bring up enough courage to rebel and resist. If they understood that poem, they would begin to have a revolutionary, political ideology. They would see, as the Black Panther Party has, that spontaneous uprisings are not what's happening.

But, as Fanon said, violence can be a strength and a weakness. The violence of the many riots that occurred before the Black Panther Party was conceived was a strength in producing an organization like the Panther

Party and also made other organizations more determined
to seek a better, more revolutionary ideology to guide the
people. They could see that so many people were getting
killed just because they were without organization. Well, I
more or less explained that poem to the brothers and sisters.
I recited the poem and they checked it out. Then I recited,
"Uncle Sammy Call Me Fulla Lucifer." This is by a cat
named Ronald Stone back in New York. I recited these
poems to the brothers in a very dramatic way. Then I
explained to them that this is the reason the man has really
got you down and you're making $1.35 an hour. "All you
cats who are from sixteen to twenty-one," I said. "He's
paying you $1.35 an hour because he knows your soul. He
knows that you have moved to resist this system. I'm trying
to show you that you don't have to move to resist this
system in that fashion anymore." They dug the poem.

On Saturdays there was an education thing for an hour
or two and then there was a baseball game. The young cats
would get paid for coming to the four-hour session on
Saturdays. After the early morning education class, some
cats wouldn't go play baseball. They'd sit down and start
playing blackjack, or some other card game. Bobby Hutton
was one of those cats. I first met Little Bobby when a friend
of his brought him around and asked me if I could get him a
job. I said, "Yeah, there's three or four more spots open
down there. They ought to have enough money to give you
a job." Bobby said he was sixteen years old, but I knew he
wasn't sixteen. I could tell by his face, but I said, "I'll just
say he's sixteen and let him have his job, because he needs a
job." His partner had told him, "We got a foreman that's
something else." This is what I heard. And his partner said,
"I know he'll give you a job. He really digs all the brothers."
One Saturday nobody in that whole program wanted to
play baseball. So I said, "Well, you cats can't gamble without me! I know all of you are thinking you can out-gamble
me. So let's get it on down then." They were betting nickels
and dimes. "Now what are you gambling for anyway," I

said. "You don't need to be gambling because the whole operation is always against you."

"Oh man, you don't know what you're talking about, baby. You're just one of those jive squares, Bobby."

"So you think gambling is where it's at, huh," I said. So I thought to myself, "Now, I don't believe these brothers are too hip. I'm going to have to teach them just a little bit of a lesson." They were playing blackjack, so I got in the game, a nickel and a dime, a nickel and a dime. Then I said, "Let's raise the stakes. Let's raise the stakes, baby. I can't win no money, man. You cats are making big money." The cats were just sitting there. "A quarter, man. A quarter," I said. "What kind of gamblers are you? Are you all tight, chintzy, jive, gamblers?" So the cat who had the deal said, "Bet a quarter, if you want to bet a quarter."

I said, "Bet a half."

He said, "Bet a half."

I said, "Right on time."

I hit down and bet a half, and I lost about fifteen halves. Finally I got to deal. I had lost almost all of the $10 I had with me. So I said, "All right. Who's gonna go against me with this piece of money?" I had seventy-five cents on me. I said, "Here's seventy-five cents right here." One of the brothers says, "I'll go." I said, "All right, let's deal one hand." Boom. We dealt one hand, and I won it.

I said, "Who's gonna go with me against this $1.50 I got here?" Everybody's saying, "This motherfucker." They were thinking that I had to lose. I could have lost, but I had a little piece of luck. I won and I built the pile up to about $5.00. I said, "All right now, the sky is the limit. Anybody can bet anything they want to. Anything they want." A cat ran out of money. He said, "I want to play payday stakes."

"Payday stakes," I said. "I'll take anything. I'm taking all bets coming in this way right here. Comin' round the board, baby. Can you hear me?" I ran it on down and flipped all the cards out. That's when I really started winning, but I lost the damn deal.

So I lost the deal and the game is spirited with payday

stakes. So I said, "The sky's the limit." One cat was going to
be slick. "What will you bet?" he asked me. "I'll bet $100,"
I said. The other cats said, "Right on time! That ol' Bobby
makes that ol' $650 a month. I'm gonna get me some of
that money."

"$100, $100," I said. Boom. I won. This cat didn't want
any more part of it. So I went down to another cat and got
him. I went and played a few more hands. I was running the
game, and things were getting tight with the little change
they had left on them. I finally got caught by another cat. I
said, "$100." I lost.

"Bet another hundred," I said.

I lost.

"Payday stakes," I said. "Bet another $100."

I lost.

I lost five more hands. I was about $700 in debt. This cat
had a shit-eating grin all over his face, man. He didn't know
what to do. So he just giggled and all the other dudes, they
wanted to deal, because they figured I was a fool.

We went on again. Payday stakes. $100. Lost again.
Payday stakes. $100. Lost once more. Then I got a black-
jack, and won back the deal.

"Payday stakes," I said.

"Oh, man," they all said.

"Oh man, nothing," I said. "I played payday stakes with
you. Now you can play payday stakes back with me. I make
the most money anyway in this motherfucking thing. Now
what are you guys gonna do? Sit up here and jive like a
bunch of little jive chickenshits, squirming? Or are you
going to gamble like men? You say you can gamble." I was
really going to teach them a lesson then, because I was
always going to out-bet them. We went way out to the
benches in the middle of the park, and we sat down and
really started gambling. We had about fifteen cats there. All
the cats who thought they were slick wanted to gamble. I
kept the deal and after a while, I must have had two of them
$2000 in debt to me.

So, I told the cats, "Now you're gamblers, aren't you?"

They said, "Yeah."

"Now see what I've been doing to you cats?" I said. "I've been outbetting you." I had one cat there $1000 in the hole. "What you need to do is bet $2000 next time. Bet $2000, man," I said. "Come on, all of you cats that are in the hole here. Come on now. Some of you have got to win. Now I've got you $600 in the hole," I pointed at one. "You, $500, you, $300."

I had all these cats in the hole and I told them they had to righteously bet, so the cats uped their bets, and I won every hand, man. I won every hand. They didn't want to play anymore. I said, "Come on, man. What's the matter?" They got to jiving. "I don't make as much money as you do. I can't pay that kind of money."

"You're going to pay me," I said. "Don't be jiving me. You're going to pay me because I get your checks. I'm the one who gives you your checks. You understand that? I'm the one who puts your hours on the books." I was serious with them, too—I sounded very serious with them. Then, I said, "All right, all right. I might cut it down on some of you, because I know you can't pay it. But you cats are going to pay me. You're going to pay me every bit of it. I don't want to have no shit out of none of you."

Man, they were kind of teed off. Payday was coming up that Monday. They got paid twice a month, on the fifteenth and the last of the month. So when payday came I got them all together. I had their names written down in a book. I had their checks put aside especially. "Come on brothers," I said. "Let's go. Get in the truck. Get in the truck." I put them all on the special crew and took them all down to the bank, and handed their checks out. I said, "All right now. You owe me, uh, $2000, right?" The cat says, "Yeah."

"All right," I said, "I want half of your check, and that'll be the end of the debt."

"Really, man?"

"Yeah," I said, "the end of the debt. Now here's your check. Cash it."

So what I did was prorate everybody who owed me less

than that. Some cats only wound up paying me a couple of dollars. But the thing is, after that I told them, "Now don't be gambling no more. The house will beat you. I've been to Reno. I know, man. The house will beat you. That's going to teach you a lesson." I took that money and donated it back and turned it toward a big party they had. Then with some of the cats who were twenty-one years old, I bought them all the beer they wanted for the rest of the summer.

Another time I caught some of them drinking wine on the job. I saw two of them sitting in a car and sipping from a bottle. I called to the brother who was supervising the job. I said, "Hey man. You see these dudes right here? They were sitting out there hiding the wine bottle. You see these dudes, man?" The cat who is supposed to be supervising looks at me. "Man," I said, "these punks are sitting up there jiving and fucking off, man, and they're not doing any work and it's your fault. But the most killing thing about it is that they have some wine in the car, man."

The supervisor thought I was getting halfway serious, but he knew me a little bit, so he started laughing and grinning. I said to the dudes in the car, "OK now. Open the door, and get out of that car." I told the supervisor, the twenty-one-year-old cat, I said, "These cats have this wine and wouldn't give us any. They wouldn't give us a bit, man. So now that they've drunk half the wine out of the bottle, the rest belongs to me and you, doesn't it, brother?" He agreed.

"Is that all right with you, brother?" I asked one of the dudes who had been drinking.

He says, "Yeah, man, OK."

So we checked around and we drank the wine. Then we said, "Everything's all right. You all go on back to work, all right?"

They said, "All right, man." This was toward the beginning of the job. They thought that I was going to turn them in. What I was trying to do was show the brothers that they have to take more responsibility, but I was trying to do it with a different technique, instead of pouncing on their heads.

I knew that those kids had been drinking wine before they ever met me. When you roll it in on them fast, like the authorities do, and beat their heads, and put them down, they only want to do it more. So the thing was to catch them with the wine, and let them know that they weren't being slick, that they weren't hiding from anybody, and have them go back to work. Now if I had thrown the wine away and spilled it all on the ground, the cats would have hated me. I'd have despised a cat who threw all the wine away myself.

This is the kind of general relationship that I built up with the brothers. Some of the brothers who got caught doing different things got docked on their pay occasionally. Sometimes I'd leave the pay docked but a lot of times I'd take the docked pay off if I saw that the cat was really trying to go ahead and do his work. One of the more significant things I tried to do, was to get the dudes to do the jobs real quick and do them efficiently. This would leave some time over to sit down and talk about the history of black people and the experience of black people, and how the system was really against us, and how we had to grow up and be more functional.

Bobby Hutton originally said he didn't want to go back to school, but through the summer program, I talked him into going back. Of course, when he did go back to school, he got kicked out again. I was still working on another job down at the same poverty center, and he came up and told me. I talked him into going back a second time but a week or so later he got kicked out again. He asked me to get him a job in the poverty center. So I said, "Yeah, that would be better than running the streets because that's what's going to happen to you, man." The pigs busted him one day and he told them that he was trying to get a job down at the corner, and the pigs dropped him off in front of the poverty office. I happened to be out there. I told them, "Yeah, I'm trying to get him a job here." I think they busted him with a beer can or something. So I got the head supervisor at the place to get him a job. Some of the other brothers in that program

were among the initial members of the Party, but Bobby
Hutton was the very first member of the Black Panther
Party.

What was significant to me about that summer program
was that I had built up such a good relationship with the
young brothers. One of the things that hurt that poverty
operation was that they were always trying to get the kids to
do things by pulling that authoritarian stuff. They were
citing the Marquis of Queensbury's rules and stuff like that.
And half of those brothers couldn't even read. Some of
them were already out of high school. Some of them were
drop-outs, and some of them had already graduated, the
eighteen-year-olds and the nineteen-year-olds, but many of
them couldn't even read.

Trying to teach those cats was tough. Most of the sisters
could read. The brothers could read words like this, that,
did, done, days, though, etc., but their general reading level
wasn't any higher than that. Most of the brothers were from
the streets. They wanted to be slick, they wanted to be
pimps, they were trying to get them a piece from some of
the sisters all the time. It was hard, but I was able to
encourage them to go and sit in the writing and reading
classes that went along with the program. The work crews
had to come in for a certain number of hours. They'd go to
a class for an hour or two and go back out. I tried to give
them some insight into the values of reading and the values
of learning, along with Black History. I'd try to help the
cats understand that it was all related.

POLICE-COMMUNITY RELATIONS

■ Our best experience in dealing with the power structure
in that program came when somebody in the Department of
Human Resources downtown set up a tour of police headquarters for our center. Mr. Allen, the head of the program,

said, "Mr. Seale, the young ladies and fellows on the whole crew here will be going down to police headquarters tomorrow." That was Friday.

I said, "Police headquarters?"

He said, "Yeah, they have a tour down there, and they want them to come down and tour the police station so they can understand the city government better, and so the police department can establish better human relations with the community."

"Well," I said, "OK. I'll see to it that they all get down there tomorrow." I thought to myself, "If those brothers and sisters get down there and get to talking with too many of those policemen, those cats are going to get themselves busted." I knew they were always in and out of jive, petty crimes. A lot of times, I put them on jobs somewhere in town, a crew of ten or twelve, and they might try to shoplift from a corner store or something like that. One time I had to go in and talk the man into not having them arrested because they had been in there stealing, stealing the man's stuff, when they had money in their pockets. I had to show them that it wasn't necessary to be ripping things off, when they had money in their pockets.

"Petty crimes can jack you up," I told them. "Not that I'm on the side of the system," I said, "but when you've got something going for yourself, you should use that as a functional thing as much as you possibly can." The next day I thought I'd drop back by there because I knew these brothers. They'd go down there and steal even if they had $50 in their pockets. So I drove by there, and sure enough there were two of them in the store. No sooner do I walk in than I saw somebody sticking a bag of cookies up under his belt. The cat came outside.

I say, "Hey, man, come here. I thought I told you, man, not to be jiving around here, jiving and stealing. This old man wants nothing more than to arrest you cats on a bullshit tip." Then I asked him, "Now how much money have you got on you? I'll buy you a beer. Tell me how much you've got on you."

"Oh man. What's wrong with you, man? You out of your mind?"

"No, I'm not out of my mind, man. You ain't got sense enough to see that this old stupid man here is going to get some cop." I pulled on his coat and took the cookies back to the man. Then I said to the cat, "Now come over here. Walk back there and apologize to the man."

"Man, you out of your mind?" He turned around and walked out. I thought to myself, "Well maybe I shouldn't have done that." So I went out there and said to him, "Look, man, maybe I was wrong in telling you to apologize, but what I'm trying to do is to keep the man from calling up. He's mad, man. He wants to call up and bust nine or ten of you cats who are working down here.

"I've got another job up the street from this place," I said. "Nine or ten more cats are going to be working in this general area. You all are going to come to this jive store, and the next thing I know, you all are going to get busted on a bullshit tip, because you don't have sense enough to see that you've got money in your pocket and cookies don't cost that much."

"Yeah, I guess you right, Bobby. You right, man. Shit. I'm a fool."

I said, "You sure are, if you keep that up, brother."

"Right," they said and split.

We had to go down to the police station on Friday, so I got everybody together Thursday evening. I went around to all the jobs and picked up half the cats. "Look, tomorrow you cats are going down to the police station for a tour," I said. The cats say, "Police station?" They said that really turned-offish.

"Yeah, man," I said.

"Bobby, what you doing, man?"

"Man, it ain't me," I said. "I don't want to go down to no jive police station." Some of the sisters said, "Shoot, I don't want to be going way down there to see old fools." But one little girl said, "I want to go down there. I want to see what it's like." Half of them wanted to go and half of them didn't. The half that did want to go, wanted to go just out of curiosity.

"Well we're going anyway," I said. "This is one of the tours, and you cats have got to go, so we'll go. But when you get down there, don't be talking to no policemen. They are going to try to ask you questions. I know these cops. They're going to try to ask you questions in some kind of way, about yourself, gangs, and people in the community, so they can focus in on you cats. That's trying to use you like Germany used little kids," I told them, "although it's not that heavily organized. But I know them. Don't answer any questions. Just observe things there and whatever the tour is about. I don't know what it's about, but I'll be with you."

"All right, man."

"Right," I said.

"Right. OK, man. Beautiful."

We bussed down to the police station the next day. We went inside, and they took us into a big room, a kind of police room. It had a lot of chairs in it. Some lieutenant who was the head of the juvenile division was sitting up there, along with the chief of police. This lieutenant jumped up and said, "Well, it's good to have all of you here. Come down and see the police station. We've got a lot of things you're going to see today. You'll be able to go up to the crime museum, and you'll see the firing range, and go around and see the communications operations here." His voice was real coppish-like. "And the communications section upstairs, and generally look over the police department, because this is all related to establishing, er a . . ." It wasn't in a human tone at all. "And uh, establishing community relations with the people in the communities and uh, and uh, and . . . and . . . so that we can better get along in our society."

Then this cop went right off into it. "I know a heck of a lot of you guys out there are in gangs." Now he sounded real toughish-like. He went on, "And a lot of you are in different organizations and groups. And uh, I want to ask a few of you some questions." I noticed the other three or four cops in the room, they've got pads out, sitting up there. They've got pads out. There was another one sitting over off to the side and he had a note pad sitting on his lap.

I said to myself, "These motherfuckers!"

"And uh, a lot of rioting. Things been going on, and uh, some of you guys are good guys, and you know we've got some good jobs down there for you guys this summer, and uh, if you know any guys who've been running around here looting and things like that we want you to, uh, give us their names, and, uh, the names of the different organizations and groups out there, and uh, and uh, let us know where they're staying, and . . ."

I jumped up and I said, "Hold it! Hold it! Hold it right there!" I said, "Not one more word! Don't you brothers say a word! Don't anybody say nothing!"

This cop looked at me and I looked at him and I said, "No sirree!"

"Well," he said, "this is just a part of the tour."

"No, uh-uh. You ain't gonna jack these cats up here like that," I said. "You've got them informing on other people in the community and half of the cats are getting shot and brutalized when you cops go pick 'em up.

"No sirree!" I said. "You're not going to turn us into no operation where the police department makes us inform on ourselves. You're talking about community relations. This ain't no community relations operation. This is a jive criminal investigation, and you're not going to use them to do it!

"We know how to start encouraging these brothers to stop committing crimes and things like that, and how to organize them to teach themselves, but we're not going to have this!"

They didn't like that, man. So Mr. Allen came in and said, "Seale, I think you should let the officer continue."

I said, "Yeah, OK."

So he tried again, this cop. "Well, has anybody got anything to say out there?" Nobody said a thing. "Well, does anybody have any questions about the police department?" Silence. "Does anybody have any questions?" Nobody said nothing. "If anybody's got any questions about the police department just raise your hand, just raise your hand, and we can talk and have some general discussion here." Nobody would piss a drop. The brothers and I and the sisters, we all had that together. They weren't saying a thing. Then the police walked out, and the chief of police walked over and talked to Mr. Allen. They walked outside.

As I walked down the aisle, I spotted a brother over to my left. This cat had a big, big old long switchblade. He had the blade down on his lap but he was cleaning his fingernails with it, with this big, long switchblade, about four-and-a-half inches long. "Goddam," I said to myself. "Sitting right up here in the middle of the police station!" I walked over and I bent down and whispered to him.

"Brother."

"Yeah, Bobby," he said, "what is it, man?"

"Don't raise your hands up. Keep 'em down," I said, "and close that knife, and put it in your pocket. Man, do you realize you're sitting right in the police station and you've got an illegal knife on you? And when you get home, man," I said, "leave that thing in your house. What's wrong with you?"

"Yeah, man. OK. I'm sorry. You right, man. You right." He got kind of shaky there. He realized that he could get busted on a bullshit tip.

Some of the other brothers next to him heard us talking and they started giggling, "Ha, ha, hee, ya damn fool." They ridiculed each other a lot. So I said, "You ain't got no business calling him no fool, because you'd have probably done the same thing. Why don't you cats stop laughing at each other."

Then they called me outside and the lieutenant said, "Well, Bobby, uh, it seems like you've got things under control here. Uh, don't you want to let us ask any questions?" Mr. Allen said, "Bobby, uh, I mean uh, you have to let them ask questions. You have to tell those kids out there

. . . I know they like you and everything, Bob—but uh, you have to uh, at least let them ask questions, uh and let these officers here see if they have anything to investigate."

"Well I'm not going for the investigation, Mr. Allen," I said, "because the way police departments work, half of the stuff that they get is trumped up. They're trumped up because one kid will say, 'Joe might have done this, Jim might have done that.' Most kids don't know what they're saying and they don't know anything about the law."

The police tried to say, "Well, we're trying to teach them about the law."

"No, you're not teaching them about the law," I said, and we got into a little argument right there. "You're not teaching nothing about the law. Not one of them, probably, has ever opened a penal code book. They don't generally know what a law is or what law is being broken. Some of them are wrong, some of them do illegal things maybe, but I don't see any reason for you railroading them.

"You police departments work erroneously anyway," I told them. "Because what you cats do is get skimpy information here, and skimpy information there, and Joe said that, and Joe said this, and Jim said this, and Jack said that, and the next thing you know, half the cats you have arrested haven't even committed real crimes, or any specific crime that you're trying to charge them with, because what's-his-name will mention such-and-such a person's name on such-and-such a night. That's what you're trying to get those cats in there into, and I'm not going to let them do it. We're together, we're going to stick together. Even if you fire me, Mr. Allen, I know I'm right because I'm protecting them."

Then Mr. Allen said, "Well, I still think that the kids should ask some questions to go along with the community relations program."

I said, "All right. We'll let them ask a few questions, but I'll go with you to tell them." So what I did, instead of telling them, "Go ahead and ask questions," I said, "Do you guys want to ask questions here or not?"

One of the brothers said, "Aw, man, I don't want to ask no questions here."

So I said, "Well, we'll see what we can do about setting up something because I still think that you brothers have something to say about what the police do in our communities, instead of always letting them dictate to us."

Somebody said, "That's right, because a whole lot of stuff has happened, man, that I know about, that a whole lot of these police have done." All the brothers were saying, "Yeah, yeah." They were carrying on, man.

I said, "All right. Hold it. Hold it. Hold it." I raised my hands up. They always got quiet when I said, "Hold it." I said, "All right. I'll talk to this lieutenant some more and see what else we can set up in the future." I went over and said, "Mr. Allen, why don't you just let them finish the tour, and if we just work it out together, we could have them send some of the regular patrolmen off the streets to talk to the kids at one of the Saturday morning lecture sessions."

"All right, Seale," he said. "That makes sense."

So they finished taking them on the tour. I was running around the tour with them, looking at different things all over the building.

Along the way, I saw one of the regular sergeants, a cop that we knew, a black cat Huey and I had known for a time, and he complimented me. "Bobby," he said, "you did right, because these cats really will trump up a lot of shit on a lot of brothers." Huey and I dug him because he had told us that the only time he'd shoot a cat was if his own life was really in danger, if he saw somebody else's life in danger, or where the cat was actually committing a criminal act. "But like in riots and stuff like that," he told us, "cats breaking windows. I'm not going to shoot nobody over nobody's property, but I will arrest them." Me and Huey had definitely respected that fact about him; the fact that he said that if he was ordered out on a riot, he'd quit his job before he'd go out there shooting and killing.

This particular cop always felt that he could do a lot from the inside, but he was isolated, isolated from that whole department. He gave us a lot of statistics, and a lot of information about the entire Oakland police department and how 75 to 85 percent of them were racists. This black cop came up to me during the tour, and told me that they wanted to talk to me upstairs. I said, "OK, I can talk to them." So I went upstairs and Mr. Allen was up there, the woman foreman was up there, and another member of the Department of Human Resources was up there. They didn't like me because I had stopped it. The police chief and Assistant Chief Gain (he's the chief now) were sitting there, and they'd filled up their heads with certain attitudes they were trying to get off.

"Well, Bob, uh, I think that was, uh, not a good thing, you know, uh, that, uh, the officers weren't able to talk to the kids."

"Well, I think that the officers should come to the community. Come down to the park where we meet on Saturdays. If you want to establish some community relations come down and listen to the kids. They've got grievances too. They want to ask the police some questions instead of the police bringing us here and asking us questions. They're always trying to ask us questions," I said. "Now we want the community and the youth to ask *them* questions. That's a better way to establish relations.

"Both of them can ask each other questions, but we want to stand on our own ground. So you send four or five regular officers off the beat, young ones and old ones, and we'll go from there. I'm pretty sure they'll go for that, the Saturday lecture class right before the baseball game."

They came down the next day. That next morning they were there, man. That same lieutenant came. They had some pamphlets stacked up with three policemen standing at attention in a very dramatic photo. They took the picture from a ground angle, with the modern police headquarters building and the American flag in the background, and these policemen in the pictures were smiling, and on top in big letters they put "POLICE-COMMUNITY RELATIONS." Then you flip the book over and you see all nicey, nicey things.

You see pictures of a policeman helping a little white girl across the street. She's nice and neat and clean. There were no black people in the whole motherfucking pamphlet. I was checking that out, man.

"Oh goddam," I said to myself, "Isn't this a front and a phony situation. The police chief is saying all kinds of nicey, nicey things, and he doesn't say a word about the police brutality going on in the communities, and he doesn't say a word about racists and bigots." They had pamphlets and passed them all out. Then the lieutenant said, "Well, uh, Bob, do you want to set the tone here?" He was trying to be friends with me in front of the kids.

"Yeah, I'll set the tone," I said. "Hey, you cats. All the questions we talked about yesterday after we left the police department. I just want the true facts, things that you remember, or that you heard people talk about that sound pretty true to you. Not exaggerated things. You can ask these policemen about those cases of police brutality and injustice that some of you have witnessed. You can go ahead and ask them about that. They say they want to start this community relations program and I know you can document a heck of a lot."

I hate the day that I didn't tape that session. I hate the day. Man, those kids tore into the cops. They just tore into them. They talked about cops. They really talked about the police brutality that half of them had actually witnessed. Then they talked about stories they'd heard. I always made the point of asking, "Is this something you witnessed, or is this something you just heard? Now be honest and say if you saw it or just heard about it." I was trying to get them to be as objective as possible, although the things they had heard were very significant, too. Man, it made the cops mad, and they looked mad.

"What about the time," one little girl asked, "down on Fourteenth Street in front of the dance hall down there on the other side of Cypress, when a black woman was snatched by three cops and knocked down to the ground with a billy club?" She was angry, too, when she said it. She made one cop just turn red. "Now do you think it's right for a big six-foot cop to throw a five-foot woman down to the ground, and hit her on the head with a billy club?" One of the officers, kind of half nervously and trying to be serious and objective, said, "Well, maybe she had a weapon in her hand."

"Yeah, she had a weapon, and they took it away from her. But after they took the weapon away from her, that's when they beat on her and that ain't right. I don't think no cop got no right to be beatin' on no woman." That sister was mad, and she put that over with every piece of emotion she had, and she sat down, man. Ooh, that tore those cops up.

Some of the guys were articulate, and some were very serious about what they had to say. Some were mad, and some weren't. Some just presented cases they'd heard, and argued their cases as to what was right and what was wrong. There were a few points of law that the policemen were citing wrong. One cop actually stood up and said, "No, you don't have a right to defend yourself." I said, "Wait a minute. Are you telling me, are you telling us, are you telling all these young people here, that if a policeman unjustly, criminally attacks and brutalizes them, they don't have a right to defend themselves?"

"No, you don't have a right to defend yourself," the officer said. "What you should do is take it, and come down and file a complaint."

"Well, what about some of the ones who are dead?" I asked him. Man, that upset the whole place! "They can't come down and put in a complaint," I said.

"Well, uh, you know, uh, that, that those cases are exaggerated."

"Exaggerated, my ass!" I said. "Fifty percent of them, 50 percent of them, man, are outright cases of police brutality and police murder! Maybe the other 50 percent of them are related to some kind of criminal activity because we know that the brothers do commit crimes. We're not trying to hide that fact. But 50 percent of those cases are outright police brutality!" Man, that upset that whole place.

Then this little girl got up and she said, "Say you!" She was about sixteen, and she pointed at this one policeman.

"You don't have to treat him like that," I said.

"Bobby, I'll treat him like I want to, because they done treated me so bad."

"Well, excuse me, sister," I said, and I sat back.

This cop she had pointed to, he was red. He was shaking. She said, "Have you ever been to see a psychiatrist?"

That's what she said to this cop. This cop just looked at her and the lieutenant got ready to say something, but she started speaking again.

"I heard that policemen are supposed to go see a psychiatrist to see if they are psychologically capable of being a policeman. Have you ever been to a psychiatrist?" He really got to shaking then, man.

"The way you're shaking now," she said, "the way you're shaking now and carrying on, you must be guilty of a whole lot! And I haven't got no weapon, or nothin'. This is just an ordinary meeting between police and people in the community, the youth here on this program, and you're shaking. Not only do you need to see a psychiatrist, you need to be off the police force!"

Man, that cat was mad. That was a hell of a scene. I have never witnessed anything so beautiful. Those kids knew cases. They know, man. They know. That was so beautiful. And that was when I knew I became an enemy of the Oakland Police Department. This was about three or four months before the Black Panther Party got started.

Most of the brothers really dug the poverty program, and the way I ran it. I'm pretty sure that most of those kids learned a lot. I even found brothers who knew drafting. Since I dug drafting myself, I began to advocate to the advisory committee that the brothers should learn more skills in these programs, and that we should set up more

programs in the community so brothers who wished they
had skills like brother Huey P. Newton, could learn them.

"They should be taught by people who are really concerned with the brothers and not by those old-time white
racists who are trying to control them and misguide them
away from unifying black people and serving black people."
That was that scene, and it was something else, man.

HUEY:
GETTING THE
PARTY GOING

THE PANTHER PROGRAM

■ One day Huey said, "It's about time we get the organization off the ground, and do it now."

This was in the latter part of September 1966. From around the first of October to the fifteenth of October, in the poverty center in North Oakland, Huey and I began to write out a ten-point platform and program of the Black Panther Party. Huey himself articulated it word for word. All I made were suggestions.

Huey said, "We need a program. We have to have a program for the people. A program that relates to the people. A program that the people can understand. A program that the people can read and see, and which expresses their desires and needs at the same time. It's got to relate to the philosophical meaning of where in the world we are going, but the philosophical meaning will also have to relate to something specific."

That was very important with Huey. So, Huey divided it up into "What We Want" and "What We Believe." "What We Want" are the practical, specific things that we need and that should exist. At the same time, we expressed philosophically, but concretely, what we believe. So we read the program one to one. Point One of "What We Want" and Point One of "What We Believe." Point Two of "What We

Want" and Point Two of "What We Believe." This is the way the people should look at it. It puts together concisely all the physical needs and all the philosophical principles in some basic instructive thing that they can understand, instead of a bunch of esoteric bullshit.

I don't care what kind of cat is on the block—if he doesn't relate to anything else, he can relate to the ten-point platform and program of the Black Panther Party.

Huey said, "Black people and especially brothers on the block have to have some political consciousness."

We wrote it out and Melvin Newton, Huey's brother, came over and proofed it for corrections in grammar. We put it together, and we took all the paper we needed out of the poverty program supplies late at night at the poverty office. We were writing out the ten-point platform and program inside the back office.

Huey said, "Now, what's the first thing we want?" And Huey answered his own question. "WE WANT FREEDOM."

And I wrote down, "We want freedom."

Then he said, "We want the power to determine the destiny of our black community."

I said, "Right, brother, that's good. What's the next thing?"

"We want full employment for our people."

"What else?"

"Nothing else."

"OK, brother, right."

I thought about it and he was right. That's what we want. We want full employment for our people. This is a basic program for our people, because the people are going to relate to the fact that this is exactly what they want and they ain't going to settle for nothing else—they ain't going to settle for a bunch of esoteric bullshit and a long essay.

Then Huey said, "We want the white racist businessman to end the robbery and exploitation of the black community." So, we wrote that down.

Then we wrote, "We want decent housing, fit for shelter of human beings."

"What else, brother Huey?"

Huey sat there and he thought for a few shakes. He said, "Now we got to get off into the area of education. I think that's important. We got employment, the power of our own community, and decent housing. Now we want decent education that teaches us about the true nature of this decadent American system, and education that teaches us about our true history and our role in present-day society."

After that he went right into, "We want all black men to be exempt from military service."

That's the way we put it. We didn't have to go into anything else because we knew that the black people on the block would understand and that's what we want. Basically nothing else.

Then Huey said, "Look at the racist power structure. We have to deal with that. We have to understand that we want an immediate end to police brutality and murder of black people."

I wrote that exactly like it was.

Huey went on to the next one. "We want all black men and women to be released from the federal, county, state, and city jails and prisons."

I said, "Right," and wrote that down.

Then brother Huey said, "We want every black man brought to trial to be tried in a court by a jury of his peer group as it is defined by the Constitution of this United States."

For a black man this means people from the black community.

Then Huey said, "Let's summarize these points. We want land, we want bread, we want housing, we want education, we want clothing, we want justice, and we want some peace."

That's the way Huey put it and I wrote it down. We went over the ten points and put in our commas and periods, and then we got into "What We Believe." We went through everything we believed that was correlative to everything that we wanted.

Huey said, "This ten-point platform and program is what we want and what we believe. These things did not just come out of the clear blue sky. This is what black people have been voicing all along for over 100 years since the Emancipation Proclamation and even before that. These things are directly related to the things we had before we left Africa."

When we got all through writing the program, Huey said, "We've got to have some kind of structure. What do you want to be," he asked me, "Chairman or Minister of Defense?"

"Doesn't make any difference to me," I said. "What do you want to be, Chairman or Minister of Defense?"

"I'll be the Minister of Defense," Huey said, "and you'll be the Chairman."

"That's fine with me," I told him, and that's just the way that shit came about, how Huey became the Minister of Defense and I became the Chairman of the Black Panther Party. Just like that.

With the ten-point platform and program and the two of us, the Party was officially launched on October 15, 1966, in a poverty program office in the black community in Oakland, California.

We got my wife and Huey's girl friend LaVerne together, and they typed it out for us on stencils inside that poverty program office. The next night we took them and we ran off over a thousand copies of that ten-point platform and program.

Huey said, "The brothers and sisters have to relate to this because this is what they want. This is what they've told me. This is what they've told every other leader in this country."

You always have to understand that Huey understood the difference between reform and revolution. Huey understood that you answer the momentary desires and needs of the people, that you try to instruct them and politically educate them, that these are their basic political desires and needs, and from the people themselves will rage a revolution to make sure that they have these basic desires and needs fulfilled.

That's what Huey P. Newton put forth, and that's what Huey P. Newton understood to be political, and that's what Huey P. Newton understood to be the reason why people who are oppressed will wage a revolution. That's what I remember, that's what I know, that's what I feel, and that's what I'll never forget about Huey. He never forgot about the people. He'd bring it right down to the food, and the bread and employment, decent housing, decent education —the way the motherfuckers, the President, and all, fucked over us in the military service; the pigs, the murder, and brutality; the courts; the brothers who are in jail, how they had to be released.

While he was in jail, a year-and-a-half later, Huey said to add something to Point Ten. He was reading brother Eldridge Cleaver's thing about a black plebiscite in the United States conducted by the United Nations (which is directly related to what Malcolm X said). Huey related not to the personality alone of Malcolm, or Mao Tse Tung, or Fanon. He related to what all these revolutionary leaders of the world said we must do, what we must establish, what we must institutionalize. That's very important. This is the way the program was written. Huey always had the people's desires and political needs in mind. He always had the revolutionary tactics and the revolutionary means in mind as to how the people must go about getting these things, getting these basic desires and needs.

This is where the shit boils down to—to what the people want and not what some intellectual personally wants or some cultural nationalists, like LeRoi Jones, want, or some jive-ass underground RAM motherfucker wants, or what some jive motherfucker in some college studying bullshit says, talking esoteric shit about the basic social-economic structure, and the adverse conditions that we're subjected to

so that no black man even understands. Huey was talking
about some full employment, some decent housing, some
education, about stopping those pigs from brutalizing us
and murdering us.

Then Huey came on the street with some guns. About a
month and a half after this program was written, Huey P.
Newton tried to tell the intellectuals that it's time, it's time
to go forth in the revolutionary struggle. That it's no time to
be bullshitting. "Pick up some guns and don't be bullshitting." Huey wanted brothers off the block—brothers who
had been out there robbing banks, brothers who had been
pimping, brothers who had been peddling dope, brothers
who ain't gonna take no shit, brothers who had been fighting pigs—because he knew that once they get themselves
together in the area of political education (and it doesn't
take much because the political education is the ten-point
platform and program), Huey P. Newton knew that once
you organize the brothers he ran with, he fought with, he
fought against, who he fought harder than they fought him,
once you organize those brothers, you get niggers, you get
black men, you get revolutionaries who are too much.

We went off into this ten-point platform and Huey went
forth to take a pulse beat of the black community, using
Oakland, California where there's nearly 40 percent blacks
and as a black community typical of any other in this
nation. I don't give a damn if a black brother's in the South
because we have brothers from the South all the way up
here in Oakland, and we have brothers from New York,
brothers from Chicago, what have you. Huey understood
that Oakland was a typical black community, so we took
the ten-point platform and program—a thousand copies of
it—and went to the black community with them. He didn't
just pass out the platform in people's hands. He stopped,
talked, and discussed the points on the ten-point platform
with all the black brothers and sisters off the block, and
with mothers who had been scrubbing Miss Ann's kitchen.
We talked to brothers and sisters in colleges, in high schools,

who were on parole, on probation, who'd been in jails, who'd just gotten out of jail, and brothers and sisters who looked like they were on their way to jail. They would cite cases. Huey was always interested in any kind of case anyone who looked like he was going to jail had inside of the courts. Huey was always interested in that. Huey would talk about this brother possibly being railroaded off into jail or prison. Huey knew this because he experienced it and because he understood the brother's predicament in terms of the power structure railroading him there.

So, we had a thousand copies of the ten-point platform and program being circulated through the black community by myself and Huey P. Newton. Little Bobby Hutton came along, and for one-and-a-half months, Bobby stuck with me and Huey, helping us articulate this ten-point platform and program, and the fact that we have to arm ourselves against these pigs who've been murdering us and brutalizing us, how we have to arm ourselves against these racists, Birchites, and Ku Klux Klaners infested in the police departments, the pig departments who "occupy our communities," as Huey P. Newton says, "like a foreign troop." We have to defend ourselves against them because they are breaking down our doors, shooting black brothers on the streets, and brutalizing sisters on the head. They are wearing guns mostly to intimidate the people from forming organizations to really get our basic political desires and needs answered. The power structure uses the facist police against people moving for freedom and liberation. It keeps our people divided, but the program will be what we unite the people around and to teach our people self-defense.

When we started passing the platform around the poverty center there, they'd ask, "Why do you want to be a vicious animal like a panther?"

Huey would break in. "The nature of a panther is that he never attacks. But if anyone attacks him or backs him into a corner, the panther comes up to wipe that aggressor or that attacker out, absolutely, resolutely, wholly, thoroughly, and completely." They didn't *want* to understand that.

Here is the ten-point platform and program as it appears each week in our paper:

OCTOBER 1966
BLACK PANTHER PARTY
PLATFORM AND PROGRAM
WHAT WE WANT
WHAT WE BELIEVE

1. We want freedom. We want power to determine the destiny of our Black Community.

We believe that black people will not be free until we are able to determine our destiny.

2. We want full employment for our people.

We believe that the federal government is responsible and obligated to give every man employment or a guaranteed income. We believe that if the white American businessmen will not give full employment, then the means of production should be taken from the businessmen and placed in the community so that the people of the community can organize and employ all of its people and give a high standard of living.

3. We want an end to the robbery by the capitalist of our Black Community.

We believe that this racist government has robbed us and now we are demanding the overdue debt of forty acres and two mules. Forty acres and two mules was promised 100 years ago as restitution for slave labor and mass murder of black people. We will accept the payment in currency which will be distributed to our many communities. The Germans are now aiding the Jews in Israel for the genocide of the Jewish people. The Germans murdered six million

Jews. The American racist has taken part in the slaughter of over fifty million black people; therefore, we feel that this is a modest demand that we make.

4. We want decent housing, fit for shelter of human beings.

We believe that if the white landlords will not give decent housing to our black community, then the housing and the land should be made into cooperatives so that our community, with government aid, can build and make decent housing for its people.

5. We want education for our people that exposes the true nature of this decadent American society. We want education that teaches us our true history and our role in the present-day society.

We believe in an educational system that will give to our people a knowledge of self. If a man does not have knowledge of himself and his position in society and the world, then he has little chance to relate to anything else.

6. We want all black men to be exempt from military service.

We believe that black people should not be forced to fight in the military service to defend a racist government that does not protect us. We will not fight and kill other people of color in the world who, like black people, are being victimized by the white racist government of America. We will protect ourselves from the force and violence of the racist police and the racist military, by whatever means necessary.

7. We want an immediate end to POLICE BRUTALITY and MURDER of black people.

We believe we can end police brutality in our black community by organizing black self-defense groups that are dedicated to defending our black community from racist police oppression and brutality. The Second Amendment to the Constitution of the United States gives a right to bear arms. We therefore believe that all black people should arm themselves for self-defense.

8. We want freedom for all black men held in federal, state, county and city prisons and jails.

We believe that all black people should be released from the many jails and prisons because they have not received a fair and impartial trial.

9. We want all black people when brought to trial to be tried in court by a jury of their peer group or people from their black communities, as defined by the Constitution of the United States.

We believe that the courts should follow the United States Constitution so that black people will receive fair trials. The Fourteenth Amendment of the U.S. Constitution gives a man a right to be tried by his peer group. A peer is a person from a similar economic, social, religious, geographical, environmental, historical, and racial background. To do this the court will be forced to select a jury from the black community from which the black defendant came. We have been and are being tried by all-white juries that have no understanding of the "average reasoning man" of the black community.

10. We want land, bread, housing, education, clothing, justice, and peace. And as our major political objective, a United Nations-supervised plebiscite to be held throughout the black colony in which only black colonial subjects will be allowed to participate, for the purpose of determining the will of black people as to their national destiny.

When, in the course of human events, it becomes necessary for one people to dissolve the political bands which have connected them with another, and to assume, among the powers of the earth, the separate and equal station to which the laws of nature and nature's God entitle them, a decent respect to the opinions of mankind requires that they should declare the causes which impel them to the separation.

We hold these truths to be self-evident, that all men are created equal; that they are endowed by their Creator with certain unalienable rights; that among these are life, liberty, and the pursuit of happiness. That, to secure these rights, governments are instituted among men, deriving their just powers from the consent of the governed; that, whenever any form of government becomes destructive of these ends, it is the right of the people to alter or to abolish it, and to institute a new government, laying its foundation on such principles, and organizing its powers in such form, as to them shall seem most likely to effect their safety and happiness. Prudence, indeed, will dictate that governments long established should not be changed for light and transient causes; and, accordingly, all experience hath shown, that mankind are more disposed to suffer, while evils are sufferable, than to right themselves by abolishing the forms to which they are accustomed. But, when a long train of abuses and usurpations, pursuing invariably the same object, evinces a design to reduce them under absolute despotism, it is their right, it is their duty, to throw off such government, and to provide new guards for their future security.

WHY WE ARE NOT RACISTS

■ The Black Panther Party is not a black racist organization, not a racist organization at all. We understand where racism comes from. Our Minister of Defense, Huey P. Newton, has taught us to understand that we have to oppose all kinds of racism. The Party understands the imbedded rac-

ism in a large part of white America and it understands
that the very small cults that sprout up every now and then
in the black community have a basically black racist philosophy.

The Black Panther Party would not stoop to the low,
scurvy level of a Ku Klux Klansman, a white supremacist,
or the so-called "patriotic" white citizens organizations,
which hate black people because of the color of their skin.
Even though some white citizens organizations will stand
up and say, "Oh, we don't hate black people. It's just that
we're not gonna let black people do this, and we're not
gonna let black people do that." This is scurvy demagog-
uery, and the basis of it is the old racism of tabooing
everything, and especially of tabooing the body. The black
man's mind was stripped by the social environment, by the
decadent social environment he was subjected to in slavery
and in the years after the so-called Emancipation Proclamation. Black people, brown people, Chinese people, and
Vietnamese people are called gooks, spicks, niggers, and
other derogatory names.

What the Black Panther Party has done in essence is to
call for an alliance and coalition with all of the people and
organizations who want to move against the power structure. It is the power structure who are the pigs and hogs,
who have been robbing the people; the avaricious, demagogic ruling-class elite who move the pigs upon our heads
and who order them to do so as a means of maintaining
their same old exploitation.

In the days of worldwide capitalistic imperialism, with
that imperialism also manifested right here in America
against many different peoples, we find it necessary, as
human beings, to oppose misconceptions of the day, like
integration.

If people want to integrate—and I'm assuming they will
fifty or 100 years from now—that's their business. But
right now we have the problem of a ruling-class system
that perpetuates racism and uses racism as a key to maintain its capitalistic exploitation. They use blacks, especially

the blacks who come out of the colleges and the elite class system, because these blacks have a tendency to flock toward a black racism which is parallel to the racism the Ku Klux Klan or white citizens groups practice.

It's obvious that trying to fight fire with fire means there's going to be a lot of burning. The best way to fight fire is with water because water douses the fire. The water is the solidarity of the people's right to defend themselves together in opposition to a vicious monster. Whatever is good for the man, can't be good for us. Whatever is good for the capitalistic ruling-class system, can't be good for the masses of the people.

We, the Black Panther Party, see ourselves as a nation within a nation, but not for any racist reasons. We see it as a necessity for us to progress as human beings and live on the face of this earth along with other people. We do not fight racism with racism. We fight racism with solidarity. We do not fight exploitative capitalism with black capitalism. We fight capitalism with basic socialism. And we do not fight imperialism with more imperialism. We fight imperialism with proletarian internationalism. These principles are very functional for the Party. They're very practical, humanistic, and necessary. They should be understood by the masses of the people.

We don't use our guns, we have never used our guns to go into the white community to shoot up white people. We only defend ourselves against anybody, be they black, blue, green, or red, who attacks us unjustly and tries to murder us and kill us for implementing our programs. All in all, I think people can see from our past practice, that ours is not a racist organization but a very progressive revolutionary party.

Those who want to obscure the struggle with ethnic differences are the ones who are aiding and maintaining the exploitation of the masses of the people: poor whites, poor blacks, browns, red Indians, poor Chinese and Japanese, and the workers at large.

Racism and ethnic differences allow the power structure

to exploit the masses of workers in this country, because that's the key by which they maintain their control. To divide the people and conquer them is the objective of the power structure. It's the ruling class, the very small minority, the few avaricious, demagogic hogs and rats who control and infest the government. The ruling class and their running dogs, their lackeys, their bootlickers, their Toms and their black racists, their cultural nationalists—they're all the running dogs of the ruling class. These are the ones who help to maintain and aid the power structure by perpetuating their racist attitudes and using racism as a means to divide the people. But it's really the small, minority ruling class that is dominating, exploiting, and oppressing the working and laboring people.

All of us are laboring-class people, employed or unemployed, and our unity has got to be based on the practical necessities of life, liberty, and the pursuit of happiness, if that means anything to anybody. It's got to be based on the practical things like the survival of people and people's right to self-determination, to iron out the problems that exist. So in essence it is not at all a race struggle. We're rapidly educating people to this. In our view it is a class struggle between the massive proletarian working class and the small, minority ruling class. Working-class people of all colors must unite against the exploitative, oppressive ruling class. So let me emphasize again—we believe our fight is a class struggle and not a race struggle.

OUR FIRST WEAPONS

■ Late in November 1966, we went to a Third World brother we knew, a Japanese radical cat. He had guns for a motherfucker: .357 Magnums, 22's, 9mm's, what have you. We told him that we wanted these guns to begin to institutionalize and let black people know that we have to defend ourselves as Malcolm X said we must. We didn't have any money to buy guns. We told him that if he was a real revolutionary he'd better go on and give them up to us because we needed them now to begin educating the people to wage a revolutionary struggle. So he gave us an M-1 and a 9mm.

There was a law service section up in the poverty program office, and Huey studied those law books, backwards, forwards, sideways, and cattycorners; everything on gun laws. And I was right there with him, trying to study them too, run them down, and understand them. Huey knew that he could carry a rifle or a shotgun. His probation officer had run this down to him—he could carry a rifle or a shotgun, but he couldn't carry a pistol. So I carried the pistol, and Huey P. Newton carried the M-1.

The advisory councils of each one of these four poverty program target areas—which consisted of over thirty members from each area, a cross section of the community—had voted unanimously that there should be a citizen's review board of the police because of the police brutality and the murder that had gone down recently and in the past.

We got these two guns together and decided to carry them to a party we were going to. Huey said, "We're going to carry our guns, and we're going to patrol these pigs, on the way to the party." We didn't see any pigs on the way to the party. When we got to the party, Virtual invited us in. We went into the party with our guns. We got inside, and here come the bootlickers—scared niggers, niggers who were jiving, niggers who were talking shit. But Huey is such a humanistic brother that he wants to educate people, and I don't blame him. They have to understand.

"What're you doing with the guns?" a few people asked.

"We have the guns," Huey P. Newton said, "because we're instituting a new organization, a revolutionary organization, that has a ten-point platform and program, that emphasizes the basic political desires and needs of black people throughout racist decadent America."

A few people got upset about the guns. At this party, there were predominately *Negroes* and a few black-minded

people. And they said, "Check your guns." They had been
brainwashed to the position that a black man couldn't have
a gun, but a cop could. That's what was wrong with them,
that's exactly what was wrong with them. Huey P. Newton,
Minister of Defense of the Black Panther Party, said, "All
right, we'll check our guns." So we checked our guns. We
put them in closets, and proceeded to party.

But before Huey checked his guns, he told them, "These
guns are not here to brutalize black people or to intimidate
black people. They're just to let you know that there's a new
organization established called the Black Panther Party for
Self-Defense. Its ten-point platform and program outlines
the basic desires and needs of black people, and this revolutionary organization intends to see that black people receive
those basic political desires and needs." That's what Huey
ran down to them. They couldn't understand it, they were
so damned brainwashed. But we checked our guns, and we
proceeded to party.

It wasn't fifteen minutes, before some bootlicker inside of
that party, some Uncle Toming bitch or nigger—and I
mean to say bitch or nigger—decided to call the police. We
didn't know it was happening but they called the police.
There they were, about ten or fifteen outside the house.
Three or four of them came up inside. One of the "Negroes" pointed me out, and one of them pointed Huey out. I
don't remember what they said to Huey, but I do remember
the pig that came up to me and said, "You have a gun."

"Yeah I have a gun," I said, "what about it?"

"Well, the person who owns this property and who re-
sides in this apartment does not want you in this apartment
with a gun."

"All right, I'll leave. I'll go get my gun and I'll leave," I
said.

I found out later that Huey said the same thing. But as
Huey was leaving, Huey called the bootlickin' nigger, and
his sister, a bootlickin' sister, both bootlickin' bastards. He
told them they were wrong. They'd called a racist dog pig
upon us, who were trying to establish an organization, a

political party to defend black people against the decadence and the racism in this system, against brutality and murder and all other political, economic, and social injustices.

So we walked out, and walked down the stairs. There were pigs on the stairs, pigs on the balcony, pigs downstairs, and there were pigs in the streets. With our guns loaded to the gill, we walked to our car on the corner, me with my wife, and Huey with his girl friend, LaVerne. The pigs were trying to harass Huey and me verbally, but Huey harassed them, verbally. He cited laws and cited points of rights, and put those rights in context about black people's right to defend themselves, and bear guns, and be armed, by the Second Amendment of the Constitution. "If you don't like it," he said to the pigs, "later for you." And all I could do was dig on Huey's technique, listen to him, and reiterate what he said; and back him up with the 9mm I had.

Huey put his M-1 in the middle of the car, between the two seats in the Volkswagen, and I had my 9mm. After the pigs tried to shout at him through the car window, I told him to just cool it. I always had a habit of telling Huey to split and it's the truth. Man, that shit got so hot, and Huey was the kind of a cat who'd be ready to vamp on the motherfucker; and I'd be telling Huey, "Wait a minute, man. We got a lot more work to do. We got a lot more of this to do. Come on. Let's go."

Huey would ask me, "You think we ought to, man? These pigs are trying to harass us."

"Let's split," I would say.

One thing about Huey—he'll listen to the dudes around him. He won't listen to pigs, and he won't listen to people acting the fool; only those with levelheaded sense. But his close brothers, his partners, he'll listen to them because there's something he detects: if you're with him you're with him; if you ain't you ain't—and if what you have to say is not a bunch of bullshit. He doesn't relate to bullshit, but at the same time he'll go right out front and before you know it—whoom! Don't mess over with Huey. That's the way he is.

I remember I called him down a whole lot of times, and I'd say, "Look Huey, let's do this here." He'd talk to David Hilliard, who is now Chief of Staff of the Party, "Hey man, what was I doing in this kind of situation? What do you think we should do?" And Huey'd have his shit and right down with it. And David'd say, "Well, I think you ought to do so and so and so." Huey'd know who is his partner, who's with him. And he'd say, "OK," and he would go along in a kind of unity with those around him. That's the way Huey is, man.

At the same time, if you get him off in a room and discuss politics, organizing people, and the political machine, the necessity of it, etc., he can relate to that, too. That's what's so beautiful about Huey. He can relate to any kind of situation, whether it's death on the streets or organizing the political machine, you see? That's what's so beautiful about him. You can't get around him on that.

That was the first confrontation. The pigs asked Huey if he was on probation. He said, "No!" But he was on probation. They asked me if was I on probation, which I was, and I said, "No!" Huey told me, "Don't tell 'em nothing', because if they find you're on probation, they're gonna shoot to the probation officer and find out." I was on a judgeship probation, from the court, and Huey was on a probation with an officer. Anyway, we drove away and they followed us for three or four blocks. We went on. I guess we were crazy then. They called us "crazy niggers," but fuck it. We just went on. And that was the first implementation of armed self-defense by black people, black brothers, led by Huey P. Newton.

I was proud to be with that brother, beginning to deal with pigs, beginning to educate people to self-defense, because Huey handled it so beautifully. We were going to back off, but at the same time Huey knew his law, he knew his points, he knew his rights, and he knew his ten-point platform and program. It was a motherfucker, because Huey'd start reciting the Party's ten-point platform and program to a pig in a minute. Before the pig knew it, Huey could be finished with the ten-point platform and program. He wouldn't recite the whole program, but the basic things of what we want and what we believe, would be in the context of everything he had to say.

So we floated around the streets, and we patroled pigs. We followed pigs. They wouldn't even know we'd be following them. That's the way that shit went down in the very beginning. That went on for a month, back there in December 1966. Sometimes we'd just be high, going to a party. We might not have guns. Other times, we'd have guns. Still other times we weren't even going to a party. We'd just be going to a meeting. We'd have our shit with us, and while we were going to the meeting, we'd patrol those pigs, trying to catch them wrong. We'd see a pig, we'd get keyed off the meeting. We'd just forget about the meeting, and patrol that pig, just drive around behind him, a long time. After that, we'd go to the meeting. That's how interrelated that shit was. We went to a lot of meetings.

About this time Huey said, "Let's get these brothers together and let's get us an office." That was very important to Huey, because the establishment of an office meant that something was functional. The people in the black community could relate to it. Around the corner from my house, about a block and a half away, there was a vacant store. Huey and Bobby Hutton went and got it for us. Bobby Hutton said, "I'm a member of the Black Panther Party." And Huey says, "You're the first member, a righteous member." He righteously came in then as a righteous member. From there, we got our little pay checks from the poverty program—Bobby Hutton, Huey, and I. We put all our money together and paid the first rent on the first office. We rented that first office for $150 a month on Fifty-sixth and Grove in Oakland.

We got off in that office and we painted a sign in the window—BLACK PANTHER PARTY FOR SELF-DEFENSE. This is what it was named at the time and a lot of people came by in those first days that we opened that office. We opened it January 1, 1967. We announced that we were going to have a first meeting of the Black Panther Party on Saturday, one week later. We opened up the office with the new name on the window and brothers came into the office and sat down and heard what we had to say. We passed out the ten-point platform and program of the Black Panther Party. We weren't even using the Red Book then.

At the next meeting, about a week later, Reginald and Sherman Forte came in. Sherman Forte was in junior college. Huey said, "We're gonna have political education classes on Wednesday night but before you go through political education you have to go through use and safety of weapons for one hour, and at Saturday meetings you have to go through use and safety of weapons for one hour."

We met a drunk brother named John Sloane on the streets. Drunk, he was drunk. He didn't know where to go and he lived about a block from the Party office. He'd say he was going to "righteously get himself together." Later John Sloane righteously stopped drinking. He wouldn't drink a lick because Huey told him he didn't want him coming in the office drunk. "Don't come in the office high or drunk," Huey told him, "because all you can do is be destructive to the Party because you don't know what you're doing in the first place." We found out that John Sloane had been in the military service and that he was the best man to teach brothers field stripping and shooting of the M-1 rifle. He did that for two or three months. He was out of sight on the weapons and rifle in terms of getting the brothers down. He wasn't jiving. He was with us.

Then other brothers began to come in. We had a Saturday night meeting about three-and-a-half weeks after we opened that office, and we had about twenty-five brothers there. It was me, Bobby Hutton, Huey, Mark Johnson, a brother I knew from the poverty program, John Sloane— we made John Sloane a captain—and then about four weeks later, Warren Tucker came in. We got another .38 from a brother up at Cal. He said he wasn't doing anything with it. We told him we wanted it, we needed it. We were going to defend our people. We said we weren't giving it back to him. He didn't raise any arguments about it. We said we weren't bullshitting. He gave us an old broke-up shotgun too. The next thing we knew, we had about thirty, maybe forty members of the Party. Richard Iokey came in —the Japanese brother who gave Huey and me the M-1 and 9mm—and he got to talking about how he had a .357 Magnum. We got the .357 Magnum from him and a couple more pistols, and the brothers got to getting money together, and started buying weapons.

Every Saturday, we opened up a community meeting in the office and Huey was teaching dudes, brothers, and people from the community the ten-point platform and program of the Black Panther Party, in that storefront office. It was a nice, clean office, too, but it didn't have any furniture in it. Sid Walton came down and gave us twenty, twenty-five chairs, but he never panned out to be much of anything close to the Party. He was too engrossed in a lot of abstract bullshit, although he did a lot of work at Merritt College in terms of furthering the things that Huey had already instituted there.* But that's the way it all began, in that office on Fifty-sixth and Grove in North Oakland, the first official headquarters of the Black Panther Party.

RED BOOKS FOR GUNS

■ We were sitting in a car one day, in front of a doctor's office, where Huey had gone. We had just finished reading in the papers about the Red Book. The Red Book was all over TV—the Red Book of China.

The Red Book became a key thing with the Cultural Revolution that was going on in China, and Huey said, "You know what? I know how we can make some money to buy some guns." I said, "How?" "We can sell those Red

---

* Sid Walton is now principal of a Sausalito school. His appointment raised a good deal of controversy, but he was eventually hired.

Books. I know that many brothers on the block would not even buy a Red Book, but I do know that many of those leftist radicals at Berkeley will buy the Red Book." Huey went on to talk about the community of 26,000 at Cal, and how maybe a third or maybe a quarter of them were radicals or liberals who'd be interested in the Red Book, since it was being publicized so heavily.

The next thing you know, Huey asked me, "How much money do you have?" And I said, "Well, I have about $45 or $50 on me." He said, "Well, let's go buy a batch of Red Books and go up to Cal and sell them. I bet we can get a dollar apiece for them." I said, "Right on time."

You know what we did? We went over to the China Book Store in San Francisco and we bought up two batches of the Red Book, thirty in a package, and got back over here and we sold them motherfuckers at Cal campus some Red Books. We sold the Red Books inside of an hour, at a dollar apiece and that shocked us. So we took all that money and we went back to the bookstore and bought all the Red Books the man had left in the store. I think we had three or four more packages. We bought out all the Red Books, paying thirty cents for them. We made a deal with the bookstore. We told them, "We are the Black Panther Party, and could an organization get a discount?" and the next thing I knew, we had enough money to buy two shotguns. This is the way it was.

We got up to Cal the next day at 10:00 A.M., right around the time the student traffic gets heavy in front of Sather Gate. Huey did his sales pitch, "Power comes out of the barrel of a gun. Quotations from Chairman Mao Tse Tung. Get your Red Book." The books were going like hot cakes.

I was hollering, "Quotations from Chairman Mao Tse Tung. Get your Red Book. I just learned that two CIA agents were converted to dedicated communists. Get your Red Book." I said, "All you free speechers up here who lost Mario Savio must read the Red Book and do it like the Red Guards did it." Brother Bobby Hutton could hardly get the title correct. He kept coming over and asking Huey or myself how to pronounce it. Huey would tell him, but he couldn't get it. He said, "If we can buy guns with money coming in this fast I don't have to be able to say it." So he just hollered, "Red Book, Red Book," and they really sold.

CIA, pigs, Communist Party, Socialist Workers Party, news cameramen, and other people took pictures for the next two hours as we sold Red Books. Richard Iokey walked up around the time that we first got there and told us to make sure that we didn't go on campus with the books because those agents were standing all around waiting to bust us. We made our Party over $170. We thought this was where it was at, because the Muslim brothers didn't seem to be selling more than one-fourth of all their papers as fast as we sold those books. They were getting twenty cents per paper and we got a dollar apiece, but this was to get some shotguns.

And if you ever had a "Freedom Now" feeling, you would have sure got it if you saw how we took off to buy some shotguns.

Huey said, "Let's go buy some shotguns." So we went to the B.B.B. department store where Virtual Murrell was working at the time, and we bought a shotgun. Huey bought a High Standard. (That's the brand name of the shotgun.) It holds six shots in a magazine after you take the plug out. And one in the chamber. Huey says, "Let's get some double 0 buckshot." I said, "What's double 0 buckshot?" And he said, "That's the same thing that the pigs use. Double 0 buckshot." I said, "Right on." I was right behind him. This brother was out of sight. He knew what to do, when to do it, and how to do it.

We walked up to the counter and were paying for the shotgun after we requested it from the back counter where the sports material was located. We were drunk admiring those pistols, shotguns, rifles, what have you. And the woman at the counter says, and you could tell she was lying, "You know, these FBI men have been coming around to

request information and names on *everyone* who buys a gun
in our store." Huey says, "We don't care. That don't make
any difference. There is my money. I'm Huey P. Newton of
the Black Panther Party. Here's my money. I want my
shotgun." And the woman looked at him, amazed. I don't
know who she thought she was tricking, because she wasn't
tricking Huey P. Newton—he couldn't give two goddams
about who she thought she was intimidating with some
supposed FBI investigation.

That's very important about Huey's attitude and his personality and the way he's going and the way he knows he's
going. That's very important. Because Huey said, "Here's
my money. My name is Huey P. Newton of the Black
Panther Party," and we picked up that shotgun.

So we sold the Red Books, made the money, and used
that money to buy guns. Me and Huey and the brothers in
the core organization used the Red Books and spread them
throughout the organization, because Huey made it a point
that the revolutionary principles so concisely cited in the
Red Book should be applied whenever they could. That is,
whenever they could be applied within the confines of this
system. Huey would say, "Well, this principle here is not
applicable to our situation at this time." Where the book
said, "Chinese people of the Communist Party," Huey
would say, "Change that to the Black Panther Party.
Change the Chinese people to black people." When he saw
a particular principle told in the Chinese terms, he would
change it to apply to us. So, from there, we righteously used
the Red Book, because we talked about it, and Huey had us
practicing the principles. And we used Fanon and Malcolm
X—his autobiography and other material on him. Huey
integrated all these principles of the other revolutionaries.
We taught from all these materials, and from Che Guevara,
too.

We had initially used the Red Book as a commodity.
Huey P. Newton knew the brothers well enough to know

that they would not pay a dollar for the Red Book. Huey did know that the radicals on the campus would pay a dollar for that Red Book if we had it. And we were the only ones who had it. I remember SWP's (Socialist Workers Party), CP's (Communist Party), and a lot of people, asking very inquisitively, "Where did you get those books?" And we would say, "That's for me to know and for you to find out. You wanna buy one? Only one dollar. *Get your Red Book Quotations from brother Mao Tse Tung.* Aw come on." I would holler, "I know you're wondering what in the world are those Negroes doing with those Red Books?" And I would sell three or four.

We knew that at first the guns would be more valuable and more meaningful to the brothers on the block, for drawing them into the organization; then in turn we taught them from the Red Book. Huey was something else. Huey was out of sight. He knew how to do it. Huey was ten motherfuckers. He would say, "Bobby, you and I know the principles in this Red Book are valid, but the brothers and the black folks don't, and they will not pay a dollar or thirty cents for that book. So what we have to do is to get the white radicals who are intellectually interested in the book, sell the book, make the money, buy the guns, and go on the streets with the guns. We'll protect a mother, protect a brother, and protect the community from the racist cops. And in turn we get brothers in the organization and they will in turn relate to the Red Book. They will relate to political, economic, and social equality in defense of the community."

That's the way the shit went. At the same time, Huey would go off into Fanon. He would get off into Malcolm X. Huey would relate these principles. He was a motherfucker. You couldn't get around Huey. He knew the Red Book sideways, backwards and forwards. There are brothers in the Party that got to know the Red Book cattycorner. The brothers know that book sideways, backwards, forwards, upside down. Turn that book any way you want to—they tell you in a minute. "The Red Book and what else? The gun! The Red Book and what else? The gun!" That's what Huey would say.

Our last major selling escapade of the Red Book to radicals, leftists, and liberals was many months later at that big, 65,000 strong march against the war in Vietnam that wound up at Kezar Stadium in San Francisco. Huey and I had met Eldridge Cleaver by then. Eldridge spoke at that rally that day and the only time Huey and I took out time from selling the whole while we were there, was to listen to Eldridge's speech.

At the end, we made about $850 and had books left over. We had heard from the China Book Store man that he had received a shipment of 5,000 books, so we picked up about 1,200. They all could have been sold, but the man-power we had was short. Only about fifteen or sixteen brothers showed up that Saturday morning at the Black Panther Party office. First we followed the march up Market Street when it started that morning and followed it for about twenty-five blocks. All I could think of was books, dollars, then guns for us motherfuckers. *"Get your Red Books, old liberal ladies."* You know, the kind who decided to go against "Lynching" Baines Johnson because brother Martin Luther King finally went against the war.

The old broads, looking at me, amazed, couldn't figure it out. Probably asking themselves, "What are those colored boys doing with those 'communist books'?" As they walked along the street, I walked out into the ranks and held a Red Book up to them and said, "I know what you're thinking, so why don't you buy just one book and satisfy yourself." I gave one a slight smile, and she said, "OK." Her marching partner also wanted one. Hell, the first thing I know, ten books are gone and I'm working up a sweat running back and forth to the bundles that we had to keep moving.

Dollars for Red Books, and I mean those brothers who were working knew this meant more guns so we could defend ourselves and educate all black people to pick up the gun. Just like the Red Book itself says. The Party was in motion. Dollars for books to be able to get more guns.

HUEY BACKS THE PIGS DOWN

■ Huey was on a level where he was ready to organize the black brothers for a righteous revolutionary struggle with guns and force. It came to a point where, every day, we walked in and out of the Black Panther office, around to my house or around to Bobby Hutton's house, or somebody's house, with guns on our sides, and got in a car, or two or three cars, or four or five cars as it built up, and patroled the pigs on Friday and Saturday nights. Sometimes when we went to a meeting during the week we patroled the pigs. We had a camera or two, a law book, and were working on getting some tape recorders in patroling the pig cops.

One day, as we were walking out of the office (I guess we'd been there about a month or so), a pig passed by. He saw us coming out with shotguns and pistols on our sides. About six or seven of us came out of the office there, in the daytime, and we looked at the pig as he passed by, and he jumped on his radio because he saw us coming out of the office with those pieces and stuff. We had just finished field stripping weapons, learning about double 0 buckshot, learning about the 9mm and the .45, and having a political education session.

We had a .45 and a .357 Magnum in the group, and a couple of M-1's. We had three or four shotguns by then. We bought up guns like a son of a bitch then. The pig went down two blocks and turned around, came back up the other side of the street. They were building rapid transit, BART, right down Grove Street there, and he went up the other side of the boulevard and came back. We readily assessed that the pigs were ready to see what the fuck was happening, that this pig had radioed in, and he was running it down how he had "seen some niggers come out of a place here with some guns and blah blop de bloo, etc., etc., come out of this office with guns" and stuff. He was radioing to other pigs to help "get 'em."

Huey had his father's car that day. I think he had just finished paying some bills and he stopped by the office for about a half-hour. By the time we got in the car, the pig was back around down the street and he drove up behind us. And Huey told everybody to remember what he'd said— that nobody in the car should say anything. Only the driver should do the talking, and Huey happened to be the driver. He said, "I'm the driver. Nobody else say anything, and remember the legal first aid." This was the legal aid information that we had printed for the brothers in the Party, and we were teaching them thirteen points of basic, legal first aid, legal and constitutional rights.

Huey used to teach the brothers on that; he wouldn't let them get around it, because Huey understood that the brothers had no guidelines about how to deal with the pigs. So Huey went off in the area of law and he found out the brothers respected law. Huey *knew* something about law, and he could use it to make it serve him. That's all he was doing, he was bringing them basic things in everyday life about law. That's what Huey dug; he understood that shit. Huey would take those thirteen basic points and try to show a dude where he was fucked up at *in the ghetto*. That's very important in understanding how the Party first began to function.

So he said, "Nobody say anything, because the minute somebody says something the man is going to try to arrest you. And he's going to arrest you for some jive about interfering with an officer carrying out his duty. He's going to try to prove to all the people who are subject to gather around us here that we have no right with a gun. And he's going to arrest you on a traffic ticket and the people out in the community will think he arrested you because you've got the gun. We want to prove to the people that we've got a right to carry guns and they've got a right to arm themselves, and we will exhaust our constitutional right to carry these guns." That's what Huey was trying to exhaust. Boom. Which he did exhaust, ultimately, when we look at the power structure's moves against the Party over the years.

Huey got in the car and the pig came up to the window. "You have any driver's license?" So Huey rolled the window down. There wasn't more than about a three- or four-inch crack in the window.

Huey handed his license out the window. "Is this your true name?" the pig said. And Huey said, "Yes, that's my true name, Huey P. Newton." "Is this your true address, 841 Forty-seventh Street?" And Huey said, "That's my true address, 841 Forty-seventh Street." "What are you doing with the guns?" And Huey said, "What are you doing with *your* gun?" This particular pig decided he wasn't going to argue, so he went back and got his little writing pad where they fill out shit.

"Your true name is Huey P. Newton?" Huey said, "That's right." The pig wrote this down.

"Your true address is 841 Forty-seventh Street?"

Huey said, "That's right." The pig then looked at his license. "What's your phone number?" And Huey said, "Five!" and stopped and wouldn't say anything else. And the pig said, "Five what?"

This is when all the shit between the Party and pigs began. Huey said, "The Fifth Amendment. You ever heard of it? Don't you know about the constitutional right of a person not to testify against himself? Five! I don't have to give you anything but my identification, name, and address so therefore I don't even want to talk to you. You can leave my car and leave me alone. I don't even want to *hear* you."

"What do you mean?" the pig said. And Huey said, "Just what I said. The constitutional right of any man is that he doesn't have to testify against himself." And Huey had a big M-1 sitting to his right with his hand on it. I had this 9mm sitting beside me, and Huey had this M-1 at his side. Huey was driving. Four other brothers were in the back seat, and one of them was Bobby Hutton. They were being quiet because Huey told them to be quiet. And the pig is going crazy. He's by himself and Huey had all these black niggers in the car going for a motherfucker.

Meanwhile, while the pig is trying to get bad, three cars drove up in back of us, and one in front. Some more were in the driveway. Blop, blop, blop de bloo. Then another car came up in front of us. A pig jumped out of his car, walked up to our car, and said through the crack in the window, with a hogish voice, trying to sound intimidating, "What's going on here?" And Huey said, "The same basic procedures that are supposed to go on!" Huey rolled the window down another five or six inches. The pigs were looking at the guns in the car.

"Can I see that pistol there?" one of the pigs said. "No, you can't see it!" Huey told him. I was beginning to get skeptical about what was happening because he pointed to my 9mm pistol. Huey was on probation, and if they thought that this was Huey's pistol . . . I didn't know this law stuff the way Huey knew it, so I moved the pistol over beside me real close. It had been lying in the middle of the seat. I said, "No, you can't see it." Huey said, "No, you can't see the pistol, nor this (pointing to his rifle), and I don't want you to look at it. You don't have to look at it."

"Is that your pistol?" he asked Huey. And I said, "No, it's not his pistol, it's my pistol!" I said that because I was thinking the man's gonna jump on Huey because he already told me about the probation law—if he gets caught with a pistol he's burned. But if he gets caught with a rifle, the man can't mess with him because his probation officer told him he can carry a rifle or a shotgun, and he couldn't stop him. The pig said, "Can I see it, or not?" So Huey said to me, "I'll talk." And then to the pig, "No, you can't see the pistol. Get away from the car. We don't want you around the car and that's all there is to it."

"Well, I can ask *him* if I want to see his pistol or not," the pig says. So I said, "Well, you can't see the pistol!" The motherfuckers try to get indignant. They were blabbing and oinking to each other about who in the hell we thought we were and, "Constitution, my ass. They're just turning it around." Then a pig said to Huey, "Who in the hell you think you are?"

"Look, dammit," and Huey just opened the car door, and this is where Huey got mad. I mean you have to imagine this nigger. He got mad because these dogs were going to carry on and they were bracing up like they were bad. Huey didn't go for this at all. Huey got very *mad*. He opened up the door saying, "Who in the hell do you think *you* are? In the first place, this man (pointing at the pig) came up here and asked me for my license like he was citing me for a ticket or observation of some kind. This police officer is supposed to be carrying out his duty, and here you come talking about our guns." Huey put his hand around his M-1 rifle and continued, "We have a constitutional right to carry the guns, anyway, and I don't want to *hear* it."

The pigs backed up a couple of steps, and Huey was coming out of the car. Huey had his hand back in the car, getting his M-1, and you know, if you've ever seen Huey, he gets growly, but articulate. He came out of the car with his M-1. Huey knows his law so well that he wouldn't have the M-1 loaded inside the car. When he came out of the car, he dropped a round off into the chamber right away. Clack, clup.

"Who do you think you all are anyway?" Huey said to the pigs. And the other pigs are on the sidewalk harassing all the brothers and sisters who have gathered around: "You people move on down the street!" Huey started inter-rupting. "You don't have to move down the street! Don't go anywhere! These pigs can't keep you from observing. You have a right to observe an officer carrying out his duty." And these pigs, they listened to this shit. See, Huey's citing law and shit. "You have a right to observe an officer carry-ing out his duty. You have a right to. As long as you stand a reasonable distance away, and you *are* a reasonable distance. *Don't go anywhere.*"

The pigs kept trying to move the people, saying, "You're gonna get under arrest." So Huey just went over and opened the door to the Panther office and said, "Come on in here. They can't move you out." He took his key, opened the door, and let the people go in. "Now, observe all you want to!" The pig said, "What are you going to do with that gun?"

"What are you going to do with *your* gun?" Huey said. "Because if you try to shoot at me, or if you try to take this gun, I'm going to shoot back at you, swine. Furthermore" —and he just got off into it—"you're nothing but a share-cropper anyway. You come from Georgia somewhere, you're downtown making $800 a month, and you come down here brutalizing and murdering black people in the black communities. They gave you some sergeant stripes and all I say is that you're nothing but a low-life, scurvy swine. A sharecropper from racist Georgia in the South somewhere.

"So if you draw that gun, I'll shoot back at you and blow your brains out!"

"You, you, you . . ." the pig was mad. "You're just turning the Constitution around." This is the pig trying to slough it off.

Huey said, "I'm not turning anything around. And I got my gun. What are you going to do with yours?" This blew the pigs' minds. They didn't know where to go, man. Huey just walked on around the front of the car. Got on around the front of the car, talking, then went on and opened the office door again, and let some more people in, telling the people they didn't have to go anywhere, citing their consti-tutional rights and all this stuff, then just jumped on out of the office again and said, "Now what are you going to do?"

Another burly kind of fat pig walked up to about five yards in front of Huey with his hands in his belt, the front of his belly falling over the belt. He asked Huey, "Are you a Marxist?" Huey asked him, "You a fascist?" "Are you a Marxist?" the pig asked in a louder tone of voice. Then Huey got louder. "Are you a fascist?"

Then the pig asked it in a very loud, demanding voice. Lifting his hand out of his belt, the pig said, "Are you a

Marxist?" And Huey, louder, *"Are you a fascist?"* The pig asked three more times in a softer tone, and Huey repeated his question.

Then the pig said, like a stupid fifth-grade kid, "I asked you first."

Huey shook his head unbelievingly and said, "I asked you second. *Are* you a fascist?" Everybody laughed at the pig.

I was sitting in the car with the hammer of my 9mm cocked back. I said, "These pigs are going to be wild-eyed. I *know* they're gonna be crazy." I rolled the window down. "What's *your* name?" I say, "My name is Bobby Seale. Why?" "Want to check *you* out. Got any identification?" I laid my pistol down, gave them identification; I picked my pistol back up. I said, "My name is Bobby Seale, as it says in my identification. Want to check me out?"

"You were arrested for armed robbery at seventeen."

I said, "You're a goddamned liar. I've never been arrested in my life. I've never been arrested for armed robbery." They didn't even check me out. "You were arrested for armed robbery when you were seventeen. But since you were a juvenile, we can't arrest you for possessing a gun now." I said, "You damned liar. I've never been arrested for armed robbery. I don't want to hear it. Fuck it."

And Huey out there, man, he's calling the pigs swine, dogs, sharecroppers, bastards, motherfuckers, with his M-1 in his hand. And *daring* them, just daring them! "You don't pull your gun on *us*." And that's where Huey began to show us. You tell some motherfucker, and you *mean* it. This is what I remember. Huey was relating to one thing. When he told me, a long time ago, to remember that we might not ever come back home one day, I said, "I'm with you, Huey." I remember that. I remember I might not ever come home one day. "Fuck it, I'm with you."

We were sitting in the car, and Huey made us all stay in the car and be quiet. He was out there, the baddest mother-fucker in the world, man. Huey and ten pigs. Three or four of them trying to run kids off bicycles and tell the people

they didn't have the right to stand around, and Huey was
going out there, interrupting, "No! Come in the office."
Little kids on bicycles got inside the office. We had a big,
wide, clear picture window. Niggers just got all over the
front of the window, man. They were leaning on it, kissing
the window just to listen to this shit. And they would holler,
"Go 'head on, brother," and "Run it on down. You know
where it's at," and "I can dig it," all the while Huey was
letting these pigs know where it was at. The brothers observing would see that those pigs were scared of that *big*
gun that a bad black but beautiful nigger had in his hand.
Every time Huey would say, "If you shoot at me, swine, I'm
shooting back," niggers would have to holler something
like, "Tell it, *do* it, brother." That would let Huey know
that he was revolutionizing our culture; educating black
people to be revolutionaries; that the gun is where it's at and
about and in. A white man two doors down smiled. He was
the only one around but he seemed to respect Huey.

Then some people came up after that, after Huey had
made this display of going into the office. Other people were
standing around and the pigs weren't even moving anymore. And Huey just daring them to do anything. Huey had
an M-1 with him, one of the eight round clips in it. What
do you do, man? All you do is back up a nigger like that.
You do nothing else but that. Anything that happens, this
nigger's the baddest nigger you ever seen. Because this
nigger is telling *ten pigs,* "I don't give a damn what you do,"
and making us all shut up and be disciplined. And we have
our shit ready, sitting in the car.

So I said to myself, this is the baddest motherfucker in
the world! This nigger is telling pigs, "If you draw your gun,
I'll shoot you." Telling this to the pigs standing there. When
the pig says, "You're just turning the Constitution around,"
Huey says, "I'm turning nothing around. I'm exercising my
constitutional right. I've got the gun to back it up!" And the
pig *sees* the gun. The nigger told the pigs that if they act
wrong or get down wrong, I'm going to kill you. I'll defend
myself!

So what do you do? You say, this nigger is bad. This nigger is crazy. But I like this crazy nigger. I like him because he's good. He doesn't take bullshit. You back him up.

So that was the very major incident that happened with the Black Panther Party in front of the Black Panther Party office. And after *that,* we really began to patrol pigs then, because we got righteous recruits. I think ten or twelve, maybe thirteen extra members in the Party that day, just came and put applications in. We went down to the poverty office again—I was still working there—and drew up a formal application form for enrollment to get into the Black Panther Party. And from there, what did we do? We just patroled pigs.

BADGE 206

One night Huey, Little Bobby, and I were patroling this pig in North Oakland. We had been patroling him for a couple of hours. We'd be about a block away from him wherever he'd go. Sometimes we'd stop and lose the pig, but ten, twenty minutes later he'd make it around again, he'd be back where he was, and we'd patrol him some more. Little Bobby had an M-1, I had a .45, and brother Huey had a shotgun and a law book on the back seat. Brother Huey was driving my old '54 Chevy. I guess we patroled for quite a while, then on Fifty-eighth Street we saw the pig stop up at the corner. We stopped at the corner, and he backed up and parked right in front of the stop sign at the corner of Fifty-eighth and Grove. I remember us saying we were tired of patroling this pig, "Let's go in." It was about 8:30 or 9:30 when we drove down the street and stopped next to the pig. We were stopped at the stop sign. I looked over at the pig. Naturally we were carrying guns in Oakland in those days. The shotgun barrel was sticking up. I was holding on to the shotgun while Huey drove. I was on the right-

hand side of the front seat and the shotgun was to my left,
next to my left leg. It was standing straight up resting on its
butt. I looked over at the pig, the pig looked back and
looked over to me and to Little Bobby, who had his M-1 in
the back seat between his legs, the barrel of it showing
through the window, too.

Huey had completed his stop and he started off again and
started turning right, right in front of the pig's car. As we
were turning right, the pig flashed his lights on and he
flashed his high beams on. Huey kept moving. He didn't
stop and didn't speed up. See, those pigs don't shake Huey
at all. I guess we drove no more than twenty feet when we
could see the red light flashing. He was starting his engine
up and pulling out of the spot where he was parked, making
a right turn right behind us. Huey kept moving. He got
ready to make a left turn right there at the next little corner.
He made his left turn and said, "I'm not going to stop till he
puts his damn siren on because a flashing red light really
don't mean nothin', anything could be a flashing red light."
Well, the pig cut his siren on as he was turning the corner
following us and when he cut his siren on, Huey stopped.
We'd been stopped by pigs a number of times, pigs who'd
seen us with guns and didn't know what to do. We were
down with it because Huey had put us together and knew
how to handle the situation.

This pig surprised us because he stopped his car as soon
as we stopped. He stopped his car about twenty-five feet in
back of our car. Some pigs stop right up behind you, but he
was twenty-five feet from us. He got out of his car and as
soon as he did, and came walking from his door, we could
hear this pig hollering, "What the goddam hell you niggers
doing with them goddam guns? Who in the goddam hell
you niggers think you are? Get out of that goddam car. Get
out of that goddam car with them goddam guns."

I said, "Huey, this motherfucker's trying to get killed,
man. Listen to him."

As he walked up to the car, he said, "Get out of that car."

Huey said. "You ain't putting nobody under arrest. Who the hell you think you are?"

The pig snatched the door open. When he snatched it open, he said, "I said get out of that goddam car and bring them goddam guns out of there."

Huey said, "Man, what the hell?" By this time the pig came all the way up, his head inside the door, and he's reaching across Huey real fast. This all happened so fast. He was grabbing hold of the barrel of the shotgun, and I tightened up on it and pulled it away from him. At the same time I was pulling the shotgun away from him, Huey grabbed this pig by the collar, pushed his head back up against the roof of the car, then shifted around and got his foot and kicked him in the belly, shoving him all the way out of the car. The pig fell backwards about ten feet from the car but as he was going out, no sooner had Huey finished putting his foot in this pig's belly, kicking and pushing him out of the car—and the pig was being propelled and off balance, away from the car—than Huey was grabbing hold of the barrel of the shotgun. No sooner did brother Huey's feet hit the ground, but he was jacking a round off into the chamber, "Clack upp," and taking three quick steps.

The pig looked up and looked around, and Huey P. Newton was standing there saying, "Now, who in the hell do you think you are, you big rednecked bastard, you rotten fascist swine, you bigoted racist? You come into my car, trying to brutalize me and take my property away from me. Go for your gun and you're a dead pig." The pig folded his hands up. By this time I'd gotten out of the car on the other side, put the .45 in my hand, and pulled the hammer back. As soon as Huey finished saying what he had to say, Little Bobby jumped out on the back of our car and jacked a round off in the M-1. The pig heard these clicks and looked back at Huey, and the pig folded his hands up. In other words, he was taking his hands away from his gun. Huey had said, "Go for your gun and you're a dead pig. Don't you know by the Fourteenth Amendment of the U.S. Constitution that you can't remove a person's property from them without due process of law." Huey was mad, loud, and articulate.

The pig began to walk and he kind of did a half-moon, walking around and away from Huey, trying to walk back to his car. Huey just stepped back holding his gun on him and the pig came walking back to his car hollering, "They got guns. They got guns. They got guns." He got on his radio, "Niggers down here got guns. Get me some help down here. Niggers got guns, they got guns." This pig was scared.

Black people began to come out of their houses, wanting to know what was going on. Huey said, "Come on out, black people. Come on out and get to know about these racist dog swine who been controlling our community and occupying our community like a foreign troop. Come on out and we're going to show you about swine pigs." People got to coming out. It must have been around 9:30 because we were in the back of Merritt College and people in night school were coming out, and I guess seventy or eighty had gathered up there before the other pigs got there. They had about fifteen cars come down there—fifteen cars and pigs everywhere. So me and Huey and Little Bobby were there with our guns. The people were there. I think Little Bobby placed his gun right back on the back seat again. He was sitting in the seat and he shut the door and got back out. Huey and I had been warning Little Bobby about keeping in his possession the written permission he had, and to carry with him the written permisson thing from his father to carry and keep the gun because he was still under eighteen at the time, and I think he didn't have it. He realized that he'd better lay the gun down.

Huey was talking to most of the people and running it down to the people about how racism was rotten. How these pigs were brutal and murderous racists. And every time Huey said something I'd say it right behind him, I'd say the same thing, I'd say, "That's right." And he would say,

"Racist dogs pigs occupy our community, come down here to brutalize and kill and murder us. I'm tired of it," and I'd say, "That's right, racist dogs, pigs occupying our community like a foreign troop that occupies territory. Black people are tired of it." Every time Huey said something, I'd say something. The pigs must have thought that we was crazy niggers. A pig walks up and says, "Let me see that weapon!"

Huey says, "Let you see my weapon? You haven't placed me under arrest."

"Well, you just let me see the weapon, I have a right to see the weapon."

Huey says, "Ain't you ever heard of the Fourteenth Amendment of the Constitution of the United States? Don't you know you don't remove nobody's property without due process of law?" Huey got loud at those last words. "What's the matter with you? You're supposed to be people enforcing the law, and here you are, ready to violate my constitutional rights. You can't see my gun. You can't have my gun. The only way you're gonna get it from me is to try to take it."

Then another pig walks up to me, "Come over here by the car."

"I ain't going no goddam place. Who the hell you think you are? You ain't placed me under arrest."

"But I have a right to take you over to the car."

"You don't have no right to move me from one spot to another."

Huey P. Newton, the Minister of Defense, teaches us and runs it down to us that whenever a cop moves a person from one spot to another, then he's technically under arrest, and if the cop states that you're not under arrest, or doesn't say you're under arrest when you ask, then he has no right to ask you to move from one spot to another.

"You just got through telling me I wasn't under arrest, so I'm not moving nowhere, I'm staying right here."

"Well, you let me see that gun."

"I said you can't see my gun," and I ran down the

Fourteenth Amendment of the Constitution just like Huey
had run it down. The pigs were frustrated, mad, and didn't
know what to do.

"Well, I got a right to look at the serial number."

"I already know what the serial number is," I said.

"I got to make sure it has a serial number." So I held my
gun in my hand and he looked at it with his flashlight.
"Hold it up, let me see."

"No, I ain't holding up nothing. You got a flashlight so
you look at it from that distance right there, because you
don't get near this gun." So I read the serial number, and I
said, "There's the serial."

The pig took the serial number down and after that a
police lieutenant came down, and he kept saying, "Well, if
we charge him, we'll probably lose the case, just for them
having guns, we'll probably lose the case because they turn
around the Second Amendment of the Constitution about
them having a right to carry guns as long as they ain't
concealed."

Then one big fat pig says, "Well, we gotta find something. We gotta find something to do to them." He was
looking down, he started looking the car over and he said
that the license plate was being held on by a coat hanger. It
was secure all right, but it was just put together with a coat
hanger. "Let's give them a ticket for this here, this here
license plate is not adequately secure." He asked Huey for
some identification and Huey handed him his license. They
said his license looked kind of old so they gave him a ticket
for not having a good new license. Huey later went to court,
pleaded not guilty on both counts, and beat both tickets.

The pigs jumped up and left the scene and the black
people were asking what was happening. While Huey was
calling the pigs all kinds of names and stuff, a lot of the
brothers said, "Right on time, Huey. Tell it. Right. Run it
down, Huey." Huey talked to the people some more and a
lot of them said they were going to come down and join the
Black Panther Party. And we did get some of the older
brothers and sisters and some young brothers and sisters out

there to join. Even a number of white people had a chance to watch that.

Badge 206 was the cop. The cop who almost got his head blown away that night. I kept telling him he was acting a fool. Badge 206. Badge 206. We never forgot his badge. I remembered his badge, Huey remembered his badge, and Bobby Hutton remembered his badge. We put his number on the front page of our newspaper.

HUEY AND THE TRAFFIC LIGHT

In its embryo stage, early in 1967, the Black Panther Party was working with the advisory committee of the poverty program to get a traffic light at the corner of Fifty-fifth and Market Streets in Oakland, because kids were getting hurt and killed regularly on that corner.

I used to work near this corner when I was working on the poverty program. Almost every other day, there would be some kind of accident—a wreck or somebody'd get hit crossing the street, etc. Huey and I found out that two kids coming from the Santa Fe School, which is only a block from that particular corner, had been killed and another injured. Shortly before this, a girl had been killed there around seven months before; a young white girl, riding a motorcycle, got hit there, too. A car hit her and her leg was all busted up. Someone started to talk about how our kids were getting killed on this corner on their way to school. So Huey said the city should have had a street light here on this corner a long time ago, and we should work to see that we get a street light.

A lot of kids were getting out of school when this young girl got hit. A bunch of them saw Huey, and they ran up to him, and asked him was he the Minister of Defense of the Black Panther Party? They all gathered around Huey—he had about twenty, twenty-five of them around him—and

Huey was telling them, right then, that there ought to be a street light on this corner. Huey had already more or less organized little Pennywell, twelve-year-old Pennywell, because he hung around the office. Huey told him that he was the captain of the Junior Panthers, and to organize the brothers to understand the basic political desires and needs of black people and to learn the revolutionary principles, and to tell them that when they're sixteen years old, if their mother wants them to carry a gun, she could sign a statement to let them, and we would teach them how to use a gun and defend themselves and the people of the black community.

But right then Huey was concerned about this light. When a few older people walked up, Huey got into a conversation with them. You know, when an accident happens, people will come around and naturally voice their opinions. "Lord, somethin's got to be done about this. There's always a wreck goin' out here," an old woman said. "Somethin's gotta be done about it. Every time I turn around I hear some brakes squeakin' out here, and an ambulance comin' down."

Huey said, "Well, they shoulda put a light here a long time ago," and through conversations with the people, Huey learned about the two kids who got killed and the one who had been injured coming from the school.

Three days later there was an advisory committee meeting at the North Oakland Poverty Center. Huey said we had to bring this up to the people, that we had to make a grievance concerning the light. The whole staff of the North Oakland Service Center was concerned about it because so many accidents had taken place and because people's conversations had begun to center around it. There had also been one accident where a car had literally run into the poverty center building on a weekend when we weren't working there. We came to work one Monday morning and the stairs were all banged up and half the building torn apart and busted in, so people became very concerned. So

Huey, walking around talking about how we have to have a signal light there, began to arouse the interest of the people in and around the service center. At the time he was a part-time community organizer with the North Oakland poverty program.

Huey was actually what they call a neighborhood organizer. He was supposed to go out and get names and addresses of people who wanted to relate to the multiservice poverty center at Fifty-fifth and Market. He really got fed up with just getting names, but he saw the real validity of getting names and making contact with the people, to inform and educate the people, not only about the multiservice center but about the ten-point platform and program of the Black Panther Party.

So Huey, some of the people on the staff, and some of the people on the advisory council of the local poverty center, brought the light up and decided that we were going to get up a petition. Somebody found out some legal facts concerning people who lived two blocks each way from an intersection. We got the petitions together. Huey and I went around and got all these people to sign the petitions concerning the necessity of a light there, and then gave it to the advisory council, and the advisory council submitted it to the Oakland City Council. The Oakland City Council sent information back saying that, based on a report from the street engineers, they couldn't put a traffic light on that corner until late 1968.

But Huey P. Newton says, "Well, we're gonna have to have a red light there. If we don't have a red light there, the Black Panther Party is gonna come forth, and the Black Panther Party will direct traffic there until you get a light put up even if that means that we tie traffic up for fifty blocks. We think the light should be here readily, and we also think we should have an officer here to direct traffic when the traffic is so heavy. Many of the people passing Fifty-fifth and Market," Huey said, "are middle-class white people going to their homes after work in the evening, and many of them are coming by when traffic is heavy, around

3:30 when our kids get out of school. We've already had two children killed here, and one injured, and there's an accident on the average of one every other day. It's very dangerous. We want a light or we're gonna direct the traffic ourselves. The Black Panther Party's gonna come forth. We'll have our guns with us, and we're gonna stop the cars so our kids coming from school and other people in the community will be served by the Black Panther Party."

This got out in downtown Oakland, and I guess about a month-and-a-half or two months passed, and it came back to the poverty center and came through the staff there. We got off into other things with the Party, but we went back and checked, and people in the poverty center said a few of the members of the advisory committee were still making efforts to make sure the light got there, by late 1967, instead of late 1968. Right around August 1, they begin to drill holes, and knock holes in the ground and put the light up, and the light was up by late October 1967. So that was the Panther Party in another type of initial phase, working in conjunction with members of the community.

The kids who were standing on the corner that day when one of the big accidents happened, the twenty-five or so who crowded around Huey, had in a sense already been organized. They were relating quicker, they were relating more meaningfully—of course their minds hadn't been destroyed yet by this racist power structure and all its brainwashing—than the cultural nationalists and the jive intellectuals in the colleges. So Huey organized what he called a Junior Panther group. He would never let these young brothers come into the office, because we always had guns in the office at Fifty-sixth and Grove. He said we were going to set up a place—one of the churches maybe—where we could teach them some Black History and some revolutionary principles, teach them how to use them and how to apply them. This is very important, knowing how to apply the revolutionary principles. This is what Huey was all about in placing the Panther Party in motion. These young brothers began at twelve, thirteen, or fourteen. Junior Panthers. Everyone from sixteen years of age and up was treated like a man. If he wasn't a man, he could get on out of the Party.

Then we had an intermediate group going down from twelve to eight years old. Little twelve-year-old Pennywell was trying to organize them like Huey was organizing, because he related to Huey, he loved Huey, because Huey was the defender of the black community. So Huey told him he was captain of the Junior Panthers in North Oakland. These young brothers were crazy about Huey. They used to come up to me: "You Bobby Seale, ain't you? Huey's partner?" I'd say, "Right, brother, I'm Bobby Seale. I'm Huey P. Newton's partner. We stick together. Huey's our Minister of Defense." Brother Huey was a symbol to these brothers and sisters, in a way that other black organizations had never been.

Those twenty-five kids standing on the corner there might see a pig drive by, look at his marked car, and say, "Racist cop, you swine!" Huey had a term. He used "swine" a lot. "Swine, racist cop!" They would imitate Huey. There were just those twenty-five young brothers—twenty-five little Huey Newtons. That's what is so significant to Huey's name. He would see these kids walking home from school, anywhere from twelve or thirteen all the way down to six, maybe five years old. He'd play with them a little and teach them. The signal light that was needed so badly was not there, and two kids had been killed on that corner and one had been injured. This is what Huey related to. This was *survival*.

Huey would talk about laws being made by mankind to serve mankind, and once those laws stop serving mankind, they must be changed so they *do* serve mankind. This is Huey P. Newton. It was necessary to make political pressure, so that change, revolutionary change, ultimate change, could take place. We have to understand this change that Huey was talking about. Huey would say, "If people are getting killed on a corner, you have to change it. You have to alter it *completely*."

How do you alter it? Huey says some law has to be made, some law has to be instituted or something has to be initiated by the lawmakers to say that the situation that exists here now, at Fifty-fifth and Market, has to be grossly changed. "Go to the lawmakers and tell them that we want a signal light here. Hear ye, hear ye, lawmakers, would really be the cry. We need a signal light here *now,* we want it here *now,* because young children are getting killed; the same young children who must mold the world to change it; young children on the streets who are coming home from school, from a school where they're getting brainwashed, or getting killed and murdered. You lawmakers are not making laws, are not making propositions or resolutions, are not instituting things to serve the people." This is the meaning of the children. You have to understand Huey in this fashion. He liked them.

There was a little boy who lived next door to him. They called him Junior. Every time me and Huey'd drive up there, he'd run up to see the car. Huey was trying to help him learn how to ride his bicycle. Huey said, "Let him go. He'll learn. He'll learn." Huey has faith in children. He has faith in small children, growing up in the confines of their environment. I guess the reason he has faith in children is because he has faith in himself, and to have faith in yourself is only to be human, and only to be human is the foundation of why and where faith comes from.

Faith is not a mythical bullshit thing. Faith is where you directly relate yourself to reality. Huey could perceive a young brother trying to ride a bicycle. Even with training wheels on, he'd fall off of it. Huey'd help him back up, and say, "Go on, ride it! Go on, now, Junior! *Ride* it!" Sometimes Junior would get bad, and Huey'd threaten to spank him, but Huey didn't spank him. Huey wasn't thinking about spanking him, Huey was trying to get him to relate to his environment. That little boy Junior was only four-and-a-half or five years old. Huey could understand the difference between children learning and living in their environment. That's why these brothers in the Santa Fe grammar school, having to cross that intersection there, wanted that light there. They wanted it so that they could *survive*.

Huey P. Newton wanted that light there on the corner, and worked to see that the light was there. If the power structure didn't put it there, the Panther Party was going to come out, block traffic, and direct traffic so that our young kids wouldn't die; so they would *survive*. It's that simple and it's that basic. These are the things that brother Huey is dedicated to. I know he is dedicated to them, because I felt it. I respected Huey, I highly respected him, just for that little small gesture—because he saw that the light, the signal light on the corner at Fifty-fifth and Market served the people, served the black people living in the black community. It helped to keep young kids from dying, helped to keep the young brother named Junior from dying, and would give him a chance to learn to live and survive and exist. It helped to keep them surviving and keep them living so that they would understand that they have to mold the world, to change the world, so that they can voice their basic desires and needs as human beings. Huey is so human. He wants those kids to survive. But some people didn't know or understand this.

Some teachers got together and said that Huey was teaching young kids to use *guns*. They lied to the parents. Huey didn't let kids in the office. He didn't let them in because we had guns there. He told them they had to learn Black History and revolutionary principles and grow up to be men, and defend their people in the black community. Huey finally had a whole little Black History class going on at the service center when he was a community organizer, because he convinced the people there that he could bring those little brothers in there, and teach them a lot of things that are going to be very related to their future survival as human beings—as black people in the black community. Then the little kids would be able to oppose the lies the teachers were telling them about their history, and the teachers—many of whom were white—with their egos, with their misconceptions of the black community, spread lies about Huey. I say white not in the context of the color of their skin, but white in relation to their puritanical views, to the absolutist concepts they were trying to drill into the kids' heads. These absolutist concepts are very directly related to racism.

These kids would speak about things that Huey had taught them about Black History, about great men in Black History. The teachers would oppose them, and many times the kids would mention that Huey P. Newton teaches them, and shows them the true way of thinking and understanding ourselves and our lives, helping us survive, etc. The teachers were trying to oppose Huey P. Newton by trying to hurt the children. To oppose Huey, they called up the mothers, and told the mothers that Huey had them in the office using guns, which was a lie.

So this is the meaning of that red light at the corner. How Huey taught the young brothers to survive; how the teachers in the school told lies to the mothers and other people about Huey. Just as Huey saw the gun as a necessary tool of black people's liberation, he saw the young people as the basis and foundation of it.

A GUN AT HUEY'S HEAD

■ A short time after we began to organize around the traffic light, a little kid came running up into the Black Panther Party office, and said that down the street, a whole lot of cops had broken into a brother's house, and that the Panthers better get down there. He came down to the Panther office to get us down there to stop the cops. I think for some reason Huey's shotgun was at home—he was only passing by the office because he was headed somewhere else. Huey broke out of the office, and Truman Harris and Warren Tucker were with him. Warren Tucker had a .45 strapped to his side and Huey happened to have a twelve-inch dagger that had a metal cover to put the knife in. It was a dagger. It came straight to a point.

Huey got down there and asked the cop why he was searching this man's house and breaking the furniture all up. He asked him if he had a search warrant. The brother had just come home and found the pig in the house. Huey said, "You ain't got no search warrant. You ought to get out of the man's house." Then the pig looked at the black citizen, the brother there, and said, "You gonna let him tell people what to do?" The brother told the pig to get out of his house. The pig got mad because the citizen saw Huey was working in his interest and the pig was not working in his interest by breaking into his house without a search warrant or anything.

Then Huey went outside, and the pig and two other pigs snuck up behind him. There were about ten pigs. One of the pigs walked up to Huey and said real low to him, "Motherfucker," into his face. He thought he was going to provoke Huey, but Huey just laughed out loud.

A lot of people were standing around, and Huey said, "You're a swine! You had no business breaking into this home. You broke into this man's home without a search warrant. You acted in a manner other than a police officer is supposed to." And the people said, "Right." The pig thought that Huey would jump up and attempt to strike him just because he called Huey "motherfucker," but Huey is very hip to the necessity of educating people to what the pigs are.

Then these other two pigs grabbed Warren Tucker's arm and snatched his pistol out. The pig walked up to Huey and put the gun at Huey's head and said, "You're under arrest." Huey turned away and walked away from him and walked towards his car. He said, "You goddamned right. If you're gonna have to fool like that, then I've got to be under arrest. In fact, I'd better be under arrest." Huey just walked on away and left the pig standing there holding the gun. The pig was booed and he just walked off and got in the car. Huey said, "I got to be under arrest, you damn fool swine." Anyway, Huey was placed under arrest.

A brother and I went and got some money, $25, $30. I

went by my house first. I got hold of Little Bobby Hutton
and Sherman Forte. I got a couple of pistols and a shotgun,
and we broke down to the jail. We always said that every
time the pig arrests somebody, we'll go right down there with
our guns and bail the brother out of jail; and after we bail
the brother out of jail, we're going to take the brother right
back out on the streets. Let the people know that this is a
unified organization. Let the pigs know that we're right
back here. We'll be here. We're going to organize and
educate our black people to revolutionary principles. Huey
used to talk about this all the time.

So I was only doing what we had already agreed was
always necessary to be done. At the same time we couldn't
afford to have Huey in jail. Any time we can get him out,
we're going to free Huey. Well, I went down and LaVerne
was there. I gave her the $25 that we had picked up,
and told her to add it to the bail. I went around to the bail
bond office and came back. We finally got Huey out of jail.

Before we got Huey out of jail, some pigs came up and
tried to get me to give them my shotgun. I wouldn't let them
have it. I told them, "You haven't placed me under arrest so
you're not gonna get my shotgun from me." I looked to the
left to see Little Bobby. One pig standing close on my right
snatched my right arm, and another one snatched the
weapon out of my left arm. They opened it up and were all
surprised because they saw some double 0 buckshot shells
in it, loaded and ready to go. They gave me back the
shotgun and left. I had cited my constitutional rights and
argued with them till they left, all ten of them and a lieutenant.

Anyway we got Huey out of jail. We went upstairs and
Huey said, "Let's go upstairs and get the gun back and also
bail out Warren Tucker and Truman Harris." They had
been busted also. We went and got some more money and
had those brothers bailed out. After bailing those brothers
out, we went upstairs to pick up Warren Tucker's weapon.
One pig came talking about Warren Tucker was arrested

for carrying a concealed weapon. When Warren Tucker got arrested, the brother was wearing a T-shirt and some tight Levi's with a belt. That's all he had on. The weapon was strapped to his side in broad daylight. Everybody could see it, but they told us he had a concealed weapon. And then Huey asked, "What kind of concealed weapon did the man have?" "He had a knife on him," a cop said. It was just a regular pocket knife with a blade a little less than three inches. A knife over three inches is illegal, here in California at least, if it's concealed.

We all went upstairs. Bobby Hutton had a shotgun and someone else had a pistol. We went upstairs to the police detective division. A pig saw us coming down the hall while on our way up there. Bobby Hutton had his shotgun, I had a pistol, and I think Sherman Forte had a pistol. We were walking down the hall and this pig turned around, ran the other way, and disappeared around the corner.

We just kept walking right on into the detective division, made a left turn, and got to one of the doors there. We made another left turn and walked right up in there, and these pigs, these fat pigs, they call themselves detectives, got to looking up and wondering what the fuck was going on. Talking about, "Can I help you? Can I help you?"

Huey P. Newton said, "We've come to claim a weapon of Warren Tucker's. You took the man's property from him and we want to see that the man gets his property back. You had no right to take it. You say he was arrested and charged with carrying a concealed weapon, namely a knife." "Well, we're holding the weapon in evidence," the pig said. "Well, how can you hold a weapon in evidence when in fact the weapon is not any evidence concerning the particular charge?" Huey asks him. "The charge is that the man was carrying a concealed weapon. The specific type of weapon that was named was a *knife,* and a *gun* is not a *knife.* Now if you want to just take something to hold as evidence, why didn't you just take the man's comb? The man needs the gun to defend himself and wants to claim the weapon."

"I'm sorry, we just can't give it up, and blop de bloo," the pig says. Then Huey said, "Well, then you're all gonna die. You're all racist dogs. You're all racist swine . . . pigs . . . dogs . . . that's what you all are. And you're all gonna die, and you're gonna be run out, driven out of the black community, because you have no respect for the human being. You have no respect for people's property and lives. You have no respect for anything, when it comes down to the survival of black people . . ." Huey just went on and on, and we just walked out. He was really running it down to them. Really telling them what they were, what kind of scurvy reprobates they were.

THE PARTY GROWS, ELDRIDGE JOINS

THE PAPER PANTHERS

■ In San Francisco, there was a group of cultural nationalists who had named themselves The Black Panther Party of Northern California. We called them the Paper Panthers. (David Hilliard first called them that.) Their name, the Paper Panthers, is directly related to Mao calling the coward running dogs of the imperialistic power structure of the West "paper tigers." But there is also a more direct reason. We were called the Black Panther Party for Self-Defense, and they, the cultural nationalists, called themselves the Black Panther Party of Northern California. We don't know who had the name first, because around October 1966, around the time we had printed up our ten-point platform and program, they went and printed up something, maybe a periodical. We went to them and said, "What are you doing for the community in regard to the revolutionary struggle?" "If you're doing something for the community in the revolutionary struggle," Huey told them, "we'll join your set, but we don't see you doing it so let us alone." They had printed something that was an attempt to cut us up intellectually.

Roy Ballard came over to our office and gave us a long line, that the Northern California branch of the Black Panther Party, these cultural nationalists, were having a conference in Hunter's Point, the large black ghetto over in San Francisco, a Malcolm X Memorial Day Conference. This was held on the date Malcolm was assassinated. He asked if we would come over and provide security for Betty Shabazz. He stood there and bragged about the fact that the Black Panther Party of Northern California had all kinds of brothers over in San Francisco with guns. In fact, he had twenty dudes with guns, he said. In that very first conversation he mentioned twenty dudes, then he mentioned sixteen dudes for sure, and said they were all ready and he wanted to know if we would bring thirty or forty of our Panthers over.

After we had talked about the fact that Betty Shabazz was coming into town, and we wanted to have security for the sister and escort her around town, Huey said that a small group of dudes was best—that we'd just bring over eight brothers at the most, and the most he should have is another eight cats. But Ballard was running around talking to us like, "Man, we got more guns than that. We can bring all of them." He was trying to brag about numbers, but you could see through it. We said to ourselves that since these cats had decided to pick up guns, we could go forth to try and work with them. Huey always said we're ready to unite and work with any brothers anywhere, because the name of an organization doesn't mean anything, it's what an organization *is* that's important; and if these guys finally had realized that we'd been on the street patroling the cops already and had been trying to implement a program to educate black brothers, if these guys were ready to pick up the gun, if they were making an effort to do so, that we should work with them for the sake of unity in our black community.

Roy Ballard went on and went off at the mouth, and asked us to come to one of their meetings over in San Francisco. So we decided to get up and go on over to the meeting, about three or four days later at the Northern California branch of the Black Panther Party's office, the Paper Panthers' office. We got over there and there was nobody in the office. We drove around until somebody found out where Roy Ballard lived. We went to his house, and waited out front. He drove up and we went upstairs. He was talking to us and he was explaining about how he had eight men.

We said, "I thought you had sixteen, although we don't need but eight."

"Oh well," he says. "It really ain't but eight cats."

He was explaining some more details about this conference. He was really trying to manipulate. But we were concerned about the changes in the amount of men he had, the brothers he had with guns. Well, the brother didn't have much to say that evening, no more than that we're going to have to get together and have the gun laws checked out thoroughly. Huey P. Newton, of course, had checked out all the gun laws very thoroughly, because we read those books, law books and the penal code, in the law section of the legal aid service of the poverty center where we worked, and Huey was going to law school at night. But Roy Ballard made a big play about how he was doing all this work in the black community for black people, and I suppose they did have some statistics down and that kind of stuff.

Another meeting was set for a few days later, and this time we all went in our uniforms. Me, Huey, Bobby, Reginald Forte, Sherman Forte, and Orleando Harrison, we all got down our uniforms—the blue shirt, with black leather jacket, black pants, and black beret. We loaded up and got out guns and things, and went over to their office that evening about 7:30. We walked into the office and there was a bunch of what I've always known to be jive-assed intellectuals sitting around. I'd run with some of them— Douglas Allen, Kenneth Freeman in West Coast underground RAM, and some other dudes there were just shits. The dudes whose doors I've told about breaking in were just jives, like the cats that ran with Kenny Freeman. I didn't know it till later, but Eldridge was sitting in there too. (I didn't know Eldridge then.) Roy Ballard and Kenny Freeman and the others were all sitting in a circle, and they seemed to be going through their everyday business. I remember Kenny Freeman saying some simple shit like, "If black people don't get together, we're just going to have to get uptight on them, and make them get together." And I said to myself, "Now who in the hell does he think he can *make* get together?" So me and Huey and Bobby and Reggie and Sherman and Orleando, and I think there was another brother with us, all sat down and listened, and after we had been there for about twenty-five or thirty minutes, listening to them go through their little intellectual changes, feeding off of their ability to articulate, and, as they put it, run it down to each other, looking at them acting like a bunch of armchair revolutionaries, I made a gesture to Roy Ballard and asked him when we were going to settle this thing about how we were going to handle the escorting of sister Betty Shabazz.

He said, "In a minute, brother. In a minute, we're going to take care of that," as an intellectual always does to a field nigger.

Roy Ballard did come around to it in the context of his conversation with Kenny Freeman and the rest of the intellectuals in there. The point was, that the conference was coming down and Betty Shabazz needed to be escorted here, and the Black Panther Party for Self-Defense would handle the self-defense aspect of the operation. He asked us if we wanted to speak at the conference, and Huey said, "Yes, we'll speak."

Vince Lynch said, "That's good, because you can go into the history of self-defense."

Huey said, "I'll be talking about politics."

Kenny Freeman popped up and said, "Do you want to speak on self-defense or politics?"

Huey said, "It doesn't make any difference, they're both one and the same." They went through some intellectual changes, with a few statements here and there—Roy Ballard, Kenny Freeman, and a couple of other people—and came back to the same question that they had asked Huey about a minute before. "Do you want to speak on self-defense or politics?" Huey said that they're both the same thing.

"If I'm talking about self-defense, I'm talking about politics; if I'm talking about politics, I'm talking about self-defense. You can't separate them."

They didn't understand Huey when he said, "Politics is war without bloodshed, and war is politics with bloodshed, a continuation of politics with bloodshed." They didn't understand antagonistic contradictions and non-antagonistic contradictions both being lodged in the arena of politics. They didn't understand that the plight of the black people's struggle here in the confines of decadent America is a political-military whole, unified within itself.

Then Vincent Lynch said, "You could talk about Nat Turner, then you can bring it up to date. You could talk about brother Robert Williams, then you could talk about the Deacons for Defense in Bogaloosa, Louisiana, and you have that whole historical thing put together. Then we can speak about the politics." Huey said, very firmly to all of them, that we would speak, and when we speak it won't make any difference if we're talking about self-defense, or if we're talking about politics. If we're talking about politics and the survival of black people, it's the same thing. They finally decided to shut up. They didn't want to mess with Huey because Huey was sitting there with a big 12-gauge shotgun, and he had his men all around him, decked down, sharper than a motherfucker, sharper than two tacks, and Huey wasn't about to sit there and lollygag with these jive dudes who call themselves revolutionaries who didn't even have the understanding of integrating the gun for self-defense with politics. I'm pretty sure this is what frustrated brother Huey, and made him not want to deal with those cats, but we tried to anyway.

I made a gesture to Roy Ballard to get on with the thing because we had come over to lay down some plans about operations for security for Betty Shabazz, and we wanted to know how many men they were going to provide for the operation. We got up and went outside and they got to talking about how they had five men, with pieces and guns and they'd be loaded down, ready to go, and that they would let us know when sister Betty Shabazz was coming in. They talked to me and Huey alone. They told us that she would be coming in on a Monday, so we split. Then we got a phone call from them Monday saying we would have to come over there. So we rushed over and they told us she'd be there that Thursday. When we got over there on Thursday to the Northern California branch of the Black Panther Party, Roy Ballard, Kenny Freeman, Isaac Moore, and Douglas Allen were there, along with some other cats. We come to find out one of them was a special nigger pig.

Huey says, "Look, we are not going to go and give any security to Betty Shabazz with pigs around—with nigger cops around. I don't give a damn if they're black or white, they're cops for the system."

One of those guys said, "Yes, but he's blacker than you. He's blacker than you!" (He was referring to the cop's skin color.)

I said, "It doesn't make any difference, we aren't going with any pigs, and that's all there is to it."

Huey P. Newton said, "We aren't going with any of them. It's not possible. We can't function with cops, in any way."

Kenny Freeman called Huey to the side, and told him that he didn't know Roy Ballard had set this up. So I said, "How many guns do you have?"

They said, "Five."

I said, "When Roy Ballard first came over he come talking about twenty men with guns, and the next statement he made before he left that first time was sixteen with guns, and after that he says he has eight with guns, and after that he said he had five with guns. Now I wonder if you guys got any guns at all or anybody with guns. You've been talking this shit, so have you got anybody at all with guns or not?"

Huey said, "Right on. You be here and have some guns

with you tomorrow, or what you guys think you're handling in terms of security, the Black Panther Party for Self-Defense will take over and we'll handle the whole damn thing, if you aren't here with guns. You'd better be here with loaded guns, right down to the gills."

Kenny Freeman got uptight. "Okay, yeah, man, yeah, man, we'll be here tomorrow, man. We've got five cats with guns, man, to go along with this operation, man." So we all got together, we got eight brothers together, and came over on Thursday. Just before we left, they said sister Betty was arriving at San Francisco Airport, somewhere around 1:30 or 2:00 P.M. We got over there around noon. Douglas Allen, a cat named Leo who had an M-1, and Isaac Moore with an M-1, were there. Kenny Freeman says, "Hey, man, you know these brothers here, man? They got their stuff with them, man, and they're ready. Everything is cool, and I think Roy Ballard's got a piece with him."

I said, "I thought you cats were going to have five cats, man."

"Well, man, we've got these cats here, right offhand, and I myself, I'm going to be there, you know, and Douglas Allen, you know, he's going to be there, so everything is cool. Everything's all right."

I said, "Yeah, man, okay." I didn't want to talk to him any more, because I just didn't dig the dudes. They were intellectual jivers. Intellectual cultural nationalists. Punk motherfuckers who sit in a fucking armchair and try to articulate the revolution while black people are dying in the streets. Huey defined him very well. Huey said, "I see Kenny Freeman is a dude who wants to compete with everything that's going on. That's the only thing that satisfies his little chicken-shit ego is to sit and compete."

We all loaded down in cars, caravan fashion. We had our guns. Kenny Freeman, Leo, Isaac Moore, and Douglas Allen were in another car, and Roy Ballard was in a third car—five of them. We told them to have five guns with them, but they wound up, from what I saw, only having three guns. Roy Ballard flashed his little .25 pistol sitting in his belt. Huey and I didn't have any faith in .25 pistols because they could get you killed. Anyway our eight dudes and their five dudes loaded up in the cars and drove to the San Francisco Airport, and I noticed one thing as we got in front of the terminal. Kenny Freeman was in a car behind us, a white station wagon. He got out of the car. It was three or four blocks down from the terminal drive but I could see him, stopping the car and getting out of it. He got out of the car. Then all of the brothers piled out with their guns, because we drove up there, guns showing and everything. I noticed that Leo and Isaac Moore, Kenny Freeman's boys, were about thirty feet away from us with their two M-1's.

Just then a pig came out, a head plainclothes pig. Huey saw him and some other pigs coming, so Huey told everybody, like he always tells the brothers, "Don't nobody say nothing, I'll do the talking, because we don't want too many people trying to say something at one time."

The pig came and asked, "What are you doing with these guns?"

And Huey said, "Well, you're a cop. What you doing with *your* gun?"

Then a uniformed black pig walked out and said, "What's he doing with this gun? Is that gun loaded?"

And Huey said, "If I know it's loaded, that's good enough."

"Well, where are you going?" the plainclothes pig asked.

Huey said, "We're going to the airport to get our sister Betty Shabazz. Why?"

If you understand Huey, you know Huey wasn't answering his questions as if he had to answer them. Huey was giving orders to me to get the brothers and sisters together because he knew what he was going to do. He knew what the Party was there for. He knew what the delegation was there for and that's all there was to it.

Then stupid Roy Ballard walked up and said humbly and meekly, "Why should we have all this argument? Sir, you should read *The Autobiography of Malcom X* and you can understand why we are here with these guns."

Huey said, "Aw, man, I'll do the talking. You go on back."

"Wait a minute, Huey, wait a minute, let me explain it to him."

Huey said, "This is absurd. How do you explain to a racist, ignorant bastard cop, cops of the power structure who were behind the killing of Malcolm, who kill black people, and who are here to try to tell you you can't go anywhere. This is no time to stop and read the *Autobiography*." And Roy Ballard was still, in a humble and meek manner, trying to explain to the cop that he would understand us if he would read our brother's book, when the pigs in America were glad Malcolm was dead.

The man said, "Well, you can't go into the airport."

"What do you mean we can't go into the airport. We have to be able to go in and meet our sister there, Betty Shabazz," the brothers said.

Huey said, "Be quiet. We're going in the airport. This is public property and you can't deny us our constitutional rights just because we've got guns. We're going in whether you like it or not. I'm going to exercise my constitutional rights, and the Panthers here are going to exercise their constitutional rights, and that's all there is to it."

The pig said, "But . . ." Huey interrupted him in a firm and clear manner.

"This is public property . . ."

The pig said, "It's private property and you're not . . ."

"Even if it is private property," Huey said, "if it accomodates more than 200 people at a time, then any citizen has a right to exercise his rights on it. So get out of our way. We're going inside whether you like it or not, swine!"

Meanwhile Isaac Moore and Leo were standing thirty feet or more away from us with two M-1's in their hands. Ballard was running around flapping at the jibs. He didn't know what he was doing. Huey said, "All right, brothers. In a column of two's. Get together. Bobby, put them in a column of two's." So I put everybody in a column of two's. To Leo and Isaac Moore, I said, "Come on, you dudes. Come on up here and get in the column of two's." They hesitated. Meanwhile Huey was still checking this pig, when all of a sudden, about twenty pigs spread out around us in the streets out there.

But Huey P. Newton wouldn't let that phase him at all, because he knew he had a shotgun and he knew he had some brothers with him, he knew his constitutional rights, and he was going to make sure that people got down to the nitty gritty of things. So, Huey is talking with the pig telling him we're going inside anyway and also trying to make Roy Ballard be quiet and shut up because Roy didn't know what he was doing. He didn't know how to handle the racists and Huey did. We got in a column of two's and Huey said, "Let's go." We started moving and I finally got Leo and Isaac Moore to fall in, in the rear with me. Huey was in front. The first thing Leo and Isaac started complaining about was, "Man, get the sisters outa here. Get the sisters outa here."

I say, "Why? We got guns. We can defend ourselves."

"Man, if they start shooting, man," Leo was saying, "It's bad enough having to protect ourselves, let alone having to protect them too."

I said, "I heard that one of the sisters has a pistol in her purse and she isn't worried. Don't worry about it." Leo was overly concerned about the sisters being in the column of two's. Leo and Isaac were holding the M-1's, and at the time I didn't know that these M-1's were not loaded. Later on I could see how his overconcern about the sisters being there and standing thirty feet away related directly to the fact that they did not have loaded weapons.

We all went up into the terminal and some of the pigs were walking around us. They were following us, and they were also walking in front of us, but we just barged our way in over this so-called head cop, or sheriff. They have these little security-type sheriff guys out there at San Francisco Airport. We went inside and upstairs, and from there we went all the way down to the particular gate we were supposed to be at.

Brother Hakim Jamal, Malcolm's cousin by marriage, had gone to check out the exact time sister Betty was going to arrive. Jamal came back, and by that time we were in the lobby section. It's like a hallway, about twenty feet wide, and that's where the gate area is. We walked around, we walked inside the gate area and all the brothers sat down. Little Joe, Orleando Harrison, Bobby Hutton, and me and Huey, three or four other brothers, along with the punks, intellectual, jive, motherfucking cultural nationalists, Isaac Moore, Leo, and Roy Ballard.

Kenny Freeman had gotten out of his car, and was way, way, down the street, three blocks away. He'd gotten out just before the confrontation had started. I don't know who he thought he was fooling because I heard later on that he said he was planning strategic security. That nigger was just scared! That nigger wasn't coming up there at all. That's why he had those dudes running around there carrying unloaded guns. John George, a lawyer they knew, had suggested that they carry unloaded guns, and they went and did it, but they didn't tell us that. Huey doesn't believe in anybody carrying unloaded guns.

We were waiting for the plane to come to the gate area. While we waited, something happened. Those pigs were all outside in this twenty-foot aisle to the gate section, and some old pig came over and acted like he was going to take a picture of us. Huey walked up to him and said, "Don't take any pictures." People began to look, so Huey said, "We're not going to let them take any pictures." I walked over and stood in front of the pig with the camera, more or less to block him, to keep him from being able to take pictures.

Then Huey said, "If you take any pictures we're going to take your camera away from you and we're going to smash it." The pig acted as if he still wanted to take pictures, so Huey said, "All right, people. You see this jive racist cop here? He's trying to provoke something. We told him not to take any pictures and if he takes any pictures he's going to provoke something. That's where it's going to start at, right now."

The other pigs got to looking and said, "Come on, Joe. Come on, Joe," beckoning for this pig with the camera to come on out to the far end of the lobby section. They decided they didn't want to take any pictures because Huey P. Newton wasn't jiving around. He had that shotgun in his hand and he was letting people know where it's at. I noticed Isaac Moore and Leo standing over away from us. They were standing next to the wall together. We were kind of spread out but they got away from us.

We waited for sister Betty Shabazz. The plane came up to the gate and let the people off. As soon as she came out, we surrounded her. Brother Hakim Jamal was there, and we surrounded the sister and began to walk out. The pigs —I don't know what the hell they thought they were doing —were walking out around us, acting as though they were security, but we had as many guns as they had. We came outside and sister Betty said, "Who are these fellows here?" Jamal answered her, "These are some brothers from the Black Panther Party for Self-Defense."

I noticed that Leo and those cats were nil on gun laws and the way the Party was functioning. One time Isaac Moore had his gun level, and people were walking by in front of his gun. At the time I was still thinking that the guns were loaded. But he had it level, then he kind of dropped it, very relaxed. When he was pointing the gun at people he wasn't paying any attention to it.

So I said to him, "Man, don't you point no gun at nobody like that! A loaded weapon!" I said, "That's assault with a deadly weapon. Whether you're doing it maliciously or not. You'd get charged on a bullshit ticket if the cops out here knew the law. They just don't know the law. Hold that gun up!" Then he was getting Betty Shabazz into the car. I saw Isaac Moore when he put his gun in the car. He put his gun in and slid it under the seat. We didn't carry guns like that, sliding them under the seat. It was very necessary, at that time, to carry our guns in the open, because it was exhausting a means of being able to carry guns that way and at the same time educating the masses of black people about the necessity for guns and how self-defense was politically related to their survival and their liberation.

CONFRONTATION AT *RAMPARTS*

■ We got in the cars and we drove back to the *Ramparts* office on Broadway, in the middle of downtown San Francisco. We got to *Ramparts* and went inside. Douglas Allen was sitting there looking like he was sick and scared and didn't know where the fuck to go. I can't blame him for being scared. There were just too many damn people with guns there and I don't know where Kenny Freeman had disappeared to, and Isaac Moore was hanging around somewhere. I stationed two brothers outside, Little Joe outside on the right of the steps and this other brother on the left of the steps. He had a .45 and Little Joe had an M-1. We then went inside. There were some interviews scheduled so Huey was with sister Betty all the way inside the *Ramparts* office down the hall, where she was talking to Eldridge Cleaver, whose writings on Malcolm X she had admired. I made periodical runs between Huey, where he was with sister Betty and Eldridge Cleaver, all the way back to the front door. I came to the front door one time and a couple of pigs had driven up. I stood right on the top landing of the front steps and a pig walked up to Little Joe, and said, "Who are you?"

Little Joe said, "I got nothing to say to you, and if you have anything to ask me I'm taking the Fifth Amendment." Just like that.

The pig said, "Well, all right," and when he got up beside me I was looking dead at him, looking firm right in his eyes. He kind of took a couple of steps up from the bottom steps and he said, "Who's the leader?"

I said, "I'm one of them, why?"

"Well I'd like to talk to you."

I said, "Goddamit, I don't want to talk to you, so you can go on away from here." And he said, "Oh," turned around, and walked away. Then more pigs drove up. They were plainclothesmen. They looked at Little Joe. He looked like he was too young to be carrying a weapon, but they didn't say anything else to him. Three or four more pigs drove up, so I called for a couple more brothers to come outside, and then walked halfway down the hall. Betty Shabazz was about to come out. I walked all the way to the front and there were four or five pigs outside.

A few minutes earlier, a lieutenant pig, had asked Warren Hinckle, the editor of *Ramparts,* what the trouble was. When he said, "What's the trouble?" he pointed over our way. We were standing in front of the inside door to the office.

"There's no trouble here," Hinckle told the pig lieutenant. "Every thing is under control." That seemed to make the pigs mad. They couldn't do a thing to us, because the person whose place we were in had no objection to our having guns there. We weren't doing anything illegal.

I remember sister Betty saying that she didn't want any cameras, and Huey said, "If you don't want any cameras on you that's all right." But, of course, by this time a TV cameraman had shown up, ABC Channel 7, and Chuck Banks, the news reporter. We came outside. As I was coming outside they were bringing sister Betty out and I was kind of in front there. I grabbed a magazine from a stack of magazines in the hall, to use to block the cameras. Huey grabbed a magazine too, and we came outside. I was holding this magazine up in front of the cameras and then all of a sudden Kenny Freeman popped up somewhere. We had sister Betty Shabazz surrounded but then Douglas Allen popped up from somewhere, and somehow he's walking with her.

Even before we came out the cameramen tried smashing in. They tried breaking in and that's when Warren Tucker pushed them down the stairs. Then they tried taking a picture of one of the Panthers who pushed them away with a gun. They had already been trying to provoke something, to get an incident going. Then as we came out, I walked out first and I was holding a magazine in front of the camera, about a foot away from it, and Huey came on out with sister Betty and Douglas Allen and Kenny Freeman from the Paper Panthers. While she was coming down the stairs around front, the TV dude snatched at the book I was holding, and I snatched it back. Then Huey put his magazine in front of the camera and Chuck Banks grabbed hold of Huey's magazine and pushed the book down into Huey's stomach. He didn't get his blow in good enough, but he did strike Huey. When he struck Huey in the stomach like that, Huey wasn't phased a bit. He let the magazine go and fired on Chuck Banks's head and knocked him back against the wall and against the man who was holding the Channel 7 camera. Then I looked around and saw all these pigs. I saw one of them unstrap this little strap that holds down the firing hammer on his .38 pistol. I said, "Huey, cool it, man. Let's split, man." I grabbed at Huey's jacket on his right arm.

"Don't hold my hand, brother," he said, so I let go of his arm right away, because I know that's his shooting hand, his right hand.

Then I said, "Come on, brother, let's split.

But Huey said, "All right, all you pigs, all you cops. That man assaulted me. Now why in the hell don't you arrest him? Arrest that man."

"Come on, brother, let's split," I said. Then a couple more of those cops flipped the little straps off the hook of their pistol hammers and another brother came down and said, "Come on, Huey. Let's back on up here and get outa here, man." One of the brothers had his back turned on the pigs and I guess Huey saw the cops pulling the straps off of the hammers all of a sudden, so Huey says, "Turn around! Don't turn your back on these backshooting motherfuckers!" Just like that. We all turned around. I turned around,

Little Joe turned around, Little Bobby turned around, and Huey goes, "Spread!" and jacks a shell off into the chamber of his gun. Betty Shabazz was moving and gone by then. Kenny Freeman and Douglas Allen had hustled her off across the street.

A big beefy cop moved forward. He had unhooked the strap off of the hammer of his pistol, and started shouting at Huey. "Don't point that gun at me! Stop pointing that gun at me!" He kept making gestures as though he was going to go for his gun. Huey stopped in his tracks. He was just staring at the cop. Then he walked right up to within a few feet of this fat pig and said, "What's the matter, you got an itchy finger?" The cop didn't say a thing. He just stood there.

"You want to draw your gun?" Huey asked him. The other pigs were calling for this one cop to cool it, but he didn't seem to hear them. He was looking right at Huey, staring straight into Huey's eyes.

"OK, you big fat racist pig, draw your gun!" Huey said to him. The cop didn't move. "Draw it, you cowardly dog!" and with that, Huey jacked a round off into the chamber of his shotgun. "I'm waiting," Huey said, and, man, he just stood there waiting for this pig to make a move toward his gun. All of the other cops moved back out of the line of fire. The five of us were spread out behind Huey.

Finally the fat pig just gave up. He let out a great big sigh and just hung his head. Huey almost laughed in his face, and we started backing up slowly. Huey backed up. He went near the wall and I went to the outer edge of the sidewalk, near the car. The sidewalk is at least eight or ten feet wide. Little Joe and Little Bobby were in the center and another brother got on the outside of the car in line with us and took about six or seven steps. At this point, Roy Ballard came running up the street, yelling, "Hey, don't shoot that gun. The cops are going to kill us. They're going to kill us. Please don't shoot that gun." Then the cops started talking about, "Don't you go for your guns. Don't you go for your gun."

So Huey said, "Don't you go for *your* guns."

I remember repeating behind Huey, I said, "That's right, don't you go for your guns. Don't you touch your guns." I had flipped the little strap that went over the hammer of my .38. So we were standing there, backing up, stepping off from the pigs, and the pigs were all bunched up.

It was a very tense scene. This was one of the first major confrontations and we were almost into a righteous shoot-out. You can think about a lot of shoot-outs. You can think about situations you might be in where there's going to be gunfire and gunfighting with pigs you know are racists. But I knew how Huey felt. If just one of them had gone for his gun, he would blast him, because Huey had his gun at a 45° angle to the ground and he was ready. He had the barrel of the gun in his left hand. His finger was on the trigger, he had knocked the safety off, and had jacked a round off into the chamber. It kind of shook the cops when Huey jacked that round off in that chamber.

We were just backing up then. I wasn't scared or anything like that. You don't even think about it in a situation like that because the situation is so tense. We were stepping off and the cops took three or four steps forward. Then they stopped and realized that we had them. The cops stopped. I said, "Come on, brothers. Let's move across the street." We got about halfway up the street, about fifty feet away from them when they started bottling around to our right. We backed across the street and stopped the traffic coming off and on to the ramp to the Bay Bridge. Traffic was jammed up. I know people in the cars were sitting there wondering what in the hell was going on. "Who in the hell are these niggers with these guns, and the cops all on the street. My God! My God!" I could just imagine one of them, sitting there in the traffic that couldn't move.

We went across the street and got into our cars. Betty Shabazz was gone, so we split and went back down to the Paper Panther office. We got back there, and Huey and the brothers were good. They were all talking about how we had spit on the pigs and how the pigs were all bunched up. Huey was talking about how so many of them were bunched

up and how he had his shotgun on their butts and if one of
them had gone for their guns . . . We told how we split and
how we stood those pigs off. Some thirty-odd pigs, all
bunched up on the sidewalk. How they had taken two or
three steps and how Huey told them, "You'd better not go
for your gun either." I know Leo and the rest of the dudes
standing around there weren't too enthusiastic about the
whole thing at all and I thought that they should have been.
I thought they should have been excited about how we'd
covered Betty Shabazz, how the pigs went crazy, and stuff
like that.

We went to the conference in Hunter's Point that night
and decided not to speak. We got fed up with the whole
thing, man. They were just trying to make guards out of us,
for some artwork shit sitting around there. They were trying
to give us orders. What kind of shit was that?
"You guys have to be over there this evening, man, at six.
There's a lot of art and stuff there that people might steal.
You guys get over there and, ah, guard that stuff."
Huey says, "Look, we're the security for Betty Shabazz
and we're with Betty Shabazz." So we cut out, went down,
and talked to the brothers on the block who were shooting
dice. Huey and I wouldn't think about that damn shit artwork in there. That's what's wrong with them. They want to
put guys up to protecting the cultural nationalistic artwork
when they should be organizing the brothers on the block.
Me and Huey went down there with some guns, and talked
with those brothers out there on Hunter's Point, talked to
them about joining the Party. We told them we were going
to be out there and how the brothers have got to get together and start arming themselves. We broke up a whole
dice game. About twenty dudes. Some dudes were high, and
wanted to be murder-mouthing—"Yeah, I'm going to get a
gun." But some of those brothers were serious. They wanted
to get on with it. There had been riots in Hunter's Point and
the pigs had done in a lot of the brothers. They had already
shot up brothers out on the Point, brothers and sisters had

been murdered and brutalized, there was bad housing, unemployment, rats and roaches and hunger. Hunter's Point was a typical black ghetto.

We went inside the auditorium where the conference was being held and talked to a bunch of brothers in there who were concerned about why we had the guns. Huey ran down the revolutionary program, about why we had to defend ourselves, how it was legal then under the laws of California to carry guns and how the right to bear arms is guaranteed to all citizens under the Second Amendment of the Constitution of the U.S. He also ran it down how the Black Panther Party was fixing to serve the black community with positive programs like Breakfast for Children, free health clinics, and Liberation Schools.

That's what they should have been talking about inside that conference, called to commemorate the death of Malcolm X, but the thing had been put together by these cultural nationalists who were trying to project themselves as the leaders of the black community while trying to use the Black Panther Party. Actually, they should have called the conference to celebrate Malcolm's birthday, rather than to commemorate the day he was assassinated.

Those cats didn't know the gun laws. They didn't know that trying to lead people was a dangerous thing. They only came out to the airport with us because Huey had demanded it of them. After that little set in front of *Ramparts,* we found out that their guns were not loaded.

"Not loaded?" Huey said. You've never seen cats mad like us. The brothers in the Party wanted to go over and beat their asses for having unloaded guns. They said, "Here our lives are on the line for our people and the bastards are trying to manipulate us. If a pig had started shooting, they would have run." I said to Huey, "I'm out with all these jive intellectual cultural nationalists."

That became a real thing in distinguishing the brothers off the block and those who only talk, those who have their intellectual possessions in pawn to the man, the power structure of this racist, capitalist system. That's when David

Hilliard said, "They're Paper Panthers." Jive punk Paper Panthers.

ELDRIDGE JOINS THE PANTHERS

■ Early in 1967, Huey heard Eldridge on the radio. "Damn! Who is this cat?" Huey kept saying. "This cat is blowing, man! He's been in prison!" Huey related to Eldridge as a Malcolm X, coming out of prison. Huey always respected the brothers that came out of prison. He felt that he could relate to dudes who came out of prison. That was his whole key. Huey heard that: "This cat's been in prison, man, for nine years!" That wrapped him up. We ran down to the radio station that night, because Huey said, "I'm going to talk to this cat."

He said to Eldridge, "Man, look. You got to be in the Party! It doesn't make any difference what the name is. This is where it's at! We need you. We want you." He knew Eldridge could rap, and he'd heard that he could write, that he was writing for *Ramparts*. Huey couldn't write, but you could get Huey cornered, get all his ideas out of his head, and put them on paper. He'll write if you corner him, but the shit travels fast. Huey understands the need for a media. Huey understands skills being functional for black people. That's what Huey wants. He pushed for a Panther newspaper.

That's why we got ahold of Eldridge when we heard him on the radio that night. Eldridge told us, "Look, I just got out of prison, and I'm checking around. I'm trying to see what's happening." I said to Huey, "This nigger from prison, this nigger is tired of shit. This nigger is like a Malcolm X to us, and voom! This nigger can write." One day a few months later Huey and I were in Eldridge's apartment. Eldridge had a leather jacket and a beret on. He said, "Fuck it, I'm in the Panther Party. That's all there is to it." I didn't know him then. I was looking at him, and I was saying, "Well, fuck it, this is just another nigger saying he's in the Party." But, boom! We get to pounding out that first little leaflet, and that began to mean something. Next thing I know, we're over at Beverly Axelrod's house, and we're pounding out a paper, man! * So I said, "This nigger here is where it's at."

Huey related to Eldridge more than I did, initially. I just had a tendency to follow Huey. I was never ashamed of the fact that I always followed Huey. I just followed him, and listened to him, and tried to understand what he was saying. If I disagreed with him, I tried to disagree properly.

Eldridge later told us that when he came out of the penitentiary, he was wired up behind Malcolm X. Malcolm was teaching that it was necessary to pick up the gun. Eldridge had been running around repeating what Malcolm had said, but he didn't know that there were some niggers that had already picked up the gun. He didn't know it until February when we started planning for sister Betty Shabazz's visit. Marvin Jackman and all those dudes were hiding it. They wouldn't tell Eldridge about us.

Eldridge said that when he saw all us brothers with guns, all ready and organized, it didn't take him any time at all to relate to that. The only thing he didn't want to give up was the name that Malcolm X had for his organization, the Organization of Afro-American Unity, OAAU, but then he said the name thing was complicated because Malcolm's sister had taken it and incorporated it. There was so much confusion and so many phony people had gotten involved in the OAAU, that when he tried to organize the Black House, he was sick of it already. So he just started moving with the Party, going everywhere, making all the scenes. He was relating to it and functioning, but he still had some reservations.

Eldridge just couldn't understand how it could happen —how we pulled this shit off or why niggers would be crazy

* Beverly Axelrod was the lawyer who helped get Eldridge out of prison.

enough to go out there in the streets. It looked unbelievable. Eldridge said it scared him, that's what it did. Scared Eldridge! He said that when Malcolm was teaching, he was just dealing with rhetoric about how we had to organize a gun club, we had to do this, we had to have these guns, etc. He said it was abstract and he couldn't visualize it. Or if he did visualize it, he visualized a whole army, the black race armed. But then, when he saw us out there in the process of organizing, he saw about ten, twelve dudes with some guns, and he saw all those pigs. It looked like we didn't have a chance, it looked hopeless, but then many times it looked so beautiful and inspiring, that he just had to relate to it.

What turned all that around for Eldridge was that first scene, when the brothers escorted sister Betty Shabazz from the airport, and came by *Ramparts*. That had a huge impact, a huge influence on him. He said he didn't believe it, even after he witnessed it. He said it was like observing pure instinct. What was so important to him was that when those pigs came by there, there were sisters and brothers on the street, and the Minister of Defense stepped forward, the shield between his people and the pigs, jacked off that round into his shotgun, and put his life on the line. "That was it," Eldridge said, "that was me there."

THE DEATH OF DENZIL DOWELL

■ The Black Panther Party was called to Richmond by the Dowell family. They had heard of the Black Panther Party over in Oakland. Mark Comfort came down to the office at Fifty-sixth and Grove, and told us that the Dowell family would like us to come over because Denzil Dowell had been killed in Richmond by a Contra Costa County deputy sheriff.

We went out there that day and saw the Dowell family. They began to explain all the details about how certain people had said they heard ten shots, and the papers and the local media there were saying that only two or three shots were fired. And how the coroner's office had originally told them he was shot nine or ten times, but the police department said he was only shot once or twice. How the pigs had lied about Denzil Dowell, the brother, telling about how he was trying to burglarize some place.

His brothers, Carl Dowell and George Dowell, explained how the pigs knew Denzil by name, because they had arrested him a number of times. The pigs had made threats that they were going to get Denzil. It was just a cold-blooded killing of a black man. Some pigs were trigger-happy and wanted to shoot somebody, shoot a "nigger."

They explained all this to us. Then the family took us over to the site where they killed brother Denzil Dowell, and showed us just where the bullets hit certain walls and the direction they came from, and how the pigs lied and said that he ran and jumped a fence. The blood was twenty yards away from the fence. They must have dragged his body over to the other side, and then over another fence. The blood was in two different places.

We were investigating, and a lot of black people in the black community there came out. They had noticed us Panthers, with our guns and everything. I guess there were ten or twelve of us who went out there together and went through the whole process of investigation, of looking over what had happened, and listening to the information that people were giving that contradicted all the crap that the pigs and the newspapers had run down. And the people were looking.

We were standing on the corner there in North Richmond. There were about 150 people around, some in cars, some standing across the street. Some of the younger brothers, fifteen, sixteen, some twenty years old, were asking us about the guns, and we were explaining to them about the Black Panther Party. All of a sudden, some sister hollers out, "Uh, oh . . . here come the *cops.*"

When the sister hollered, Huey jacked a round off into the chamber of his eighteen-inch shotgun with a loud click

and clack. When he did that, I unhitched the strap that held
the hammer down on my .45, and it clacked too. People
started moving back. Some of them went across the street.
Some got in their cars and drove up the street. Then the pigs
came down and Huey stepped to the curb. I followed Huey
and stepped to the curb, a few feet down from him. The
pigs were surprised all of a sudden. They looked and noticed who was ready and standing tall for them. The pigs
kept driving, drove right on off—in fact, they speeded on
up and drove on away. Then the people moved on back,
and some of them jumped around across the street, figuring
there was going to be a shoot-out, but we just stood tall,
ready to defend ourselves. We were educating the people
that we would die here for them. This was the position we
always took with brother Huey P. Newton.

We told the people there that we were going to have a
rally that coming Saturday, on the corner of Third and
Chesley, right down the street. We said we'd run down and
educate them about the fact that we'd have to start using
guns to defend ourselves, because the racist pig cops were
coming to our community and murdering our brothers and
sisters. Brother Denzil Dowell was killed, and we'd found
information out about two, three other brothers who'd been
shot up back in December, in North Richmond there. The
brothers had been shot in the armpits, which clearly showed
they had their arms over their heads. Two brothers were
killed in December and around April 1 Denzil Dowell was
gunned down by those pigs. Huey told them we were going
to have a rally concerning this, to tell the people it was
necessary for us to arm ourselves for self-defense.

We went forth to have this rally, and we got about twenty
brothers together with their pieces and their uniforms. We
had the rally right there on the corner of Third and Chesley.
We got guns and a force to defend ourselves. "Ain't no pigs
going to come down here and stop our street rally. We're
going to exercise our constitutional rights to free speech.
And we're going to have a rally right here on the corner."
Most of North Richmond doesn't have sidewalks at all. But

for that section on the corner there, in front of this liquor store, there's an eight to ten foot sidewalk between the curb and the store. We got right out there on the corner, and all the brothers out there in this community saw us with the guns. We lined up all along the streets.

Imagine an intersection now. On one corner we put four, five brothers, and they were spread out about twenty, thirty feet from each other, coming around the corner. Across the street, we put a brother on the corner, then two brothers down from him, thirty or forty feet apart. Then on the corner where Huey and I were speaking, right there in front of the liquor store, we lined that corner up going east and west. Then we lined the other corner up as you go north and south. So the whole intersection was lined up with Panthers, all up and down the corners, going north, east, west, and south on both sides of the streets. And we had our guns, shotguns, pistols, and everything.

The people began to line up and brother Huey told me to go ahead and start blowing. So I started blowing to the brothers there, running down to them about the ten-point platform and program, what kind of organization we had now, about the fact that brother Denzil Dowell had been killed by some racist dog Gestapo pigs. And the fact that we must begin to unify and organize with guns and force. That the Black Panther Party had come to North Richmond, and the Black Panther Party is there to serve the people, it's going to be a black people's party. I guess about two or three hundred people gathered around. In fact, people in cars just stopped, and the whole section on the one side of the street was just a line of cars. And on the other side, coming right up to the intersection, there was another line of cars. Some cars were still moving, by going on the other side of the street, driving up the wrong side of the street.

I was blowing there, and then all of a sudden they start sending some sheriffs in. The people had noticed that we were there, we were there with our guns, we were back again. The pigs started driving down the streets, the sheriff's pigs. Huey whispered, he said, "Run it down about the pigs, Bobby. About how we're going to hold this street rally, and how we're going to exercise our right of free speech. No pig's going to stop it." And he said, "Tell them about the reason why no pig's going to stop it. It's because we've got guns and force here to protect ourselves, to protect the people."

So I ran it down to the brothers, and pointed to the pigs, and the pigs got nervous. I noticed one of the pigs stopped across the street and sat there, and started listening. Four of the brothers came across the street and surrounded the pig car, standing about nine, ten feet away from it. One brother had a .357 Magnum, Warren Tucker had a .38 pistol hanging on him, and Reginald Forte had a 9mm pistol. One brother didn't even have a gun and he got up there too. Then the pig got nervous. He started trying to light a cigarette, but the cigarette just fell out of his hand, with all these people looking at him. The black people had guns and force, ready to deal with the pigs, and the pig couldn't take it any more, he couldn't light his cigarette he was so nervous, he just up and drove away. The people yelled and raved at the fact.

Huey P. Newton had placed the notion in their minds that we organize. I think the people respected the fact that Huey had all of the brothers organized, because he had them all stationed up and down the streets, covering the intersection, guarding the lives of the black people, while we went forth to organize the people. They respected this organization that Huey put down. Huey put down a form, a discipline, that the gun was for our protection, and not for bull jive. So the pig had to split.

Another pig was sitting there. This other pig came up in a car and some of the people's cars moved along. But one man said, "Well, I ain't moving my car. I'm going to sit here and listen." And this cop got caught in between the cars and he couldn't move and he had to sit there and listen to everything. He couldn't do nothing. And that brother didn't move his car. He had a Cadillac too, and he and his woman were sitting in the Cadillac, sitting right at the head of the intersection. So this pig's car was right in between, and he couldn't move, he just had to sit there and listen, and look at 300, that's right, he had to look at 300 mad niggers— mad at the pigs for killing Denzil Dowell. And twenty Panthers out there armed with guns, disciplined, standing thirty or forty feet apart, on every corner of the intersection. So it was tied down.

The people dug it and they said, "Right on." And Huey went on and blew to the brothers and sisters and told them how we're going to get organized and how we're going to start using guns and force in an organized and disciplined manner. In a very revolutionary manner we're going to go forth, and we're going to defend ourselves against any racist attacks. And we're going to patrol these pigs, we're going to patrol our own communities, even the old people are going to have to patrol from their homes and houses. And everybody has to have a shotgun in their home, everybody. Then George Dowell blew about how his brother, Denzil, had been murdered by the pigs. We said we were going to have another meeting over on Second Street, and Huey said we're going to block the whole street off, and ain't no pigs going to be allowed up the street . . . *at all.*

At the second Richmond rally, three or four hundred people came up. They drove their cars all inside the street, and brothers got on top of cars and top of roofs all up and down the street, from one corner to the next, and it was a pretty long block. The whole street was cluttered with cars. We were at one particular address, where I think some relative of George Dowell lived. This was right around the corner from George Dowell's mother's home. All the people came around and we had applications there for people to join the Party. I guess just about everybody out there joined the Party that day, from little young fourteen-year-olds and twelve-year-olds.

We blocked the whole street off. Brother Huey blew, I blew, brother Eldridge Cleaver came over and he blew to

the people, and the people dug it, and the people filled out
the applications.

One incident happened there. I noticed that one of the
brothers moved some four, five guns to one of the corners.
We were in the center of the block. Some more of the extra
brothers had been moved down to one of the corners. The
corner on the north end. The brother explained to me (I
was blowing at the time), that one of the pigs had come up
at the corner down there, so the brothers blocked the street
off. One of the pigs was sitting there. So a couple of other
brothers went over to a vacant lot and stood with their
M-1's and 30-.06's, looking at the pig's car. They couldn't
have been thirty yards from the pigs. Stood staring right at
the pigs' car, and the pigs looked around and one of them
saw another brother walk up near his car, and stand there
almost like at parade rest, but with his hand just a few
inches from his .357 Magnum. And the pig looked at him
when he got up there, then he looked at his partner, and he
said, "That's a .357 Magnum he's got!" And when he said
that, the pig turned his engine on and he got out of there
and didn't come back.

Then a helicopter came around. We blocked off the
whole street and held a people's rally, with power, gun
power. Gun power's the only thing that backed it up. So all
they could do was send a helicopter over, flap, flap, flapping
all day long to try and bother us. This time it wasn't only
the Black Panthers who came, but other people came there,
with their rifles, with their guns, and with their pieces. I
noticed some older brothers come out and they were shaking hands with a lot of us, and they had their pieces under
their shirts. They just carried them concealed. And some
sisters. One sister came out and jumped out of her car with
an M-1. We saw the black community people getting uptight and ready. And the helicopter kept flapping over and
Huey pointed up at the helicopter as it was going over and
said, "Always remember that *the spirit of the people is
greater than the man's technology.*" And the people said,

"Right on." I remember we got way over 300 applications.

The community people got together and George Dowell's sisters and brothers and friends got together and began to have a regular session. And everyone would come to the meeting with the people of North Richmond. The brothers had their guns on. They were tired, sick and tired, and they loved brother Huey. They thought brother Huey was out of sight. He was a beautiful leader, and Huey began to instruct them on many things, on many ways they can go about dealing with the real problems. One of the sisters brought up the problem at one of the nightly sessions that one of those schoolteachers beat up and slapped down a couple of black kids in school. She wanted the Panthers, the Black Panther Party, to go to the school, and she was going to get a lot of mothers and parents to go to the junior high school where her kids went. We all got together and scheduled it for that Monday.

On Monday we took three carloads of Panthers down to the school. All of them were armed down to the gills. We got out of the cars with our guns and stood on the sidewalk. Right at the sidewalk there's a fence to the school yard. All the little black kids ran over to the fence, and all the little white kids ran away from the fence, and went and hid somewhere inside the school. Then the mothers came driving up. They went inside the school building to patrol the halls of the school. They patroled the halls during lunch period, and went and told the principal that they didn't want any more brutality upon their kids in the schools. "We're concerned citizens, and we'll whip your ass and anyone else's that we hear of slapping our children around."

After about twenty minutes, while the mothers were patroling the halls, the pigs drove up. This little, young, rookie, jive pig, trying to look mean and thinking he was bad or something, walked up to the car; the brothers were sitting there in the car, looking back at him, because Huey had trained his brothers, don't be moving in a rash manner. And they got shotguns, four motherfuckers, M-1's. He looks in the car and sees all these pieces and he moves back in a hurry. He got all nervous. "Wha' . . . wha' . . . what the guns for? What the guns for?" And I think Huey said, "We're the Black Panther Party, why?" "Uh, uh, da, da, doo, do you have any license? Do you have any driver's license?" And Huey gave him his license.

"Well, you're Huey P. Newton."

"Minister of Defense Huey P. Newton, of the Black Panther Party." And the pig was just shaking. He didn't know what to do, so he gave Huey his license back and went and got on his radio and called up another pig. They kind of hung off, away from us, looking and not knowing what to do. Shook, because there's too many niggers and too many guns down there for them.

They called up another car and the principal of the school come out, and tried to talk to the pigs. Their cars were parked a little way out in front of the sidewalk that leads into the door of the school, about thirty, forty yards or so behind ours. All they could do was sit there and wonder. And that's all they did, was sit there and wonder. We went there with the mothers and they patroled the halls for the lunch period, and then we left.

About four, five days later, we got a call at the Panther office. There was a session going on up in the Sixth Street office in Richmond, concerning the fact that the D.A. of the county had better do something, had better charge these cops who killed Denzil Dowell.

Me and brother Huey and a number of other brothers all got together and walked off into the meeting there, with our guns. The D.A. was sitting there and he looked up and saw Huey; he saw Huey with that big shotgun. The pig could see that Huey's shotgun carried a whole lot of rounds. And Huey had a bandolier holding twenty-six shotgun shells across his chest. Huey had double 0 buckshot, and the pig was definitely checking Huey out. Huey was decked out in the Panther uniform, and he simply walked in and sat down, and he and the brothers and the sisters who were there talked about this pig, this D.A. Talked about him like he was nothing, running it down about how rotten he is and he is trying to give off some verbal sincerity.

The people saw Huey, and they felt it was no time for them to be taking shit because here's a man that we respect, here's a leader. He's armed down to the gills and he's articulate, and he knows what he's talking about. They were ready to jump over there and snatch this D.A.'s throat out, concerning this whole situation and how Denzil Dowell was killed. We blew the dude away, and told him he wasn't doing anything, wasn't serving the people, that he was jiving, that he was a swine, and that he wasn't intending to do anything for the people, etc.

But he came up and started talking about—why don't you go to the Contra Costa County Sheriff's Department, up in Martinez, and if you go to the Contra Costa County Sheriff's Department in Martinez, maybe you can get some results there. So the people said, "We're going to go to the Contra Costa County Sheriff's Department in Martinez." The mother and the father and the Dowell family wanted us to go to Martinez, and since we're a people's party, we generally go along with what the people want to do, to serve them. Especially if we think it will help them to raise their interests and unity, and get support and try to begin to attempt to change the system. So we said, "Yes, we'll go to Martinez, with the brothers and sisters here. We're concerned about this here. The Panthers will definitely be there."

Somebody called the sheriff's department from the meeting and told them we were coming up and that the people wanted to come up and speak to them. The district attorney had to back it up. I think the people put so much pressure on him that he made the appointment for them within the next two or three days. They made him make the appointment, right there at the meeting. They wouldn't let him get out of there till he made the appointment. That's what it was. He saw all these guns, and the people's power, and he saw that the people were ready for Huey to use this gun on him, and, knowing Huey, he'll defend the people.

We loaded up in our cars, the community people of North Richmond and Black Panther officers and members, and we headed for Martinez. A couple of carloads of brothers, and three or four carloads of community people, went to the Contra Costa County Sheriff's Department. When we got there, they had sheriffs standing all down the doorways, and sheriffs all around. The brothers drove up, and the first six brothers got out. I think there were three shotguns, two or three M-1's, and one brother with a pistol. I drove around the block, but Huey got out. The sheriff's car came up directly across the street, right at the corner. The pig jumped out of the car, took his key out, and unlocked that little thing that holds the shotgun in it. He got his shotgun out and jacked a round off into the chamber of the shotgun. When he did that, Huey just stopped and looked at him, and the brothers were kind of in line, right behind him, doing the same thing that Huey was doing, looking at the pig.

Soon as the pig jacked that round off, Huey jacked a round off. And the brother next to Huey jacked a round off, and another brother jacked a round off, and another. And the only sound the pig heard was, clack-cup, clack-cup, clack-cup, clack-cup, clack-cup, clack-cup, clack-cup, right down the line. The sheriff looked at these Panthers jacking these rounds off, took his shotgun, ejected his round out of the chamber, locked his shotgun back up, got back in his car, and drove away. That was the baddest set on the scene. I don't know who he thought he was. Those other sheriffs standing at the door were amazed and surprised, because Huey turned right around and turned on them, and walked up to the door. And they said, "You can't go in with no gun." And Huey said, "What do you mean, you can't go in with a gun? This is public property. This is people's property. We have a constitutional right to carry guns, and anywhere on public property anybody can carry a gun. So we're going to go in with some guns."

"If you go in we're going to arrest you."

So Huey said, "OK, I'll tell you what we do. We take one brother who's going to volunteer to go in and take the arrest, because we're going to make a test case out of this." Huey knew the law very well, knew that they couldn't charge anyone with coming on public property with guns, because public property is paid for by the people's taxes. And since we have a right to have guns, a constitutional right, they can't charge anybody.

Brother Reginald Forte said, "Here I am, brother." He jumped forward. As he jumped forward—to go in with the gun—the pigs all blocked up, about six of them. We were about twelve or thirteen feet from the door, inside the building. Reginald was getting ready to go into the elevator, and the pig said, "No, you can't go in. No guns upstairs." Reginald Forte started saying, "All right, now look, let me go in, I'm going, I'm ready to go in." As Reginald Forte attempted to go in the elevator, six pigs stood shoulder to shoulder, holding themselves against him. Reginald Forte has his shotgun with him. He walked right up to them and bumped right up into them. The pigs wouldn't move. Reginald Forte said, "Let me go in." He walked away and said, "What's the matter?" Then he walked right back, right up to them again, and bumped into them and said, "Will you get out of the way, so I can go through the elevator? What are you doing blocking the passageway where people go through?" And he bumped into them again. And the pigs are just standing there. Then Reginald Forte moved to go up the stairs, about five feet to the side. He moved to go up the stairs and some more pigs were bunched up together there. He bumped up into them and said, "Hey, what's the matter? Get out of the way so I can go in."

They just held tight, and wouldn't let anybody go by. Another pig came up and I think he said he was a detective of the Martinez City Police, and if you need somebody to protect your rights, etc. He was talking to Huey. "Well, if you need somebody to protect your rights," he says, "well, the police department, the sheriff's department, will protect your rights." Huey P. Newton said, "We don't need racist dogs who murder and brutalize us to try and protect us, because we know you're brutal murderers. Get away from me. I can protect my own rights, because I have my own gun."

At this point Huey got to arguing with him, and one of the pigs stepped on Huey's feet. Huey pushed him off and said, "Get off my feet. Who do you think you are?" Then this little jive who told us, "I can protect your rights," all of a sudden said, "Well, I think that all these people are disturbing the peace, that's what they're doing, and we're just going to have to place somebody under arrest." Huey got to telling about, *"You're* disturbing the peace," and Reggie was over there bumping into these pigs, driving his body into them, saying, "Move so I can go up," with a shotgun in his hand.

Obviously, they weren't going to let anybody go up. So I called Huey back. I said, "All right Huey, come on." I said, "Let's go back in the car, let's put the guns up, and go up here for these people because the people do want us upstairs, and the sister there is explaining that she wants us to go upstairs." I think she wanted us to bawl the head sheriff out. So we went back, locked all our guns in the car, and went to the brothers and sisters upstairs. We left one brother outside to guard the guns.

We got upstairs, and me and brother Huey and brother Eldridge all sat there, listening to this fool, one of those hog of hogs, with his fat belly hanging over his belt. Talking about how he cannot do anything for us, that he does not make the laws, and the best thing that we could do was go to Sacramento, to the legislature, where the laws are made. He kept trying to pass off some verbal sincerity, and trying to doubletalk somebody. Brother Eldridge Cleaver got up and explained. He said, "Look, brothers and sisters, this dog, this swine here ain't going to do nothing for us. This swine is doubletalking and jiving. We know he don't care about us so why don't we all just walk out on this set." Everybody was disgusted and pissed off, after this pig talked about going to the legislature, and all this kind of double talking crap. So we got up and walked out of the building, and went back home.

We went back and laid out the first *Black Panther, Black Community News Service* paper. It was two sheets of legal-sized mimeographed paper, printed on both sides. The headline was, WHY WAS DENZIL DOWELL KILLED? We printed about five or six thousand of those papers and took all the Panthers and went out to the black community in North Richmond. We got to passing the papers out and giving them to people, and children were following, about 100, 150 kids on bicycles, and some of them walking down the streets, following the Panthers, walking all throughout the community, block to block, passing out leaflets. We gave a lot to the kids and told them to put them on all the doorsteps.

One young brother drove up, on his bicycle, and I guess he hadn't seen the headlines on the paper, because he said to us, "How much will you pay me if I go and distribute all of them to the doors? Is them other little kids getting paid?" And Huey said, "No, none of the other kids are getting paid, young brother." He said, "You see who's on the front page of this paper?" And he looked and he saw Denzil Dowell's picture. He had a paper route, and he was getting ready to do his route. The little boy looked at Huey, and looked at Huey's gun, and looked at Denzil Dowell, and he said, "Brother." He was very hurt. He said, "Don't pay me nothing. I ain't even going to do my route. I'm going to distribute these to every door." And he just snatched up a bundle of them and you could see him going down the street, trying to give everybody one, because the brother was remembered.

The *Examiner* came down to the Panther headquarters,

and did an interview on a Tuesday. They said they were going to print it on a Sunday. That Saturday evening the headlines hit, about the existence of the Black Panther Party, who patroled cops in the black community. They wrote it all backwards. They said we were anti-white and were black racists. After that Huey began talking about how we needed to go straight up in front of some city hall, as we did in Martinez, and talk to the people and hold a rally there, so we could get a message over to the mass of the people. And the mass media would come along and cover it. We saw another article in the paper about the Black Panther Party about three or four weeks later. We all read the papers and realized that the news of the existence of the Black Panther Party was being widely distributed, especially in the Bay Area.

One Monday morning Huey called me up and said, "Bobby, come over to the house right quick." I went over to the house. Huey showed me the papers. He said, "Look here, Mulford is up in the legislature now, trying to get a bill passed against us. We don't care about laws anyway, because the laws they make don't serve us at all. He's probably making a law to serve the power structure. He's trying to get some kind of law passed against us." He said, "I've been thinking. Remember when I told you we have to go in front of a city hall, in front of a jail, or do something like we did in Martinez, to get more publicity, so we can get a message over to the people?" This was Huey's chief concern, getting the message over to the people.

So Huey says, "You know what we're going to do?" "What?" "We're going to the Capitol." I said, "The *Capitol?*" He says, "Yeah, we're going to the Capitol." I say, "For what?" "Mulford's there, and they're trying to pass a law against our guns, and we're going to the Capitol steps. We're going to take the best Panthers we got and we're going to the Capitol steps with our guns and forces, loaded down to the gills. And we're going to read a message to the world, because all the press is going to be up there. The press is always up there. They'll listen to the message, and they'll probably blast it all across this country. I know, I know they'll blast it all the way across California. We've got to get a message over to the people."

Huey understood a revolutionary culture, and Huey understood how arms and guns become a part of the culture of a people in the revolutionary struggle. And he knew that the best way to do it was to go forth, and those hungry newspaper reporters, who are shocked, who are going to be shook up, are going to be blasting that news faster than they could be stopped. I said, "All right, brother, right on. I'm with you. We're going to the Capitol." So we called a meeting that night, before going up to the Capitol, to write the first executive mandate for the Black Panther Party. Huey was going to write Executive Mandate Number One.

This executive mandate was the first major message to *all* the American people, and *all* the black people, in particular, in this country, who are living in the confines of this decadent system. Eldridge and Huey and all of us sat down, and it didn't take us long. We weren't jiving. No time at all, not like some of the intellectuals and punks that have to take ten days before they can write an executive mandate to put things together. I don't think it was fifteen minutes before we whipped that executive mandate out, looked it over, and Eldridge corrected it, got things together. The executive mandate was to the first message, the first major message made by the Black Panther Party, coming from the Minister of Defense, Huey P. Newton. Huey told me to organize the brothers, tell them to get their guns and be at the office tomorrow morning, at nine o'clock. "We're going to leave at ten o'clock. We're going to leave at ten o'clock sharp."

PICKING UP
THE GUN

NIGGERS WITH GUNS IN THE STATE CAPITOL

■ On May 2, 1967, we went across the bridge to Sacramento with a caravan of cars. We wound up right in front of the Capitol building. There were thirty brothers and sisters. Six sisters and twenty-four brothers. Twenty of the brothers were armed.

Huey P. Newton was not with us. The brothers felt we could not risk Huey getting shot or anything, so we voted that he would stay behind in Oakland. We voted Huey down and wouldn't let him come.

When I first drove up, I didn't know where the steps were. The Capitol looked about a block or so away from me. I didn't know whether this was the right place or not, because we were specifically looking for the Assembly of the State of California. The reason I didn't know is because of an old thing they'd taught me in school about the Capitol in Washington, D.C. The dome, a round dome, you know, it was supposed to be the "omnipotent area," as brother Eldridge Cleaver puts it. It's the top, and it was supposed to be made up of two houses.

So I assumed it was the same as Washington, D.C. I didn't know if I was going to the right place or not. But I

said, "Look, there's some cameramen up there." Huey said
there's always cameramen around these places, so I
thought, "This is probably it." The other brothers had
parked their cars and had come back around to where we
were. We got out of the car and got all our guns out. You
know we always follow the laws. As soon as the brothers got
out of the car, they were putting rounds into the chambers
because Huey and I researched those laws in the past. We
had to follow the law to the letter. There was a fish-and-
game code law that you couldn't have a loaded shotgun or
rifle in a car. That didn't refer to a pistol, but to a shotgun
or a rifle.

The loaded rifle or shotgun meant an unexpended cartridge in the chamber. The law also read that unexpended
cartridges in the magazine do not constitute a loaded gun.
That is, bullets that haven't been fired do not constitute a
loaded gun, even if they are in the magazine. But if there
is an unexpended cartridge or bullet inside the chamber
of a rifle or a shotgun, then it is considered loaded. The
brothers got out of the car, and you could see brothers, just
jacking rounds off into the chambers.

A lot of people were looking. A lot of white people were
shocked, just looking at us. I know what they were saying:
"Who in the hell are those niggers with these guns? Who in
the hell are those niggers with these guns? What are they
doing?"

One or two white people, they probably passed it off,
"Oh this is just a gun club," and this is where Bob Dylan
gets down on Mr. Jones, "You don't know what's going
on." Because this was getting to be a colossal event and
those people did not know what the hell was going on. Some
of them did look at us like we were a gun club. But a lot of
them only had questions on their faces of, "What the hell
are those damn niggers doing with these goddam rifles?"
They actually stopped and looked at us and stood up there
around the Capitol, and stared up from the grass and

looked at us. I didn't pay a damn bit of attention to them because we knew our constitutional rights and all that stuff about the rights of citizens to have guns. The Second Amendment to the Constitution of the United States, and no police or militia force can infringe upon that right; it states that specifically.

Anyway, all the brothers got up, and I said, "All right, brothers, let's roll." We started walking and moving. We didn't walk in military form. We just moved. We were scattered all across the sidewalk. We were not in any rank, but we held our guns straight up because Huey had taught us not to point a gun at anyone—not only was it unsafe, but there was a law against just the pointing of a gun.

So all the brothers had that stuff down. They all had their guns pointed straight up in the air or pointed straight down to the ground as they carried them. We were walking up the sidewalk. I remember a brother in the background saying, "Look at Reagan run." I thought that he was just referring to something symbolic, but I did find out later on, after all this shit was over, that Reagan *was* over there with a bunch of kids. We'd walked almost up this long twenty-foot-wide sidewalk leading up to the first steps of the Capitol, and one of the dudes said, "Look at Reagan run." Now this is very important, because we found out later that Reagan had had with him 200 Future Youth, Future Leaders they call them. He was speaking to them on the lawn of the Capitol. I was looking straight up at the front of the Capitol building and I saw a couple of cameramen running around up there.

I found out later that Reagan had righteously spotted us. One of the brothers saw Reagan turn around and start trotting away from the whole scene because here came all these hardfaced brothers. These brothers were off the block; righteous brothers off the block. From what they call the nitty gritty and the grass roots. You could look at their faces and see the turmoil they've lived through. Their ages ranged

anywhere from sixteen, which was about the youngest we
had there—that was Bobby Hutton—all the way down to
myself, thirty-one. I guess I was about the oldest.

We righteously walked on up to the first stairs, and then
we walked on up to the next stairs. Bobby Hutton was on
my right side and Warren Tucker was on my left side.
Bobby Hutton had a 12-gauge shotgun, a High Standard
12-gauge pump shotgun, that's what Bobby Hutton had.
And Warren Tucker had a .357 Magnum. We walked all
the way up, and they stayed right next to me.

We got to the stairs. Now personally I do not remember
reading Executive Mandate Number One on the stairs, as I
was ordered to do. I don't remember reading it there, but
the brothers told me and everybody told me that I did in
fact read it.

I'm on the stairs and I'm trying to make my mind up
about going in. It wasn't any long process by which I had to
make up my mind. Huey's emphasis on going into the
Capitol was based on the fact that there might be a string of
National Guards and policemen there, in case they found
out we were coming. I heard the security guard over there
talking to two brothers, when I glanced over there a second
time, and I heard him say, "You aren't violating anything
with your gun, so if you want to, you can go inside." And
that made my mind up for me. But I also made up my mind
in another context too. That I personally wanted to see the
area where a citizen has a right to observe the legislature. I
read in the paper that Mulford was an assemblyman from
the Sixteenth Assembly District in Oakland, so it was the
Assembly that I wanted to see. I waved to all the brothers. I
said, "All right, brothers, come on, we're going in here.
We're going inside."

The brothers were scattered all out in front of the Capitol. One of the cameramen walked up to me. "Are you
going inside the Capitol?" he said. I said, "Yeah, we're
going inside." And I snatched the door open, and me and
Bobby Hutton and the rest of the brothers, walked through

that door. Warren Tucker was on my left and brother
Bobby Hutton, with his 12-gauge shotgun, was on my
right. We walked off into the lobby area. All around, to my
right, to my left, everywhere, there were people, predominantly white people, who looked shocked. Man, they were
shocked.

As we began to walk, I noticed one thing. They moved
and stepped aside, and I saw some with their mouths hanging open, just looking, and they were saying with their eyes
and their faces and expressions, "Who in the hell are these
niggers with these guns?" And some of them were just
saying, "Niggers with guns, niggers with guns," and I
pointed those out as enemies because they were confused.
I saw three or four faces that really caught what was going
on. They must have been in the Assembly and heard Mulford talking about us because they frowned their faces up
and looked at us like a bunch of pig racists, like I've seen
racist pigs look at me and Huey, like they wanted to kill us.

I saw a long hall in front of me, a very long hall. I said,
"We're looking for the Assembly." I saw a sign that said
"Senate" and had an arrow that pointed to the right. But I
was looking for the Assembly and I hadn't seen any sign. So
I walked on. As we walked down the hall, cameramen were
running from our left and from our right, around Bobby
and around Tucker, jumping in front of us taking flicks and
clicking flicks. Cameramen with movie cameras were shooting, but that didn't make any difference. I just tightened up
and squeezed the mandate I had rolled up and kept walking. I stopped and said, "Where in the hell's the Assembly?
Anybody in here know where you go in and observe the
Assembly making these laws?" Nobody said anything. Then
somebody hollered out, "It's upstairs on the next floor."

We went up to the second floor and started walking
again. By this time there were many cameramen in front of
us, backing up and taking pictures of us walking down the
hall. Movie cameramen, still cameramen, regular cameras.

Bulbs were flashing all over the place. I got about midway down the hall when I saw a gate. I didn't relate to the gate at first, but I turned around and asked a reporter, "Could you please tell me where I go to observe the Assembly making the laws? I want to go there. I want to see Mulford supposedly making this law against black people." That's what I was thinking to myself—I want to *see this*. So he said, "Straight down, sir." I went ahead and saw this gate. As I was approaching the gate, when I was about five or six feet from it, this pig jumped out, this state pig, and said, "Where the hell are you going?" I said, "I'm going to observe the Assembly. What about it?"

"You can't come in here!"

"What the hell you mean, I can't come in here? You gonna deny me my constitutional right? Every citizen's got a right to observe the Assembly. What's wrong with you?" And while the conversation was going on, the reporters were vamping inside the gate. And so many reporters were trying to get in there, they bammed and knocked the pig all up against the wall. Trying to get pictures. The only thing that was in front of me was the pig, and just a little gate. Swing gate, like a swinging door, but it was only about three feet high. When the reporters vamped all over the pig, he just moved out of the way, and I just proceeded to move on.

As I proceeded to move, the reporters always had a way for me to travel. I noticed the way to go was to the right, so I moved to the right, and as I moved to the right, I could see a kind of heavyset short man, about five-foot six inches or five-foot seven. As I approached a big door that was three or four times as tall as I was, he was opening the door. He was opening the door in a manner of, "Yes, sir, you *sure can* come in. Come right on in, sir! You have the *gun!*" That's what he was saying. You have the gun. Come in. And he opened the door in a very humble manner. Like a servant. Like a vassal. That's the way he opened that door. He was scared.

• • •

I walked inside, and as I did, I saw a lot of what we call "back seats." Back seats in a theater. Inside the Assembly, I looked to the left and I looked to the right. I walked to my left. There was an aisle over there. Cameramen and reporters jumped all in front of me. Something funny about the cameramen and reporters getting up in that aisle to my left. A lot of them came in another door. Because I know they weren't in front of me when I hit that door. They must have come in another door.

As I was walking to my left, I remember hearing this speaker, the Assembly speaker, saying, "Get those cameramen out of here, they're not supposed to be in here." As I got to the aisle, Eldridge Cleaver was there all of a sudden. Eldridge Cleaver was there, and Warren Tucker was halfway up the aisle, with a .357 Magnum on his side. I glanced up, and I saw some so-called black representatives in the legislature who we refer to as "Toms, sellouts, bootlickers."

They were looking at the man as if to say, "Why did they have to come here?" They hated us being there, those bootlickers. I looked at those bootlickers, those Uncle Toms, very intensely. I didn't care for them because they never represented us there. And this kind of humble-shoulderedness and looking back, "Well, here they are, they're here. What are they doing here?"

Someone was saying, "This is not where you're supposed to be. This is not where you're supposed to be." We were trying to decide whether to stay there on the floor of the Assembly or go upstairs. We were trying to discuss that in a very short span of time, in less than a minute. The next thing I know, a pig and Bobby Hutton passed behind my back. Bobby was cussing out the pig who had snatched his gun out of his hand. He had snuck up behind him and snatched his gun out of his hand. Bobby Hutton was cussing the pig back, "What the hell you got my gun for? Am I under arrest or something? If I'm not under arrest, you give me my gun back. You ain't said I was under arrest." He was remembering very well what Huey had taught. Always ask if you are under arrest. And if you're not under arrest, then you stand on your constitutional rights.

So I turned and ran up to the side of the pig and said, "Is the man under arrest? What the hell are you taking his gun for?" He said, "You're not supposed to be in here. This is not where you're supposed to be." I asked him, "Is he under arrest? If he ain't under arrest, what the hell you got his gun for?" Another pig walks up and hands this same pig a gun, which I recognized as the same gun which Mark Comfort had had, a 30-.06. I walked out of those big doors—this pig, me, and Bobby. Bobby was on one side and I was on the other side, Bobby cussing the pig out, calling him all kind of motherfuckers, and telling them to give him his gun back if he ain't under arrest.

Just as we got to the elevator, the pig grabbed hold of my right shoulder. I kept asking him if I were under arrest. He pushed me, and when he pushed I went into the elevator. I said, "All right, we're under arrest, brothers. We must be under arrest. Come on in, let's go." Because just before the pig grabbed me, he said I wasn't under arrest. So I think I accepted this kind of informal thing of him arresting us at this point. Then it flashed in my mind. The mandate . . . the message that Huey sent . . . I haven't read it. I gotta read the message, I gotta read the message. So nine or ten of the brothers just crowded in the elevator with guns, and some reporters got on that elevator too. We went down to the first floor and we went to the right, into a little room with a counter. The room was about ten feet long and six feet wide. All of a sudden I saw all these cameramen poking their cameras in the doors. I said, "Yeah . . . the mandate." The message that Huey told me to read. The message. Gotta get the message over. So I pulled the message out and opened it up, and I read the whole thing. In the background Bobby Hutton was cussing the pigs out and telling them to give him his gun back: "You give me my gun back. You ain't placing me under arrest. You give me my gun back. You ain't placing me under arrest." That might have been mentioned three or four times. He called the pigs all kind of motherfuckers, which even came over on TV, I heard later on.

At this point, after I finished reading the message, right at this point, a black pig walked in. A nigger pig, a "Negro" pig walked in. As he was passing in front of me I said, "Look man, are we under arrest or not?" And he says, "No, you're not under arrest." "Then dammit," I said, "give these black brothers back their guns." At this point he said, "They're going to get their guns." I said, "Well, give them back to them!" And Bobby Hutton tore into them, "Bastard, load my gun back up. You unloaded my gun. I seen you unload. You unloaded my gun. Load it back up, just like you had it. Give me my gun back."

I glanced over at the counter there, and they were doing something to the guns, the 30-.06 and Bobby Hutton's pump shotgun. Next thing I knew they had the guns back in their hands. I was looking at all these cameramen. They asked me some questions. Somebody said to read it again. Said he didn't catch it. I read the mandate again, right inside that little room. When I finished reading it, I figured it was time to go. So I said, "Let's go." We cut out and came out the door. Then some cameraman walked up to me and asked me to read the message once more. So I read it again. First I was on the upper steps in front of the Capitol. I read it and then I got down to the lower steps and read the message still another time. I said, "All right, brothers, let's go." *

** Executive Mandate Number One
Statement by the Minister of Defense
Delivered May 2, 1967, at Sacramento,
California, State Capitol Building*

The Black Panther Party for Self-Defense calls upon the American people in general and the black people in particular to take careful note of the racist California Legislature which is now considering legislation

At that time I knew that what Huey P. Newton was saying about the colossal event had occurred. Because many, many cameramen were there. Many, many people had covered this event of black people walking into the Capitol, and registering their grievance with a particular statement. A message, Executive Mandate Number One, that Huey P. Newton had ordered me to take to the Capitol, to use the mass media as a means of conveying the message

---

aimed at keeping the black people disarmed and powerless at the very same time that racist police agencies throughout the country are intensifying the terror, brutality, murder, and repression of black people.

At the same time that the American government is waging a racist war of genocide in Vietnam, the concentration camps in which Japanese Americans were interned during World War II are being renovated and expanded. Since America has historically reserved the most barbaric treatment for non-white people, we are forced to conclude that these concentration camps are being prepared for black people who are determined to gain their freedom by any means necessary. The enslavement of black people from the very beginning of this country, the genocide practiced on the American Indians and the confining of the survivors on reservations, the savage lynching of thousands of black men and women, the dropping of atomic bombs on Hiroshima and Nagasaki, and now the cowardly massacre in Vietnam, all testify to the fact that toward people of color the racist power structure of America has but one policy: repression, genocide, terror, and the big stick.

Black people have begged, prayed, petitioned, demonstrated, and everything else to get the racist power structure of America to right the wrongs which have historically been perpetrated against black people. All of these efforts have been answered by more repression, deceit, and hypocrisy. As the aggression of the racist American government escalates in Vietnam, the police agencies of America escalate the repression of black people throughout the ghettoes of America. Vicious police dogs, cattle prods, and increased patrols have become familiar sights in black communities. City Hall turns a deaf ear to the pleas of black people for relief from this increasing terror.

The Black Panther Party for Self-Defense believes that the time has come for black people to arm themselves against this terror before it is too late. The pending Mulford Act brings the hour of doom one step nearer. A people who have suffered so much for so long at the hands of a racist society, must draw the line somewhere. We believe that the black communities of America must rise up as one man to halt the progression of a trend that leads inevitably to their total destruction.

to the American people and to the black people in particular. We walked out and got to the car and brother Eldridge Cleaver came up behind me. And Eldridge said, "Brother, we did it. We did it, man. We put it over." I said, "That's right, brother, we sure did."

So I said, "All right, brothers and sisters, let's go. Let's get out of this town." I remember telling everybody, "The sisters and brothers cooked some chicken." The brothers were crowding up. Some of them were slightly behind us, and I said, "Let's go. We gonna go eat all this fried chicken that we got here, 'cause I'm hungry and it's hot in this town. It's hot, brother." So I went and got in my car, and I looked back for those people who'd parked behind me.

I opened the car door and asked the people if they were ready to go. "Let's go," they said. "All right, brothers and sisters. Let's go," I hollered. As I pulled out, I asked, "Where's everybody else?" "They're around the corner," somebody said. "Some of them tried to park around the corner." So we drove around the corner. Further on, down a long, long block, I stopped and made sure that all of our people and all of our cars were in a line behind me. Warren Tucker who was driving the second or third car hollered to me, "Hey man, this car is hot." He was driving my '54 Chevy. "It needs some water in it, so we can cool it down." The engine was running hot because there was something wrong with the radiator.

"Later for that," I said. "We're going outside of town. We'll eat that chicken, and we'll get water later on." So I took off in the right-hand lane. Just before the corner, I noticed a sign: SAN FRANCISCO—TURN RIGHT. I stopped for the light and noticed a service station across the street. I debated in my mind. I decided that we'd go ahead and get the water. Instead of turning right, I waited until the green light came on and went straight across the street, and turned up into the service station. The rest of the brothers and sisters rolled into the station and just sat there. It was very, very hot. It was burning up. I decided to take off my leather jacket, but to take off my jacket I had to get out of the car.

As I was opening the door, I looked up and saw a pig at the corner walking south on the sidewalk from his car. He had his gun in his hand. I jumped out. I came on out of the car. I walked straight toward him. I stopped and he stopped. I said, "Now wait a minute." I said, "Now first thing you have to do is you have to put that gun away. Put it back in that holster. If you want to make an arrest you can make an arrest, but you better put that gun away." And the next thing I heard was brothers jacking rounds, jacking shells off into the chambers of their guns. When they saw the pig walking up with that gun, they started jacking rounds off. I said, "Put that gun away!" I looked him dead cold in his eyes. He was a scared pig, with his gun out. He took his gun, after hearing all the rounds, and me telling him to put his gun back, he slid his gun back into his holster, and kept his hands off of it. Right on!

Then I looked up and there was another pig who had walked up near. He'd parked his motorcycle, and jumped on his little radio. I can't remember what the hell he said on his radio but he looked back at me. "We got a right," he said, "we got a right to have identification." I said, "Maybe you do have a right to identification, but you just make sure you keep your damn guns in your holsters!" The next thing I knew, other pigs were driving up. I heard something come over that radio that said, "Arrest them all. On anything. Arrest them all on anything." That's what it said. Then he asked me where I had been. I said we'd been to the Capitol. "Why? What about it?" You know what he asked me? He said, "What are you, a gun club?" I said, "No, we're the Black Panther Party. We're black people with guns. What about it?"

As I began to move away, I saw a lot of pigs coming up; plainclothesmen jumping out of cars, cars in the middle of the streets, everything. I still wasn't disturbed by them at all.

I was just walking. Some plainclothesman came up. "You got any identification?" I said, "Yeah, I got identification." I saw a pig opening a door of one of the cars. I ran over to the car. I said, "Keep your hands off."

I turned around and two pigs were sneaking up behind Sherman Forte. Before I could say anything, they grabbed hold of both of his arms, and one of the pigs snatched his pistol out of his holster. And I said, "Is he under arrest?" "Yeah, he's under arrest." I said, "Take the arrest, Sherman."

The pig asked me again about identification. I went to my back pocket to pull out my wallet, and when I did that the pig, almost simultaneously, grabbed my right arm, and another pig grabbed my left arm and said, "You're arrested for carrying a concealed weapon." Then he snatched my gun out of my holster, holding my arms. They handcuffed me readily, and began to move me to the car.

They drove me to the Sacramento police station. As we came out of the elevator there, one pig grabbed the handcuffs and pushed them up real high—real high, so it hurt and pained. And he ran me right up against the wall and said, "Now you stand there with your face against the wall." That's what the pig said. And my face *hit that wall*. The wall was very cool. It was a soothing cool. I was glad to lay my face against this cool wall. Sherman Forte was to my left. I looked over at him. "What about it, brother?" "Ah man, it's nothing," he said. "It's all right." "Yeah," I said. "Going to be all right."

They took me to a cell. I asked myself, "Did I fuck up?" I didn't know. I was very tired. I got on the other side of the door, three or four feet away from it, lay down, and righteously fell off to sleep.

Somebody was unlocking the cell. There was Eldridge. "Oh, goddam it." That hurt me. That hurt me bad. I said, "Goddam, Eldridge is arrested!" I knew that was bad. Eldridge was on parole. I said, "Eldridge isn't going to get out of jail." I felt so bad. I said, "Man, they got you arrested. You might have to go back to prison." Eldridge said, "Fuck it. It was worth it, because we did it."

SACRAMENTO JAIL

■ Eldridge spotted a brother down inside the cell. He was bleeding. Somehow Eldridge detected more than I detected, when I first looked at him. Eldridge could see that his face was all fucked up. Then he began to groan. Eldridge said, "Hey brother, what's wrong?" He got down, looked at him, and saw that the brother's eye was almost hanging out of his head. His face was swollen all up around his right eye. The pigs had beat up the side of his head. His nose was bleeding, too.

A pig come to the door later on and Eldridge told that pig that he'd better get this man to a hospital. "You get this man to a hospital. Look at his eye. Look what's happened to him. His head's all swollen up and everything." Eldridge knows how to deal with the pigs and the prisons. The pigs went on and got themselves together, and called the ambulance and took the man to the hospital. That was very good. We got the brother out of there to the hospital. The pigs had whipped him all up inside and he was drunk too. The pigs beat cats up when they're drunk, just because they're sadistic motherfuckers, and they have somebody who's helpless and they can beat him. That was the way a lot of that shit went down in Sacramento.

A little after that, they decided to move all eighteen of us to this big tank, this big drunk tank. You had to take your shoes off, and you couldn't have any cigarettes or stuff like that. A couple of lawyers had gotten together, and they got up there from Oakland. We got one of the lawyers to go to the cigarette machine and smuggle us some cigarettes.

They called me out to try to get me to sign some jive statement. I didn't have to sign a statement, nobody signed any statements. I think one brother almost broke down and got weak, and almost signed the statement, but he held on. I was out there refusing to sign the statement for quite a while, and when I came back in, the brothers had already smuggled some cigarettes in while I was out there. The lawyers wanted to talk to me, and I talked to them a long time. The pigs seen all this smoking there and began searching for the cigarettes, trying to find the cigarettes, but the brothers hid them in a loose piece of tile near the ventilator in the ceiling.

Before they left, Eldridge and I said, "When are we going to get some food in here?" One of the pigs was talking about, "You ain't gonna get no food," and Eldridge vamped on him. "What you talking about, we ain't going to get no food? We're going to get some food in this motherfucker, or don't you motherfuckers never come up to this door no more because you come to this door, there's eighteen of us and maybe three, four, or five of you." Big Willie walked up, and the pigs looked at him. Willie was a bad-looking cat. He looked like he could knock a dude out of the picture, which he could (I saw him knock a dude out, later on, in Big Greystone). We were mad because when the brothers started getting hungry, they got to remembering the big pans of chicken everyone was going to eat. The brothers were mad about that chicken. That's when we told them, "Don't you come back in here because if you come in here you might get your heads whipped." And Big Willie walked up and put his arms up. That was a righteous protest.

Personally, I thought they weren't going to feed us. I thought they were going to lock us up and just never come back. But forty-five minutes later the dudes said, "All right. Line up. Line up. Line up. Let's go. Hit the food. Hit the food." All the brothers lined on up to get that food because you gotta live. Everybody lined up and we had a bag apiece. We had a carton of milk, a cheese sandwich, a hamburger, and an orange.

We were hungry, man. We hadn't eaten all day and it was five or six o'clock that evening. We knew they weren't going to feed us and we were getting mad, remembering that chicken. It wasn't only Big Willie jumping up talking about, "I'll knock you out," but everybody was saying, "You'd *better* get some food in here, you goddam motherfucker. Who the fuck you think you are? You better bring some goddam food in here. We've had this shit." That was a little power play we made on them. They went out and bought our food. That's the way you have to do it. Use them tactics.

That was very important, to revive the spirits. Everybody was kind of down. Except for Eldridge, most of the other brothers hadn't been to jail. Some of the brothers were sloughing in the corner while we were busted. Mark Comfort's boys, two of them sloughed out, jumped up talking about, "If I'd a known this was gonna happen, I'd a never come along." Just got to jiving. They hadn't been in enough situations with Huey P. Newton out there on the streets. There were a couple of other brothers who had been in jail before who could relate to the situation because that's all there was to it.

I personally had this goddam feeling that I had just made a big mistake. I kept running over it. But it made me feel good, too, because we were vamping on these pigs, and Eldridge just knew more about how to vamp on the pigs than I did. I'm glad he was there that day. I'd been in jail before but that was in a military stockade. I'd been in the stockade twice (for one month and eight months) when I was in the Air Force, and the most time I'd been to jail in between those times was ten days here, twelve days here, or thirty days in Los Angeles on some bullshit. But Eldridge knew how to deal with the pigs. He was vamping on them in a minute, and it always made me feel good, to know that he was there, because he wasn't going to let pigs mess over any of us. He'd remember things like food, and know how to talk to the motherfuckers.

All the brothers' spirits revived. I know most of the brothers must have thought about what we said in the last point of the program. We wanted land, bread, housing, education, clothing, justice, and peace. But the brothers knew that bread was food. Righteous food. I know they must have remembered that, because I remembered it. We were off in jail there, and the man was talking about how we weren't going to eat. Shit. He must have been crazy. Burn that padded cell up, one way or the other. We had no matches or anything but we would have found something to burn it up with, and cause shit.

Brothers started ripping those iron strips on the wall. Big Willie started ripping them off. Big Willie had lifted some powerful weights and his muscles just rippled all over his arms. He'd been in the joint before. He got most of that in the joint. He got a lot of it, I found out later on, outside on the streets. Anyway, Big Willie Thompson, the Black Panthers, and Eldridge Cleaver were all in jail there. We finally ate, and after we ate most of us laid out across that padded cell floor and went to sleep.

I went out and made a phone call. A lot of brothers went in and out making phone calls. I called the bail bondsman. I called Williams Bail Bonds. He's an older cat, about forty-five years old. He's a boyfriend of my sister's and he told me on the phone that Huey had already been to the office and he had gone somewhere to do a radio program to get some support, saying that we should be set free, we were political prisoners. I told him that I wanted him to bail out *all* the brothers. All the brothers *now*. "Just bail us out, and we'll raise the money for you." He said he'd see what he could do about getting on up there. So I said, "If you can't bail out all of them, than bail out me and Eldridge, right now." The reason I wanted Eldridge bailed out was because Eldridge was on parole.

When a dude's on parole or probation, the teletypes get to working, from city to city. They find out about the person being on parole and they'll call up the parole officer and make him put a hold on him right away. One time Huey was getting out of jail in Berkeley. He was on his way down the stairs, coming out of the front door, and the teletypes got to working. Ten pigs ran downstairs and grabbed him and said, "Your probation officer put a hold on you so you can't get bailed out." That's why I told Lionel Williams to try to bail out Eldridge, me, or anybody right away, right quick. But he didn't do it.

Anyway, we went and got some sleep. It had been a long day. We'd done a lot of revolutionary work for the Party. Revolutionary and political work. I remember George Dowell talking about how he never was going to jail no more. He didn't like jails. I can relate to that brother's feelings about jail, because George Dowell had five, maybe six children. The youngest one was about three or four years old. His wife was at home in North Richmond. His brother Denzil had been killed. He readily joined the Panther Party, because he knew it was the right thing. He understood that you couldn't call on pigs to help you. He related to that unity we were talking about, the unity of black people defending themselves against these pigs murdering us in our community. But with his wife and his kids home there, he just couldn't see being locked up in jail. George also talked about how he was supposed to have been back to work that night. That job, of course, was directly related to his family, and he just hated to be locked in jail. He never was going to jail no more. He just didn't like it.

But I kept reassuring the brothers, and I begin to ask the brothers their names, because with some of the brothers, I didn't know their full names. I wanted to remember their names, so that if I got bailed out right away, I could tell the bail bondsman which names to ask for, because sometimes, if you come up and say you want to bail some people out, and you don't know their names, the pigs won't bail them out. I asked them their names for that specific reason. Pigs will withhold information on you, while you're inside the jail, in a minute.

Anyway, we fell asleep. I guess it was about twelve or one o'clock at night and somebody came in there and called me. One of the brothers shook me, to kind of help wake me up and said, "You getting bailed out. Let's go." I looked around. I saw all the brothers asleep. I said, "Well, I won't disturb them. The best thing to do is get on out of here and start working to get some bail money to get these brothers out of here." So I got out and went downstairs. Mark Comfort was there with the lawyers. One of the lawyers was Beverly Axelrod. I explained to her the best thing to do was to run back to Oakland and get Huey, so I could get with Huey and figure out a way to get the bail money together and get all the brothers bailed out.

We jumped in the car and drove on down the ninety miles to Oakland. I didn't even go to sleep. We drove all the way down. In fact, I drove. I'd already had some sleep. They were pretty tired, and I drove all the way in. We got to my house, on Fifty-seventh Street in Oakland. Huey was waiting there and handed me a cold Colt 45 beer.

Huey greeted me and said, "Brother, you were good. You were beautiful. You were a true revolutionary. You did the job you were supposed to do." He shook my hand, wrapped his arm around my shoulder like the brother will do when he knows we've done righteous revolutionary work. We sat down, and I explained a few other things, other than what the TV had put over. We talked a little bit, talked to Beverly about the fact that we had to get these brothers out on bail. I guess it was about 3:00 in the morning by then, so we decided to take off at 6:00 to make sure we were back in

Sacramento by 8:00. I went to sleep, and somebody came back over to my house and got me up. Huey, Beverly, and I jumped into the car about 6:15 and cut out, back to Sacramento.

BAILING OUT THE BROTHERS

■ There was supposed to be a court hearing at 9:00 concerning the lowering of the bail, which had been arranged by Beverly Axelrod and another lawyer. Huey held a press conference and he blew those pigs away. He talked about the power structure like it had never been talked about before. He brought out significant things about why we had guns, the reason we had guns. We had guns to defend ourselves against the 400-year-old brutality and oppression.

They were asking him if he was anti-white. He said, "No, we're not anti-white. I don't hate a person because of the color of his skin. I hate the oppression that we're subjected to daily by racist pigs and other racists who attack and murder and brutalize us. Those who have been brutalizing us for 400 years." And Huey just ran it all down about wars. Politics is war without bloodshed—and war is a continuation of politics, with bloodshed.

You talk about antagonistic contradictions and non-antagonistic contradictions that exist between the people and those who're supposed to represent them in the government. I remember him running down that antagonistic contradictions are created by the power structure attacking the people, or attacking those who disagree with the basic political decisions that have been made by the power structure and put on the people's heads. And when the people disagree with those political decisions made by the power structure, the power structure always sends in guns and force. By sending in guns and force, attacking the people, the contradiction becomes very, very antagonistic.

Therefore the people should always stand, and they do stand, for peace. The people, the masses of the people, want peace. The masses of the people do not want war. Huey, quoting Chairman Mao, said the Black Panther Party advocates the abolition of war. But at the same time, we realize that the only way you can get rid of war, many times, is through a process of war, because war has been unjustly waged against us in our communities. Therefore, Huey says, the only way you can get rid of guns is to pick up the gun and get rid of the guns of the oppressor. The people must be able to pick up guns, to defend themselves against all forms of aggression, all forms of racism—all forms of *real* racism.

We went off in the courtroom to sit down, and the lawyer from Sacramento and Beverly Axelrod were making motions for lowering of bail, and we looked and listened. The judge didn't want to lower the bail. He started citing off the records of brothers who had been arrested before, the hardcore brothers off the block. Even Emory Douglas, an artist, who went to art college of some kind for two years, had a record on him—he'd been arrested three, four times, spent five, six months in jail.

They came down to Eldridge Cleaver's record and Beverly Axelrod began to explain how Eldridge Cleaver was arrested. That he didn't have a gun or anything. That in fact, and it was true, *Ramparts* had sent him up there. That he was a writer for *Ramparts,* and he knew that the Panthers were going, so *Ramparts* sent him up there to cover the story as a reporter. And Beverly Axelrod blew so beautiful about how Eldridge Cleaver was snatched up off the corner just because he was black. She went further to prove this to the judge about how everybody had witnessed a black woman, who was a citizen of Sacramento, and not a Black Panther, being snatched up by the pigs and taken apart just because she was black. That was very important,

I think. And she said that's why Eldridge Cleaver was arrested, a man with a camera in his hand, without a gun, who was taking pictures just like twenty other cameramen took pictures on that corner, the same corner where the Black Panther Party got arrested.

She blew a beautiful set, Beverly Axelrod did, in defense of Eldridge, that they should release Eldridge, that he's on parole, and there's no reason for them to hold him. They arrested him erroneously, etc., which they did. Because that's exactly what Eldridge was doing. Eldridge was righteously covering. Although Eldridge was a Panther at the time, he didn't have a gun, and he was functioning as a reporter. And so she blew.

They announced that the brothers were supposed to appear the next day at the Municipal Court across the street, and me and Huey went home and came back the next day and we appeared in court and we vowed that if the brothers weren't out by Friday at two o'clock, that by hook or crook, any way we can, we gonna get that money, to bail the brothers out. We were worried about the money. We figured we had a few funds coming in, but we were going to get that money, we were going to bail all the brothers out. But our most extreme worry, our major worry, was Eldridge Cleaver, because Eldridge Cleaver was on parole. He just spent nine years in prison and he could possibly go back to prison. And that's what we worried about the most.

Huey said, "The reason we're going to get those brothers out is because those brothers off the block who stuck with the organization, who took time to learn the principles of the organization, who took time to learn the ideology of the organization, and who took time to understand and follow the leadership of the organization, *they* are the real true heroes, not us, Bobby." I said, "You're right, Huey, I know that, you're right. By hook or crook I'm with you. We going to get the money to get the brothers out of jail."

• • •

The next day we came up early in the morning, and before the brothers came to court, we cornered a bail bondsman, a jive motherfucking bail bondsman. We found him out later on to be a really jive dude. He was a black one. Name was Glen Holmes, he was in Sacramento. He had a statewide license. He could bail out anybody all over the state. We called on him and started talking to him. And Huey got on one side of him and I got on the other side of him. And we got to rapping to him. We got to talking to that brother so strong and so hard and so fast, and running it down to him why he should bail these brothers out of jail, the fact that we have enough publicity to raise the money, just that we have to get these brothers out of jail *now*. And these brothers, their feet have to hit the ground. Work hard. This is something that Huey always stressed, and I really learned this from Huey, the meaning of being dedicated to pulling brothers out of jail.

Huey was rapping to that dude, Glen Holmes, and running it down to him about how he should go forth and bail the brothers out on credit. Glen Holmes was the dude who went on and bailed me and Mark Comfort out initially on half credit, because all they had put up was half the bail. But we talked to him before the court appearance came about. He says, "All right, I'll do it." And Glen Holmes did it. He said, "They'll be out by six o'clock this evening." And Huey said, "Well, we said two o'clock, but if they can hit the ground free like this by six o'clock, good." We waited for the court appearance, for the arraignment, and they arraigned the brothers, charged us all with conspiracy to commit a misdemeanor, the said misdemeanor being disturbing the peace. Disturbing the decorum of the legislature.

Conspiracy to break any law—a conspiracy is that you conspire to break a law. But we weren't guilty of any such thing. Huey only told me to go to the steps, and we went inside the place to observe the legislature. But who

disturbed it? The fact that we were running down, was that
the TV cameramen disturbed it. The first thing that the
speaker said when we walked inside, and when the cameramen flushed through another door and ran all up the aisles,
the speaker said, "Get those cameramen out of here! Who
brought those news reporters in? Get those cameramen out
of here, they have no right to be in here, and bloppety
bloppety blop," that's what he said. He never said get those
Panthers out of here with those guns, never said that all
through the whole set. It never was said. I mean that's the
legal technicality of the whole thing. Of course I served five
months in jail, and Tucker served six, along with some
other Panthers who served some other misdemeanor time
for doing nothing illegal.

Anyway, we got the brothers out of jail. Six o'clock, we
were waiting for them. They start filing them out. The filed
the brothers out, and as each brother would come out, Huey
would give him a big hug and pat the brother on his strong,
revolutionary back, hit him on his strong, revolutionary
back, and say, "Brother, are you glad you did it?" And the
brother would say, "Right on." Huey said, "We did a good
job," and hit every brother on the back that come downstairs. And Warren Tucker, the man on my left, with the
.357 Magnum, was the last one to come out. He said,
"Well, goddam. I was getting ready to say, these motherfuckers *better* let me out of this motherfucker." He saw
everybody else leaving. We got those brothers out, and
Huey greeted them as revolutionaries. Huey greeted them as
dedicated brothers. We piled them in the cars, and we took
them back home, to their home, in the confines of a decadent ghetto that we live in, in Oakland. We bought them a
beer or two, and let them drink the beer. Our juveniles were
still in jail. Bobby Hutton, Orleando Harrison, one other
brother who was in North Oakland working on the poverty
program with me, and two other brothers of Mark Comfort's.

THE BLACK PANTHER NEWSPAPER

■ A colossal event had occurred, that Huey P. Newton had put in motion. A colossal event had occurred that had significant meaning to the Black Panther Party. News of the existence of the Party went all the way around the world. A few days after we came back from Sacramento, Huey found out that the fact that we went to the Capitol was plastered across the front pages of the London *Times*. Things developed from there. We now had a case where some twenty-four brothers were charged with conspiracy: $2,200 bail apiece. When we tried to raise money at the time, we found that the Black Panther Party was known everywhere. After we brought the brothers home from jail, we went over to the Black House, which had actually been named and established as the San Francisco headquarters of the Black Panther Party. Eldridge Cleaver had named it that, and Huey and I had agreed to it. Black House was where brother Eldridge had been living.

The objective was to get out *The Black Panther*.

Huey and I had been around the Black House all day, that third day after Sacramento, and news reporters were calling us and trying to get in touch with us, and calling Eldridge Cleaver. Everyone was trying to vamp in on us to see what was going on. They called all day. One call told us that the next morning they wanted us on Channel 7, on the "A.M." program. We agreed to be there. That night, we got set to lay out the ten-point platform and program for the Party Newspaper, and to lay out the second issue of volume one of *The Black Panther, Black Community News Service*.

We had a lot of things set up to lay out *The Black Panther*. Emory Douglas, who's now our Minister of Culture, had brought over all his materials and Huey was explaining to him about revolutionary culture, explaining that the only real culture is revolutionary culture. Huey told him that if he was going to be an artist for the Black Panther Party, he had to relate specifically to the revolutionary culture, the black people. Emory explained that he had related to revolutionary culture.

I asked him a couple of questions myself. I remember trying to explain to Emory that culture is basically learned behavior, and what is involved in learned behavior, especially when you speak of black people and a revolutionary culture. The Molotov cocktail had become a significant part of black people's culture, and now Huey P. Newton had brought forth the meaning of guns, organized guns and force as a significant part of black people's culture. They had to graduate from rocks and bottles and Molotov cocktails, Huey was saying, to a level where they understood the proper use of organized guns and force, and where they understood what a political party represented when it started to go forth to liberate black people. I was hoping that he understood that the Black Panther Party was concerned specifically with the basic political desires and needs of the people and seeing that those be answered in a revolutionary fashion. The brother was all head-shaking and yeses saying, "Yeah, I can understand it, I can dig it." He just wanted to do some art.

So we sat up that night, and I sat down myself and laid out the first little Black Panther headline—THE TRUTH ABOUT SACRAMENTO.

Many people ask us where we get our money from. The power structure has been accusing us of being robbers and thieves. This is not the case. A large portion of our money comes from many groups and people who support us. That includes different sources: lawyers groups, church organizations, other types of organizations, and many people who sympathize with the Party because they have taken time to read our newspaper.

Speaking engagements are another way we get funds. Sometimes we get $500 and $1,000 for speaking, especially when Eldridge, myself, and Kathleen were moving around, but they still are being given to other leaders of the Party and these funds help the Party function.

One of the main sources of funds is the Party's newspaper. It is an organ which lumpen proletarian brothers and sisters produce. Eldridge Cleaver is the chief editor of the paper, but the quality and development of that paper has come from brothers who have previously been in jails, brothers who have previously just been on the block, lumpen proletarian everyday Afro-American brothers who became politically organized and politically conscious, and learned their skills in producing that paper.

The brothers in the Party don't receive any kind of salary from the Black Panther Party, but for every paper that they sell, they keep ten cents. We give a lot of the young brothers, the little brothers in the community, ten cents for every paper they sell. Some of the brothers were able to buy themselves bicycles from selling so many papers. This is very good because it's constructive, it helps them work, and at the same time it helps the Party get correct information about the Party to many more people.

The paper has the highest circulation of what are generally called "underground newspapers" although we're not really underground. We're very much on top of the ground. Underground is a way to distinguish us from the Establishment press. Our circulation is 125,000 copies per week at present and is rising rapidly across the country. The brothers in the Party, the paper's staff, and all the brothers and sisters who work to help produce that paper are the ones who deserve credit for seeing to it that that paper consistently moves, for gathering the news, and for becoming reporters of news in the community where they can serve the people with the truth of what's happening.

So it's not a case of some white people behind the scenes putting our paper out or some special Jewish money being the sole source of the Party's existence. This is not the case at all. It's a thing where the Afro-American lumpen proletarian has become the vanguard, and the newspaper in itself is key in teaching the people that the brothers in the community who are revolutionaries, who want revolutionary change are not about to step back from the power structure, but in fact the Party's going to go forth, and is consistently going forth.

Some very tricky methods have been used to try and stop our paper from being published. We received a letter from the Printers Union of America, which stated that since our paper had become of such "professional quality" they demanded that we have our paper printed and put together in a union printers shop. We understood that this was part and parcel of FBI and police attempts to try and stop the Black Panther Party newspaper. Howard Quinn, the place where we print the paper, is a union shop, but the Printers Union was referring to the people who lay the paper out, the members of the Black Panther Party. Since we understand the workers and we understand that we are workers, four or five of the brothers and sisters who actually do the layout of the paper, and who are Party members, joined the Printers Union, and that stopped all of that noise.

In the past, a large number of papers have been stopped, and thousands of issues were received soaking wet. This went on for a year off and on. In the process of shipping the papers, the airlines would hold them up in their freighting operations for a week or two. This included American Airlines, TWA, and United. We've got the records to prove it. We also have records of the notices we sent to the airlines saying we were going to sue them for holding our papers up like that and sometimes causing fifty or sixty thousand papers not to show up at all or to show up when they couldn't be sold, two and three weeks after the date on the paper.

There were also numerous attempts to factionalize the workers inside of the Howard Quinn Printing Company where they roll our paper off the press. Half the workers got on our side and the other half were on the side of this CIA-FBI operation, who said that they were going to quit Howard Quinn if they didn't stop printing the Black Panther Party paper. The other half, the workers who were on our side, were the ones who run the press downstairs. They were getting along fine with us because we were helping them make more money. We were running off more papers than any other underground newspaper printed at Quinn's. They said they would quit if Quinn didn't continue printing the Black Panther Party's newspaper.

Well, we survived through that and we finally started sending the papers on a C.O.D. basis so as to be able to collect insurance from the airlines. Suddenly a lot of our papers began to arrive on time, although there are still some cases where they're holding them up. In the past there were actually cases where the police department would be out at the airport waiting for the particular plane that our papers were coming in on. The airlines were checking out the papers and giving them to the police, and the police would take our property somewhere and destroy it.

It costs about eight cents to produce the paper, but with mailing and shipping costs it comes to about ten cents a paper. The paper sells for twenty-five cents but we only receive about five cents from every paper. This money goes back to pay rent on our offices, phone bills, and other expenses. We are very proud of our paper. It comes from the hard core of the black community, the grass roots.

This should let people know that we have a national organ that they can read to keep themselves informed about the Black Panther Party and what's going on in the world, in these changing revolutionary times.

HUEY DIGS BOB DYLAN

■ Later we moved to Beverly Axelrod's house to finish the paper. This was about eight or nine blocks south of the

Haight-Ashbury district over in San Francisco. It was a
nice, big house, and we moved over there for room and
space, and to get things together. We righteously got it
together. Eldridge and Barbara Auther were pounding out
some articles.

We called up a white Mother Country radical photographer, got him together, and asked him to shoot some pictures of Huey because we knew it was necessary for us to try
and get a centralized symbol of the leadership of black
people in the black community. We had to centralize it in
some way, so we decided on a picture of Huey. This photographer came over with his cameras and his tripods, and
Eldridge set the scene. The photographer took a number of
different shots. We got a wicker chair and African shields,
and we had a shotgun over there, and Eldridge said, "Take
the gun, and put the spear here." He artistically put that
picture together that everyone sees of Huey P. Newton
sitting in the chair, with the shotgun and the spear, and the
shields sitting on each side of the chair.

The shields were very important, because Huey was artic-
ulating that we use the spear and the shield, and the shield is
very significant. Huey would say many times that a long,
long time ago, there was a man who invented a spear, and
he frightened a whole lot of people. But, Huey said, the
people invented a shield against the spear. The people
weren't so frightened after all. So this is really what Huey P.
Newton symbolized with the Black Panther Party—he represented a shield for black people against all the imperialism, the decadence, the aggression, and the racism in this
country. That's what Huey P. Newton symbolized with us.
That's the way we projected it. The headline of the Party
paper was THE TRUTH ABOUT SACRAMENTO, because there
were so many lies about the Black Panther Party, and the
Black Panther Party in Sacramento. Lies by the regular
mass media—television and radio and the newspapers—
those who thought the Panthers were just a bunch of jive,
just a bunch of crazy people with guns. Many and many

an Uncle Tom and our backward brainwashed black men
had a misconception about the whole thing, when you get
down to it.

While we were laying that paper out, in the background
we could hear a record, and the song was named "Ballad of
a Thin Man" by Bob Dylan. Now the melody was in my
mind. I actually heard it, I could hear the melody to this
record. I could hear the sound and the beat to it. But I
really didn't hear the words. This record played after we
stayed up laying out the paper. And it played the *next* night
after we stayed up laying out the paper. I think it was
around the third afternoon that the record was playing. We
played that record over and over and over. Lots of brothers
stayed over there with a lot of shotguns for security. It was a
righteous security in those days. There wasn't any bullshit.

Huey P. Newton made me recognize the lyrics. Not only
the lyrics of the record, but what the lyrics meant in the
record. What the lyrics meant in the history of racism that
has perpetuated itself in this world. Huey would say: "Listen, listen—man, do you hear what he is saying?" Huey had
such insight into how racism existed, how racism had perpetuated itself. He had such a way of putting forth in very
clear words what he related directly to those symbolic
things or words that were coming out from Bobby Dylan.
The point about the geek is very important because this is
where Huey hung me.

I remember that the song got to the point where he was
talking about this cat handing in his ticket and he walked
up to the geek, and the geek handed him a bone. Well, this
didn't relate to me, so I said: "Huey, look, wait a minute,
man." I said, "What you talking about a geek? What is a
geek? What the hell is a geek?" And Huey explains it. He
says, "A geek is usually a circus performer. Maybe he was
an experienced trapeze artist who was injured. He's been in
the circus all his life and he knows nothing else but circus
work. But he can't be a trapeze artist anymore because he's

been injured very badly, but he still needs to live, he needs to exist, he needs pay. So the circus feels very sorry for him and they give him a job. They give him the cruddiest kind of job because he's not really good for anything else. They put him into a cage, then people pay a quarter to come in to see him. They put live chickens into the cage and the geek eats the chickens up while they're still alive . . . the bones, the feathers, all. And of course, he has a salary, because the audience pays a quarter to see him. He does this because he has to. He doesn't like eating raw meat, or feathers, but he does it to survive. But these people who are coming in to see him are coming in for entertainment, so they are the real freaks. And the geek knows this, so during his performance, he eats the raw chicken and he hands one of the members of the audience a bone, because he realizes that they are the real freaks because they get enjoyment by watching what he's doing because he has to. So that's what a geek and a freak is. Is that clear?

"Then to put it on the broader level, what Dylan is putting across is middle-class people or upper-class people who sometimes take a Sunday afternoon off and put their whole family into a limousine, and they go down to the black ghettoes to watch the prostitutes and watch the decaying community. They do this for pleasure, or for Sunday afternoon entertainment. Of course the people are there, and they don't want to be there. The prostitutes are there because they're trying to live, trying to exist, and they need money. So then that makes the middle-class and upper-class people, who are down there because they get pleasure out of it, freaks.

"And this goes into the one-eyed midget. What is the one-eyed midget? He screams and howls at Mr. Jones. Mr. Jones doesn't know what's happening. Then the one-eyed midget says, give me some juice or go home. And this again is very symbolic of people who are disadvantaged. They're patronizing Mr. Jones, the middle-class people. You know, they're not interested in them coming down for entertainment. But if they'll pay them for a trick, then they'll tolerate them, or else they'll drive them out of the ghettoes. This song is hell. You've got to understand that this song is saying a hell of a lot about society."

The white society and the middle-class society are surprised to see that black people will pimp chicks on the block. They come down that way because they looked at black people as freaks. They thought black people were into a big freak bag. They thought they had niggers all figured out. But black people were not even niggers. Black people were not backward and apathetic.

Huey says that whites looked at blacks as geeks, as freaks. But what is so symbolic about it is that when the revolution starts, they'll call us geeks because we eat raw meat. But the geek turns around and hands Mr. Jones a naked bone and says, "How do you like being a freak?" And Mr. Jones says, "Oh my God, what the hell's goin' on?" And Bobby Dylan says, you don't know what's happening, do you, Mr. Jones? And to hand him the naked bone was too much—was really too much.

Eldridge Cleaver explains in *Soul on Ice* that the black man has been led around by the white man, the white omnipotent administrator primarily—big businessmen who manipulate and bullshit and control the government. The black man has been led around, and was projected as being led around, with a little piece of string, cord string, that could be broken in a minute. The string was tied around the black man's neck, and the black man was projected as a big gorilla. He was a gorilla. He was inhuman, and he couldn't talk. He's not supposed to be able to think. But the gorilla beats on his chest and says, "I'm a man."

One of the symbolic things that Eldridge was pointing out with this thing was that Cassius Clay said: "I'm the greatest"—the symbolic thing of him beating on his chest. He said in fact, "I'm a man." He said, "I'm a strong man." What shocked the racists, what shocked the omnipotent administrator, is that he looked up at the big gorilla. The string had been broken and he saw this gorilla beating on his chest saying, "I'm a man." That was Cassius Clay.

Cassius Clay would brag. People misunderstood the bragging. All Cassius Clay was saying was that he was defying all this omnipotent, racist bullshit by stepping forward and saying, "I'm the greatest! I can't be hit." He beat on his chest, and when he said that, the white racist omnipotent administrator who had a hold on the string had to ask himself, "Well, if he's a man then what the hell am I?" And that's what Bobby Dylan meant by the geek handing Mr. Jones the naked bone and saying: "How do you like being a freak?" And that's the whole meaning of the question. If he's a man, if he's not a freak, and he tells Mr. Jones he's a freak, then Mr. Jones has to ask, "Am I that?" That's symbolic of saying that if he's a man, what am I?

This song Bobby Dylan was singing became a very big part of that whole publishing operation of the Black Panther paper. And in the background, while we were putting this paper out, this record came up and I guess a number of papers were published, and many times we would play that record. Brother Stokely Carmichael also liked that record. This record became so related to us, even to the brothers who had held down most of the security for the set.

The brothers had some big earphones over at Beverly's house that would sit on your ears and had a kind of direct stereo atmosphere and when you got loaded it was something else! These brothers would get halfway high, loaded on something, and they would sit down and play this record over and over and over, especially after they began to hear Huey P. Newton interpret that record. They'd be trying to relate an understanding about what was going on, because old Bobby did society a big favor when he made *that* particular sound. If there's any more he made that I don't understand, I'll just ask Huey P. Newton to interpret them for us and maybe we can get a hell of a lot more out of brother Bobby Dylan, because old Bobby, he did a good job on that set.

SERVING TIME AT BIG GREYSTONE

■ After Sacramento, we made a deal. Myself and a few other brothers who had no previous records would serve some time for "disturbing the peace" or something like that, and all the other brothers who were on parole or probation would be cut loose. We weren't guilty of anything, but we made that deal to save the other brothers from going to state prison. Warren Tucker and I served the longest sentences, six months each.

At first they had me in Sacramento County Jail, but later they transferred me to the Alameda County Jail at Santa Rita. I was in a maximum security wing of a place everybody calls Big Greystone, because the buildings are made of this drab gray stone.

Huey tried to visit me in Sacramento County Jail shortly after I went in to serve my sentence in August 1967, but when Huey arrived, I had been transferred down to Greystone. I remember Huey saying to me, just before I went to jail, "You can do six months for the Party, can't you?"

"Sure I can," I told Huey. "I can do it easily."

On the morning of October 28, 1968, I was lying on my bunk inside one of those jive cells they have at Big Greystone. Suddenly someone hollered, "Bobby Seale, Bobby Seale!" It was one of the trustees, walking on the catwalk above me. "Bobby Seale, where you at?" he called. I said, "Over here, in cell 82." This cat walked up and said, "Two Panthers had a shoot-out, and one cop is dead, and one of your boys got wounded, I think." I said, "What! You know who it was?" He said, "No, we don't have information on who it was, yet. They shot him, though. That's what one of the bulls said."

A lot of names flashed in my head, but not Huey's. I thought it might be Sherman Forte, Bobby Hutton, Reggie Forte, Orleando Harrison, any one of the brothers who went to Sacramento with us. "Who could it have been? Who could have been shot?" I remember saying to myself. I knew the *Oakland Tribune* would have the information. That's the only thing they let you read in jail; they just cram that junk right down your throat, and they won't let any other papers in. I waited, reading some portions of a book, waiting for the newspaper.

Finally around twelve o'clock, the trustee brought me the paper. There was Huey P. Newton's picture on the front page. He was on a stretcher.* The paper said he had been shot.

At first I worried if he was all right. I read the pig's lying story. Then I thought about getting the brother out. They were going to charge brother Huey with murder. All kinds of schemes went through my mind about busting up the jail or busting up the court. He had to appear in court, and I thought about walking in there, and blasting away at every judge, every bailiff, and the clerk, just blasting at all the pigs, walking over to Huey, and walking out. I had scenes in my head, of crowds of people in the court, and while Huey was there in the crowd of people, I would dress him up like a woman. I'd put some kind of dress on him and let him walk out with another dude, disguised as man and wife. The pigs would never figure that out, I thought.

I remembered that Huey had told me many times that he never wanted a murder charge where you have to be on death row. Huey described death row as a form of righteous torture. You sit on death row three, four, or five years, not knowing when you're going to die. That in itself is torture, but the real torture comes, he said, when they're about to

---

* On October 28, 1967, there was an early morning gun battle between Huey P. Newton and two policemen. Huey was wounded seriously. One policeman, John Frey, was killed, and the other, Herbert Heanes, was seriously injured.—Ed.

walk you up to the gas chamber, and five or ten minutes before the time of execution, somebody would give you a stay of execution for one month, or one year. He said that's righteous torture.

I began to intensely count my days left in jail, so that I could get out and work to get Huey free. I was scheduled, as far as I knew, to get out of this jail sometime between January 8 and 15. It wasn't very clear. I'd gone into jail on August 8, on that Sacramento bust. It was now October 28 and I had to wait all the way till January 8 to get out.

I had read the papers. I had also read about the protest over police brutality about a week or two before, in which the pigs busted up the heads of the anti-draft demonstrators who went forth to close down the draft office in Oakland. Chief Gain and his pigs, the highway patrolmen, and others from surrounding cities beat the heads of all these *peaceful* demonstrators. They were peaceful demonstrators. They'd sit down in front of the draft office and say, "If I'm violating the law by sitting down, then arrest me." And they would go to jail peacefully. But Chief Gain and the pigs wanted to beat their heads. These demonstrators called a press conference after what had happened to brother Huey and said that the racist dog policemen who attacked Huey P. Newton must be removed and Huey must be freed. Solidarity and support were shown in this article. They said that the pigs who jumped on the anti-draft demonstrators in Oakland there were the same pigs who vamped on Huey. (The demonstration at the induction center had taken place a few weeks before.)

I also read that Judge Staats held court to arraign and charge Huey in the hospital room where he was getting better from the gunshot wound. Some Panther brothers had also gone to the hospital, but it was surrounded. The pigs asked them what they wanted, and the Panther brothers said, "We come to get Huey." Six or seven brothers got busted. These brothers really loved Huey. They came to get the Minister of Defense, they came to see about Huey, to set

Huey free. A pig jumped up with a shotgun in front of
them, stopped them, and asked them, "What you want?"
And one of the Panthers dedicated to the revolutionary
struggle, dedicated to the liberation of black people, looked
at this pig and told him, "We come to get Huey." That pig
must have shit! These were crazy Panthers.

Sunday mornings, when you're in jail, you have to go to
the day room to hear some puritanical thinking, Christian
preacher preach a bunch of bullshit about how we were
wrong and we must seek for the Lord. How ironic can this
shit get! Here's some preacher in the day room cell, with
over 200 cats crowded in. This guy is just blabbing out of
the mouth and the brothers aren't even listening to him.
There are guards standing on each side, telling you to be
quiet and listen. You get mad at those pigs, especially when
you've got a minister of defense like Huey P. Newton. You
get real mad when you know there's a hell of a revolutionary leader who wants to give the land and bread back to the
people. You just want to break out of that joint; you want
to go and do something about Huey. That's the way you
feel.

There were a lot of brothers in jail who suddenly all
wanted to be Panthers. They had listened to me before, but
now they wanted to be Panthers. They saw there was hope.
They looked at Huey as a hero of the people. Huey was so
beautiful; he'd turn around, and tell the people, "You're the
heroes, you're the heroes, people. So let's unite, go forth in
unity, so we can get land, bread, housing, education, clothing, justice, and some peace."

I thought and wondered, and read the papers, and
schemed about what to do for Huey. There were demonstrations for Huey, and people showed up in court. Panthers
jammed into the courtroom, and 200 people besides
jammed the hallways. They had literature and information
concerning Huey P. Newton. They wanted him to be set

free, cut loose. They ran down how unjust this racist decadent system is, and said it couldn't do this to Huey.

I made up my mind and said that when I got out I was going to work myself to the bone, harder than I ever had before. Our first objective and first goal, working with Eldridge and the other Panthers, would be to mobilize 5,000 people, standing around in the courthouse for Huey. Then if necessary, we might have to bust him out of jail, because Huey's gotta be set free somehow. That's what I was saying. That is the way I felt. That's what I became dedicated to as I sat there in jail waiting to get out. Five weeks later, I was talking to Huey.

I had to appear in court a couple of times, somewhere around the latter part of November. They transported one from Greystone to the County Jail in downtown Oakland. I was in Tank B, and Huey was in Tank A. He sent a couple of messages around to me, like "Power! Power to the People!" The brother also sent me some cigarettes. That was kind of funny when I thought of it. Here's this brother, on a murder charge, which Huey never wanted, and he sends me cigarettes.

I had another court date, December 8. Once again they drove me from Greystone to the jail in Oakland where the court was, and they put me in Tank B. I knew Tank B was next door to Tank C. That's the hospital tank where I figured Huey was. I knew that you could holler from Tank B to Tank C, although you couldn't see anybody. I asked the trustee, "Is Huey P. Newton still in Tank C, the hospital tank?" He said, "Yes he is." Then I went to the bars, as close as I could get to Tank C, and started hollering, "Hey, Huey!"

"Yeah," he said.

"This is Bobby."

"Hey, man!"

The brother was glad to be able to talk, and I was glad to

be able to talk to him. He told me about a few things that
happened, a few things that he'd read in the paper, about
some brothers getting in a shoot-out with some pigs, and
how the pigs rammed their car. He ran down how I wasn't
to say anything around a couple of jive trustees who, he
knew, would turn words around and snitch to the man. And
I told him how the pigs came out to the jail, three days after
he'd been shot, and how they were trying to say that I knew
where the 9mm gun was, that Huey was *supposed* to have
had the night he got shot. I told Huey I had nothing to say
to the pig, that I took the Fifth Amendment on it. One of
them was a nigger pig, a bootlicker pig, who acted like he
wanted to jump me, so I just backed up against the wall,
and braced myself, and got ready to fight the pig, right in
the middle of this jive 7' x 7' Greystone cell. Huey and I
hollered around there in the Oakland jail, talking to each
other for a long time, and then I had to go downstairs and
appear in the court.

They brought me back upstairs around noon, and one of
the trustees told me that I would be able to see Huey in a
few minutes. I said, "What!" He said, "Yeah, because they
bring him around to Tank B, in the aisle over there. The
entrance is to the side." I said, "Right on, brother, right on.
I get to see brother Huey P. Newton. That's good, that's
good." I was really happy. I really wanted to see the brother
because I hadn't seen him since August 8, the day I went to
jail. I wanted to see how he was doing.

He walked around and he looked like he was in pretty
good shape. He lifted his hands to the bars, and we grabbed
each other's hands, shook each other's hands real tight and
hard. I mostly just wanted to look at the brother, and see if
he was all right because Huey was out of sight. It was just
good to see him. It was just a filling thing for me. I felt like
we were close to some kind of freedom for Huey, when I
saw the cat. We had to free Huey.

The next time I came up to court, I saw him again.
I was in the day room and he was locked in an aisle in the

hallway. He walked up to the end of the aisle, and spoke through that chicken-shit hole that the pigs set up for visitors. I said, "Go on and take your visits, brother." It was good to see him. I looked and saw some of the visitors, his girl friend LaVerne, and Orleando, and the others through that little hole on my side. They all came over to see me after visiting with Huey.

When we were hollering, before the visitors came, Huey had asked me how long I had to go. I told him that I might be out January 8 or January 15, as close as I could figure. I said, "Well, brother, you've got to be set free. Something's got to be done, and we're going to have to do it. I hope I can do it." He reassured me, "You can do it, Bobby. You can put it together, you and Eldridge and everyone. You can do it." It made me feel good. I had to relate to that, because I had to believe and understand I could do something to help the brother get free.

You sit in Greystone, in a (7' x 7') cell, all day long. Then they move you and put you in another 7' x 7' cell. They let you go to the day room every three days. In the course of an hour, you go to the day room, take a shower, shave, and then they put you in another one of the same 7' x 7's, somewhere. You get used to it, especially when you know you haven't got too much time to do.

A lot of cats naturally get pissed off at Greystone. I took mine out on thinking about the organization, and what I could do for the organization, and for the revolutionary struggle. During those last weeks, October 28 to December 8, I thought about ways to free Huey P. Newton, and about the fact that we have to get this brother free somehow or other. This brother's got to get cut loose, he's got to beat this case, because these pigs are trying to jack him up, and they're trying to jack the Panther Party up.

On December 8, after I came back from court, they called me out of the bullpen, and I walked back down the hall, to change out of my civilian clothes, that I used to appear in court, back into those regular jail clothes. There are three security prisons there really—Big Greystone, which is maximum security, 7′ x 7′ cells, and Santa Rita (farm work for sentenced inmates), or Little Greystone, where there's barracks and compounds, maximum security, and you can walk around. Most of the cats in Big Greystone have felony cases, or have gotten into fights and have been put over there. Mostly, those in Little Greystone have smaller cases and are unsentenced. I knew one thing through that routine of going back and forth to court—if you go to Big Greystone, you aren't allowed to wear any shoes. When you go to Little Greystone, you put on shoes, because you can walk around. The shoes are very significant.

I stepped forward, took off my coat, and the pig wrote down the color of my jacket, my slacks, and my pin-striped brown shirt. He looked at a list of the jail clothes I was supposed to get and said, "Shoes." I said, "No, you got it wrong, no shoes. I'm at Big Greystone." "Nope," he said, "here it says, shoes." "Uh uh," I said, "I'm in Big Greystone. You got it wrong." He said, "Shoes, Seale!" I said, "All right."

They have some special shoes they give you, brogans. I told the pig, "Wait a minute, I have to wear shoes?" He said, "Yeah." I said, "Am I going to Little Greystone?" He said, "Yeah, I guess so," in a real snotty way. I said, "Well, then, I can't wear those brogans." I took my sock off and showed him my left foot. My left foot is about three-quarters of an inch shorter than my right foot, because I was hit by a car when I was thirteen. I said, "This is a skin graft you see on the top of my foot. Those brogans will rub the skin graft, and the next thing you know I'll run around infected. The shoes are too heavy. I'd rather wear my regular civilian shoes." So he said, "OK, let's go." So I dressed, put my shoes on, climbed on the wagon.

He took me over to Little Greystone, dropped me off, and

assigned me to one of those jive-assed barracks with barbed-wire fences around it. I went inside, looking for Warren Tucker, because he was supposed to be serving time there. I couldn't figure the whole switch out, and I really wanted to talk to Tucker. I inquired around, asking all the brothers if they had seen a brother, a Black Panther, named Warren Tucker, but they didn't know him. So I settled back to get my bunk straight, and get bedding from the trustee. Some brothers were singing some soul music. It was nice the way they were putting the harmony to it, putting the real soul into it. I lay there listening to them about forty-five minutes, thinking about brother Huey, and about how we were going to get him out.

Then one of the guards walked inside the barracks, and said, "Seale?" I said, "Yeah."

"Let's go, you're bailed out. You're out on bail."

I said, "Uh uh, you got the wrong man."

"Seale?"

"My name is Seale, that's right."

"Well it's supposed to be Seale."

"You got the wrong man, I can't get out of jail till January 8. Maybe you're looking for somebody else with the same name as mine. Who's got a name similar to mine? Any of you brothers know anybody who's got a name similar to mine?"

Some brother said, "There's a cat in here named Scales."

"That's who you're looking for, man," I said. "Well," the bull said, "I don't know, let me go check."

I rolled over and almost fell asleep, and about five or ten minutes later, the pig came back. "Let's go, Seale, it's you!"

"Now wait just one goddam minute," I said. "You dudes got Huey P. Newton in jail! You dudes pull all kinds of schemes, to mess up our Party, to mess up black people. To kill them and murder them."

"I don't have nothing to do with that," he said.

"Regardless of that," I ran on, "you're telling me I'm supposed to be out on bail, and I say I can't be out on bail because I can't get out till January 8. I'm going to be honest. You know that me and a lot of the people want to free Huey P. Newton. We want to do a lot of work in the black community. Get rid of you pigs. All you cats want to do is to say I'm out on bail, take me somewhere, say I escaped, and then give me a year and a half, so later!"

"I don't know anything about that, Seale, you just come on."

"All right, goddamit, let's go. But I know damn well I can't get out of jail till January 8, and that's even with *good* time. I can't get out of jail till January 8." I ran it down to him, "I got sentenced to six months. It's *impossible* for me to get out. I went in August 8, and now its only December 8. The only time I can get out, is by January 8. And that's with thirty damn days of good time." I argued with the cat, I didn't believe him. But I jumped up and put on my shoes.

We walked all the way up to the discharge place. I argued with the lieutenant. I argued with the captain. I argued with the sergeants and everybody else. I wanted to see some definite proof. They showed me a teletype message from Sacramento, where I had been sentenced, which said that they couldn't hold me any longer, that my time was up.

I snatched that teletype message and looked at it. Meanwhile some more brothers were coming through the bullpen. I told them, "Hey, brothers, remember. You see this discharge here? It says I'm out of jail, and I wasn't expecting to get out of jail till January. But you remember that all these cops came down here and said I was supposed to get released. You remember that, you hear?"

The brothers said, "Right on, Bobby. Right on. We understand."

"Brothers, I'll catch you later on." Then I said to the pigs, "OK, let's go."

The pigs were very upset, about why Bobby Seale wasn't going to leave jail. I was tired of the pigs, and the power structure scheming on us. I was very apprehensive about them saying I was discharged, because I didn't really believe it. I called my father and waited for an hour and a half. He came out and picked me up, and took me home.

My wife was in the car. When I saw her, I remembered that I told her that she was going to have to be ready to sacrifice, when I got out of jail. She said she understood. Now she was in the car, and she'd brought Little Stagolee with her. He was about a year and a half old. I had to get used to the idea that all of a sudden I was out of jail on my way home. I had to do a hell of a lot of things now, to try to help get Huey out of jail. Before I'd just been sitting in the cell, day after day, thinking about things to be done, but now it was time to implement them. Huey P. Newton always said, "Unite theory with practice. Unite your ideas with practice, by applying those ideas.

Of course, the first thing I decided to do when I got out of jail was to make love with my wife. Then I'd call everybody else up. It can be bad for a man's mind when he's locked up and taken away from good loving and good screwing.

THE SHIT COMES DOWN: "FREE HUEY!"

FREE HUEY

■ I got out of jail on December 8, 1967. I came out with the feeling and desire to get brother Huey P. Newton out of jail and to keep them from sending him to the gas chamber, because this was the Party, and the Party was my life. It was like a musician learning how to play a horn and blowing some jazz and really being with it in such a way that it's your life, it's part of you. This is the way I always felt about the Party. I don't generally go into things about the Party from the way I might subjectively feel about them—I try to project them objectively. But I also came out of jail with a feeling that I had a wife and I had a little baby. My wife wanted me to go to work. I have nine trades—musician, comedian, community organizer, carpenter, builder, drafts-man, journeyman sheet-metal mechanic, general machine-shop work, and non-destructive testing of machine and aircraft parts. I have a number of trades like that. But going to work wouldn't give me enough time, I felt, to work to free Huey. Before Huey had gotten shot, I was contem-plating that half of my time would be taking care of my family, and the rest of my time would be used to work diligently in the Party. I felt that we would have to have some kind of financial support that would help back up the Party.

I knew I was a good draftsman, so before Huey got shot, I made up my mind to do the kind of work that I'd need to support my family, at home. I would try to get private drafting jobs that I could do at night. If I could do private drafting at home, I could make money to take care of my family, and the rest of the time, if I could be flexible and be my own boss, I could do work for the Party at any time, and in any way it called upon me to do so.

I was only into having a family for two years at that time, but I really related to my family. This was my first experience at being married and having a family, and having this responsibility. I never really was afraid of the responsibility, but at the same time, I knew that life and living were not really secure with all the racism and all the exploitation black people were subjected to.

After I had been out of jail a couple of days, I was riding down Grove Street with Eldridge, David Hilliard, Artie, and a couple of other people. I told Eldridge that we had to do something for Huey, but said that I also felt that I had to go to work, get a half-assed job, and possibly do some drafting at home to make some money on the side, and put some specific scheme together to bust out Huey.

Eldridge ran it down that our real work was organizing people. "Man, don't worry about doing any work," Eldridge said. "We've got a lot of work to do. This isn't like leaving your family. We'll take care of that, all together. But let's organize the people to free Huey."

"You're right, man," I said. "I don't have time for a job." Before I came out of jail I had actually known, deep-down inside me that we didn't have any more time to be hung up on jive jobs, with all this stuff happening to us, and these pigs trying to railroad brother Huey.

So we really went into motion, using every means we had, taking every speaking engagement we could, and rallied the community. The Party moved rapidly to the campuses, and held rallies and forums. We had funds and donations coming in. A lot of brothers were flocking to the Party. There were a lot of brothers, a lot of Party members who worked doing leafletting, announcing rallies, raising money, and stuff like that. Brothers and sisters would come back and report how they went out to collect funds on the streets of the Fillmore district. They would have buckets and cans to collect donations and funds. Some of the pimps would throw a five or ten dollar bill in, and some would drop two or three dollars in.

The pimps would say, "Is this for Huey Newton?"

"Yeah, brother," the brothers and sisters would say, "You know you're making money. You gotta come on and cough up some of them coins, so brother Huey can have some righteous legal defense."

The brothers threw the money in. I think Huey knew three main pimps very well. You know there's no really successful pimp, but there were about ten of them who you could call successful in the Bay Area at the time, and I think Huey knew most of them. He knew most of the cats in and around the black community.

So Eldridge, David, and I were all working, and figuring out different things that were necessary to be done. A couple of days later, there was a court appearance for Huey. We went there and I did a couple press interviews about how we were trying to mobilize people for the defense of Huey. And that's how we launched our campaign to free our Minister of Defense.

A WHITE LAWYER FOR A BLACK REVOLUTIONARY

■ Shortly after I got out of jail, I went over to San Francisco to check out Charles R. Garry, the lawyer the Central Committee had tentatively chosen to defend Huey. I had never met Garry before and I guess, to be honest about it, I had a little tingling bit of racism still hanging onto me. It wasn't that I hated white people, but I had to find out if I could trust this white lawyer to fight for Huey's freedom. Everyone had said that he was very good. He was recommended to us by Beverly Axelrod.

We had been considering a number of lawyers—Donald Warden, Clinton White, and a couple of others. White and Warden were both black cats, but Warden had too many guys who went to jail, some of whom we thought were on death row. The way Warden operated wasn't cool, we thought, because he would tell you one thing out of the side of his mouth, and then go and do another thing behind the scenes with the police department and the people downtown. Clinton White had the reputation for being a good lawyer and a good fighter, but I was fearful that they would try to manipulate him, and Huey and the Party would become political football. I really don't know if he decided not to take the case, or if the Party decided not to hire him, because when I got out of jail, Garry had already been tentatively chosen.

So I went over to meet Garry. He told me about the kind of law firm he was running, and why these political cases related to him. I popped up right away and asked, "How much money is it going to cost?"

"Let's not worry about that," Garry said. "Let's worry about the fact that we want to free Huey." He seemed to be a very honest person, from everything I could detect about him. "Well, let's see how he works out in practice," I said to myself. I generally hold back on my judgment of people until I see how they work out in practice.

A couple of days later, another lawyer was being considered. We went up to see him, and right away we decided that we didn't like him because he wanted ten to twelve thousand dollars in advance, off the cuff. We judged that Garry's firm was a better firm and that Garry himself was a better lawyer. We looked at the man's record, the number of people he had kept off death row, the number of murder cases that he had won, and those in which he had actually proven people innocent. From all this, and because of our concern for brother Huey, we felt that it was Garry who was needed.

Three or four days after we made our final decision, I went to a meeting of the defense committee for Huey P. Newton, and there were less than ten people there. I had read in the papers that there were hundreds of people on the committee. The problem was a bit of black racism which was hanging on and which was very bad. The people who were originally on Huey's defense committee were all black people, naturally. But it turned out that they were mad because Huey's family and the Black Panther Party had decided that Charles Garry was the best legal technician available. Our argument was that we couldn't judge the man by the color of his skin. We wouldn't choose a lawyer *just* because he was black. We would choose him on the basis of his ability. We said that if you had cancer or another bad disease, you would want the best medical technician that you could find. This was our argument, but they didn't understand it.

We tried to show them that you could not judge Garry by the color of his skin. We tried to show them that Garry had no reason or desire to be a tool or a puppet of the power structure. We had to remind them that Garry had been viciously attacked by cops in the past when he fought for the labor unions in San Francisco, and that a lot of corrupt people in the local power structure didn't like him. The man had integrity, we said, and his record and everything else about him were all in Huey's favor.

But they still wanted to hinge it on a little old thing like, "He's not black." Someone even had the nerve to say that we should hire John George, a man who had never handled that kind of case. Those two kinds of politics developed in the black community: one on the basis of a racist line, another on the basis of our progressive line. Later, we didn't get along with John George at all, because opportunistically he sided with the hundred or so people who only wanted a "black" lawyer and were trying to form a Huey P. Newton defense committee, but who didn't really have any power in the community. When it turned out that there wasn't going to be any black lawyer, most of them stopped worrying about saving Huey's life, but some worked to free Huey.

So the Black Panther Party hired Garry, and when I went to this first meeting of the defense committee, there was only David Hilliard, Eldridge, myself, Huey's brother Melvin Newton, Sid Walton, and three or four other people who showed up. There were only about eight or nine people actually functioning on Huey's defense committee right after we hired Charles Garry.

Eldridge and I were very pissed off at some of those people who had their little racist hang-ups. So many of them, about sixty or seventy, used to crowd into meetings before I got out of jail, Eldridge told me. They used to stand near the door trying to get out what they had to say, just running off at the mouth. They weren't really interested in doing any work. When we hired Garry, they all dropped away like a bunch of little scared rabbits and racists. I didn't like that at all. Some of those people had been to college, and had talked about all of the oppressive conditions black people were living under. The way I looked at it, their actions were tantamount to selling out the black community.

Some of the local black lawyers and black cultural nationalists tried to attack Garry publicly. "You guys have got to have a black lawyer," they told us. We just wanted the best one we could get. Those black lawyers had some kind of a meeting in Berkeley and tried to condemn Garry. That kind of stuff even hit the newspapers.

We realized that half of those lawyers were just thinking about money. They were thinking that we were going to raise a lot of funds for Huey's defense, and they wanted to get their hands on those funds and stick them in their own pockets. When we hired Garry, we didn't have any money. Garry's firm didn't get any money from us for a long time and went into the hole on Huey's case. Most of those black lawyers who condemned Garry never would have stuck with us when we were without funds. They would have gotten rid of us. But they really had to get up off Garry's back after he got Eldridge out of Vacaville in June, and later on when his legal and political work together with our community efforts kept Huey out of the gas chamber.

Black racism is a fault of a few within the black community. Black racism is a very selfish thing. It is definitely not a progressive or a productive thing.

COALITIONS

■ Three weeks after I got out of jail, we formed a coalition with the Peace and Freedom Party. Eldridge called me and told me to come over and meet some people who wanted to give us money to help Huey out. When I got there he told me an organization, the Peace and Freedom Party, was trying to get on the ballot, and they wanted to know if they could come into the black community and register people into their party. We thought about it, and talked about what Huey had said. Huey thought that we should not become an official party on the ballot at that time, because he knew political repression was going to come down. The Black Panther Party wasn't massive at that time and hadn't yet spread across the country. Remembering what had happened to the American Communist Party, he was afraid that the government would take every person who was registered or attempted to register as an official Black Panther Party member, and try to trump up charges on them. At the same time, we wanted to spread out a lot more and get a massive group of white people to work in their communities because Huey had always held the position that white people should work to end racism in their own community.

Eldridge told me that the Peace and Freedom Party would give us money and also give us $3,000 for Huey's defense fund. They not only wanted to register people for the Peace and Freedom Party in the white community, they also wanted to do it in the black community and saw us, the Black Panther Party, as representatives of the black community. I thought that that was correct and right in line with "White Mother Country Radicals," an article written by Eldridge. I decided we should form the coalition. Eldridge agreed that we should form a coalition for a specific purpose, which was an idea Huey had talked about. Later we went to the jail and asked Huey about it and he agreed.

We had a number of rallies in the black community, in Hunter's Point, the Fillmore, and West Oakland, with the Peace and Freedom Party supplying sound and technical equipment which the Black Panther Party did not, at that time, have at all. With the $3,000, we were able to pay a fair retainer to Charles R. Garry for Huey's defense. In the white community as well as the black, we initiated a broad campaign for increased concern about the problems of the black community, centered around our leader and Minister of Defense, brother Huey P. Newton.

There were a few black members of the Peace and Freedom Party, and they always said they represented the black community in the Peace and Freedom Party. We would look at them and say, "What do you mean? Huey P. Newton represents the black community." It got to be a hassle, and they would sometimes ask us what we thought they should do. We would say that they should join the Black Panther Party. We looked upon the Peace and Freedom Party as a predominantly white organization for the white

community. At the same time we saw that it was valuable to
form a coalition for the specific purpose of encouraging
black people to register in the Peace and Freedom Party
instead of the Republican or Democratic parties who were
oppressing us. With this understanding we formed the coalition and later announced that we would run brother Huey
P. Newton for Congress from the Seventh Congressional
District and myself for the Assembly from the Seventeenth
Assembly District, districts that were half white and half
black.

There were attempts by the power structure to limit the
Party's activity with this coalition. We had a lot of clashes
with a lot of different groups of people, but there were
thousands of black people coming into the Black Panther
Party because of what was happening. The coalition was a
working coalition, not just a verbal one. There was some
very good work done in the community. When the university students were being viciously attacked by the Berkeley
police, the students understood that the people in the black
community were being attacked, murdered, and brutalized
all the time.

The Peace and Freedom Party came to the realization
that we had to do something about the police, on a political
level. The Black Panther Party agreed, and they asked us
what we thought should be done. Eldridge talked to Bob
Avakian, Rick Hyland, and quite a number of others about
the concept of community control of police. We began to
work jointly on this with members of the Peace and Freedom Party, because it would not only be community control
of police in the black community, it would also be community control in the white community.

It was at this time that I began to think that some members of the Peace and Freedom Party weren't really concerned with brother Huey P. Newton as a political prisoner
who needed to be free. Many people worked on our campaign, and showed concern, but *some* of them just weren't
interested. Some of the leaders looked at it as a political

lever, or something to use, but others were earnest and really wanted to free Huey. It became apparent that many Peace and Freedom Party members would have to become more radical and more revolutionary. Many people did not understand that the very police who attempted to kill Huey were controlled by the Democratic and Republican parties, so they weren't very concerned with community control of police. They didn't understand that Huey's situation was inseparable from the needs of the community. We also saw that they didn't have a real interest in the community control of police. We weren't in good communication about it, so we just naturally worked on our own with the petition.

This didn't make us against coalitions. It mostly placed us against people who allow themselves to stagnate, who think they don't have an issue, when there's a lot of hard work to be done.

There were some 25,000 votes cast for Huey P. Newton for Congress in the Seventh Congressional District. For the people who still thought like the old politicians, if a candidate lost, it was over. Some of the leaders felt that running Huey was a losing tactic, but that was not the case. They misunderstood how much Huey was interlocked with every black man in the black community who suffers from oppression. We'd run Huey again because ours is a revolutionary struggle. They acted like social democrats and were not able to advance to a higher level and continue working. The coalition began to split up. I still believe that if the Peace and Freedom Party would really rally its people together, their membership alone could place the community control of police issue on the ballot; but they wouldn't push for it.

We will continue to have working alliances with other groups like Los Siete de la Raza, a group supporting the seven Latino brothers who are accused of killing a cop in San Francisco. Alliances with groups like Los Siete have worked out a lot better than coalitions with white liberals because the brown American people are suffering from the same things black American people are. The Young Lords, a Puerto Rican gang that turned political, works in alliance with the Black Panther Party in Chicago and New York. They're suffering the same oppressive conditions that black people are subjected to. There's also the Young Patriots who are a vanguard in the poor white communities. We can relate well with them because they are in opposition to the power structure's oppression.

Alliances between poor oppressed peoples work out readily. It is the poor oppressed people who have to dictate their political desires and needs, and explain what should be done and what should not be done. The organizations of the lumpen proletariat are the ones we can relate to. We even have a problem with black students sometimes because they tend to have a detached understanding of the realities in the black community.

A lot of people don't understand that when we make coalitions, we're not trying to shuck people. We have no time to be shucking and jiving. When we get three or four brothers shot up and killed, we can't say that it was bad, and forget about it, because we know the pigs are coming back tomorrow. They'll try to attack us again. We know that because of our historical experience as black people.

We are not against intelligence. The Party is very intelligent, and we read the same materials that the college students have read. But it's different when cats like Huey P. Newton and Eldridge Cleaver write and talk, because it is coming out of a lot of experience. It comes from the guts of their souls.

STOKELY COMES TO OAKLAND

■ Early in January of 1968, we decided to have a huge rally in Oakland in support of brother Huey's freedom. We knew that a rally for Huey would fill the Oakland Auditorium, and we went about securing it. The auditorium is

owned by the City of Oakland, and they said they couldn't
rent it out to us because they didn't want "black power
advocates" coming to Oakland to cause riots.

We went back down there with a lawyer, and he told the
auditorium manager that he should rent the place to us for
any date he had open. "Well, I can't give it to them," he
said. "If you don't give it to them," our lawyer told him,
"we'll get a court injunction on you for violating the right of
the people to be able to assemble in the auditorium. Now
there must be some date open, so you'd better just cough up
a date." He decided to cough up a date, so they arbitrarily
said, "Well, the only date we have open is next month some
time . . . February 17." Eldridge quickly said, "We'll take
that date, any date."

When we came out of the auditorium, Eldridge ran back
across the street to the County Jail, where Huey was being
held, and told him we were going to have a big rally for
him, for him and his freedom, and that we were going to
pack the Oakland Auditorium. "The rally is going to be on
February 17," Eldridge said. Huey looked up at him and
said, "Hey, that's my birthday." Eldridge had had no idea
Huey's birthday was in February. So right up there in the
County Jail is when Eldridge got the beautiful political idea
that it would be a birthday rally for Huey, a birthday rally
for the freedom of our Minister of Defense.

I wasn't allowed to go into the jail to visit Huey. They
have some kind of jive rule, that after you get out of the
County Jail, you can't go back in to visit someone else. I
didn't go up that time with Eldridge, but a number of times
after that, I disguised myself, and went up and saw brother
Huey. They have a little booth up there where you're supposed to identify yourself, but sometimes when I came up in
the elevator, there were so many visitors and supporters of
Huey that the brothers just shifted me sideways away from
the booth, and I went in and visited Huey. I don't think it's
illegal, but they have this jive rule. If they want to try to
prosecute me on it now, let them try it.

Eldridge came out of the courthouse (the holding section of the Alameda County Jail is on the top floor of the Alameda County Courthouse) and ran it all down to me about how we were going to have a birthday party for Huey. We only had about a month before the rally.

We went down to the Peace and Freedom Party and told them that we needed some money because we wanted to go see Stokely Carmichael in Washington, D.C. Stokely had just come back from his world tour of Vietnam, Cuba, Africa, and other places. We felt that Eldridge and I should go directly to Washington, D.C., and sit down and talk to him, and run it down to him because he really hadn't committed himself to coming to the rally yet, although we had told him about it. We asked the cats in the Peace and Freedom Party to finance that trip for us. They financed it, but not before we went through a few changes.

When we first asked them, they said that they didn't have any money. Eldridge and I told them they were a bunch of liars. "How can you tell us you don't have any money?" we asked them. "If you don't have it, you can raise it." We said, "We need $500 in plane fare and $100 in expense money to go and see Stokely so we can secure this whole rally." So they said, "Well, we can get about $200 but we can't get any more."

"Well, you're damn liars," we said. "You cats are talking about working with us in a coalition and you want to go into the black community and want us to be key spokesmen there for the Peace and Freedom Party. But at the same time, we are talking about Huey's freedom. The reason we entered into this coalition was to talk about Huey's freedom. That's what this rally is all about; politically educating the masses of people that Huey P. Newton must be set free now.

"Are you cats going to be racists and jiving around and go back on your word, or are you cats going to be able to go out and hustle that money? We don't have much time because we want to start getting some other things together and we want to raise some more money to print our posters."

Then I got mad and I told them I didn't want to talk to them. "Don't talk to me," I said. Eldridge would do this all the time. He would get mad and cuss them all out and say the hell with them sometimes. Later on I didn't do that, but at that time I was overtly concerned with brother Huey and I didn't want to be jiving around with anybody that was going to be bullshitting. We knew they had enough money to help us out. We were so concerned about Huey and the organization and black people that we felt that we had to use these "tactics" to make those cats see that it was important.

Eldridge came back out of the office and sat in the car. Then they went back inside the office and got $500 and brought it out. I said, "No, no, no!"

"We can make it with this," Eldridge said.

"We haven't got any expense money," I said.

"We can get some."

"If they're going to have a coalition with us," I said, "then they can get the other $100. I'll bet they've got it with them!" So Mike Parker and some other cats raised that extra $100 in thirty minutes.

That night, Eldridge and I got on the plane and split. When we got to Washington, we rented a car to get around with. We drove to this address we had for Stokely, and when we got there we went up and knocked on the door. It was kind of early in the morning, about 8:00 A.M., but when we knocked on the door, the guy who answered it was uptight. The FBI and the CIA had been trailing Stokely consistently. But the cat looked at us and he had to know that we weren't FBI or CIA agents. Eldridge told him we were from the Black Panther Party. So they said, "Stokely is sleeping now. Come back later on."

"Well, wait a minute," we said. "We've come to sit down and talk."

"Well, you have to go to somebody else's house," the cat said. He wrote something on a piece of paper and said, "Go to this address."

"Now what kind of shit is this!" we thought. These cats are crazy. These cats lack understanding, placing their egos before the struggle. But we decided to go to the other address. When we got there, those cats were a little bit more hospitable.

About two hours later, we went back to talk to Stokely. We talked a little while about different things, about going around the world, asking about Cuba and things like that. We went on for a while. We tried to relax, had some coffee, and then somebody brought in half a gallon of wine, and we righteously relaxed. After that we got into the car we had rented, to talk to Stokely about what we really wanted, his coming out to Oakland for the big rally.

We let Stokely drive. He drives like he's crazy. We looked back and noticed that some cops were trailing us. They looked like FBI agents. "Man, look at those cops trailing us," I said.

"Don't worry about it," Stokely said. "They trail me like that all the time."

"But they're not even hiding themselves."

"Well, they know that I know that they're following me, and they don't care if I know or don't know that they're going to follow me."

"You mean they're right there on your bumper all the time? And if you speed up, they speed up? And if you slow down, they slow down? And if you turn a corner, they turn the same damn corner?"

"That's the way they do it," Stokely said. Meanwhile, he's driving real crazy.

I told Stokely that we didn't allow any cops to be following us around like that. "Aw, just leave 'em alone," he said. Then he took off and just started driving wildly, speeding down the streets and everything. He actually lost the cats and left them out of sight. He'd drive all the way up a street and stop. About four minutes later, the same cops would come after us in the same car. Then Stokely would turn around and drive back down the street. As he drove back down the street, the cops would see him coming that way. They would turn into a driveway and back out and have their car sitting in the same direction that Stokely was going. We would pass them and they would get right back on our tail again. They were never more than thirty feet away from him.

They followed Stokely around wherever he went, twenty-four hours a day. Another time, Stokely cut out and completely lost them. We waited ten minutes, then they drove right up behind us.

"They've got a beeper on the car," Stokely said.

"What do you mean, a beeper?" I asked.

"They've put a beeper on this car already. That's what I was trying to find out," he said. "You all just got this car and they checked you out when you came to see me. While you were upstairs, they put a beeper on the car, some kind of radar-type beeper that can find this car, wherever it is. They've already put it on and can find you guys wherever you are. That's how they keep up with my car."

We cut out again and lost them. We lost them for a number of blocks, but they almost caught up with us. Then Stokely went into a park and wound his way up a road. It's not a big hill, but it's got a good slope to it. You go up the road, and it makes a complete circle and comes back into itself. Stokely sped up this road and made a complete circle. Then the road came right back into itself. So here was Stokely barreling down this very narrow road, coming right back down on the cops. They saw him coming so fast, and they just swerved off of the road and let Stokely go by. Stokely cut out while they were hustling to turn around and get their car off the dirt and back onto the road so they could continue following him.

Stokely drove to another part of the pack, almost a mile away. We just sat there in the parking lot, and watched them from a distance wind their way toward us. We turned the radio on to try to drown out any bugging of the car that might have taken place.

We talked about the fact that we wanted Stokely to come out to Oakland and speak, and that we probably would have five to six thousand people there. Stokely agreed to speak, and we wound up our meeting with him.

Eldridge and I went down to the SNCC office later that night. We talked to a lot of different organizations. They had heard about our coalition with the Peace and Freedom Party.

"Why do you trust white people?" some SNCC members and cats from black nationalist organizations wanted to know.

"We don't trust white people in the sense that you're talking about," we said. "We judge everybody by what they do."

They asked us why didn't we get a black lawyer for Huey. We told them it wasn't necessarily true that if Huey had a black lawyer he would automatically be well defended and not become a political football to kick around. We told them that we readily went forth to secure legal defense for Huey and that the coalition with the Peace and Freedom Party was not something based on just "trusting" white people, just because they were white. They should at least respect the fact that at one time there was a John Brown and that the John Browns had done a lot more than some black college intellectuals had ever done. We respected John Brown for that, we said, but we live in the spirit of Nat Turner, Patrice Lumumba, and Malcolm X. And Malcolm denounced every kind of racism in his last days.

They were unable to understand this. They had a basic psychological block, because, as Fanon put it, their intellectual possessions were still in pawn to the man's system. A lot of cats down there were college students. They couldn't

see it when we told them that a lot of their ideas were black
racist and that we couldn't operate in a black racist thing.
They couldn't see it because they were trying to say that
there was no such thing as black racism and we were trying
to show them that there could very easily be such a thing as
black racism. Black racism is not overt in most people in
the black community, but it's the way a lot of those cats in
the colleges think. They think about their own selves being
free, and they think with the same racism that a lot of white
people project on to them. And you're not going to end
racism by perpetuating more racism.

We also told them that ours was a working coalition to
get white people to work in the white community against
racism, to destroy it, and ultimately get rid of it there. Our
aim, we said, was to educate the masses of people to understand that they have to get rid of the system that exploits us,
get rid of the oppression, and create some real government.
Well, all in all, the cats there, the SNCC people and the
others, didn't accept what we were saying.

There was also a rally planned in Los Angeles, on the
day following ours. Ron Karenga of the US organization
had sent two of his bald-headed black racists to Washington
because he had found out in some kind of way that we were
going to see Stokely. He flew them in that evening. Those
cats were trying to get Stokely to see to it that Ron Karenga
would get to speak at our rally. Stokely was going to be on a
forum with them in Los Angeles, the next day. We didn't
object to it. We didn't even want to argue about it. We said
we would check it out when we got back to Oakland.

The next day we talked to Stokely again and secured
everything. We agreed upon when he would be out, when
he would receive travelling expenses, and who was coming
with him. We were aware that Stokely and James Forman
weren't getting along at all at that time. There had been a
dispute of some kind, because Stokely traveled out of the
country without the approval of the central committee of

SNCC. But even with Stokely at our rally, we still wanted a working alliance with SNCC so as to better unite black organizations around the country. We felt that they should come forth in this working alliance to further the defense of Huey and lay a broad foundation of unified organizations across the country.

We proposed this, against their arguments that they didn't want to work with white people. We reminded Stokely that he himself set in motion the idea of white people working in the white community when he spoke at Berkeley about a year before this. The Black Panther Party had adopted the idea, and saw it as something that was in opposition to all forms of racism. Huey and I respected it and used it. Now Stokely was saying "down with white people." He told us that many people around Washington, D.C. didn't want him to speak in Oakland because there were going to be white people on the platform. We told Stokely that there was going to be a Peace and Freedom Party member speaking from the platform and we thought it was very necessary that he speak. The person from Peace and Freedom was going to set forth their understanding of what white people have to do to end racism in the white community, which is something black people have to understand.

Stokely definitely agreed to come. We drove around for the rest of that day and talked in the car. The next day we left Stokely off at the SNCC office, cut out to the airport, and flew back to Oakland. We told the Peace and Freedom Party that everything was set up and that we were going to have a major rally. We knew that Stokely would definitely speak, so we could put things into motion. We publicized the event in the black community and they did the same thing in the white community.

We brought Stokely out a little early to visit Huey. There was a lot of press coverage, and a lot of people realized that it was time to come out for Huey P. Newton. It was one of the biggest rallies that ever took place in Oakland. Besides Stokely, Rap Brown and James Forman of SNCC showed up. It had become clear to Stokely, to James Forman, to Rap Brown, and to a lot of other people that brother Huey P. Newton, the Minister of Defense of the Black Panther Party, had become the central leader of the revolutionary movement that was coming out of the black community on a new and a higher level than it had ever been before.

The place was packed. Stokely, Eldridge, and I could hardly get into the Oakland Auditorium ourselves. When we first announced the rally, we said that we didn't want any cops in or around the auditorium. We said that we would take care of all the traffic direction ourselves, and that we had enough Panther Party members to do this. We said the community would support us in this. A few days before the rally, Chief Gain of the Oakland Police Department called up the Party. Eldridge and Emory Douglas went up to talk to some of his lieutenants and captains. Eldridge told them flat that we didn't want any cops on the premises and that we would take care of the whole thing. The cops tried to shake hands with Eldridge, but Eldridge told them, "I don't want to shake hands with you. I'm just letting you know that we don't need any cops around the auditorium." And there were none. Not a pig in sight. And naturally, there was no rioting.

It was Stokely's first speaking engagement since he returned from his world tour. It was very important because it linked up SNCC with the Black Panther Party, although many people in SNCC were in disagreement with Stokely at that time.

We had met with James Forman in Los Angeles about a week after we came back from Washington. We had talked about his working with the Party and we told him that we wanted that kind of alliance. But Forman was definitely against us making Stokely Carmichael the Honorary Prime Minister of the Black Panther Party. He thought we should

make Rap Brown the Honorary Prime Minister. We saw
then that there were factional differences inside of SNCC.
There was Rap Brown running on one end with James
Forman directing things, and Stokely on the other end,
directing his own thing.

So we decided that if they all accepted the ten-point
platform and program, we'd make Stokely Carmichael the
Honorary Prime Minister, James Forman the Minister of
Foreign Affairs, and brother Rap Brown the Minister of
Justice of the Black Panther Party. We thought that would
give us a good group of black revolutionary leaders to unify
the black liberation struggle across the country.

So we had an SNCC-Panther alliance. The alliance was
supposed to be practical and functional. They wholly accepted being special kind of officers in the Black Panther
Party, which indicated that they saw the Panther Party as a
revolutionary organization which a lot of black people were
sitting up and taking notice of, with regard to both our
political line and our stand on the right to self-defense.

We felt that these brothers should work with the Party.
We were attracting thousands of young brothers off the
streets, cats who in the past had been in riots and what have
you. We were also getting people from other organizations
who were dropping their old groups and coming to check
out the Panther Party, except for the bootlickers who were
deathly afraid of cops and weren't about to mess with them
whatsoever. James Forman was going to be the head of a
most profound and necessary political education program.
He had spent a lot of time with me and Eldridge while we
were down in Los Angeles. We asked Forman to come to
Oakland too, and he said he'd definitely be there.

Forman was playing politics, though, and his strategy
was to try and keep the Panthers weak. Stokely at this time
was only a field marshal in the Black Panther Party. We had
drafted him as a field marshal seven or eight months before,
and he accepted the draft. Forman told us again that he
thought we should make Rap Brown Prime Minister, in-

stead of Stokely. So what we wound up doing was to try to bring them all into the Party. This was going to be the basis of the alliance, a working alliance, where united we would work together for the liberation struggle. They accepted this idea.

At the rally, Eldridge announced that we were making Stokely Carmichael Prime Minister, James Forman Minister of Foreign Affairs, and Rap Brown Minister of Justice of the Black Panther Party. Forman and brother Rap Brown were also the heads of SNCC, at the time, and we respected them as that. Everyone turned out—there was a huge crowd at the rally. Rap Brown showed up by surprise. Nobody actually knew he was coming until the last minute. James Forman set that up to strengthen SNCC.

The rally came off. It came off real good. As Eldridge put it, it was the biggest line-up of revolutionary leaders that had ever come together under one roof in the history of America. That was just about the truth, because Eldridge and myself, Alprentice "Bunchy" Carter, David Hilliard, Stokely, Forman, and Rap Brown were all there. We set Huey's chair in the center, the wicker chair that many people have seen in the picture, where he's holding the spear, the shotgun, and the shield, exemplifying the right to self-defense. This in itself made a big impact, a very big impact. We raised some $10,000 at that rally, for Huey's defense fund. It was the biggest fund-raising operation in Huey's behalf that had ever gone down. At that time, it was the largest we'd ever had. We really needed the money, because Garry's whole firm was working on Huey's case almost on an around-the-clock basis. They must have been in the hole for $30,000 on us by then.

After Stokely spoke at our big rally, we had numerous speaking engagements throughout the San Francisco-Oakland Bay Area, down in Los Angeles, and all over California. The last speaking engagement we had was on a Saturday night down in Palo Alto. That night, the Berkeley police raided my house and arrested me.

BREAKING DOWN OUR DOORS

■ Early in the morning, a number of brothers and I had talked in my house about the fact that we had raised $10,000 for Huey's defense fund, and about organizing bigger rallies to raise the thousands of dollars we needed to keep our legal machinery together to get Huey out of jail. I left the house at about 12:30 P.M. and I know I left a back window open.

That night the cops busted into my house and found a sawed-off shotgun. In court it came out that my fingerprints weren't on it and my wife's fingerprints weren't on it. The shotgun was planted. They charged me with having an illegal weapon and, to poison the atmosphere, they originally also charged me with conspiracy to commit murder. Some cop said he overheard someone in my house saying, "We want Rap." He said that later that night he heard the clacking of guns in my house. I didn't know anything about it because I was asleep. I was very tired from the preceding week of running around, and going to different speaking engagements with Stokely. When I got home that evening, I went to bed.

My wife woke me up around 2:00 A.M. and told me the cops were outside. The cops tried to pull a slick operation, calling me "Mr. Seale," and trying to sound polite.

"We would like to speak to you about a disturbance in the area."

"Well, I don't know anything about a disturbance," I said. "I don't want you in my house. If you want to find out about a disturbance in here, go see the landlord who's upstairs."

"No, we want to talk to you in your apartment," they said. "There was a disturbance around here."

"There was no disturbance in my house and I don't want

you in my house. If you want to see somebody about a
disturbance, then go see the landlord."

I had been talking to them through my apartment window. I was about to open the door all the way up, step out
and show them where the landlord was, but no sooner did I
get the door two or three inches open when they knocked
me up against the wall, put a shotgun at my belly, and
started pointing a gun at my wife. I got mad and started
hollering at the top of my voice, "Don't shoot my wife."
They handcuffed me, sat me on the bed, and went all
through my house. I didn't see any shotgun the night I was
arrested, but I heard them say, "We got it." They expected
to find it. We were made to sit on the couch handcuffed,
while two cops stood over us with guns trained on us.
Sitting there, I couldn't see who he was talking to, but a cop
said, "Look what we found." The cop near me answered,
"Yeah, we expected to find that." Then they took me out.

The lady next door, who was later a witness, came to us
after the bust and said a man had rented a room in her
building two weeks prior to the bust. He was a white guy, a
racist, this woman said, and all he did was watch our house.
She had never paid too much attention, but had seen him
out there fooling around watching us. After the bust, she
realized what was happening because she knew this guy had
called the cops. The next day she asked him why he did it.
He was packing his bags and leaving at the time, and he
told her it wasn't any of her damn business, and then he
split. That was the last we saw of him. The cops say he's the
one who called them.

I was charged with possession of illegal weapons. I had
an Army .45 and I know there was a serial number on that
weapon, that it was not illegal. In court, they delivered a
gun with the serial number ground off, which is against the
law.

At the station, I thought about the arrest and I asked the
cops what they were doing searching my house without a
search warrant. "We didn't need a search warrant," they

said. "We've been listening to you all day." If they were listening to me, the main thing they heard was that we had made over $10,000 for Huey's defense fund.

In jail I thought that over again. They had our bail high —$6,000 on me. "They're planning to drain our funds," I said to myself. "That must be what they're attempting." It was only a week after the rally for the defense of brother Huey, and that is the only reason I could see for arresting me and my wife on such trumped-up charges.

The charges against me were dropped by Judge Lionel Wilson. He quashed them on the basis that the policeman was lying, that he was contradictory in his statements, and because they had no reasonable cause to bust into my house at two o'clock in the morning. They said they had reasonable cause, but the judge ruled that if everything was peaceful and quiet, as they testified it was, they had no reasonable cause to break into my house. It was illegal search and seizure.

A month before my arrest, the San Francisco Tactical Squad had busted into Eldridge Cleaver's house, trying to intimidate and harass him. They were trying to find a gun. When Eldridge first came into the Party, Huey let it be understood that Eldridge couldn't have weapons because he was an ex-felon. The Party had set that policy because we understood that we just couldn't get into a lot of illegal activity. Huey always said our activities should be legal. Eldridge followed orders and didn't himself have guns. One night after the search, Kathleen said, "What if we actually got attacked and didn't have anything to defend ourselves with?" Eldridge said that she would just have to get herself a gun, because the Minister of Defense had told him he couldn't have one because he was an ex-felon. So Kathleen went down to the store and purchased some guns. Eldridge told his parole officer that his wife was definitely buying some guns, and as they lived in the same house, there was nothing he could do. Eldridge stayed completely legal about this and also stayed within the policy that Huey set.

. . .

Huey made a lot of policies like that one, so we would have a legal organization. At the very beginning of the Party, Huey had done a lot of research in law books and he had also been in law school for a year. Huey would go to the law library downtown and he also studied the case histories that were in the North Oakland OEO poverty center, where we were able to obtain a lot of information. It was a multipurpose poverty center and one service was legal aid. They had two full walls of law books so we could check into all possible laws the cops might charge us with breaking. We were very aware of the laws related to illegal possession of weapons, so that we wouldn't get caught in the snares and traps of the system.

At the time of my arrest, thousands of members were coming into the Party. Seattle started a chapter and the Los Angeles–Southern California branch was already operating. My arrest was not only an effort to drain the Party's resources but was also an attack on the leadership of the Party. Chief of Staff David Hilliard; Deputy Minister of Defense Alprentice "Bunchy" Carter, who has since been murdered; Bunchy Carter's brother, who's now dead also, and a girl who since dropped away from the Party were also busted the same night I was. I first realized that other people had been busted when I came into the jail. I saw this girl in an interrogation cell. I was completely confused because I couldn't understand what she was doing there. She had been working with the Party almost a year. Because I had been asleep at my house, I didn't realize what was going on. I heard one of the officers say, "We've got the other four and we're booking them." When I was in the booking cell, they brought Bunchy out. They were going to book him, too. He said twenty cops surrounded them with shotguns pointed at the car, and busted them for nothing.

I finished getting booked and made my phone call. When Bunchy was booked we were put in a cell together. I really began to worry about Bunchy because he had been in prison with Eldridge, and he was on parole. One of the things Huey and I dreaded was brothers in the Party who were on parole getting busted, because the California fascist operation just sends them back to prison for practically no reason at all. I told Bunchy I had just made a phone call and that I would probably be out soon.

"You'll be the first one I come back and get out," I said, "because you're on parole." My brother, John Seale, came to bail me out. My wife was in jail too, but I knew we could always get her out. The thing was to get Bunchy Carter out. Three hours later we bailed him and his brother out.

They told me everything that had happened. There had been a pistol in the glove compartment of the car and there was another pistol in the car, but it wasn't concealed. They told me how the bust had happened and what they were charged with. We got our lawyer and about $100. I told Bunchy to go back to L.A., to continue organizing, and to lay low. He said he would try to deal with his parole officer down there.

In March, the cops busted into Eldridge's house for the second time. For that reason Huey P. Newton wrote Executive Mandate Number Three, concerning Gestapo cops busting down our doors. It stated that we had a right to defend our threshold, and that everyone must defend his threshold. If the police come up to our door acting in an unorderly manner, it said we could only consider them as a danger to our lives. Huey was aware that members of the John Birch Society, Ku Klux Klanners, and many other sick, "patriotic" racists join the police force, and also work with racist vigilante groups. Information had also been sent to him that a number of these people disguise themselves. Huey set forth Mandate Number Three, for all Party members, that said that when someone came to our door acting in a manner other than as a police officer should, kicking in our door and attacking, we were to defend ourselves.

By that time we had chapters in Seattle, Southern Cali-

fornia, Los Angeles, San Francisco, and our national headquarters in Oakland. Every time they attacked us, the Party
grew. At that time, early in 1968, they were mainly interested in the leaders, like Huey, Eldridge, David Hilliard,
Bunchy Carter, and myself. When arresting us failed to stop
the growth of the Party, the power structure escalated its
attack and began shooting us down in the streets, in our
offices, and our homes.

SHOOT-OUT: THE PIGS KILL BOBBY HUTTON

■ One day in the middle of March 1968, Eldridge called
me up and said, "Hey, man, come over here. I've got
something to hip you to about the pigs plotting to attack
us." I went over to *Ramparts,* and they took me into a
room. There was a white girl standing there. Eldridge said,
"Tell Bobby what you told me." She ran down to me that
she had been sitting in a bar and heard two cops talking
about the Black Panther Party. One was saying that on
April 2 they would have something for us. They said they
were going to get rid of all the Panthers. I asked her if that
was all she heard. She ran down some other things they had
talked about, mostly negative things about the Panther
Party. She said they went over April 2 again, and talked
about doing the Panther Party in. I looked at Eldridge and
we walked out of the office.

"What do you think, man?" he asked me.

"Man, they're going to try and attack us," I said. I asked
him if this chick was reliable. Eldridge thought she was
pretty reliable, so we knew we'd have to check it out.

Three days later, an ex-policeman, a black cat, came
over to the office and told me that he had heard some cops
saying that sometime in April they were going to get rid of
us. He had heard these rumors going around and he thought
he'd come down and tell us.

I talked to Eldridge and I told everybody that we were going to have to get some guns, keep the guns in our houses, and keep them clean and ready, because there's no telling what they might do. We had had some guns before, but I told everybody to be prepared, and to make sure that if somebody didn't have a gun, to see that they got one because there was no telling what was going to happen. We might get attacked at any time.

At the birthday rally for Huey, we had announced that we were running him for Congress from the Seventh Congressional District. The primaries to get Huey's name and my name on the ballot as Black Panther Party candidates running on the Peace and Freedom Party ticket were coming up in June. I was running for the State Assembly for the Seventeenth Assembly District. We had scheduled a rally in the black community at De Fremery Park for April 7, a Sunday. It was to be a barbeque-picnic rally for the Huey P. Newton Defense Fund, and for campaign funds to run Huey and myself. We were already getting a lot of good response from the people. Many people had already said that they were going to be there for the dollar-a-plate barbeque. We had sound trucks and all sorts of publicity out in the community. We even got a radio station to announce it. We'd been getting donations from stores of barbeque ribs, things we needed to make potato salad, barbeque meat and stuff like that; we got chickens and boxes of weiners and lots of other food that people had donated to us for this barbeque picnic. At the same time this rumor had gotten around inside the Party that the pigs were going to attack us.

Threatening notes had come to me from members of the sheriffs' department—I assumed it was the Alameda County sheriffs. The notes just said, "I'm the sheriff and when you come into court, you're going to get it." This kind of stuff had been going on for a while. I had to appear in court on April 1, and we were trying to speculate on which one of the deputy sheriffs had written the notes. We were used to getting threatening notes, but the cats would never say who they were. If you get a threatening note from the American Nazi Party you don't pay any attention to it; but when you get threatening notes from fools who say they're in the sheriffs department, you begin to speculate a little bit because you know the cops want to deal with you. So I holed up in an apartment while we were doing some quick investigation on whether one of the deputies who act as bailiffs in the Alameda County Courthouse in downtown Oakland, had actually written the notes. We wanted to check out who was wearing guns, and try to case the courthouse, and look around all the buildings before I showed up in court, to see if anybody was going to shoot me on the courthouse steps. It was all related to the rumors that they would try to get us April 2. I didn't show up in court and the judge issued a warrant for me. We were going to try to expose this possible plot, and we figured the judge would eventually have to see why I didn't appear. But it didn't work out that way.

Thursday evening I was at the house where I was staying. I did some reading, got a phone call from Eldridge, and went to sleep. Then I woke up and decided to turn on the TV to catch the news. Someone said, "Martin Luther King was shot today," but I was in the back room of this apartment and it didn't really dawn on me that Martin Luther King was shot. The sound wasn't up very high. I had just turned on the TV and walked out of the room. It didn't dawn on me that Martin Luther King had been assassinated, because here I was, hiding out in this room until we finished our investigation. Well, I came back into the room and some other kind of news was on but all of a sudden it was announced again. "Martin Luther King has been assassinated." I said, "What!" and turned up the TV. Martin Luther King assassinated! It really got off of me.

I went to the window and saw a lot of cops. The cops weren't supposed to know where I was, but I saw cop cars coming down the street, four cops in a car. I didn't know what was happening. Then I saw two more cop cars coming down and going back up the street, four in a car, and I went back in the room and thought, "Goddoggit, maybe they're trying to surround this place." So I went and looked around in back. I was in the upstairs apartment just below the attic. From the little bathroom window, I was able to see an empty lot to the side with a lot of trees around the driveway of the house and I could see a stairway going down. If I crawled across the bathtub and out the window I could reach the platform. I went back and shaved and then called my brother up and told him to bring his clippers over. When he got there, I said, "Cut my hair."

"Why?"

"Just cut my hair."

I checked out the closet of this apartment where I was staying. (It belonged to a friend of mine.) There were some clothes in there other than the ones I had been wearing. My brother left, and later that evening I got a call from Eldridge who told me everything was all right.

But the next day it was bad, man. I began to think the monkeys had surrounded the place. I saw police cars every five or ten minutes, and it looked to me like they were circling the block. Then I saw two cars drive up, and this is the thing that got me off. While I was looking out the front window, one car drove up four doors to the right, and when the guy got out of the car, he unbuttoned his suit coat. He walked across the street and started knocking on the front door of a house right across from where I was staying. "That's a cop," I said to myself. "I know that's a cop. Dammit, these bastards are trying to surround me up here." So I changed clothes right quick, put on some shades, crawled out the back window, and came down among the trees. Then I cut across the lot to the right and on to the street and I just walked down the streets of Berkeley.

I saw cops everywhere. I hadn't heard any more news and I didn't know about the riots that were taking place. I

speculated that there was going to be some trouble though.
I ran into a cat I knew who didn't recognize me because I
had completely shaven and had cut my natural way down. I
walked up to him and said, "Hey, man, what's happening?"
He just looked at me. I said, "This is Bobby Seale." It had
been in all the press that I hadn't shown up in court, so he
looked at me and said, "Man, what's going on?"

"Look, man," I said, "I want you to drive me somewhere.
At least out of this vicinity, because I think the pigs are
surrounding the place I just left. I snuck out the back way
and if they bust in there now, they might come looking for
me, and I need somebody to drive me away from here." So I
got into his Volkswagen and we drove down to San Pablo
Avenue and Dwight Way. That corner was *flooded* with
cops, man. It was flooded with cops, twenty-five or thirty.
There was a police telephone on the corner that a cop was
talking into. They seemed to be watching cars but I just
looked at them. I had my shades on and acted normal, and
the cops didn't recognize me.

We drove down and got on the freeway, went across the
Bay Bridge, and drove out onto the Peninsula. We drove in
the hills for an hour and I talked to the brother a long time
about the Party and Martin Luther King and what was
going on. I began to hear more about the riots and everything that was happening. I finally told him to take me to
Palo Alto where I knew somebody. When we got down to
the sister's house there, I told him to take a message back
to Eldridge Cleaver and David Hilliard. I gave him the
phone number of the place where I was and told Eldridge to
call me about the investigation of the possible plot. Eldridge
called me late that night and told me that Judge Staats had
pulled the warrant off and just didn't want me to "start
anything," as he put it.

Early the next morning, April 6, the brothers and sisters
were cooking the food and preparing salads and stuff for the
rally and barbeque at De Fremery Park. There were sisters

down at Father Neil's church, and over at David Hilliard's house cooking potato salad, and also in back of the office, barbequeing ribs. We had a real operation going with sound trucks throughout the community, four or five of them. We had leaflets everywhere, and a big bus, the Peace and Freedom Party's big sound truck, telling people to be at De Fremery Park for a one-dollar-a-plate barbeque to raise money for the Huey P. Newton Defense Fund, and for campaign funds for Huey and myself. We had a beautiful thing going and we knew it was going to get thousands of black people out there.

Since the judge had withdrawn the warrant on me, I came down to the office. A lot of cops were floating around the office. There were cops everywhere, many more cops than usual. That whole day the brothers were saying that if they attacked us we would defend ourselves. One of the captains said he was going to transfer some weapons over to San Francisco. I told him to make sure they weren't loaded, to keep them all in the trunk, and to keep everything legal. But I said, "If it looks like you're going to get attacked or something like that, you might have to use the weapons, because you've got a right to defend yourself."

That afternoon I met Eldridge at the Peace and Freedom Party office and he said he was going to David's house that evening. I told Eldridge to take me down to the church because I wanted to talk with Father Neil about going to Martin Luther King's funeral. Eldridge had the white car that the Peace and Freedom Party had picked up cheap and given to us. That was in the late afternoon. I asked Eldridge where he was going, and he said he was going over to David's house. I told him I was going over to Father Neil's house and I left with Father Neil in his car.

After I was introduced to Father Neil's family, we sat down and ate. We were talking about the Party and the Party's philosophy. Father Neil was in a clergyman's organization that was set up so that whenever there was a disturbance in the community, this little group—a minister, a lawyer, and a doctor—would be taken to the trouble. Each group had a section of the city that it was assigned to. The organization had been set up for quite a while. Father Neil got a phone call and all of a sudden he jumped up and said that we had to go, that they were shooting at somebody. His wife asked where he was going, and he said, "There's a shoot-out going on somewhere. The police attacked somebody and shot two or three people." Then I began to think about this April 2 thing and those threatening notes from the so-called sheriff. I naturally thought about the Party. We jumped in the car and drove all the way up to Berkeley where the switchboard office was. They said the shoot-out was between Panthers and police on Twenty-eighth Street in Oakland. At that point I was wondering who the supposed Party members were. I knew a lot of people just didn't have any guns. I got as much information as I could and then I told Father Neil I wanted to go down there. The other ministers started saying that they didn't think we should. Then, information came over the radio that the shoot-out was over, and that they had all been arrested. The radio report said that Eldridge Cleaver had been arrested and that Bobby Hutton was shot (at that point they didn't say he was dead). It also said David Hilliard had been arrested and two or three other Panthers had been shot.

It was late at night by the time we got the final report— David and Eldridge were arrested and Little Bobby was supposedly shot. I felt the best thing to do was to sit down and start trying to figure out some way to get them out of jail. I gave Kathleen Cleaver and a number of other Panthers a phone call and told them to stay in their houses, and if they got attacked, they ought to defend themselves.

I went to my father-in-law's house. I began to think about everything I could, about what had happened, and how to go about getting the brothers some political defense. Father Neil called me up about two hours later, about 2:30 or 3:30 in the morning and told me that Bobby Hutton had been killed. He told me that Eldridge Cleaver and Bobby

Hutton had somehow been forced into a house. As they were coming out of the house, Bobby had his hands up, but they shot him in the head. Eldridge and I had been spotted twice by cops in the white car that day. We saw them looking at us and carrying on. I really felt that they shot Bobby Hutton thinking they were shooting me.

I was mad. I knew Huey had said that we didn't believe in spontaneous riots, but I was so mad at that point that I felt that I was going to tell all those people at the rally the next day to turn Oakland upside down. I was going to tell every black person who came to the rally to tear up the town. I was going to tell them to hit the big man, the big-time businessman's businesses. That's what I was going to tell them. I kept thinking about the fact that Huey had said, "no spontaneous riots." But I felt differently with Bobby Hutton dead, and feeling that they thought they were killing me, and instead they murdered Little Bobby Hutton.

Maybe I shouldn't have felt that way but that's what I was thinking. The next morning I went over to Garry's office so he could take me up to the police station where we had called a press conference. Before we went there Garry went to visit Huey at the County Jail in Oakland, and Huey sent a tape back, and told me to remember to tell the people not to spontaneously riot, but to tell them to organize themselves; that the cops occupy our community like a foreign troop, and that we have a right by the Constitution of the United States to have guns and weapons in our homes. He urged me to tell them not to spontaneously riot because that's not the correct method, and because all it would do, would get fifty or a 100 black people killed, maybe 200 wounded, and thousands arrested as in riots in the past. He said we had to think of the safety of our people, even when brothers were murdered like brother Bobby Hutton was murdered. He said I knew that, and shouldn't act on emotions, but should act on the correct methods of the struggle. Huey told me to tell the people to arm themselves and put arms in their homes, and to say that if they see

racist cops brutalizing and murdering our people, that we
have but one alternative—to go forth as an organized force
in our community to defend ourselves against unjust, fascist,
brutal attacks.

I went over to June Hilliard's house (June is David
Hilliard's brother), two blocks from De Fremery Park
where the rally was being held. A large crowd was moving
toward the park. Garry came to June's house and took me
up to Oakland police headquarters where he had arranged
for the press conference. I wasn't too happy about having it
there, but I thought, "Well, if I'm with Garry and they
arrest me, they'll just have to do it right." So we held the
press conference and told the press what Huey had said. I
knew Huey was right, and I made it a point not to function
off of emotions because emotions won't guide a correct
revolutionary struggle.

Then I went back to the park and spoke to the people
and told them exactly that. I told them we were not going to
spontaneously riot, but not because we were with the power
structure. We're against the racist power structure of the
pigs and the murderers. I told them that if we rioted the
only thing that was going to happen was that maybe fifty
would get killed, 200 would get shot up and wounded,
and three or four thousand arrested. And that's too
many warriors gone. I told them that in those past riots
and rebellions, people were exposing their disgust with the
social evils that exist in society, but that now, we had to
organize ourselves, and learn to defend ourselves with guns
when we were unjustly attacked. I told them that we should
go to our homes and make sure each home had a shotgun, a
.357 Magnum pistol, and a .38 pistol. "Be safe with weapons," I said. "The Black Panther Party isn't going to get
hundreds of our people shot up, killed, and wounded. Even
though they murdered Bobby Hutton and we don't like it,
Bobby Hutton was a freedom fighter." And I ran it all down
to them about Bobby Hutton.

And you know what? Those people really applauded at

what I had told them. It showed me that the people had learned from the past riots; that they had really learned that when they go out in big riot form, the only thing that happens is they are surrounded by Gestapo policemen, and that they're herded around and shot up like cattle. People related to the idea of being spread out in the community. I told them that if the pigs come down in our community in vicious force, then we should move around in small groups of threes and fours in defense of ourselves. I explained to them that if the pigs bring tanks down to our community, the young brothers are going to have to use guerrilla tactics and learn how to take those tanks, because those tanks are brought there only to slaughter and kill our people.

The people clapped, man. The people really dug it. They really dug this understanding, and that got off with me and made me feel like I was doing right. It showed me that the people had learned, and what the people had learned is what the Party had learned. That's the reason the organization came to exist in the first place.

GETTING ON THE BALLOT

■ After the April 6 shoot-out, we buried Bobby Hutton as Fanon had said we would, and tried to get Eldridge out of jail. He was being held in Vacaville State Prison about fifty miles east of Oakland. We began to mobilize people for the primaries that Huey and I were running in that June. Huey's trial had already been postponed several times, but the Peace and Freedom Party had been officially placed on the ballot.

In May, while Eldridge was still in jail, Kathleen and I went to New York to help raise funds for Eldridge. I made a speech then that a lot of people wondered about. I said in my speech, ". . . we hate you white people . . ." and I didn't put it in the proper context of what I wanted to say. We didn't hate anybody for the color of their skin, but at

the same time we were reserved toward a lot of white
radicals who wouldn't move or do anything. A lot of people
got upset over that part of the speech.

I laugh about it sometimes because I'm truly not a die-
hard cultural nationalist. That night I wanted to knock a
play we had seen in New York in which LeRoi Jones and
some others got on stage, silhouetted in shadows, and hollered, "Black black black black black black black black
black . . ." That went on for nine or ten minutes and it
just got absurd. It kept going over and over, "Black black
black black black black." Every once in a while a voice
would change pitch, but it went on and on. It didn't make
any sense. It didn't convey anything. We called Jones and
Ron Karenga the high priests of cultural nationalism because they didn't really produce anything except fanatics.
They would have been better off, if they were going to
express anything, to talk about revolutionary culture in a
way that would change something. Four or five Panther
brothers and I sat in the audience and ridiculed it among
ourselves.

When I made that speech, a lot of people asked questions. Take everything else in that speech, and when you
come to that statement, "We hate you white people," weigh
it with everything else I said. I was ridiculing the cultural
nationalism of Jones and his "black black black." They
were embedding a form of black racism in the minds of the
people rather than giving them proper perspective on the
revolutionary struggle.

In New York, people were interested in brother Eldridge,
brother Huey, Huey's trial, and in the fact that the cops had
murdered Bobby Hutton. Cops attempting to attack and
wipe out the Party had caused the Party to grow, and when
we left New York, on May 22, 1968, their first chapter was
forming.

The primaries were coming and we did a lot of campaign
work. We had acquired a new office before the April 6
shoot-out. The Bay Area Committee to Defend Political

Freedom raised some money and printed up 50,000 broadsides about what the government was doing to Huey. Half of the reason we ran Huey was to let people see that Huey wasn't what the power structure was trying to picture him as —a small-time hoodlum. Throughout the primary campaign, there was a lot of conflict. We had trouble with other black groups who were trying to run in the Seventh Congressional District, with some Peace and Freedom people over $1,300 we thought we were supposed to have, and with some of the brothers and sisters who still didn't understand the significance of running Huey P. Newton for Congress.

The night of the primary, our workers went out to get tallies of the vote, and the power structure gave them the run-around. They were told that votes weren't counted at the polls, but were counted downtown at the county clerk's office. They went down to the county clerk's office and were told votes were counted at the polls. The brothers and sisters got very discouraged when they came in that night, and could only give estimates of the vote. When they tallied them up they came up with only seventy or eighty votes. They thought Huey was not going to get on the ballot, and everybody was disturbed, thinking that not enough people would even take time enough to vote Huey's name onto the ballot. But I said, "What are you talking about? We're going to be on the ballot by three or four times the votes we need." They didn't believe it.

I went down to the Peace and Freedom Party office and I took the votes they had tallied up from the black community and put them together with the ones that had come in for the Peace and Freedom Party in the white community. We stood there and watched, and a *lot* of people started coming in with votes from everywhere. The next thing we knew, we were way over what we needed, so I called up the brothers and sisters told them, "Hey, we're on the ballot." They felt a little better then. We still believe a lot of the votes went uncounted. In the actual election, Huey got 25,000 votes, but I think the votes were tampered with because they definitely wouldn't let us anywhere near the counting.

The primaries were important to the Free Huey campaign. We talked about the trial and educated the masses of people about who Huey was, so the people could come out to support him. A vote for him was a vote of support. One thing we found out for sure, was how many thousands of voters really support the Party. A person would have to support the Black Panther Party and know something about our basic ideas to vote for a member of our Party who was on the ballot. Although presently we aren't running any candidates, we will work for candidates who support the ten-point platform and program of the Black Panther Party.

HUEY IS TRIED FOR MURDER

■ We knew before Huey's trial began in mid-July, that the whole power structure wanted to hang Huey. We understood that William Knowland (the publisher of the *Oakland Tribune*), the mayor, the other politicians, the D.A., and the cops were all so treacherous that they would do anything to get a conviction and send Huey to the gas chamber.

We asked Charles Garry a number of times what he thought would happen. He would run it down, how Huey was really innocent, and how the two cops had shot each other in an attempt to kill Huey. He knew that defending Huey was the most necessary thing that a lawyer could do to save human integrity, because the power structure was attempting to crucify a black man who was the heir of Malcolm X—Huey P. Newton, the man who put in motion a revolutionary movement to bring the struggle to a higher level. Brother Malcolm had educated black people to the need for a political party like the Black Panther Party, and Charles Garry understood this.

Charles told us that Lowell Jensen, the D.A. prosecuting

Huey, knew that Huey wasn't guilty. He said that even though these cats were going to do everything possible to get a guilty verdict, and that even though he shared our understanding of how corrupt we felt the legal system was, he knew that we should get a not-guilty verdict. We should definitely get a not guilty.

The trial started and Charles defended Huey. The way that trial went down, the so-called kidnap charge had to be dropped right away. The person who was supposed to have been kidnapped came forth on the witness stand and refused to testify. Later, he said that he had been intimidated by the police to make false statements.

They tried to set Huey up as the "only person who could have done the shooting." Gene McKinney, who was with brother Huey on the evening when the cops tried to kill him, came to the witness stand, and Jensen and the judge tried to force him to testify. He refused. He took the Fifth Amendment. The judge is supposed to be impartial, if nothing else, but he was working with the D.A. through the whole trial.

The main prosecution witness Jensen put up against Huey was a bus driver named Grier, who said that he *had* gotten a clear look at the shooting. Garry found a passenger who was on the bus who completely contradicted Grier's story and said that Grier couldn't have seen anything. Apparently, months before, when the police first asked Grier questions, he had initially stated: "I *didn't* get a clear look as to who it was." He said he *didn't* get a clear look. However, on the police report that Jensen had entered in as evidence for the jury to have and read over, this particular statement had been changed to, "I *did* get a clear look." It had been changed by the D.A. and the cops. Grier was lying on the stand and Jensen knew it.

It came out during the trial that Grier's first interview had been taped by the police department. Garry got hold of the tape, duplicated it, and brought it to court while the jury was trying to decide on our Minister of Defense. Garry

argued in court that the tape recording showed that somebody had tampered with the written transcript and that the
D.A. had knowingly submitted that crap as evidence.

Garry didn't take any crap from the judge. He played the
tape recording, argued with the judge, and finally got the
judge to recognize the tape recording as the real evidence,
and order that a new transcript be made, in which Grier
said, "I *didn't* see who did the shooting." Even though they
brought the new transcript into the jury room, no one on
the jury was told that this was *new* evidence, so they didn't
bother to read it.

Garry's a hard-working revolutionary lawyer who really
goes after the facts. All during the trial, he worked in the
evenings investigating and digging up evidence to prove
brother Huey's innocence.

We waited in those days when the jury was out on
brother Huey and we knew that they had to come up with a
not-guilty verdict, especially if they read the last piece of
evidence Garry had submitted. We didn't really know it at
that time, but we speculated that Judge Monroe Friedman
was really working in conjunction with the power structure
which was trying to get Huey railroaded, and that, because
of him, the jury didn't know about the new evidence. We
didn't put it past the power structure to try to buy out a
member of the jury or anything like that. But we felt that
someone on that jury would know the real facts, after
having read them, and would realize that brother Huey
wasn't guilty, not even of voluntary manslaughter.

That night, we heard that the jury had reached a verdict.
We had said, "If they kill Huey P. Newton, the sky is the
limit." We meant every word of that. "If they kill Huey P.
Newton, the sky is the limit." We were going to go down
with brother Huey because Huey was the leader of our
Party. But "the sky is the limit" also meant that we would
go to the highest court if necessary. They had thousands of
cops around in those days when the jury was deliberating so

that you couldn't go two blocks anywhere throughout the black community without seeing a regular city police car or highway patrol car. I had also heard that they had secretly placed National Guardsmen in different places around Oakland and San Francisco. You couldn't go two blocks in that city day or night, especially in the afternoon, without seeing a cop car with two, three, or four policemen in it, with shotguns and helmets and all that riot equipment. That's how tight the cities of Oakland, San Francisco, Berkeley, and Richmond were.

I was at home, at my mother's house and my mother came in and said, "Bobby, Bobby, did you hear that on TV? They said that the jury has reached a verdict on Huey P. Newton." I jumped up and got into a car and drove over to David Hilliard's house. When I got there, it was on the radio that they had found Huey guilty of third degree murder, "voluntary manslaughter." I just couldn't see that. That pissed me off. It really made me mad. And some brother started saying, "Let's burn the town down. Let's burn the town down." At that point I remembered that there had been a press interview on TV a few days before the jury came out. Huey was asked, "What do you mean by 'the sky is the limit'? " Huey had said that he was sure that he would not be convicted at all, but that if he was, the Party would fight it all the way to the Supreme Court. Huey also had sent a message to us that we should defend ourselves if unjustly attacked, but that we just didn't believe in spontaneous rioting.

I was sitting in the house and this brother was talking about, "Ah, man, let's go burn it down. Let's go burn it down." I told them no, that they couldn't do it. A lot of Party members were calling up from all over town, asking, "What should we do? What should we do?" We told them, "Cool it and don't do anything. We're not supposed to be doing anything. They haven't killed the brother," I said. "We said that if they kill Huey P. Newton, 'The sky is the limit.' But right now the sky is the limit in terms of the legal fight, because they just got Huey in for two to fifteen years and we're going to have a one-and-a-half or two year fight on our hands trying to get Huey free. We're going to fight it all the way to the Supreme Court. That's what Huey P. Newton said and that's what we're gonna do. Don't be running out in the streets there," I said, "because there's so many cops out there now that if you turn your head wrong, man, you might get shot down—you'll just be brutalized and murdered."

From there, we started getting petitions signed demanding that Huey P. Newton be given appeal bond, because a third degree conviction allowed a man to have bail. But Judge Friedman, racist and punkish as he was, wouldn't give Huey the bond. Huey is now in some jail in San Luis Obispo. They have denied him bail while the case goes to the higher courts. He is nothing but a political prisoner.

The whole ten-point platform and program and the Party's true ideology and philosophy really came out during Huey's trial, although much of the press didn't want to print it. It would have been in our favor if people had learned the truth. People would have known the real objectives of the Black Panther Party. Charles Garry is the man who really brought all that out, and was able to set forth the philosophy and ideology of the Black Panther Party. A lot of judges in the future are going to try to cut it off, but they can't separate our ideology and our philosophy from ourselves, when they trump charges up on us and try to railroad us to prisons and jails.

PIGS, PURITANISM, AND RACISM

■ One Tuesday night around midnight, right after the verdict on Huey had come down, two Oakland pigs just drove up in front of the Panther National Headquarters office, and emptied twelve rounds into it. One shell shot the window all up, and another went in the café next door. Luckily, no one was in the office at the time. *They* talk about law and order! It's a felony to shoot inside of any building where people are living. There are apartments in the back of the building, and apartments upstairs. You dig where it's at? These dudes are breaking the law, but they keep saying *we* are the lawbreakers.

Huey always made us follow the law to the letter, because within the confines of following the law to the letter, Huey had a principle. The principle was that "laws are made by mankind to serve mankind, but once those laws stop serving mankind in any society, anywhere in the world, the people are supposed to move forth to change those laws so those laws *will* serve them." That's how intensely the whole Party has related to this system. That's what people never know. It's very dangerous to try to bring about this change, especially when you are messing with a tyrannical, despotic system. Most people, most middle-class people, don't understand that the system is very despotic and very tyrannical.

Now those pigs were there, *waiting*, waiting for something to happen in Oakland because of the guilty verdict. You dig? They were on the look-out for a Panther, for any cat in a black leather jacket, to shoot him, to blow him away. They had murder and malice in their hearts. When you read the law book on the charge of murder, it says malice and intent. That's what it says. The same bulls were waiting there, but they couldn't find any Panthers, so they decided to shoot up the office.

Even Police Chief Gain saw that the incident could be politically destructive to the whole police department. We'd been down on the police department for two years, talking about the acts of brutality and murder they'd committed in the black community. Two hours later, Gain suspended them from the force. Boom! Then he charged them with a felony (shooting into an inhabited building), and fired them from the police force. Gain was running around

trying to defend himself by doing these two pigs in. Later
the court let them off with two or three years probation.

He didn't use the excuse that they were drunk. He said
stuff like, "Well, they're human and they didn't like the way
the verdict came down, and blah blop de bloo . . . And I
want all you other police officers not to feel this way. *But* at
the same time we must remember that these were only two
police officers, etc." He also had to appeal to all the police
officers; he's got over 1,000 cops. He appealed to them
through the newspapers and the mass media. "Don't do
anything else. Let us keep our heads, blah, blah,
blah . . ."

All that stuff exposed those pigs. The racism was placed
out front, where it belongs. You dig? The people saw it for
what it was. There's a lot of good cops on the police force,
but you don't go around depending on 20 percent of the
force, on the good cops, when 80 percent of the force is
fucking you up. Every time we turned around those pigs
would be blasting people away, arresting dudes, railroading
them, and attacking cats. So you can't depend on them. We
attacked that racist aspect of the police department.

Then we had a big scene about Gain hiring cops from
the South. We found out that one of the Oakland pigs came
from Florida. Down South it's a bitch. The average white
person down South really envelops himself in this superiority bullshit. That's very important to understand. "Really
I'm a liberal." All that's a bunch of bullshit. Black people
know it. They don't want to hear it. Don't be calling me
"colored," and "these Negroes," and speak articulately with
a lot of verbal sincerity around it. Fuck that, because black
people don't want to hear it. That shit's 100 years old, as
old as the Emancipation Proclamation. Later for that.
Down South, the cops get an orientation that is really laid
on by the local power structure, and they project all these
ideas and misconceptions about black people. It's just a
perpetuation and institutionalization of racism.

We don't practice racism. We practice dualism, two ways

of thinking. Most people don't understand what the Panther Party means by this. What we did was research a lot of history. This is what Huey did. This is what Eldridge did. We researched it all the way back to Europe. Not only are we down on white racism, but we are down on black racism. You know, the cultural nationalists say, "I'm black, I'm beautiful." Most of those cats will project a puritanical concept of blackness. They relate only to the purity of blackness, of being a black person. When we say blackness we mean relating to black culture. These cats, they hang themselves up. White people have always projected, in their educational institutions, etc., a very puritanical, very absolute, superiority thing. This is projected in what they teach us in the school systems. So what do we get? I'll give you a few examples to show you what I mean.

You're looking at a soap opera:

"Mary, you cannot marry John."

"Mother, why?"

"John has an illegitimate child."

"Oh, Mother!"

Wow, they go through all these goddam *fucked up* changes. But this is directly related to something. Sometimes during a speech, Eldridge would say, "Power comes out of the lips of a pussy." Just like that. Then twenty minutes later he'll turn right back around, and say, "Power comes out of the barrel of a dick." People don't know what the fuck he's talking about. But I tell him, "Eldridge, I understand exactly what you're saying because I *know* what's happening." In *Soul On Ice,* Eldridge says it's very necessary to relate the mind to the body. They both must function together to survive. That's key. So take the analogy of a human being, these very practical things of the mind and the body functioning together, and relate them to a whole society having a government with people in it who are supposed to serve the people. The government becomes the mind, that leads the people, that represents the people, and gives them proper representation.

When you start talking about relating the mind to the body of each individual, practicing this dualism, this two-way thing, you're talking about man. Then you have a thing where the power structure, the government, masses forces and guns, goes to Vietnam, kills poor people, masses forces in the black community, police forces are doubled, tripled, and quadrupled, and murdering and brutalizing goes on around the world. The people, who the government is supposed to represent, want to bring themselves into a part of the government, but the government is cutting them off. In an individual, if his head were cut off, it would be a very direct tragedy, a mind being separated from a body. Neither would survive. Neither would function without the other. So when you're talking that way, you're relating to the essence of the body. The dick on a man—we say it just like that— and the pussy on a woman, are related to reproducing human beings. This is what this all relates to. This is how human beings come about. But we have to check out history now, see how in the fuck we were taught that sex, pussy, and dicks were bad and nasty things.

In California now there's a controversy about whether or not sex should be taught to kids. Why do we have to go through this controversy? Three billion people on the face of this motherfucking earth got here through good old downhome human screwing. You got here that way. I got here that way. Everybody got here through good old down-home screwing. How in hell can sex be nasty and bad? Who in the fuck would project such an image? So you ask the question, "Why the fuck did this happen?" All you have to do is relate back to history, and see how different societies develop, and see how different concepts took over those societies and became dominant, and pervaded the society, the minds of its people, and how they were perpetuated up to now.

So, as Huey said, let's go back, back, back. Let's go to Europe. Let's take Europe and let's take Africa. Let's take two different peoples, even before they met each other. Let's take Europe. Europe had the one-headed god concept, the all-pure god, right? The pure blood, and my son of pure blood will become king, and my daughter of pure blood will become queen. This is the thing that went down through history. This is directly related to this purity of god bullshit, the single-headed god, the one-headed god. It's not just the idea of the one-headed god, but what people projected and put into it. People said, "I'm made in the image of god." Boom. They're made in the image of this pure head who's absolute, who's all superior, who's all pure, so goddam pure that people began to read things into the bullshit, and they began to reject their basic animal drives.

But even the masses of people in Europe screwed. They had a tendency to accept the so-called bad things about themselves. It was that monarchy, that government, that king, queen, and hierarchy that laid the rules out, and they themselves projected themselves in this puritanical image of god. They were created in the image of god and they had the power and the guns and force to see that everybody stayed pure. And if you didn't stay pure, then you were a witch, and you were burned at the stake. This happened even before they met black Africans. Europeans were lynching people then.

I'm not saying all societies in Africa didn't have this puritanical concept, but many societies they call primitive, even some outside of Africa, had what many people define as pagan gods; a two-headed god system or a three-headed god system, but they also said they were made in the image of god. You look at the society, and the way people develop, and you look back in history, and you can find these things out. This head was a three-headed god, with a neutral head, a bad head, and a good head. They said they were made in the image of god, so they were able to accept the bad things and the good things about themselves; but the European monarchies perpetuated this purity bullshit, tabooing things, like sluts or those who were downgraded and under their feet. "You're a vassal!" This projection by the monarchy of "I am the greatest" and all that shit was very bad for human society, because it was a process of chopping the head from the body, of the government heads being cut away from the masses of the people.

The Africans mostly had the two-headed god system, bad and good, and said they were made in the image of god. Maybe it developed out of the fact that they had so much fucking food and fucking land down there, they didn't have to worry about a bunch of bullshit. It may be related to industrial development and poor peoples, I don't know. So when the European met the African, when the whole economic development of using slaves came about, these taboos were ingrained in the minds of the people in European society, especially with the monarchy projecting that purity for the people.

"Ah, he's different than I am. He's *black.*" In the kind of system that has a two-headed god, that's impossible. But if god is one-headed, pure-headed, he's absolute. They put taboos on the Africans the same way they put them on their own people, in their own society, with the witch concept. They were burning white people at the stake in their own society even before they met Africans. That even got transported over to America, this thing about witches. They even have a tendency to carry it on now. They superficialize the witch, like the one on TV. Samantha. A good little puritanical witch. It's a thing with them. You have to understand society and have a concept of how human beings function, to be able to see them, and to be able to define how things will go, especially if you try to relate directly to it.

When the Panther Party first came on the scene, the man said, "They're all anti-white. They're a bunch of black racists!" We *never* considered ourselves a bunch of black racists. "They're going to come up in our communities and they're going to shoot us all up!" This wasn't the thing at all. We're saying, "We aren't going into the white community shooting up white people. We're going to defend ourselves against those racists who already occupy *our* community, those pigs, and others who come down and shoot *us* up. We're going to defend our community because we want the power to determine our own destiny in our own black community. We have a right to this, brother, the way we've been treated for 400 years. This is what we want.

"At the same time," we say, "we hope to civilize all of those who are racists in their own communities, or who relate to it, who don't understand what the fuck's going on." Boom.

"Oh no, they can't do that. They have guns. They've *got* to be racists." They accuse us of being what they are.

What we're saying is, you don't fight fire with fire. You fight fire with water. The thing is to define what the fuck is the water. We're saying it's the mass of the people. We say that the water represents a very defensive thing. We say that the people have a right to pick up guns. They're the water. All the people—the hippies, the yippies, the whites, the blacks, the Vietnamese—they have a right to pick up guns to defend themselves against the fire of aggression.

That's why we go through a long process of trying to educate the people. All of them. The hippies, whites, blacks, everybody. We try to organize them. We're talking about revolution in the Mother Country. We have a tendency to parallel the Mother Country with relating only to the mind, and the black colony being related to the body.

Eldridge says that the closest this country has ever come to relating the mind to the body symbolically was when we heard rumors of Jacqueline and John F. Kennedy doing the twist inside the White House, because to wiggle your butt is *very* low-down in white society. Elvis Presley is a white boy who wiggles his legs and wiggles his ass. What is he doing? We felt something was happening, a change was occurring.

A lot of hippies appeared. The hippies denounced their mamas and daddies. "You're a bunch of capitalist exploiting bastards and you relate to racism. I don't even want to hear you. I don't even want to talk to you." They tried to

escape. We respect them because they were trying to re-
deem themselves in their own way from the racism that
they'd been caught up in. But you can't look at them as
individuals. You *have* to look at them as a collective group,
and a development. If you don't look at it that way, you
won't see it.

I can always talk about myself as an individual. Huey
can talk about himself as an individual. At the same time,
we're still a collective group, because we always tell black
people, "We don't give a fuck whether you're wearing a
pimp suit, whether you're wearing an African gown,
whether you've got a natural on, whether you're wearing a
Black Panther uniform, whether you live in Africa, whether
you're over in Vietnam, because wherever you are, the
racists and the imperialists will brutalize, murder, and oppress you, because they've been doing it for 400 years and
they're still practicing it."

Many leftists, hippies, and yippies, will go out to redress
their grievances against something they see that's dead
wrong—"Appears to me that war is wrong"—but what
happens? The same, goddam things that have been perpetuated against all the colored peoples of the world. The pigs
whipped their heads, and cracked their skulls. They stopped
and they said, "Wait a minute. You guys are really right.
Police brutality's a motherfucker. It's something else. It's
bad."

All we're doing is saying we want some land, some bread,
some housing, some education, some clothing, some justice,
some peace. When we say that, they go through a bunch of
sincerity bullshit, that you hear on the radio. "So and so
from the NAACP in conjunction with Governor Reagan
and representatives from so and so, are now investigating
the school integration problem. They are also concerning
themselves with how welfare recipients receive their checks,
blah, blah, blah." That's all we hear.

Bob Dylan sings about one of these cats, you don't know
what is happening, do you, Mr. Jones? OK, so he eats his

motherfucking salami sandwich on sour French bread with
cheese and mayonnaise and lettuce and all this motherfucking bullshit in the middle of a TV program. Meanwhile,
while he's doing that, either there's a pimp on the block
thinking about robbing some joint, or he's pimping some
chick, or he's beating somebody's ass, or there's a mother
over here, wondering how she's gonna feed her kids tomorrow morning. Or the mother's tired, black, and broke.
She had to work twenty years, like my mother worked. She
used to scrub kitchens, like that woman you see over there.
You've seen her over there, that black woman, right next
door there. She sweeps and I don't know what kind of pay
she gets. She may even get paid good. I don't know. But my
mother used to work for a buck an hour. I even remember
when my mother worked for seventy-five cents an hour,
scrubbing those floors. She'd come home with shopping
bags. She's *tired*.

So you have a woman like that, another cat going to jail,
hundreds of them getting busted by the pigs. Some cop
walks up to them and says, "Nigger, where you going?"
And this black man stands there and says, "I'm not a
nigger. What you mean. Don't call me that." Or if he
doesn't want to defend himself, he says, "I'm going down
the street, *sir*." It doesn't make any difference whether he
rises up and defends himself or whether he tries to use the
technique of meekness and acquiescence; he's still being
brutalized or murdered.

We read in the papers that so and so was allegedly
committing a burglary. I'm not saying that some of the
brothers aren't committing burglaries. I'm not even condon-
ing them committing a burglary, because I know why he's
doing it in the first place. He'll walk off into a bank and say,
"Stick 'em up, motherfucker, this is a hold-up." When a
brother gets mad, after living in this confinement, in these
ghettoes, twenty or thirty years, and walks up and says,
"Stick 'em up, motherfucker. Up against the wall. This is a
hold-up," he isn't asking anybody in there what the color of

their skin is, because there's some black tellers in there too. All he wants is that money to relieve himself of that oppression he's been subjected to for so many years.

Talk about dualism. Talk about the mind and the body. I think this is the key thing. And sometimes when the teachers say, "You talking about the mind and the body," you're really talking about the pussy, the dick, the mind, the body. The pussy, the dick, the mind. We're talking about the babies that come out of the pussies of women. We're talking about the dudes that put their dicks in the pussies of women. We're talking about the minds being related to the correct social order. Stop all this existing bullshit. We're talking about human beings beginning and surviving. That's what we're talking about.

ELDRIDGE IS FREE!

■ Eldridge finally got out of prison after the April shootout on June 6, 1968. The day Eldridge got out of Vacaville was a beautiful day. It was a great feeling to see Eldridge free once again.

Stokely Carmichael, while he was out to California for Huey's Birthday Rally, said some stupid things to me and Eldridge like, "You guys might as well forget it, because Huey will never get out of jail. They're going to send Huey to the gas chamber and that's it."

"Man, are you crazy?" I said. I got mad at the cat. "Man, you're out of your damn mind. I'm going to keep working for Huey, and Eldridge is, and all of us are." Eldridge was pissed off at Stokely too. He wouldn't say a word to him. Eldridge just looked at him like he was a goddamned fool.

Before Eldridge got out of jail in June, Stokely came out to California again. (This was in May 1968.) He brought a friend of his, George Sams, with him then. Later on, Stokely cut George Sams loose, because he suspected him of being an agent of some kind. Stokely told me again that I might as well forget about Huey, that they were going to put Huey in the gas chamber. He told me this crap a second time! He also said they were going to keep Eldridge in jail for the rest of his life.

I got mad again. I didn't hit him or anything, but I was pissed off at him. And man, when Eldridge's feet hit the ground, you talk about a dude being happy—I was really glad. Before Eldridge was released, we went to work, and started calling people up, telling them that Eldridge was coming out and that we needed some bail money and some securities to get him out right away. The bail was hanging at $50,000, but we got him out. "I wonder what the hell that stupid Stokely Carmichael is talking about now," I said to myself.

A lot of people were talking about how we couldn't get along, and how we really needed unity. Yeah, we need unity. I'm not denying that, but Stokely Carmichael said some weird things to us. If you can't stand up for the leaders and if one leader can't support another leader, then you'll never have an organization because the leaders will always be jiving. That's very important. That's why the Black Panther Party, first and foremost wants to free our leader, Huey P. Newton. The Minister of Defense is the man we want to free along with all the other political prisoners. This is what Stokely wasn't able to see. My analysis of it is that Stokely is an opportunist.

Chief of Staff David Hilliard, Kathleen, and a couple of other Panthers went up to get Eldridge. I stayed down at Charles Garry's office in San Francisco, waiting for them to bring brother Eldridge in. They drove in, and we had a big press conference. The pigs had shaved Eldridge's face, and had cut off all his hair, but the brother was in righteous good spirits, like most revolutionaries are who are involved in the struggle. Even before he knew he would be released, Eldridge was in good spirits. I had gone up to Vacaville to visit him along with Stokely and some other brothers a few weeks before he got out, and Eldridge was feeling real good. This was shortly before Judge Raymond Sherwin of Solano County released him on the grounds that he was being held solely for political reasons, that he was, in fact, a political prisoner.

That day, after we had visited Eldridge in jail, I noticed Stokely running around talking a whole lot of crazy stuff, about how he was going to organize the Party and discipline the Party and things like that. About half of the stuff he was talking about was cultural nationalism. It didn't relate. We needed brothers to help organize and educate more members, but Stokely still relied on that cultural nationalism, and cultural nationalism will not educate people. It makes racists out of them.

Cultural nationalism is trying to popularize dashikis, the natural, the wearing of sandals, and African dress. There's nothing wrong with having a natural. I have a natural and I like it, but power for the people doesn't grow out of the sleeve of a dashiki. That is something the cultural nationalists just don't understand.

Stokely's game was that every Negro was a potential black man. But what we were trying to show him was that every black man must be a revolutionary if he intends to change this decadent society. A lot of Africans know that, but Stokely didn't seem to be aware of it at all.

Well, they brought Eldridge down to San Francisco the day he was released. Kathleen, David, and the other Panthers brought him down to Garry's office where I was waiting. We had a big press conference there, and then went over to Eldridge and Kathleen's house on Pine Street. After a while, Eldridge got Kathleen and told me, "Look, Chairman, I've got to go."

"Right on, brother," I said. "I sure can understand it. It's just like when I got out of jail a few months ago."

"I'm going to hide out for a day or two," he said.

"Right on. I'll see you, man."

So Eldridge and Kathleen cut out. They went to stay with some friends, and that was beautiful.

OUR MINISTER OF INFORMATION

■ When the higher court overturned Judge Sherwin's decision to release Eldridge from the Vacaville State Prison Facility, and Eldridge was informed that he had to go back to prison, I guess he must have made up his mind right then that he just wasn't going back. He stated in speeches that he wasn't going back. He knew that they were planning to kill him there. I also think that he felt that we didn't want him to go to prison. And I didn't. I was always opposed to it.

Eldridge never would say anything about what he was doing. All of us were hoping we could work out something legally to keep Eldridge from going to prison. We were really hoping for the State Supreme Court decision to come down in favor of Eldridge. But in those days before he left, Eldridge was in another big dispute with the state and with Ronald Reagan concerning the lectures he had been hired to give on "Racism in America" at the University of California.

Between early September and November 27, 1968, Eldridge spoke on college campuses up and down the State of California, to 3,000, 5,000, and 10,000 people at various homes. There are eighteen state colleges and nine university campuses in California alone, and he was speaking not only in California but also on other campuses all over the country. He had students cussing out Ronald Reagan by the thousands. The students were opposed to Reagan because of the rotten, underhanded politics of the rich men who were directing him. Eldridge was telling it to the students and they were beginning to understand the truth about politics.

Eldridge said, "I've cussed my way all across this country and back again. These pigs are really scared of what I'm saying. They're sacred because the people are listening.

They've got to shut me up, and they know the only way they can do that is to put me in prison again, and kill me there. They think I'm going to go back to that goddam prison," he said, "but I'm not going."

"Eldridge," I said, "if you decide you're going to split— don't tell me. Just split. You've done what was needed. You've got us all cussing out these dogs, and they've been needing cussing out for a long time. But it's been an issue, you know. Brother Huey P. Newton has said that we shouldn't cuss."

"I know, man," Eldridge said. "I guess I should try to obey what the Minister of Defense says. But they got Huey isolated, he's been down almost a year. Somebody's gotta cuss these pigs out for doing that to Huey!"

I said, "Yeah, man, you're right. I feel like cussing them out, too."

Huey always said that the older people in the community wouldn't understand the cursing. He felt that that kind of language would cause the older people, especially the mothers, to misunderstand the real program of the Black Panther Party. So one day I asked my own mother about that.

"Mother," I said, "what do you think about Eldridge?"

She said, "Ooh, I think Eldridge is beautiful. He's one of the best persons around." She told me she voted for Eldridge for President. After voting for all those Democrats and Republicans for all these years, she voted for Eldridge Cleaver.

I said, "Mama, I love you. You're really seeing the revolution in your late days." Mama's about sixty.

"Well, I like everything that Eldridge is saying," she said. "And he's right. He's telling them the truth. But I wish he wouldn't cuss so much."

I said, "I hope that don't turn you off."

"Oh, no, it sure doesn't," she said. "I just always wanted y'all to do right, and I know you're doing right. I understand your getting mad sometimes at the way these"—she

hesitated for a moment, and then went on and said it—
"these racist pigs—the way they treat us and all our people."

Mama was always a Christian woman. She never talked
hate or cursed the oppressors. But she said, "I hate the way
they do. I just hate the way they murdered Bobby Hutton. I
just hate them for being ol' low-down nasty dogs. They been
treating us like this for so many years, just mauling over our
people, killing and stomping on our people. Eldridge
Cleaver is a very beautiful person and he's got a very
beautiful and wonderful wife. I respect him. I understand
why he cusses those low-down politicians out. Still, I do
wish he'd stop cussin' just a little bit."

I said, "But are you with us, Mama, in spite of it?"

She said, "Oh, yes, Bobby, I'm with y'all, I'll always be
with you, because I know you're doin' right. Way back
yonder, in the days when my mama was just mauled over,
and our peoples was owned like animals, I remember my
mother tellin' me that we shouldn't have to be over here in
this country treated like we was, and that somehow or other
we should be back over in Africa."

"Mama," I said, "you know we ain't ever going back to
Africa. We can't."

"Sure, I know that," she said. "I'm just telling you what
my mother felt. But also I know that you and Huey used to
talk about Africa and going back, and visiting over there
and so on, a long time ago. I guess all our people sort of
dream like that, even you young generation. But I know
y'all all are trying to do what you can, and I just hope
nobody hurts y'all. But if y'all can just do something for the
people—"

She sighed. "I'm old now," she said. "I wish I was young.
I'd get right out there with you and Huey and Kathleen and
Eldridge and all of you. But I'm old, and I just can't be in
the Panthers, can't do your young ways. But I sure voted for
Eldridge Cleaver."

Of course, being my mother, she was bound to take our

part and be on our side. But I hope that she was telling it the way a lot of older mothers felt. I hope they understand that when we cuss those politicians out, we're not cussing out *our* people. It's only against the power structure, and never shows disrespect of the people. We're honestly calling them what they are for messing over us. I hope the mothers understand what we feel against those who maintain this exploitation, this rotten capitalism and racism, the brutality, and all the political, economic, and social evils. I hope these older people know that we have to stand up for ourselves.

Some of them have said, "Well, you wouldn't be getting attacked if you didn't say 'pigs' and all," but we point out to them that our people have always been attacked and now we have to let the other people know what these racist pigs are. We have to redefine them for exactly what they are and stop letting them fool us. And mostly, I think, the older people do understand and *are* for us.

Well, Huey wanted the people to understand the real ten-point platform and program, so Eldridge, in his position as Minister of Information, was laying it on thick, but with a creativity and a sense of humor that was only Eldridge's.

I remember one evening Eldridge was due to speak on Channel 44, a television station in San Francisco, on some talk show. I had arrived at the station first, and they led me back to one of those rooms with mirrors on the wall, with stools and chairs to sit in and wait for the program to come on.

In came one of the guys who direct or produce that show. He said, "Look, tell Eldridge please, please do not do any cussing on the program. It's live."

"Well, I don't know," I told him. "You know how Eldridge is. He just gets so fed up with these politicians . . ."

When Eldridge arrived, I said, "Huey said he'd be watching this, so I don't think you ought to be cussing on the program. Besides," and I couldn't help laughing, "this ol' jive producer came by here, and he was really worried about you cussin' on the program. After all, it's live."

Then Eldridge jumped up and said, "What! What! They can't tell me what not to say! I'm gonna cuss all of them, every avaricious businessman, every pig, every last one of them who has ever committed brutality on black people. That's what I oughta do, Bobby." He went on, saying, "I gotta do it, I gotta do it," but actually he was kidding of course, putting them all uptight. He didn't say one cuss word on the program.

But one time Eldridge and David had just come back from a series of speaking engagements, across the country, and David told me, "Man, that Eldridge. You just wouldn't believe that cat. He was at a Catholic girls college, a place where they train girls to be nuns, and, Bobby, he had 5,000 girls singing, 'Fuck Ronald Reagan.' "

"I just don't believe that, David," I said. "He must have been blowing some heavy politics to get them to see it."

David said, "He was exposing the politicians for what they are, man. He was exposing them ninety miles an hour. He was talking about the pigs something terrible! The next thing I knew, right in the middle of the speech, Eldridge had 5,000 chicks out there singing: 'Fuck Ronald Reagan! Fuck Ronald Reagan! One, two, three, four: Fuck Ronald Reagan! Fuck Ronald Reagan! One, two, three, four: Fuck Ronald Reagan.' I've got a tape recording of it."

"David," I said, "let me hear it. I'll believe that tape when I hear it."

Eldridge was doing everything he could to expose the power structure. You could see signs all over that he wasn't going back. You could see by the way he was moving, and by the way he was talking. He was exposing Ronald Reagan. He'd go to other cities and expose other demagogic politicians, and he was doing it in a hurry. It was good that he did it. Eldridge knew that he had to do everything he had time to do, to expose this fascist power structure for what it really was.

Before Eldridge left, I think everybody contemplated it, trying to figure out what effect it would have on the Party if they sent Eldridge back to prison. Then when it was announced in the papers that Eldridge was gone, it made all of us more energetic, trying to move to get things organized. One of the principles that we really began to place forth was the one that brother Huey had run down about the oppressor. The oppressor has no rights that the oppressed people are bound to respect. Eldridge's action was a clear example of this. By not appearing, he was refusing to respect the oppressor's right to lock him up unjustly after he had already been bailed out and released from jail. He was being held as a political prisoner by the government of California, led by Mickey Mouse, fascist Ronald Reagan.

I think most of us had read *Soul On Ice* already. But I made it a thing that brothers should reread *Soul On Ice*, reread what Eldridge was running down. That book is very key and very clear when one looks at the massive brainwashing of America as a whole. We know about the brainwashing of black people, but this is not really separate from the brainwashing of the proletarian masses of America. I think that many times the cultural nationalists miss this point.

We want to unbrainwash our people by telling them the true history. One must tell the true history in terms of the class struggle, the small, minority ruling-class dominating and oppressing the massive, proletarian working-class. When I say working class, I mean those who are employed and unemployed, living below subsistence and at subsistence level.

This book, *Soul On Ice*, really shakes loose the misconceptions that exist. When you read that book, you'll see that, in the beginning, it was a brainwashed black man who was in jail. He had only the white ideals, the Western ideals, and the white woman. When he put the *Playboy* picture on the wall, he was saying that, psychologically and personally, he fell in love with that woman. Then this racist cop guard inside the prison rips the picture down. Eldridge tells the guard that he doesn't have any right to rip it down because everybody's got pin-ups. The guard tells Eldridge, "If you had put up a pin-up picture of a black girl, I wouldn't have said anything." And because of that, Eldridge's consciousness changed, and he began to become what he is. The first essay in the book is called, "On Becoming."

This is very significantly related to the other things that the book sets forth. When one gets to the chapter, "Primeval Mitosis," we see how all this is interlocked with the political sphere and the psychological makeup of the omnipotent administrator, the psychological makeup of the Nixons and Johnsons and Aliotos and Ronald Reagans—those who aspire to this peak of mind—and the black man, who is relegated to a low level. I think Eldridge unbrainwashed *everybody* in society with his book; black, white, blue, green, yellow, red, polka dot, regardless of ethnic differences, etc. Eldridge unbrainwashes anybody who really reads with an open mind.

In the revolutionary struggle today I say Eldridge brought history to the threshold, to the front of a libertion movement here in the midst of the most fascist operation on the face of the earth, right here in the belly of the whale, in the belly of the monster.

While Eldridge and I were in Carmel, something occurred that showed how Eldridge, digging on Huey, could make all the brainwashed past history relevant to the present-day situation.

Way back before they announced that Eldridge had to go back to prison, Eldridge had talked to me about writing a biography of Huey and the Party. Eldridge said, "Bobby, you knew Huey longer than anyone in the party. You and he founded the Party together, so you've got to give us all the information, everything about brother Huey and about

the Party, how things developed." Eldridge said that Huey
P. Newton followed Malcolm X like Jesus Christ followed
John the Baptist. That made a heck of a lot of sense to me.
So Eldridge got some tapes and a recorder and a typewriter,
and took me down to Carmel to a little cabin to work on the
book.

Now in front of the cabin there was a big swimming pool
with a lot of lawn around it, with fruit trees and stuff like
that. We came out of the cabin about ten o'clock one
morning. There was a green hose coming around the front
of the swimming pool. It went down to the far end of the
pool and wound up right under a tree, an apple tree. On the
other side of the swimming pool were some lawn chairs.
Bob Scheer and a young white girl were sitting in those
chairs. Now Eldridge and I had just been talking about how
brainwashed the society was and how history has messed up
the minds of the people. Just as we stepped outside, Scheer
said to the girl, "Hey, baby, go over to that apple tree and
get me one of those apples."

So she went over and picked this apple, and Eldridge and
I watched. She came back and gave the apple to Scheer.
Just as Scheer got ready to put it in his mouth, Eldridge
spoke. "Hey, man, you better watch it. You just sent her
over to the apple tree for apples."

Scheer bit into the apple. "What are you talking about?"
he said, holding it away from him and looking at it.
"There's nothing wrong with this apple."

Eldridge said, "No, it was a goof-up."

I said, "Eldridge, what are you talking about?"

Eldridge said, "History has got society messed up. Our
Minister of Defense is in prison, and history has messed up
society's mind with these puritanical notions."

So Scheer got up and walked around the pool toward us,
bringing the girl with him. He said, "I don't know what you
mean."

Then I looked at the green hose lying there like a big
snake, and I said, "I get it. He's talking about Scheer in the

Garden of Eden, and this girl going to the apple tree. You're in the Garden of Eden," I said to Scheer.

Eldridge said, "And you didn't defend it. You didn't defend the Land of Paradise."

Scheer's a white cat, and he's supposed to be a liberal. He still didn't know what Eldridge was talking about.

Eldridge said, "What you did is, you let the omnipotent administrator send down a pig angel. His name was Chief Gain or any chief of police in the country. You let him come down with a flaming sword. With a weapon, you let him drive you out of the Garden of Eden. And you didn't defend it, you and your woman."

This developed into a very creative moment, and being there with Eldridge, I said, "Yeah, that's right. You jived around, and the omnipotent administrator was wrong. He told you to replenish the earth, and just about the time you got ready to replenish the earth, he turns around and drives you from the Garden into the wilderness. He sent down an angel with a flaming sword." Symbolically, it isn't really an angel, you see, it's really a pig. "And you didn't defend it."

Eldridge said, "You let the pig drive you out into the wilderness."

I said, "Command the pigeon to fly, and then clip his wings. That's the policy of the omnipotent administrator."

"But if it had been Huey Newton in the middle of the Garden of Eden," said Eldridge, "and the pig angel came down after the omnipotent administrator had told Huey to go forth and exercise his constitutional rights and replenish the earth—if it had been Huey P. Newton and this pig had been swinging the flaming sword at him, Huey would have jumped back and said, 'No, I'm defending myself. If you swing that sword at me, I'm shooting back.' "

Symbolically, Robert Scheer was the liberal white who wouldn't defend the Garden of Eden, the Land of Paradise. We see that mankind was driven out of the Land of Paradise, to sweat by his brow from sun-up to sundown. Whereas if Huey P. Newton had been in the Garden of

Eden, he would have defended himself. He would have defended the land. He wouldn't have been driven out after he had been commanded to go replenish the earth. It was no reflection on Scheer, nothing that Scheer had done, as we weren't speaking of Scheer himself. We used Scheer in that situation as symbolic of the liberal who won't do anything and really wants to sit around and jive and talk, when the next thing you know, the vicious fascist system which calls itself God, and the omnipotent administrators at the top, will have done in the people, and taken away the Land of Paradise, and the right to live in happiness and peace on the face of the earth.

You have to defend the needed new system that's coming forth. Talking isn't enough. You have to fight for it, you have to work for it, if you intend to have it. If you do anything other than that, you'll just be oppressed.

That incident helped me to see the significance of *Soul On Ice,* and how people are brainwashed. Many people have heard me talk about the Superman notions. I try to make this relevant to an everyday situation by talking about the concepts of the comic books; the Donald Duck comic books, Mickey Mouse, Archie and Jughead etc. These put forth puritanical notions and symbols that are directly related to racism. I began to see that Superman was a punk, that Superman didn't relate to replenishing the earth, like Huey Newton and other real people do. Superman is really a superficial fantasy that relates to a steel man. Steel men can't relate to any reality because steel doesn't produce real human life and real human flesh. I talked about how Superman never related to Lois Lane, and that Tricky Dick Nixon and Lynchin' Baines Johnson and those types were the ones that were trying to play Superman, the almighty gods with their anti-tank weapons, and anti-anti-missiles, and hydrogen bombs and missiles that really destroy life. In essence, Superman is a phony and a fake. He never saves any black people in this country in any comic book stories. And this thirty-year-old figure and the other figures of Donald Duck, all should have beards on. They are older than the hills. They are phony and absurd.

The *fact* is that a man and a woman relate to each other, that through sexual relations they produce another real human being. Mickey Mouse and Donald Duck never tried to have sexual relations in the comic books with Daisy and Minnie Mouse. Archie and Jughead never tried to relate sexually to Betty and Veronica in the comic books. These thins are very important in terms of how people are brainwashed in society—two-and-a-half billion people on the face of this earth came here through the process of a man and a woman having sexual relations. The ominpotent administrators taboo these things. It's this kind of brainwashing that produced the kind of people who believe that sex is nasty, and talk about "illegitimate" children. A child, a human being, cannot be illegitimate. These things come to be understood clearly when you read Eldridge Cleaver's book.

Eldridge shows how homosexuality becomes rampant and is really part of the psychological makeup of the omnipotent administrators, to such an extent that they're cut off from the body. They use the concept of the mind being all superior and forget about the body. After reading *Soul On Ice,* I used to say often in speeches that you have to use both the mind *and* the body, both together. Eldridge points out how the mind has got to work with the body and how the black man was stripped of his mind and left with his body only, and the omnipotent administrator stripped himself of his body and recognizes the mind only. Eldridge shows how homosexuality is an offset and how this identifies the existence of a class system. The class system is highly related to a woman and a man trying to relate to each other more fully and more totally, and oppressive social obstacles, political and economic, affect this totally.

It is very necessary for the masses to understand *Soul On Ice,* so they can recognize and pinpoint the oppressive ad-

ministrations of the government here, and realize that this
system has to be changed to a more progressive system that
serves all the people. The Party, as a whole, is involved in
this, and many millions of people are becoming more
aware. The book has sold way over a million copies and is
still selling at a fantastic rate.

We are very close to brother Eldridge. We know that he
and Kathleen were forcibly separated from us. It's not a
thing of him leaving us. We understand that oppression has
put Eldridge where he is now. We know that the power
structure wants to kill him. They don't want him back here.
Eldridge was and is one of the key brothers in the Black
Panther Party. Of all the brothers on the Central Committee, Eldridge was the key brother.

Before Eldridge left, he did a magnificent revolutionary
job as Minister of Information, educating the masses of
America, hipping black people to the need to work together
in some unity, and showing the white people that the omnipotent power structure and administrators are the enemies
of all the people. I think that after he left, it made even more
people become Black Panther Party members. Thousands
of black people really began to check him out, much more
closely than they had checked him out before.

Some of the Party members had been very superficially
relating to Eldridge, not really understanding him. But Eldridge's objective was to try and get people to be more
concrete. He wanted those black brothers and sisters
who ran off to the side and really don't work closely with
the people in the community, to become part and parcel
with the people in the community, and he wanted to move
the liberal whites, too, to be revolutionaries.

BUNCHY CARTER AND BOBBY HUTTON

■ Bobby Hutton was the first member of our Party murdered by the police, and Fred Hampton and Mark Clark were among the latest. Between those murders there was a long line of black brothers gunned down by racist cops and black racist, cultural nationalists working with the power structure against the revolutionary program of the Black Panther Party.

Bobby Hutton loved Bunchy Carter. Bobby Hutton used to develop alter ego relationships with different Party leaders—Huey, Eldridge, myself, and Bunchy. His latest, at the time he was killed, was imitating Alprentice "Bunchy" Carter. He tried to become more politically educated like Bunchy was and he really dug brother Bunchy, because Bunchy had been in prison. It wasn't a boasting, kind of absurd, "I did this much time," and "I did that much time," thing that Bobby related to. Bobby related to Bunchy because Bunchy was the brother who had come from prison and was back in the community, working to serve the people.

Bunchy also had an air about him that was stylish in the manner and the environment of the black community that Little Bobby readily communicated with. This manner is in the poetry that Bunchy would write and recite, and also in the sharp way that Bunchy dressed—the clothes of the people. We all have some sharp clothes, but Bunchy was always sharp—clean, with a sharp suit, pimp socks, and shined knobs.* Little Bobby would see Bunchy with a big natural that was kept very neat, a big moustache, a sharp suit, and some clean clothes on, and he really dug the way Bunchy looked.

* Knobs are up-to-date, stylish shoes, with well-shined toes. Pimp socks are men's socks you can almost see through. They are usually nylon.

At the same time, Bunchy wasn't a selfish person. Deep down inside he really loved his people and he loved them so much that when he saw them doing something wrong, he would cuss the brothers out to try to get them to understand the need to survive, to unify, to defend ourselves, and to be revolutionaries and work in the community to serve the people.

This is the thing that surprised Bobby. Little Bobby was only sixteen years old, and he wanted to be sharp. Living in poverty and seeing brother Bunchy somehow stay sharp, and at the same time be a service to his community, kind of showed Bobby that he didn't have to get out of the Party. He didn't have to say, "Well, I'm gonna give up the Party just to get me some sharp clothes," as some brothers would, out of selfishness. Bunchy had arranged it so that on his parole he was receiving a fair sum of money working at a poverty program as some kind of assistant director. That's how he kept himself sharp.

When one would first see Bunchy, one might think that Bunchy was a pimp or some kind of hustler off the block, but he wasn't. Not that he didn't know the pimps and hustlers; Bunchy was very well respected and well known throughout Watts and the black community in Los Angeles by many, many people. When he was murdered, the Party had to go down and try to talk to some of the brothers, because there were some five or six hundred brothers throughout Watts that put shotguns in their cars and were looking for anything that looked like a member of Ron Karenga's US organization that had murdered him. We tried to tell the brothers that we didn't want a jive war in the black community among black people, but at the same time we wanted to see to it that those cats who did the killing were prosecuted. We felt that if the power structure didn't prosecute them, or if they used some kind of trick to let them go after prosecution, in the long run this would prove to the people that the US organization, black racism, and cultural nationalism were ultimately the tools of the power structure, and that they stagnate the people's revolutionary struggle for needed change in the community.

One of the cleanest things about Bunchy was his deep seriousness and honesty about the need for revolutionary change. When Eldridge, I, or someone from Central Headquarters would give him an order to stop doing something, he would stop. If he thought he was right, he would come and sit down and argue with us, not in an antagonistic manner but in a manner that showed that he wanted us to show him where he was wrong, because he still felt that it should be done. But he would stop if ordered to. Bunchy also respected organization, which is another thing that Little Bobby picked up from him.

Alprentice "Bunchy" Carter was killed because a group of blacks—black racists and cultural nationalists from Ron Karenga's US organization—became the enemies of the people and, in essence, sided with the capitalist power structure. These pig, black racists really work with the power structure against their own people, and do it out of a psychological need to hate white people just because of the color of their skin.

Bunchy had been working in Los Angeles organizing the Black Panther Party throughout the city. In January of 1968, Bunchy had some arguments and small conflicts with the US organization. Bunchy was concerned about the fact that the US organization had been running around intimidating, threatening, and beating up a number of the people in the community, in the B.S.U. (Black Student Union), and other small factionalized black organizations. Bunchy and the Black Panther Party were not about to be intimidated by anybody. These other small groups asked Bunchy to stop Ron Karenga, and take over the Black Congress of Organizations that had been formed there and that Ron Karenga was in control of.

Bunchy called up and told us that he was going to go and corner Karenga and his boys and tell them they better stop their intimidation of those people. We told Bunchy to forget

Ron Karenga because most organizations like his are boot-licking organizations, not representative of the community, and that the people will choose the organization that serves them most. I told him on the phone, "What you should do is get out in the community, and forget Ron Karenga and the Black Congress too, and go and set up those community offices. You should have five, six, or seven offices set up down there, in all the different black community areas throughout Los Angeles. Work from there at serving the people and move to implement the Party's ten-point plat-form and program, and politically educate the masses of the people. That's what has to be done. Forget Ron Karenga."

Bunchy followed orders. He flew up on a plane a week later and wanted to argue his point, but Eldridge and I told him to forget Karenga and US. Bunchy felt that Karenga was going to cause some grave danger to the black commu-nity. Our argument was that if he attacked the black com-munity, the black community would attack him and remove him.

Some months after that John Huggins was made Deputy Minister of Information of the Southern California chapter of the Party, to replace this jackanape Earl Anthony who wasn't relating to the duties of that area of work. John and Bunchy worked very closely to pull the Party together in Los Angeles. The incident that led to their murder was part of this work.

The Black Student Union at UCLA had been having problems with US for a long time. A $20,000-a-year job opened up, director of some kind of community and student program, and the US niggers wanted the job and wanted their puppet placed in control. The B.S.U. did not want them to control the program, and since the Black Panther Party had grown to be an integral part of the black commu-nity in Los Angeles, the Black Student Union asked Bunchy and John to come up to a meeting about it on the UCLA campus. The B.S.U. asked them what they thought about

Karenga's attempts to control their group, and Bunchy and John just spoke for about five minutes. All they said at that meeting was that the students had a right to control their own destiny, and "Power to the Students!" Then they left. Two days later, on Friday, another meeting was called. John and Bunchy repeated the same five minute "Power to the Students" rap. That was the day they were killed, murdered right there in the meeting room by those racist, murderous pigs from US.

Of course Ron Karenga has no political power base with his cultural nationalism and black racism in Los Angeles. He runs around, and has a little jive office stuck up somewhere, but everybody is aware of his game and his capitalistic set of little jive businesses, mainly service stations. Those businesses are not cooperatives; they're not there to serve the people. From his past record and his meeting behind the scenes with the Rockefellers,* we know that he got those little jive businesses as a handout, to trick the community on the concept of blackness and black is beautiful. Ron Karenga had no intention before and has no intention now of working in opposition to the power structure to change the system for the needs of black America.

All the murders of Party members, Bunchy, Little Bobby, John Huggins, Fred Hampton, Mark Clark, Tommy Lewis, and the brothers who were gunned down prior to Bunchy, plus a host of other brothers who were shot up and killed by cops and racist cultural nationalists across the country, have not destroyed the Party. The arrests of our members have not destroyed the Party. We pay a tribute to these dead brothers of ours, and every Black Panther Party member and the people in the community honor them. We will fight against the racist pigs and the black racists who work together to try to destroy the Party. .

* An article from the *Wall Street Journal* on the meeting between Karenga and the Rockefellers can be found in *The Black Panther* February 2, 1969.—Ed.

CHARLES R. GARRY: THE LENIN
OF THE COURTROOM

■ If the power structure tried to stop Charles Garry from going into the courtroom and defending people's basic human and legal rights, and stopped defendants from seeing their lawyers and having their constitutional rights, Charles Garry couldn't be stopped at all. He's the type of man who would go down to the pawnshop and buy himself a gun to defend his home and himself, because he's got enough insight to know that this system is corrupt. I even heard him say that he doesn't ever want to be a judge, not with the way this system is going. He never would want to be a commissioner or a politician.

The way he explains it, the institutions are being used by big money, and rich businessmen who control them, and he doesn't want to be a puppet for any of them. He said that he made up his mind a long time ago about whether he was going to do his fighting in the streets, or go ahead and work for the people and try to do it in the courtroom. We always respect the fact that he made that decision and we're glad he did, because the people need somebody like Charles R. Garry, who is able to come forth and stand up for the people when he sees things going wrong, and to defend the underdog. That is something that we know that Charles Garry has dedicated his life to. I have never seen a person like that, even in the Black Panther Party.

Charles doesn't interfere in our politics. Sometimes he can almost see us making a mistake on some specific thing or situation, but if we disagree with him, he doesn't interfere in our politics. He doesn't try to run them or anything like that. Sometimes we found that our political relationships with some organization or group were slightly off-key and didn't work out. Often it would be something that Charles had run down and told us we were making a mistake about.

It's good to have a person around like that who will tell you you are making a mistake and if you don't agree with him, he's willing to let you learn, and still be a beautiful friend and comrade who's dedicated to defending you and who knows you're right.

Just to go to Charles Garry's house! His wife is a very loving and very beautiful person. You're very welcome there. You're a human being. A lot of times we would go over to their house and if we wanted a beer, we got a beer. If we wanted something to eat, it seemed like it was a real pleasure for Mrs. Garry to be able to fix us some food. A lot of times we would be rundown. We wouldn't have eaten. Charles knew it, and I suppose he told his wife quite often that we were running ourselves to death. Sometimes when we got over to their house, we'd be so rundown and hungry that she could see it, and she'd start preparing food, putting things on the table, and telling us to help ourselves. This is the relationship we developed with Charles Garry and Mrs. Garry. It is a very human relationship and one we cherish very much.

Charles is a cat who doesn't back up from things. Back in the days when he was defending the unions who were striking or moving forth for better wages and better conditions, a lot of police pressure and big-time political pressure was put on many of the unions and the cats who were moving for a higher standard of living. Charles defended them to the end. We heard stories about Charles getting caught out at night by himself two or three times, and cops jumping out of their cars, and snatching Garry out of his car, and brutally beating him. A man who took the time to be a lawyer to defend the people, realizes and understands the pressures that come from the corrupt government when you try to stand on the side of the people. By finding these things out I began to understand why Charles never wanted to be a part of the corrupt governmental system.

Charles comes from poor, oppressed people. He's of Armenian descent, from people who were destroyed by being scattered throughout Europe and around the world, when Hitler went forth to massacre and slaughter them during his regime. We don't know every detail of Charles' life, but we can see that he is a man who is dedicated to the survival and the existence of the right to self-determination of human beings. We need a lot more history on Charles R. Garry so we can understand what motivates a man to be such a defender of the people's human rights.

One time when we were in Judge Lionel Wilson's court in Alameda County, Charles was defending my wife and me on charges that came when cops illegally entered our house. When Charles cross-examined this Berkeley cop who was trying to show that he had reasonable cause to come in and search our house and arrest us, Charles caught him in a whole lot of lies. Charles knows so much law, it comes off the top of his head. He showed that the pig didn't have any reasonable cause because he got him to admit that our house was quiet, that there were no disturbances at our house that night, and it was way over an hour before they came back to arrest me. Artie and I sat there all day in court and didn't say a word. We watched Charles handle it and listened to all the proceedings. Artie felt from the way Charles handled that, the way that he would get up at certain points, and from his style of cross-examining, she felt that "Charles was better than Perry Mason." She felt this even before the judge decided that the police had no reasonable cause to be searching our house. The evidence was squashed and the judge said we should be cut loose and acquitted on the charge.

Artie really had a lot of confidence in Garry because Charles sometimes helped us out with family problems. Often I would be very busy, jumping on planes, going to New York, flying back to L.A. the next day, or going away for three or four days around the country speaking at colleges and rallies. A lot of times my wife would get very disgusted, and I tried to get her to work more with the Party. She had a tendency to want to look at TV and take care of the house. I was trying to show her she has to be a revolutionary politician, too, even though we have a little boy. She would become very disturbed and make it known that she was very disturbed and didn't like it. She would go and talk to Charles, and Charles would try to get her to understand why I had to be away so much. At the same time Charles would sit down and tell me that I was going to have to take some time off and be at home as much as I could, because my wife was frequently upset because I was so busy with the Party.

Charles is not the kind of lawyer who isn't one and one with his clients. During Huey's trial, he'd get out and investigate the situation himself. He would talk to people and do a lot of personal investigation. When Bobby Hutton was murdered, during the April 6 shoot-out in which the cops tried to ambush the Panther brothers, Charles was down there on the spot. When our house was raided, he was there investigating the house—how they surrounded it, the size of the apartment, etc. He's always getting into things and digging down in the guts of a case. That's the kind of cat he is. If he couldn't get there, he'd have somebody else do it. Sometimes he'd even get together with Chief of Staff David Hilliard and have David do some investigation work in and around different charges leveled against us, or he'd get some of the brothers to look for evidence.

When he leaves the courtroom, Charles is always ready to sit down and talk to us at his office, if he has time. He doesn't have much time these days, but when he has time he is always ready to be one and one with us.

Charles is the chief counsel of the Black Panther Party. When I say he is one and one with us, it's based on some kind of practice, it's not just on words or trying to sell somebody something. When there's a brother in jail, he makes it a point to get up to see him and talk to him and interview him. He doesn't let brothers and sisters sit in jail without having some contact with them. He's gotten the other lawyers on Panther cases to see that they have to be one and one with their clients in the Black Panther Party. He lets the other lawyers who function with and work with the Party know that this is the way you have to function with a political organization like ours. He lets the other lawyers know that they have to be one and one with us and work right along with their clients, visit their clients, see their clients, interview their clients, and know their clients.

When we hired Charles to defend Huey, Charles went into Black History. He took time to study and read up on Black History and know it. He met Huey P. Newton and he expressed to me a number of times how beautiful Huey was, and how he was glad to know that Huey had the political perspective and the insight and human understanding that he had. He said meeting Huey inspired him to really want to know black America better. From time to time I would drop over to his office, books and other material on W.E.B. DuBois, Nat Turner, the history of black America, Marcus Garvey, Malcolm X, and other things. Charles really studied and learned. He didn't only study books—he studied and learned in relating to us.

The man is so dedicated to defending us. He sees that we're being persecuted. He knows that it's repression. He knows that the underdog is being denied his human rights to live and survive. When he walks into the courtroom, he doesn't have a gun. He doesn't have a firearm or anything like that, but he's got something that is just as effective. Huey used to say that a newspaper could be sharpened like a double-edged sword. I think that the legal defense that is being placed forth by Charles R. Garry for us is just as effective as a gun to defend ourselves from unjust attack. You see that man work in a courtroom, and all of a sudden the procedure of things is clear in your mind. When you see a D.A. move and use racist tactics or when you see a judge literally turn his head and deny your rights and let racist operations and maneuvers go on in the courtroom, Charles Garry is setting forth law that seems clear to you, so clear you could recite it yourself. You're not saying anything, but you feel you want to call that judge or D.A. who's doing you wrong, a racist. And all of a sudden Charles R. Garry has got the human gall to let the judge know that he's a racist right to his face. It makes you feel good to know that that man is standing up and defending you. In the context of law and legality, he can place forth a man's feelings and a man's desires, a man's innocence, a man's right to survive and live as a human being. He places forth the people's rights. This is what's beautiful about Charles.

In studying Lenin's works, his writings and materials, one learns a lot about Lenin's ability to use language to set forth a correct philosophy of life as a human being on the face of this earth, and also about the tactics for achieving a correspondent world through revolutionary socialism. We turn it right back around and we look at Charles Garry and say that this man is the Lenin of the courtroom.

At first Charles was Huey's lawyer, and then he became my lawyer. As more attacks and more arrests came down, we got Charles on all the cases. Pretty soon he was the lawyer for the entire Panther party. We've seen Garry's whole firm—Bernard Dreyfus, Al Brotsky, Frank McTernan, Fay Stender, Jim Herndon, and the other lawyers who are associated with them working on Panther cases. They're all very good lawyers. I went over there one day and they were all working on my case, Huey's case, the April 6 shoot-out, all those brothers' cases, and Eldridge's case. We were filing suit against the city of Oakland and they had a lot of court appearances to make. The whole office was involved in our cases. They began to handle other legal matters for us, helping us to get our income tax out, and other things like that. That office was humming. We used to go over there off and on. The cats were working ten hours a day, and we hadn't had the chance to raise their fees for three or four months at times! But they stuck with us.

That's the thing we respect about Charles Garry, about that firm. Those people, the secretaries and everybody, took time to know us. Fay Stender did a lot of beautiful, heavy legal work for us on Huey P. Newton's appeal brief to the higher courts. The next thing we knew, Charles couldn't handle all the cases. Now, McTernon handles cases, other lawyers across the country, like William Kunstler, Francis Andrew, Gerald Lefcourt, Sanford Katz, Bill Crain, Arthur Kinoy, and a number of others are also handling our cases. I hope those lawyers see Charles setting an an example to defense lawyers, using the legal and proper tactics of the courtroom to bring out the true philosophy and ideology of the Party, and of any other progressive, revolutionary, and liberal people fighting for human rights and survival in a country that's growing more fascist every day.

Charles is always ready to defend us. We've got communication with him on a human level. He's even lost a couple of cases, when we actually saw overt racist tactics used in the courtroom. But we didn't jump up and say, "Oh, he loses cases." The human relationships you have with a person are the best thing, and we know that brother Charles Garry will sit up and fight. He is where it's at. When the black lawyers tried to attack Charles just because he was white, we defended him. Charles kept Huey out of the gas chamber. We rightfully give him the credit. Charles turns around and gives it to us for organizing community and political support. But we give it right back to him.

The only time that Charles was with me in Chicago was when I was arraigned and charged in federal court in April of 1969 in the Chicago conspiracy case. When we got there, the hallways and corridors of the Federal Build-

ing were packed with about a thousand people, predominately black people. We finally made our way through the
crowd to the courtroom, but there were a lot of federal pigs
at the door who said everybody had to be searched.

"I don't have to be searched," Charles Garry said. "I'm
one of the lawyers here."

"It doesn't make any difference," the pig said. "You get
searched. Judge Hoffman said everybody gets searched."

"You're not searching me," Charles said. "You're not
going to destroy my integrity in court. I don't have any guns
on me. You're the one who has the guns on you. You're not
searching me."

"Well, you can't come in the courtroom," the pig said.

"We're coming in," Charles told him. "If I don't come in
there's not going to be an arraignment. You're not searching me."

I was on the other side of the marshal, inside the courtroom. A couple of them were searching me, and I said,
"Right on, Charles!" Charles got all the other lawyers together outside and he said, "We're not coming in!"

I was sitting in there and Jerry Rubin came in and they
pat-searched him. One of the other defendants came in
behind Jerry. I think it was John Froines. While they were
pat-searching Froines, Jerry Rubin started pat-searching
him too. The marshal was patting down one leg and Jerry
Rubin started pat-searching the other one. "Oh, he's all
right, let him go," Jerry said.

"What are you guys doing?" I asked.

"These guys are pat-searching people," Jerry said. "Here,
let me search you," he said, and walked toward the marshal, pat-searched him a little bit, then walked away. I
cracked up.

"It looks like we're not going to have an arraignment
today," I told Jerry, "because if I know Charles he isn't
going to let them be running through his briefcase and
searching him. He's already told them he won't let them
destroy his integrity as a lawyer and an officer of the court."

All eight defendants were sitting there. We looked up, and guess who was coming into the courtroom from the rear door where the judge comes through? Charles R. Garry and all the lawyers!

"Hey, Charles, did they search you?" I asked him.

"Heck, no, they're not going to search me or anybody. None of these lawyers were searched." Then he walked around and said, "The judge didn't like it because we weren't going to come in, so he decided to let us come through the back way."

That was one of those things with him. Lawyers are officers of the court, and you're not supposed to treat them like they're not. That's what he's stuck on, those ethics. Because they have the human integrity to argue for justice, Judge Hoffman treated the defense lawyers like criminals, throughout the trial.

You have to imagine Charles Garry in a courtroom. He's a tough lawyer, but he's not tough in the sense that you see the D.A.'s trying to act tough. The D.A.'s also try to act smooth and sneak and slide and pull little legal tricks. But Garry's a tough lawyer and he doesn't let those little jive, sneaky tricks on the part of the D.A. slide by. I think Shultz and Foran would have folded up in Chicago under Garry. And Judge Hoffman wouldn't have insulted Garry consistently, as he did Kunstler and Weinglass. Hoffman later sentenced them to years in jail for their real human integrity.

Garry's got so much law on the top of his head that in the courtroom he comes out fighting. There's no bell rung, but there's a gavel struck. Somebody hollers, "Order in the courtroom," or "All rise, this court is now in session pursuant to adjournment." Well, Charles is there, he's agile all day long. He's always moving. From the way he acts you'd never know that Charles is sixty years old. When he's sitting there and he jumps up to expose a sneaky trick that a D.A. might pull, they have to watch out, because Charles is coming off with so much law, and it's going to be so explicit, short, to the point, and clear. He's telling the judge that such low-life courtroom tactics shouldn't even be allowed, or words to this effect. This is where Charles is, and if you know Charles, you know he believes in what he's defending. He knows that he's defending something that's right, and he's defending someone who's right.

He's really there to defend the trumped-up cases, at least those that we've been in, where you know that railroad operations are going on. He's ready to bring the facts out on matters where you just don't expect it. If you sit up in the courtroom and watch Charles work, he'll come out with certain things in defense of his defendants that you just don't expect. He doesn't take shit from anybody. He doesn't take crap from judges, D.A.'s, cops, sheriffs, bailiffs. They don't mess over Charles, because Charles knows the law and he knows that he's defending it right. Some lawyers will let judges and D.A.'s get away with a lot of crap but Charles doesn't allow this. He won't let them get away with a lot of junk. If there's a judge who respects law and real justice—I don't mean railroading and I don't mean judges who only *say* they respect justice—but if there's a judge who respects justice, Charles respects him. If there's a D.A. who believes he's right, Charles doesn't run over the man. He's able to say, Good evening, Good morning, Hello, and How are you doing? He's that type of person. He never forgets that there are many people who can be wrong but they are still human beings and he will treat them in that manner. But he won't let any bigots, racists, or fascists, whether they be sheriffs, cops, judges, or D.A.'s run over him, and he won't let them run over his clients.

There have been cases where Charles has caught judges or D.A.'s trying to pull slick tricks and has exposed them. He has brought the stuff out in courtrooms in some of the Panther cases. I've also seen Charles take a cop's testimony apart on the stand. I've seen him make three cops who think they're telling the same story tell three completely different stories so that it sounds as if they happened in three differ-

ent places. This is just a way of saying that Charles is
something else when it comes to a lying cop on the witness
stand. Especially when he catches a cop masquerading as a
victim of an unprovoked attack, or when he catches a cop
who has violated a defendant's constitutional rights. When
Charles finds them masquerading like that, he can really eat
them up. He takes cops' testimony apart. That's one of the
beautiful things that Charles is good at—catching one of
those pigs on the stand, lying.

Besides being our lawyer, our chief defense counsel,
Charles Garry is also an honorary San Francisco police
officer. He has a special police department badge. Dr.
Washington Garner, a black doctor who knew Charles very
well, was appointed to the Police Commission in San Francisco several years ago. Doctor Garner made Charles an
honorary police officer and gave him a gold badge. It hit all
the papers in the Bay Area. That upset cops all over California, the bigots and the racists, because at that time
Charles was right in the middle of Huey P. Newton's trial.
We heard wild, crazy, upsetting racist remarks and stories.
We read them in the newspapers as far south as Los Angeles. They were really mad. But Charles kept his honorary
policeman's badge. He began to receive a lot of threatening
letters right after that and we suspect most of those letters
came from racist bigots who are on the police force. Charles
started to give the honorary policeman's badge back, but
when the bigots, racists, and fools started to scream,
Charles decided to keep it.

When he was defending Warren Wells, who was involved
in the April 6 shoot-out, Charles took his gold honorary
policeman's badge out, during a recess, and started waving
it all around. Warren figured it wasn't a real badge and was
frantically trying to whisper to Garry, "Charles, Charles,
you better put that away, because they're going to arrest
you. They'll bust you, man. You can't impersonate a pig—
especially nowadays." You can imagine Warren Wells'

mind going through all kinds of changes, with Charles Garry being the chief counsel for all the Panthers and the head Panther lawyer. You can imagine Warren's mind going twenty-one ways, thinking that if one of those deputies saw Charles with the badge, his own lawyer was going to get thrown in jail. Warren got real excited when Charles was playing around with a few of the people in the court corridor during the recess, holding his badge up and saying, "See, I'm a pig, too. I'm a pig, too."

Charles didn't want to upset Warren, and Warren couldn't call Charles a pig at all. No one could ever do that, because Charles R. Garry is a great revolutionary lawyer, a brother, and, to our way of thinking, the Lenin of the courtroom.

CHICAGO: KIDNAPPED, CHAINED, TRIED, AND GAGGED

KIDNAPPED

■ On the evening of August 19, 1969, we were returning from the wedding of Ray "Masai" Hewitt, our Minister of Education, and Shirley Needley, one of the sisters in the Party. The wedding had been held at the Berkeley Free Church, which is about half a mile from National Headquarters. After the ceremony was over, we all piled into Eldridge's car, the one with the telephone in it, and headed back toward the office.* We were about three blocks from the office when a car sped up from our left, and swerved in front of us and stopped at the light. The people in the car all seemed to be looking at us through the rear-view mirror.

"Those cats look like . . ." Masai was saying.

"Pigs!" June Hilliard finished the sentence for him. June was driving. I looked to the right and saw a Volkswagen blocking the entrance to the service station at the corner. Two other cars came up on our rear. "There's pigs all around us, in unmarked cars," June said. All of a sudden the doors of those cars opened, and agents and policemen began to flood out into the street from all directions. They

* Eldridge had told Kathleen to make all the payments on the car, turn it over to the Party, and to join him in Algeria. When Eldridge had the car, a Plymouth Fury, it had been gold, but we had it painted blue.

were running toward our car yelling, "Get out of the car! Get out of the car!" They were holding .38 revolvers, .357 Magnums, and shotguns on us. There were at least fifteen cops surrounding us. "If they're going to shoot, they might as well start shooting, because we're just dead," I thought. They were still screaming, "Get out! Get out!" Then I thought they were just going to search the car for weapons, and thought it was good we didn't have any, if they weren't going to shoot us after all.

June had gotten out of the car, but the car began to roll, because the emergency brake wasn't on. Masai got out of the car also and I hollered to June to pull up the emergency brake. The door on the side where Shirley was, was snatched open and a cop pointed a gun in and said, "Get out! This is the FBI. Out of the car! Out of the car!"

"Well, they're going to harass us and arrest us, and that's what it's all about," I said to myself.

When June had gotten out of the car, he had been pushed around, away from the door. One of the agents reached in and grabbed the emergency brake. I watched him as he snatched it up. Then he pointed a gun at me and said, "All right, Seale, get out!" I pulled the lock latch off, opened the door, and stepped out, with my hands hanging down at my sides, palms open, looking at him, cursing him with everything I could think of, because at that point all I could see and think of was a form of general harassment. Readily, someone said, "Hands over your head," and "Turn around." They grabbed my shoulder, spun me around, and pushed me toward the car. They began to pat-search me and one cop snatched my right arm and pulled it back and put a handcuff on it. Another snatched my left arm and pulled it back from across the trunk of the car and twisted the back of my hands toward my back and said, "Let's go. Let's get out of here. Let's get out of here." They had guns in their hands and they were pushing me around. They didn't show me any identification. There must have been fifteen, twenty more police and plainclothesmen there. They all had guns. Some were even dressed in blue jeans, T-shirts, and short sleeve shirts. I didn't see any uniforms.

I was rushed into a car and stuck in the back seat, an agent on each side of me. Three of them got in front with shotguns and they drove toward San Francisco. One agent said, "I'm informing you of your rights." He told me everything, except that I had a right to contact my lawyer. They asked me if I had anything to say. I didn't answer. They were talking to each other. They were giggling with each other saying, "This was so easy." In my estimation they were getting some kind of erotic sensation. They got on their radio and said, "All Berkeley Police Units and other units surrounding the Berkeley house (I assume they were referring to the house where I live) can leave. We have suspect in custody."

I was brought to the San Francisco City Jail and booked. Prior to the booking and after I took everything out of my pockets, the FBI took my little phone book away from me. That was my property. They didn't give it back to me at all. I don't know where it is now. I looked around at them and one of the FBI pigs said, "Now I've informed you of all your rights."

"You haven't informed me of all my rights!" I said.

"Yes, I did," he said, "I did it in the car."

"No, you didn't. You're a liar, and you know it. You haven't informed me of all my rights." I noticed another pig standing there. I'd seen his face before, a number of times at press conferences and speaking engagements. I know his face very well, because one time at a press conference I walked up to him and asked him if he was a government agent. "No," he had said, "I don't have anything to do with the government. I'm just a newsman. Can I come to this press conference?"

"Sure you can," I said. "I just wanted to expose you if you were an agent so that the rest of the newsmen can let people know that there are agents and provocateurs working for the government all around us, who want to take things out of context and tell lies." Well, he was one of those cats.

From everything I gathered, he must've been an FBI agent because he was there at the jail when they dropped me off. "Haven't I seen you somewhere before?" I asked him.

He looked at me and just grinned. He really thought he was Superman. You can just look at a cat and see how he's psychologically goofed up with Superman notions, so brainwashed that he thinks he's defending the so-called "free world." There is no "free world." How in the world can America be free when somewhere between forty and fifty million poor, oppressed people are living at subsistence and below?

The dude was grinning and he said, "Yes, you might have seen me before."

"I've seen you at a couple of press conferences I've had," I told him, "and you got exposed by some of the legitimate members of the press. That's where I've seen you before— and then you denied that you were an agent for the FBI or that you were a member of any racist organization."

"Well, Bob, that's how it goes," he said, a shitty grin on his face. I guess he thought he was James Bond or some great white hunter.

They tried to get me to sign a statement. "No, I'm not signing it," I said. Then they tried to get me to sign something else. I don't know whether it was an attempt to get me to sign some stupid crap about waiving extradition rights or what it was. "I'm not signing anything," I told them. "I don't have to sign anything."

They took my fingerprints and a mug shot, and told me to go down the hall, and they would give me a cell. I walked down there and spoke to a black cop who said he was a member of the Officers for Justice. He told me to sit down, and I sat down in a little office there. He offered me a cup of coffee and I drank it. I was rather tired and wanted to go to sleep. I knew that I'd have to wait overnight before getting bailed out, so he gave me some blankets, put me in a cell, and I fell off to sleep.

The first indication I had that I was being railroaded on some trumped-up charges in connection with that Connecticut frame-up—what I call a criminal agent, Mission Impossible (Mission Imperialism—domestic) plot to try and destroy the Black Panther Party—was after I'd been handcuffed on Shattuck Avenue in Berkeley. They were walking me toward a car. They said, "You're under arrest for conspiracy to commit murder, and conspiracy to kidnap and murder, in connection with Connecticut."

"What are these damned fools doing now?" I thought right off. "Now these cats are out of their minds."

"And for unlawful flight to avoid prosecution," as they put it.

I lay on my bunk in jail, and I said to myself, "These damned fools! Trying to railroad me. They're trying to railroad everybody they can out of the Party. They're trying to stop the Party from functioning. We knew it was coming, but now they're gonna try and trump up something else, and of course on me. I expect to be attacked by the pigs and the government, because we know that where we're going is correct and will expose the power structure for its continued oppression of the people."

Charles Garry came in about an hour later and they woke me up. I had made a call to the Black Panther Party headquarters before I went down to the cell and told them that I was in the San Francisco City Jail, so they'd know where to send Charles. Charles Garry came in and we started smiling at each other because we knew that the racist cops had really gone overboard again in their attempts to try and destroy the Party and the Party leadership.

The next day I was taken over to the federal building. It

was the day after the arrest. McTernan, Garry's partner, came in to see me and I said, "We'll have to post the bail, won't we?"

"Yes," he said.

"Well, let's just get a bail," I said. "We'll go from there." They really didn't have a warrant yet. The next day they still didn't have a warrant. I appeared in the federal court in front of a U.S. commissioner, and McTernan argued that bail of $25,000 was too high and that I hadn't fled anywhere to avoid prosecution.

McTernan said that I was watched twenty-four hours a day, that I'd been in the public eye continually, making speaking engagements, on TV in Los Angeles, speaking to 4,000 people at the National Committee to Combat Fascism convention, holding press conferences everywhere, even in that very building—so what did the government mean by claiming that I was fleeing to avoid prosecution.

The commissioner said he had no jurisdiction over that and could only set the bail, which he said would be $25,000. So I went back to the cell in the federal building.

I could see a whole crowd of San Francisco policemen and also what looked like plainsclothesmen coming up with prisoners. At that point I couldn't tell whether they were local San Francisco plainclothesmen or federal marshals. They were running around in a frenzy and trying to look over at me every once in a while. They'd shake their heads and all this kind of stuff and run around.

Two hours after that first appearance in the federal court I was called back again and bail was posted—$25,000 in a cashier's check. And at that point I said, "Good, now I can get out of here and get this crap straight, and go talk to Garry and everything." Charles was in the middle of the Warren Wells shoot-out trial, so McTernan was substituting for him. When I got ready to leave the commissioner's court, the marshals said, "Will you step back here first?" I thought to myself, "Now, wait a minute. They have already booked me." They repeated, "Step back here!"

I remembered that the last time I was there, (for the Chicago thing), when I posted bail I had to come back through there, and I thought that that was where they processed you out. But no sooner had I gone back than they said, "Well, you can wait in the cell right there." So I stepped back into the cell. The door was still open, and thirty seconds later, a cop in plainclothes walked back and said, "I'm from the San Francisco Police Department, and you're under arrest!"

"What kind of crap is this?" I said to myself. "These cats are really out to railroad me. I just got through posting bail. What the hell are they going to arrest me for now?"

They brought me back and put me in the city jail. They said they had a warrant from Connecticut on the trumped-up charges of murder, conspiracy to murder and kidnap, but they didn't actually get it until several days later. As soon as they had me in the county jail they dropped the phony "unlawful flight" charges. They just used that as a pretext to kidnap me.

Garry had put in a subpoena to get an assistant to Attorney General John Mitchell to appear but the judge revoked the subpoena, which I didn't dig. Here you are—you need to be able to subpoena somebody and get some information and try to find out who's plotting what. But the power structure and the courts operate like that, they stick together against the individual who has certain rights. You have to have a right to subpoena a person. I don't give a darn if it's the President of the United States. He should be subpoenaed.

The reason we had subpoenaed one of Mitchell's assistants was that McTernan attempted to call the U.S. Department of Justice in Washington, D.C., and ask them some questions concerning the Chicago case that they had against me. They told him on the phone that this assistant attorney

general, Victor Worheide, was in Connecticut. Worheide is
the head of the special "Panther Unit" in the Justice Department. That was about a week before I was arrested,
which puts the federal government there in Connecticut
working in conjunction with the state and local officials of
New Haven and Connecticut to plot this thing against me.
So naturally we wanted to have him in court as a means of
bringing out some of these erroneous charges. It also came
to light in court the next day that there was no warrant out
for me when I was arrested, but they had used this "unlawful flight to avoid prosecution" charge to hold me.

It didn't make any difference. They set a date for extradition and I was put in the San Francisco County Jail which is
on the floor above the city jail. I sat up there for three
weeks, and Garry visited me when he could, and McTernan
would visit me and give me information. A few days after
all this, McTernan came up and told me that it looked like
Garry might have to go to the hospital. I'd have to send in a
motion to Chicago that I wanted to have my lawyer, Garry,
as the only lawyer to represent me. He was the one lawyer I
had chosen, and the only one I had conferred with. I was to
respectfully ask the court to postpone the date of the trial to
a later date until my lawyer could appear. I also signed a
document, by which I was informed that it was mandatory
that Garry go into the hospital before he try another case,
unless he wanted to risk his life.

Garry came to see me a couple of days later and told me
that he had been in Chicago and that the judge had denied a
postponement. He said the judge was going to try and
choose a lawyer for me.

TO CHICAGO IN CHAINS

■ I was sitting in San Francisco County Jail one evening,
when Charles Garry rushed in and said, "They're going to
move you tomorrow."

"Tomorrow?" I said. "They can't move me. They're not supposed to move me if I'm waiting for an extradition hearing. They're plotting a whole operation to get me to Chicago and try to extradite me from there. I know that rotten Mayor Daley is going to see to it that the State of Illinois extradites me to Connecticut."

Before Garry left that evening, I told him, "Look man, when I get to Chicago I'm not letting those cats choose a lawyer for me. Someone I've never spoken to. They don't have any right to do that. I think I'll be better off defending myself if you can't make it there."

He said, "Well, we'll have to confirm it, but it looks like I'll have to go to the hospital for a gall bladder operation."

"All the other cats have lawyers," I said. "The only thing I'll agree with those other lawyers on, is that they can handle my pretrial motions—but the only person I'll go into court with is you. The judge will have to see my point of view, because I'm going to fire any appointed lawyers. I'm not going to let the judge choose anybody else for me either."

Garry said, "OK, you have the legal right to do that," and he also told me that I had a right to request the lawyer of my choice. The sheriff and the jailers didn't know anything about my being moved, so I told them that I wanted a shower early in the morning and that I wanted to get all cleaned up, because I was being taken out. At first they kept telling me I didn't know what I was talking about, but later they allowed me to take a shower and shave.

I packaged what little property I had—cigarettes, writing paper, handkerchiefs, etc.—and they put it in a box, tied it up, and took everything out of my pockets. After I was dressed they put a chain around my waist. It had a little clip on it, with an extra piece of seven-inch chain hanging down. Then they put two sets of handcuffs through one of the links in the chain, and put both sets of cuffs on me. They brought out two more prisoners and put some leg irons on all of us. I had a leg iron on the left leg attached to another prisoner's right leg, and a leg iron on my right leg attached to the other guy's left leg.

They walked us to the elevator like that, took us down to the basement, and put us into a federal government paddy wagon. Three of the guards got in front with their pistols drawn and two more got in back with shotguns.

They drove us over to the federal building where they took our chains off, then put them right back on again. We had the same type of chaining around the waist with double handcuffs and leg irons on. The cat who sat in the middle had leg irons on both legs, so each day throughout the trip we would trade places. The leg irons cut at your legs. I happened to have boots on, and I persuaded the guards to put the irons around the boot so they wouldn't cut my legs. The other two prisoners caught it a little more. They caught it real bad. Their irons were way down on their legs, and if somebody happened to accidently pull the chain it would cut into your skin. They hustled us into a regular car, a sedan, put a shotgun on the floor, and one of the cats sat on the right-hand side in front, and the other marshal sat on the left-hand side and drove.

They drove out through the city and as we went up the ramp on the freeway and started toward the Bay Bridge, a highway patrolman was right there and he fell in behind us. As we went by the main police station, another highway patrolman got in front of us. That's how we went across the bridge. At the toll plaza a third highway patrolman pulled in behind us. We then headed north on Interstate 80 to Sacramento.

One of the other prisoners was a white guy named George, and they were taking him back to a Midwestern federal penitentiary. He had been in some big shoot-out on the West Coast. They were taking him to a maximum security prison because he had already escaped once. That's what he and the marshals started talking about as we were going north toward Richmond and Vallejo.

The third prisoner was a young cat named Joe who had

supposedly robbed a payroll. After the robbery, he had walked up to an airlines office and asked for a ticket on the next plane going to Canada. When he was told there were no planes going to Canada right away, he asked where the next plane was going. They said, "Mexico," so he said, "Give me a ticket on that right away." He had a bag full of money, and the way he told it, he took the money right out of it and paid for the ticket. He flew out and was picked up a few months later. He's a white cat, of course. If a black man had asked for a ticket to Canada and then taken a ticket completely in the other direction and reached into a bag full of money, he would have been surrounded by police in a minute. That just goes to show you the racism in this society, the way people's minds function. They were taking him to a federal medical center, for some kind of observations. He was supposedly considered wacky. What he did was walk into a department store and say, "Give me your payroll," and then walk out. But if he'd been a black man he wouldn't be wacky. He'd be dead or railroaded into prison.

While we were going past Berkeley on the freeway, and for the next ten or eleven miles after we got out of Richmond, five highway patrol cars were escorting the whole scene. Most of the cars had two cops inside.

George got to talking to the marshals, and he said, "You know I want to escape. I escaped before, and if I get a chance to I'm gonna do it again." The marshal said, "Yeah, we know it," and they talked about the way in which they transport prisoners. I didn't have much to say at all to anyone at that point. All the marshals would say to me were things like, "Well, when it comes down to it, whatcha wanna eat?" They had to stop at hamburger stands. That's all we ever got. A dollar a meal was allocated to us. Usually we got a hamburger, a milk shake, and maybe some French fries, and that'd be about it. We'd eat with our handcuffs on, in the back seat. We weren't chained to the inside of the car because there's a federal law against that.)

. . .

As we drove on, I watched the countryside. I always liked the outdoors, until it became too vicious, when crazy, trigger-happy hunters killed people while deer-hunting. My father used to take me to the mountains when I was younger. I wasn't really too hip to it, because we were really living in poverty; but every time my father would make a little bit of money, he and his friends would go hunting. All I wanted to do then was go hunting with him. I did a lot of travelling up and down the State of California, from Los Angeles to Mount Shasta. As we drove I saw landmarks that I knew, and places where I had done farm-labor work when I was young.

After Sacramento we drove through Marysville, a small town where I had once been picked up in a railroad station when I was seventeen years old. I had jumped a freight train with Steve Brumfield. We roamed the state together, hitch-hiking around for two or three weeks at a time without any aid from anybody and living on wild fruit and stuff like that. When we were picked up in Marysville, we were on our way out to South Dakota because we identified with the American Indians. My mother is part Indian. We wanted to see the Black Hills where Custer had got his head whipped by Sitting Bull and the Blackfoot Sioux who roamed those areas of Montana, Wyoming, and the Dakotas. When Steve and I were picked up, we stayed overnight in a juvenile detention place until my father came and got us out.

The marshals stopped in Marysville and we ate there. The marshals let us sit down at a table and eat. One of them asked me what I considered a silly question. He said, "You guys wanna eat out here? Some guys don't like to let other people walk up and see them chained down and everything."

"Man, it don't make me no difference," I said. "I'm a political prisoner. It's up to these cats here." They said they didn't care either, so we sat out there and ate for about twenty minutes.

At that time I didn't know it, but Allan Brotsky, one of Charles Garry's partners, had been arguing in court back in San Francisco for me, and the judge had ordered that I not be taken to Chicago. The U.S. marshal kept on stalling. He said I was gone and they couldn't get in touch with our car. All they had to do was contact the highway patrol escort which followed us all the way to the Nevada border. I did notice that once when we stopped, the marshal who was in charge made a phone call. This was around noon. The judge had given the order at 11:00 A.M., I found out later, and at noon we were still in California. Legally, I should have been taken back to San Francisco. The marshal must have called San Francisco, because the next morning after he got us out of the jail in Reno he told me that a lawyer had gone to bat for me yesterday and had done a pretty good job. He asked me if I knew an Al Brotsky.

To go to the bathroom with leg irons and handcuffs on is a motherfucker. The other two guys have to wait. We were all still chained together with the leg irons. There's a little play on the chain that drops down from the chain around your waist—you have about seven inches to move your hands up and down. The handcuffs are attached to the seven-inch chain. After I opened my pants and urinated, I would step to the side and let the other guy go and then the third guy, and then we'd go on around and one of us would slowly hobble to the face basin and bend real close. We'd have to get right up on it and get the water turned on and wash our hands. If the towels weren't too high, we could reach up and pull the towel. If it was too high, the marshals who were watching us had to get us the towels. That was the kind of situation I was in for seven days on the way to Chicago. You just couldn't sit on the toilet if you had to. The only place I could have a bowel movement was inside the jails where we were left overnight.

The first night we stayed in a very filthy jail in Reno. I was put in a one-man cell by myself. There was only one little blanket full of holes, a bunk attached to the wall, and a foam rubber mattress about two inches thick.

Before I was put in that jail, I told the marshal that I wanted to call my lawyer because no one knew where I was. All he had to say was, "Well, we'll see about it." "Don't I have the right to call my lawyer?" I asked. "We'll have to see about it," he repeated. He didn't see about anything, so every day throughout the whole trip I asked to call my lawyer and was never allowed to do so.

In the Reno jail, one of the trustees—a brother—came around. I tried to talk to him, but the guard was looking. It flashed into my mind that maybe the trustee was allowed visitors and I could get him to tell somebody to call Oakland and tell my lawyer where I was. The guard was still looking at me, and when the trustee saw me trying to talk to him, he shook his head slightly, moving it a half-inch or so, to tell me, "Uh uh, they're on to you."

The next day we were chained again and drove all the way across Nevada, eating lunch midway across the state. We were again escorted by state police cars, one in front and one in back. During the day I had one short conversation about what the Black Panther Party is all about. Both the marshals were white, and Joe and George were white dudes also. I ran down the ten-point platform and program, and afterwards they asked questions. I tried to show them all the misconceptions about the Party that had been printed in the Establishment news media. We drove across Nevada, through the Salt Flats into Utah to Salt Lake City, where we were placed in a jail overnight.

Each time we were taken inside a jail they took off the handcuffs and chains, booked us, and took mug shots. Every jail did this, except for a few, like one in Wyoming and a small-town jail in Hayes, Kansas.

All the way to Salt Lake City I thought of the Mormons and of Lowell Jensen, the district attorney in Alameda County who prosecuted Huey. Jensen is a Mormon. I thought about their racism. If Jensen at all represented their outlook, these people were rather backwards too, with racism manifested in them. I went over in my mind the facts I knew about the Mormons. For one thing they say black people cannot go to their heaven. A few black people are stupid enough to join their church, but they are treated no better than slaves or animals. Their avowed concept of a race category shows the basis of their supremacy doctrine. This idea has survived from the old one-headed god system of Europe. In Salt Lake City, I saw the Mormon symbol everywhere. There were pictures of a seagull, like those who supposedly came down and did in the locusts who were destroying the crops in the days of Brigham Young.

I also thought about the fact that what Brigham Young and the early settlers talked about were cooperatives, which are very socialistic. If you're going to build a socialistic system, or if you're going to establish socialism, racism has to be rubbed out completely. It's impossible to have a so-cialistic system and racism together and maybe that is the real reason the Mormon cooperative concept wasn't able to survive. They have people like Lowell Jensen who railroad Huey to jail by changing the trial transcript. I thought that when I got inside that jail, they might treat me badly, but all they did was book me.

The brothers inside that Salt Lake City jail knew that I was there that night. The information got around. It was a very modern jail. When I say modern, I don't mean to say that I like jails, but this jail would cover a square city-block. Half the jail's down underground. The tiers are built from under the ground up. I looked at the jail and I looked at the little nozzles and things around. The jail in Salt Lake City reminded me of a streamlined concentration camp. Very much so. The tier I was on was twenty-five feet under-

ground. There were very long aisles and very few people
around me. All the doors opened and closed electronically.
It's a completely electronic jail.

I was put in a cell by myself, isolated from other prisoners. This particular tank did not seem to have been used
much. It had little skinny mattresses that went on small steel
bunks riveted to the wall. I requested a shower and I got it.
Then I washed my shorts, T-shirt, and socks, and later they
brought me some food. The marshal was trying to be nice
and went out that night and bought me a seventy-nine cent
box of chicken and a twenty cent milk shake, with a few
French fries thrown in. I had been so cramped up in the car
all day that I did 100 push-ups in sets of tens to exercise
and loosen myself up.

It wasn't until I tried to go to sleep that I got pissed off
again because I knew that I was really in a kidnap situation
and I couldn't call Charles Garry in San Francisco. When I
arrived at that jail, I again asked the marshal if I could call
Garry and he said, "We'll see about that," but he still
wouldn't let me do it. The next morning, they came and
completely shackled us down again. We ate breakfast in the
jail before we left that morning.

After we were shackled down that morning we were
driven all the way across the state of Wyoming. As soon as
we came to the Utah-Wyoming border, the Wyoming highway patrolmen got right in behind us. Those cats were
really feeling their oats. I can tell when cops are itchy and
trigger happy. We'd stop to eat lunch, or get out to go to the
toilet and these cops would stand twenty feet away from us
in a guarding position, their arms folded, ready to draw
their guns. If I looked at them, they dropped their arms
down to their sides. I knew they had weird notions and
misconceptions about the Black Panther Party. Maybe they
thought I was going to whip out a gun or something. Here I
am all shackled down and everything, three of us all hooked
together, we can't move or anything, and they're standing

twenty feet off ready to draw their guns. They called it "security."

As we drove, one of the marshals was telling me about transporting some other prisoners, three brothers, who asked him, "What concentration camp you taking us to?"

"Why do these guys think that?" the marshal asked me. "We weren't taking them to a concentration camp. We were just transporting them from one prison to another. Where did they get these ideas?"

"Well, the basic fact is that concentration camps do exist in America," I said. "There are some laws on the books that say concentration camps can still be used. They'll probably use them for the Black Panther Party."

"No, it'll never happen," the marshal said. "America will never let black people be exterminated."

"Are you kidding?" I said. "Black people been slaughtered and murdered and lynched and brutalized for centuries. Fifty percent of the people in prison and jails don't even need to be there. Twenty-five percent are hard-core criminals who really need some type of rehabilitation. The other 25 percent are just sick, and need really good psychological treatment in hospitals." I told him the 50 percent who don't need to be in prison just need jobs. "There are over a million people in the prisons. Those are the initial concentration camps." I told him I thought that the cat was right in asking what concentration camp he was being taken to.

"The Southern work farms are nothing but concentration camps," I said. "Some cat down in Texas got ninety-nine years in prison because he drew a gun in the process of holding up a store. Nobody was killed or anything like that. No shoot-out occurred, but because he held up a liquor store and was black, he got ninety-nine years. Another cat, Lee Otis Johnson, got thirty years in Texas because the cops found one marijuana joint in his possession. Johnson is a political prisoner too. His real crime was that he was a SNCC organizer.

"In prison those guys go out and they work like dogs. They are enslaved. These are our initial concentration camps," I said. "The prison system doesn't rehabilitate and doesn't really serve society."

But the marshal still said, "I don't know what you mean, talking about fascism. America's not like that."

"Well it's happening right before our eyes," I said. "It's on a small scale, but it's rapidly growing."

We drove all the way to Laramie. When we got there a funny thing happened. The Laramie city police joined right in with the two highway patrol cars, the one highway patrol car in front and the one highway patrol car in back. So as we came into Laramie, two city police cars joined us, one drove in front and one came on in back. It was a real big thing with them, I guess, to have me overnight, but I have to give the old sheriff in that town credit. He didn't treat us badly. He lives at the jail with his wife and family, and they cook the food there. The prisoners get the same thing that the sheriff and the police eat. The jail itself was clean and roomy.

We witnessed an accident from the jail window down below us. What I noticed about the police really inspired me.

Three or four cars collided. When the city police arrived, I saw community control of the police in action. The police knew the guys who were in the accident. They were all part of one community. Just like when we say community control of police, we want the police to live in the neighborhood that they patrol. These policemen didn't treat the people who were in the accident brutally. A couple of them were drunk and were talking loudly and foolishly.

"Aw come on, cool down," the cops said. The police didn't mess over them. Nobody was beaten or dragged off to the goddamned jail. I'm pretty sure Indians get treated rotten in Laramie, but among the white population there is community control of police. That's what I told the other two cats, who were in the same cell with me.

This was the first time we were in the same cell, Joe, George, and I. It was a small-town county jail so they just stuck us in together. I talked to George and Joe that night, and I told them a lot about the Black Panther Party. After hearing me they realized that they had misconceptions about us.

George was about thirty-five. He was out of the South. He wasn't innately prejudiced though, and he was interested, so we talked and transferred different ideas back and forth. His misconceptions about the Panthers were from the press. At first he actually thought we just hated white people. But he learned that we didn't, that what we hated was the brutality and corruption of the society. I even showed him where poor white people were impoverished and oppressed, not as bad as black people, but they were impoverished and oppressed too. When I said they should actually oppose the system he readily agreed with me. George was a righteous bank robber. He and his partner had gotten on the ten most wanted men list of the FBI. They were outright bank robbers. There aren't any other words to describe the cats. The way George ran it down, they had already been sentenced to fifty years in a federal penitentiary.

Joe was about twenty-one. He was a bank robber too. This kind of political conversation was quite different from the conversations they had with other prisoners. Generally they talked about how to pull a bank robbery, or something like that. I tried to project their minds into the political situation in the society. We went into what causes a cat to be a bank robber. They agreed that this society, as a whole, oppresses people, that it brainwashes everyone. They agreed that racism was in this society and needed to be removed. They said they never had any real ill feelings against black people, nothing like that. But in the past they had been brought up with a misconception of supposedly being superior to black people. They even said they were surprised to find out that the Black Panther Party seemed to have an intelligent perspective about what's going on in America today. I'm pretty sure that neither of them, especially George, felt that I was a threat just because I was a Black Panther. They realized I wasn't a black racist. We talked things over and came to an understanding.

The next morning they chained us down again and we took off. We went through Colorado, and passed a place called the Cooperative Farmers Association. I thought to myself, "I wonder if that's anything positive, something socialistic. All the farmers in America shoud be in some type of cooperative."

We didn't stop in Denver. We passed by the airport and then the marshal pointed out the county jail. That's the only place those guys know. Naturally, I had already been thinking about whether or not we were going to stop there. Langdon Williams and Rory Hithe, both Panther leaders from San Francisco, were in the Denver jail. They're both in on the same Connecticut charge that I'm on. They were visiting Denver, and the FBI raided the Denver Panther office and arrested them, charging them with conspiracy and murder.

We stopped at a service station outside of Denver and the marshal made a phone call. They didn't have any escort, but they let us get out and stand up and stretch. It was kind of isolated. Big fields on the side of the service station right off the highway. I said, "How come you guys don't have an escort across Denver?" He said, "Oh, this county here and the federal government and some other people here in Denver disgree with a few things, including the price the government pays county jails to hold federal prisoners overnight. They have some disagreement about a few things." I gave this a thought—maybe the governor of Colorado was mad enough at the federal government not to extradite brother Langdon Williams and Rory Hithe. We got back in the car and drove and drove.

. . .

We went from Colorado into Kansas. The trip took us across Nevada, Utah, north through Wyoming, down to Denver, Colorado, and then east across Kansas. That's the first time I'd ever been in Kansas in my life. We finally came to a city named Hayes, Kansas, and stopped at the Ellis County jail.

The jail was a large building. They put us in a cell with three other prisoners. We ate fried chicken, peas, everything the jailer and his family had. He lived in the jail and his wife cooked the food. He was an older cat who didn't like hippies and long hair at all, but he seemed to be a nice person. In that jail they had TV in the tanks for the prisoners, and there were razor blades and after-shave lotion, magazines, cards, checkers. You name it, they had it. The guards wore civilian clothes. There were four tanks with four bunks in each tank and a large day room. It was a clean jail because the prisoners had painted it. You went out across the hall after you came out of the tank, into the day room. Close behind the bars was a telephone. The sheriff said, "If you need anything just pick the telephone up and let me know." You could stay up as long as you wanted. It was the best jail I've been in, in my life. But I still hate jails.

One of the prisoners got into a conversation with me about how to make "millions of dollars." They said all the hippie and Yippie stuff could be profitable. "Bobby, with your organization, boy, we could really clean up, you know," one guy said. He was a Southern white cat. Deep down inside I knew he was a racist, the way he was relating to some wild capitalistic adventure. But that's how he'd been oriented in this society.

The other prisoners talked about three black people who had recently pulled a jewel robbery in that town. Hayes is a college town with only about ten blacks at the school. It's a very isolated place. Some blacks were driving through the town and went into a jewelry store and one cat picked up a

pouch of jewels, went out the door, got in the car, and drove
off. It wasn't an armed robbery. They were caught right
away. One white guy in the jail said, "Man, them black
guys, they sure shouldn't a done that in a place like this. I
can understand doing it in Chicago or somewhere where
there's a whole lot of colored people, but a place like this is
so isolated that they got spotted at the drop of a hat and
busted. It was a big thing on TV when they got caught."

The next morning we had breakfast in the jail. The
marshals came and we were handcuffed, double handcuffed,
shackled, and chained again. We drove across Kansas all
the way to Missouri.

I had never really seen that type of countryside before. It
was completely flat with a lot of tall corn growing throughout the area. One of the things about travelling across the
country is that you see the vast, vast amounts of land we
have. I thought about how this government continues with
the private property concept with all that unused land,
when there are black people, brown people, and American
Indians cooped up on reservations and in ghettoes. With
modern technology available to irrigate and build reservoirs
why is it that black people can't have some of this land? We
were promised forty acres and two mules when we were
freed from slavery. This was the thing that really hit me on
that trip. I thought, "Here I am kidnapped by the federal
government and all I'm doing is fighting for some land. I'm
trying to contribute to the struggle so we can have some
freedom which is manifested in having some land, bread,
housing, education, clothing, justice, and peace." These are
the things I thought, looking at all that tall corn grow,
looking at all the vast amount of land that wasn't even being
used, and there are our fifteen million people hungry in this
country.

We were driving on a narrow two-lane road in Missouri.
It was raining and I thought, "What if they have a wreck?

What would happen to me?" I thought to myself about Everett having escaped before. He would probably try to get that gun from one of the marshals and then he'd definitely get the handcuff keys and escape. But I didn't have to escape. I was on a political charge. If I escaped, everybody would believe I was guilty of all that jive, those trumped-up charges. At the same time I knew darn well the power structure is going to move and do everything they can to try to convict me and railroad me into prison and the electric chair.

We finally arrived at the federal medical facility. As we drove in, they stopped us by this little microphone through which a cat talked sitting in a tower twenty feet above us. While they unlatched Joe, a guy with an M-1 rifle stood above us. One of the local marshals came outside and got him and they took him in through a basement. Then the marshals got back in the car and drove on over to the county jail.

This was the dirtiest, filthiest jail I'd ever been in. The sheriff was an old cat with an old gun slung off his hip. I have never seen such a filthy place. When I say filthy, you have to imagine what I'm describing, and I'm not exaggerating one pound. The cells had crud in all the corners, an inch and two inches thick. It smelled like it'd been there for years. The bunks were only two feet wide with little mattresses that were ripped open and filthy, with bugs crawling all over them. You could knock some bugs off, you'd look down at your hand, and there were some more bugs. When they hand you your food there's flies and shit in it. It looks like slop. It was just a rundown, filthy, no-good, dirty jail, a place that almost made me vomit.

In that raggedy little jail, the guards didn't bother us. The trustees wore blue jeans and T-shirts. The other prisoners had their regular civilian clothes, and had to sleep in them. There weren't any blankets, no blankets at all. About four or five trustees gathered up in front of the cell that me and

George had been put in. They asked us who we were and where we were going. Most of them seemed amazed at George's adventures and would ask him questions. They asked me who I was, and I told them I was Bobby Seale. They didn't know the name. Then George said, "This is Bobby Seale, the Chairman of the Black Panther Party."

"A Black Panther! Hey fella, are you really a Black Panther?"

"Yeah, man, I'm a Black Panther. I'm one of the members of the Party."

"Gosh, those guys that got the guns and shoot at the police," one white trustee said. "I know a fella here who's a Panther. He didn't take nothing from nobody around here and boy he shot it out with them cops. I tell ya, man, I'd be out there too if they got to messing with me like they mess with y'all. I heard they really mess witch y'all." He seemed to be on this vicarious relationship trip about some weird stuff he'd probably read in the sensationalized local papers. Another trustee got to talking about how he was doing thirty days, and how he'd lost his hog farm and his wife was having a baby. He was in there for pushing a lollipop down the mouth of one of his kids.

There were two more prisoners in our cell. One black brother was getting ready to be sent to the penitentiary for three years. He said he had committed a burglary, got cut loose on the first one, and when he needed some money, he went back and committed another burglary. He had heard about the Panthers and I tried to talk to him about the Party a bit. There wasn't a chapter in his town. I was told there are quite a few black people in that town, but a lot of them go to jail because there aren't a lot of jobs around. He also said there was a lot of racism and police brutality. There was another tank where they kept juveniles. They separated them from the other prisoners, who were mainly just regular everyday poor white cats, Southern-type cats who still don't understand the fact that the power structure oppresses them.

The next morning I noticed I was scratching and itching. Bugs were all over my body and I had to shake my shirt out. Later on at Cook County, I found out I had caught the crabs in that filthy jail.

Our next stop was the Saint Louis city jail where the marshals left me for an hour-and-a-half.

The place was crowded with black cats, about 150 of them were being processed. While I was getting out of the car in front of the jail, I could see prisoners hollering down at the people walking outside on the sidewalk. One of the cats said, "Black Power, brother," to me. A white man was walking along there in the city and the same prisoner hollered, "Where you going, honky?" I knew that these brothers were getting turned into black racists. They still didn't understand. That sounded like he hated the white man because of the color of his skin. Brothers like that lash out emotionally in a racist manner before they realize the necessity for politically organizing the people. We're all products of this racist society and need more revolutionary consciousness.

Inside they had some Uncle Tom-type cops helping to run the jail, processing in all kinds of black cats. There were very few white prisoners in the Saint Louis jail. One brother in my cell asked who I was. He wondered why I was brought to the jail in leg irons, shackles, double handcuffs, and a chain around my waist. I told him, "That's the way you travel when you're a federal prisoner." He kept asking me what my charge was until I had to tell him that I was Bobby Seale, Chairman of the Black Panther Party. At first he didn't believe me, because he said, "Aw, man, you're trying to jive somebody." I said, "No, man, I'm Chairman of the Black Panther Party." I don't like to go out and brag that I'm Chairman of the Black Panther Party or anything like that. But this brother, being a disbeliever, I talked to him. After a while he was kind of believing, but he was still unsure. He had been busted for possession of some stolen property of some kind.

I talked to him and some of the other brothers in there. They seemed to be really out of it. I haven't ever been in a jail down South, but there was something about that jail that gave me the feeling that I was in the South. The brothers' ways and attitudes weren't in connection with anything. On the West Coast, New York, or Chicago, the average cat has heard of the Black Panther Party, whereas these other guys just look at you. It's something they don't have any information on. I think that their information is so limited, so narrow, that they have a tendency to look at the Black Panther Party as something farfetched, something that they're not going to be involved with because they assume they'd probably go to jail. One of the brothers I was talking to said, "Man, most of these cats down here, they're out of it, man. They don't know where it's at yet, man." That was the brother's opinion, and that brother lived in Saint Louis.

I was there less than two hours when the two marshals came up. They wrapped a chain around my waist and put on just one set of handcuffs, attached the handcuffs to the chain around my waist and put me in the back seat of a car. I was the last one. While they left me off in Saint Louis, they took George on to one of those maximum security places. Then they drove me north to Chicago.

COOK COUNTY JAIL

■ We arrived in Chicago at about 7:30 that evening and went straight to Cook County Jail. Inside the jail they pat-searched me and took me downstairs. The assistant superintendent, a white cat, started telling me on the way downstairs that he had gotten to know Fred Hampton very well, while Fred was in jail there one time.* I asked the cat what his job was. He told me he used to be a police officer in charge of gang intelligence. Naturally, I didn't trust him one bit. So instead of offending him, I just let him go on and present himself, to see what his attitude really was. He went on to say that he had liked brother Fred Hampton very much. I was not impressed. That sounded like "gang intelligence" work.

He took me downstairs into a hall, and there was a black cat standing there. I had heard that there was a black man who ran the jail, Moore was his name. He was the head superintendent there, and they called him "Warden Moore."

Moore told the assistant, "Bring him in here. I want to talk to him." So I walked into the little room. He said, "Sit down over there in the chair." I sat down in the chair. "Now look here," he said, like he was supposed to be very tough, "I'm the warden of this jail, and I run this jail. You got a lot of notoriety and we don't want any trouble in this jail."

I looked at him and I said, very straight and very directly, "I know you don't want me to organize in your jail. Most people don't want me organizing in their jails when I am there."

Moore said, "We haven't got any Panthers in this jail, we haven't got any Muslims in this jail, we haven't got any gang members in this jail. We got *inmates*. You understand that?"

"Yes," I answered. "I also understand that I'm still the Chairman of the Black Panther Party. I want my cell and my legal papers, so that I can work on some legal matters."

Moore said, "You'll get your cell, all right."

Another guard came in, a black cat, and took me into another section where they do the booking. They strip-

* Fred Hampton, 22, Chairman of the Illinois Black Panther Party, was shot and killed in his sleep on December 4, 1969, at 5:00 A.M. when the Chicago police raided his house, allegedly looking for an arsenal of guns.—Ed.

searched me, then gave me my clothes back. I noticed that
there were a lot of black guards at Cook County Jail. After
this procedure was finished, they had some sheets of paper
that I had to fill out; one for my property and for receiving
mail, and one for listing all my arrests. The last one is called
a rap sheet. I took the sheet and started filling it out. I didn't
have to give this information to them, and the average cat
should just flat take the Fifth Amendment and refuse to give
any such information. But in my case I knew that this kind
of information is already known by every FBI agent, so it
would have been silly to refuse to run it down.

Well, the next thing I knew, about thirty black guards
crowded around and began to ask me questions about all
the past arrests I had. I guess they were curious from having
heard so many lies in the newspapers. So, really enthusiasti-
cally, they gathered around to hear what I would tell about
what had happened in the past, about what they would call
my criminal record.

Some of them seemed to think that I had been arrested
for some vicious, vicious crimes. When I mentioned that I
had been arrested for having a gun adjacent to a jail, there
were "oohs" and "ahhs" and expressions toward each other
as if they thought that this must have been some fantastic
feat or criminal act that I was trying to pull, which was not
the case at all.

The fact was, this was right after one of the times Huey
had gotten busted. At the time of Huey's arrest, we were
carrying weapons, and I was waiting outside the jail for him
on a public sidewalk with a shotgun in my hands. The next
day I was arrested. These are the kind of things they didn't
know, the fact that I wasn't even arrested initially, and that
I wasn't trying to break anybody out of jail. We just carried
the guns in the open at that time to show the people that it
was legal to carry these guns, and that we would defend
ourselves. We had been on the streets with guns for six or
seven months by that time, and the cops hadn't arrested us
because they couldn't find anything to charge us with, until

we happened to get too near a county jail. So I explained to the guards, "Don't look at that like it's something fantastic. It's perfectly legal for a person to arm himself, and have a shotgun. We just got too near a county jail."

They looked at me skeptically and said, "Aw, come on now. What else you been arrested for? C'mon, what else?"

I realized that they didn't know any of the facts about my arrests at all, just that there had been a lot of these arrests, and they made a long list on the rap sheet, looking very sensational. They wanted to know, who is this Bobby Seale person who has all this notoriety? Most of them were thinking that I was really a gangbanger, and stuff like this, which I wasn't at all. I had never been a gang leader. I was just another cat who grew up in the community. But they were looking for a lot of theft and other bad things.

So I told them I'd run it all down in detail, but I wouldn't say anything about any case that was still pending. Anything they wanted to know from the past, I'd freely tell them.

I've been arrested five times in the last two years on major things that were trumped up by the government to try and put me in jail. But other than that, before these last two years, and before the Black Panther Party, there was nothing more serious than traffic warrants. Since the Party was founded, there was the guns on grounds adjacent to a county jail charge, then my wife and I were both arrested for possession of illegal weapons. The initial charge on that was a so-called kind of conspiracy to commit murder, which they had to drop the next day. The guards grabbed onto that. "Why'd they drop it?" they asked. "What you mean? What happened then?" But I wouldn't go any further into that because it's still pending on appeal. Then there was the bust in Sacramento and then the Chicago thing, and the Connecticut murder charge, which hasn't come to court yet. These are all my arrests.

Finally the guards were satisfied. I was ready to be taken up to my cell.

A black guard who knew Oakland told me he was taking me up, and I told him I wanted my own cell. I explained that I could work better that way. He said, "Yeah, man, I'll make sure you get a place where you can work and do your things." As we walked to my cell, he talked about Oakland, but it was like we were talking about two different places, because he hadn't been there for a long time.

He was a lieutenant. One thing I found among those black guards was that even though they were being used by the system to check and corral their own black brothers, half of them were doing it just for the sake of having a job. There's so much unemployment in the black community, that regular everyday cats will take a job as a guard just to be able to get by.

Some of the older cats and a few others try to play policeman and be tough. They're so brainwashed, they can't see beyond the man's system. But this one cat, this lieutenant, happened to have grown up in Berkeley and Oakland with me when I was younger. He remembered the same people I remembered at Berkeley High. When I was working in the poverty program, way before the Black Panther Party was formed, he was the head of a local poverty program. But he was the type of cat that's just going to take him a job, get a position, and not really be that concerned with black people and black America and the struggle.

Some places in the jail, I saw some filth around the walls that really needed cleaning. When we got to my cell, I was relieved to see that it wasn't filthy around the walls and floor. The cell was a maximum holding cell, tiny and certainly not comfortable, but at least it was empty and clean. The guard left and I went to sleep.

The next morning, Warden Moore came to pay me a call. I heard some steps. Somebody was walking down the hall, trying to be very quiet. I sat with my back to the steel door. I remembered the sound it had made the night before, when the guard pushed the button to open it—very loud, very startling. A good way to scare a person, and make him jump. A good way for a soft-stepping warden to intimidate a prisoner, by startling him and putting him on the defensive.

Sure enough, the soft steps stopped. *Blang!* My door opened. I waited for a few seconds, and then looked around slowly. It was Warden Moore.

He stared hard at me, then said, rather arrogantly, "How you doing?"

"I'm doing fine, warden, how are you doing?" I answered. I was just sitting sort of casually on the top bunk.

He looked at the papers I had spread around me, and, nodding at them, demanded, "What are you doing?"

I said, "I'm thinking about my legal matters, working on that stupid, trumped-up charge there," and I pointed to a legal document that Garry had given me.

"What charge is that?" Moore sort of growled, and I handed him the charge from Connecticut.

He looked at it and read it. Then he handed the paper back to me and stepped back, putting his hands in his belt, trying to look authoritative. "We've got over 2,000 prisoners in this jail," he announced. "We run this jail just fine. We got over 90 percent black guards in this jail."

"Good," I said. "In fact, I was surprised to see that many black people running a jail."

He cleared his throat. "You want to go outside?" he asked.

"It doesn't make any difference," I told him. "I can be locked up, or I can go outside, or I can just stay right here."

Then he said I could go watch television if I wanted to, with some trustees. "No, thanks," I told him. "I don't have to watch TV. I'd just as soon stay locked up, right in here."

He stared at me for a few seconds. He looked a little confused when I said that. Then he turned and left.

That was a little trick I had learned from Huey. Huey would upset the guards in jail. Huey understood the guards. He knew that psychologically most guards couldn't stand to

be locked up. Most believed they would go mad if they had
to be locked up. So what Huey would do is, when they put
him in the day room, all of a sudden he would jump up and
say, "Hey, officer, come here and lock me back up in my
cell." He pulled a reverse on them. Where most prisoners
would do nearly anything to get out of their cells and into
the day room, Huey would say, "Lock me up in my cell."

Huey said the guards are really the ones who fear jail,
and fear the things they do there, because they would fear
being in the same situation as the prisoners. The worse they
treat the prisoners, the more they fear—that's the mind of
the Establishment.

There were other experiences Huey had told us about to
help us deal with the situations we would find in jail. One
time—a long time ago, before the Black Panther Party—
Huey was put into the hole. They brought him some mush
in a cup, for him to eat, and some water; the mush was
green. So he took the stuff and threw it out the porthole,
and then got down and started doing push-ups. He was
already in the hole, the worst punishment they have—they
couldn't put him anywhere else. The most they could do is
come in and brutalize him. So they did. They actually came
in and beat the shit out of Huey. About two days after that,
the guard who came around on the night shift turned out to
be an old friend of Huey's. They hadn't seen each other for
years, until this guard came down and found Huey in the
hole. He sneaked some sandwiches down to Huey. After
that, every night when this guard came on the night shift,
Huey could eat. Then, in the day, when the other guards
came down, Huey would be doing push-ups. Every day he'd
throw the food back and say, "I don't want that crap. That's
not fit for human beings to eat." Huey went on like that for
ten days. It was blowing the guards' minds. Finally, one of
the guards said, "How do you do this?"

Huey said, "The spirit of the people is stronger than the
man's jails. My spirit is stronger than yours."

That's the kind of thing Huey pulled off in jail, even

before the Black Panther Party was organized. So from the ways he taught me to deal with the jail experience, I was able to deal with Warden Moore. Of course, that doesn't mean that I like jail. I abhor it, I'm pissed off at it. But I learned to take jail, and I let the guards know that being locked up doesn't change my revolutionary spirit. And usually, when the guards discover this, they become quite interested in the philosophy of the Black Panther Party, and come around asking questions and asking me to run down the ten-point platform. That's how it happens, what Warden Moore calls organizing.

In the next couple of days, I wrote a number of letters. I felt that I was isolated from everything that was going on on the West Coast, being in Chicago. So I wrote letters home to communicate. One of the guards came around and told me to fill out this thing to my lawyer, and I'd be able to get in touch with him right away. I filled that out, and the guard promised to mail it immediately. By now the guards realized that I wasn't either a mad killer or a fool, as the papers depict all Black Panther Party members.

The second day I felt something crawling on me and I realized I had caught the crabs. The only place that I could trace it to was that filthy county jail in Missouri that I had to stay at all night one night. So I went and got completely soaked down with DDT, all through my hair and my natural—everything. I had that stuff running off me like water.

The next Tuesday morning, they took me out, saying I was going to court. Actually we ended up going to the Federal Building in Chicago. On the way, I saw Jerry Rubin. I hardly recognized him at first, with his hair all cut off. We stood in the federal processing tank in Cook County Jail for two hours, and got to talk for a while. Jerry told me he was being kept in a tier across the hall from me, but Cook County Jail is so huge, that it's like being in another jail. Cook holds as many prisoners as they do in some of the major prisons. I found out that Jerry had to stay in jail until twenty-five days were up. He was serving the time for blocking a Navy recruiting table in Berkeley.

Jerry told me Warden Moore had been down the aisle that morning, hassling him a little, and had said, "Bobby Seale is an Uncle Tom." I laughed and said, "Oh, man, ain't this a gas. The other day he was treating me like I was the most notorious criminal in the world. Now that he's found out I'm not a notorious criminal, I'm an Uncle Tom. Well, we can't expect Warden Moore to understand the positives of revolutionary principles."

Then I told Jerry how Warden Moore had sought *me* out in the aisle that same morning. "Bobby Seale!" he had called out. "Jerry Rubin said he would get you to beat me up."

I had said, "Jerry Rubin might say anything. He might say that he's going to get Westmoreland to jump on Nixon." Jerry laughed at that.

Then Moore himself came inside the tank. He sat down and began talking about how SDS runs the Black Panther Party. I said, "You're crazy, man."

He said, "It's true. They do."

I said, "I don't know what kind of papers you've been reading."

Moore was walking around inside the tank, not in a uniform but in civilian clothes. Now, just outside the tank, they process guys who are going to court. Many of them don't have handcuffs on, but everyone knows they are prisoners going to court. The way Moore was sitting there, a man had no way of knowing that he was the superintendent of the jail. This cat who was getting processed for court saw Moore sitting there smoking a cigarette, so he said, "Hey man, can I get a cigarette from you?" I realized the prisoner had mistaken Moore for another prisoner, and the look of outrage on Moore's face just cracked me up laughing.

Moore looked real mean at the cat, and said, in a very harsh tone, "I advise you, young man, not to say one damn thing to me." The cat looked at Moore and then at me. He didn't understand this at all. Moore just turned back to me and started talking.

I found out that Moore did this a lot. He'd go walking around the jail, in civilian clothes. In Cook County Jail, all the prisoners wear civilian clothes, and all the guards wear uniforms. Moore goes around wearing an old T-shirt and some pants. You'd swear up and down he's a prisoner. Therefore a lot of prisoners going to court and coming back from court won't even know who he is. They may not be very careful of what they say around him.

Moore has a Ph.D. in psychology and sociology. He figures people will always react in a certain way, so he's developed all kinds of methods of getting whatever reaction or information he wants from a prisoner. I was hip to his methods, so they didn't work on me.

The next day, Wednesday, I found that I had developed an infection in my testes. The doctor examined me and said that I must be put in the hospital for some treatments. I was moved out of my cell and into the hospital ward.

MY CONSTITUTIONAL RIGHTS ARE DENIED

■ Jerry Rubin and I were taken to the federal court on Wednesday morning, September 24, and William Kunstler filed a motion to see me in the jail over there. He came in and said, "I heard you were talking about firing all the lawyers unless you had Garry."

"Yeah," I said, "because all you cats were supposed to do for me is file motions. As far as I'm concerned, Garry is going to be my trial lawyer. He's always been my lawyer."

Kunstler said that if I did that, Judge Hoffman would appoint some kind of public defender. So I told him, "Well, they can appoint a public defender, but I ain't working with a public defender. I don't want a public defender. I want Garry. I don't want anybody but Garry.

"You call Garry," I told Kunstler, "and see if I have a legal right to fire a public defender. Don't I have that right?"

"Yeah, you can."

"Well, that's what I'm going to do," I told him. "And if Hoffman tries to appoint you or anyone else as my lawyer, I'm going to fire you cats anyway."

So Kunstler said, "The jury is about to be picked now, and you can get in touch with Garry later."

"You guys get in touch with Garry for me," I said, "and then I'll sum up exactly what I'm going to do, because before this trial starts, I'm going to make sure I have proper legal defense."

After that, I had a chance to meet with all the other defendants. The trial finally got under way the next day. I was in the hospital at the time, and I was allowed to keep my legal stuff with me. I saw them pick a whole jury in just one day.

Meanwhile I was waiting for a message from Garry. Finally I got a phone call through to Garry's office on Thursday from Cook County Jail. Warden Moore called me to his office and dialed the number himself. I talked to Barney Dreyfus, Garry's law partner. I asked him if Garry was definitely going into the hospital or if he had changed his mind. Dreyfus said that the Wells case was over, but that Garry definitely had to go to the hospital the next day. His doctors had said that he'd better have that gall bladder operation right away because it would be a real danger to his life not to.

"Well, I'm going to ask the judge to postpone my part of the trial so that I can have Garry," I said, "because I can't function without Garry, and I don't want these other lawyers here. Let Garry know what I'm doing, and then maybe after he gets out of the hospital we can go on." Dreyfus mentioned that they had talked to the Panther Party Central Committee about my situation, and the Central Committee also agreed that since I had a legal right to fire the lawyers, I should do it.

And boom! That's what happened. That night, in the hospital, I wrote out my first motion, a request that I be allowed to fire the lawyers and postpone the trial until Charles Garry could defend me. The next morning, Friday, I got up and went to the trial, and when I got to the defense table I told Kunstler that I was going to fire everybody.

He said, "What?"

I said, "Yup, everybody gets fired because Garry's definitely going into the hospital and I'm going to ask for a firing on the basis of my part of the trial being postponed. This judge," I said, "seems to be kind of rotten. I already consider him a racist, seeing the way he's running this thing. So I've got my statement all written out." I let them read it, and one of the defendants said, "Man, that's going to make it look like all of the defendants are splitting."

I said, "Man, the defendants aren't splitting. I'm not splitting from you cats. It's just that my situation is very different, man, in a lot of ways. These cats stuck me on the tail end of this indictment to try and railroad me to prison, so I need Garry here and everybody knows it. Garry's my lawyer. I haven't confirmed any of these other lawyers. I'm not going to be letting Hoffman pick and choose my lawyer for me, when he knows that Garry is my lawyer, my attorney of record."

They said, "Well, OK."

"That's what I'm doing," I said, so I proceeded to exercise my constitutional rights.

The marshal waved the gavel and said, "All rise," and everybody rose. "This court is now in session pursuant to adjournment." Boom. Boom. Boom. "The Honorable Julius J. Hoffman presiding." At that point I got up and walked to the podium and told him, "I'd like to read a statement concerning my legal defense."

"Don't you have a lawyer?" Hoffman asked.

"No," I said. "I want to read this statement concerning my defense." So I read the statement. I got to the point in the statement where I said, ". . . and if you don't respect my constitutional rights then I'm going to have to consider you a blatant racist who's prejudiced against all the other defendants and myself in particular."

Hoffman interrupted me. "What did you say?"

"A blatant racist," I replied. "I consider you a racist just like all the other judges who saw people's constitutional rights violated in the South throughout the history of this country."

He didn't know where I was coming from. I was coming from the fact that he'd already denied the motion that Charles Garry had made a month before the trial started. Garry had flown to Chicago in August to try to make a motion for a postponement on the basis of the fact that he had to go into the hospital for an operation.

Hoffman said my motion would be denied. Kunstler got up and said something, but I don't remember what he said. Then Len Weinglass, the other lawyer, and the other seven defendants said that they wanted to meet with me. Weinglass told the federal marshals that this and each day after the court was over in the afternoon, I would meet with them. I told the other defendants what I was going to be doing with respect to making motions concerning my constitutional rights and things like that.

Every time my name came up, I stood and said, "Judge Hoffman, I don't have my lawyer here."

"Well, young man, you have a lawyer. Mr. Kunstler's your lawyer."

"No, he's not my lawyer," I said, and I argued the point. During the first week or so, I got up four or five times in this manner. I tried to argue, and when I'd start saying, "But Judge Hoffman, you're wrong. I have a certain constitutional right," he'd say, "Take the jury out!" When I made that first motion that first Friday morning, not one witness had been sworn in on the part of the prosecution. Not one. This is very important, because by law, the trial isn't considered to have begun until a witness is sworn in. After Schultz made his opening statement to the jury—this is still before a single witness had been sworn in—Kunstler got up and made his statement. Right after he got through, the judge asked if there were any other statements.

I got up from my chair and walked to the podium. I was just getting ready to reply to what Schultz had said about how he would prove that I was guilty and that I had made a speech telling people to get pistols, rifles, and shotguns, and then told them to riot. What I really said—and we have a transcript of the speech—was that every black man should put a .357 Magnum pistol, a shotgun, and an M-1 rifle in his home. In essence what I talked about in the speech was that we have a right to defend ourselves against unjust attacks by pigs, and "if the pigs attack us in an unjust manner, then we have a right to barbeque some of that pork." That's exactly what I said. But I didn't tell people to go out and riot. I told them we had a right to defend ourselves against unjust attacks, and the words in my speech say *unjust,* but Schultz turned it around.

"And we'll prove that Mr. Seale made this speech, telling people to pick up guns, .357 Magnums, shotguns, etc., and go out and riot." And Schultz emphasized to the jury that "Mr. Seale is a very effective speaker. He's very *effective.*"

When I got up to the podium, I was going to say, "Mr. Schultz has just made a reference to me being a very effective speaker, but I want it known to the jury that I intend to prove that if I am an effective speaker, speech is directly related to my constitutional rights, and everybody's constitutional rights." That's what I was going to say at first, and move on from there.

But all I said was, "Mr. Schultz . . ." At that point, Hoffman said, "Just a minute, young man," and peered

down at me. I looked up at him. "Who is your lawyer?"
Hoffman asks.

"Mr. Charles Garry," I said. I was getting ready to say,
"Mr. Charles Garry who's in the hospital in California," but
when I said, "Mr. Charles Garry," Hoffman said, "Take the
jury out! Take the jury out!" He rushed the jury right out,
and got them out of the way. He didn't want the jurors to
see the crap he was about to pull. After the jury went out,
he went on to argue, and then Kunstler got up and started
arguing.

"You're not my lawyer," I said to Kunstler, and I argued
my own case. Hoffman said something to the effect that he
didn't want to listen to me, that I would not be allowed to
make an opening statement because Kunstler was my lawyer.

"Kunstler is not my lawyer," I said. "I fired the man."

Now I had nothing personal against Kunstler, because I
know that Kunstler is in the struggle and that he is supposed
to be a good lawyer. I was just upholding the principle that
I had a right to my own lawyer. From there on, for about
two or three weeks, it was me standing up whenever my
name was mentioned. Most of the time when I stood up,
Hoffman would say to Kunstler, "You are the lawyer for
Mr. Seale." And I'd say, "No, he's not my lawyer. I want to
request the right to have my own lawyer, Charles R. Garry
here, or the right to defend myself."

Hoffman didn't even investigate; he didn't care. A judge
is supposed to at least investigate a person's position, especially in regard to legal defense. But he didn't.

At this point I tried to find out every piece of legal
information that I could. There was a young black girl at
the trial who was in law school. She came up to the defense
table every once in a while, and I asked her to get me all the
legal information she could. Weinglass said he would get
me all the legal information he could. So they both worked

it out to get me legal information concerning my right to defend myself and my right to have my own lawyer. And as I got more legal information, I began to argue more and harder.

I got hold of material about an old Reconstruction law, Section 1941 of the U.S. Government Code, that says a black man cannot be discriminated against in any manner, in any court in America, concerning "legal defense." When I got hold of that, man. Oh, man! It was a real thing with me, because I knew I was right by the laws, and by the Sixth Amendment.

Before I was gagged, Hoffman actually got to the point where he'd shout over me. I'd jump up and start talking rather fast, saying, "Judge Hoffman, you know darn well I have a right to have my own lawyer here or else a right to defend myself." He'd start talking real loud over me: "Take the jury out! Take the jury out! I don't want to hear this man. Mr. Marshal, set that man down! Take the jury out! Take the jury out!" He did this so the court reporter could only record what Hoffman was saying and not what I was saying. But I got hip to him. I saw the tactics he was using, so every time he started raising his voice I'd raise my voice up too.

Then four or five days after the trial started, the thing came up about the threatening notes to the jury. Man, that was rotten. I was sitting there in the court that morning, and all of a sudden Schultz said something about the lawyers and the prosecution going into chambers to talk something over. Boom! So the marshals took me with the other defendants into a room and the lawyers came into the room and said that the jury had received some threatening notes saying, "You're being watched," signed, "The Black Panthers."

"What?" I said. "Aw, man!"

Kunstler said Schultz and Foran didn't want any publicity about it.

"Don't want any publicity about it?" I said. "Well, later for them punks, man. We're not going to send any stupid notes like that, man. Somebody's railroading us."

I felt that Schultz and Foran knew about the whole thing. But I said to myself, "Even if Schultz and Foran don't know about it, then it's a government-CIA operation, because they figure that Schultz and Foran would discover it and use it against me to try to prejudice the jury, because I'm the one they have absolutely no evidence against, so they need this, the U.S. government needs this thing to railroad me."

"I'm going to publicize this and accuse the government of doing it," I said, "because that's the only people I think would do it."

Somebody said, "Well, how do you know some quack didn't send it?"

"Some quack might have sent it," I told them, "but you guys get a copy of that, a Xerox copy of that stuff, and send it to a handwriting expert, and find out what kind of person wrote the notes, and I'll bet ten to one we're going to find a person who relates to some kind of authority in this system."

So I wrote out a statement saying that I believed that the U.S. government sent the note to trick us, and that the Black Panther Party never signs anything, "The Black Panthers." If we sign anything, it's signed, "Black Panther Party," and we don't send notes. It's some of the same crap that happened during Huey P. Newton's trial when they railroaded Huey—the same business about threatening letters and threatening notes. When Huey got on the stand during that trial, and when Huey really started explaining the true philosophy of the Black Panther Party, a lot of those jurors took time to objectively check Huey out. They found out that Huey was a very intelligent person. He wasn't what the D.A. was trying to make him out to be. More than likely, I thought then, they are hip to this now, and the government wants to destroy me in the minds of the jury before I can take the stand, or gain the right to defend myself.

I reacted very strongly to that note, realizing that no one else but the CIA or the FBI could have sent it. If Schultz and Foran did know about it, then they sent it; but I thought probably the CIA did it. The CIA has done some dirty rotten work. They started the Cuban thing. They were behind Vietnam and escalating that war. And in all the other murders and operations that they've been involved in, they just sit on the side and never say a thing. We would compare the SS in Germany with the CIA, because the government uses them as a behind-the-scenes police state operation.

Anyway, that's the way I saw it and felt it. With all the infiltrating operations that they tried to pull on the Black Panther Party, I could only see it that way, and that's the way I reacted to it. From there on I began to get a few legal points about my right to defend myself, and I argued more vigorously. Judge Hoffman started shouting over me so the recorder wouldn't hear things, but I'd talk loud enough so she could hear me, and argue with him to the point of calling him a fascist, a racist, and a pig, and using that right in the context of my argument.

No judge wants to be called a fascist, a racist, and a pig, but that's what he was acting like, running over my constitutional rights like that, and just ignoring them. "I'm going to use this in my arguments at every point," I said to myself, "and that just might persuade him to understand that I really want him to investigate."

He finally did investigate, three days after he'd gagged me. Tom Hayden and Len Weinglass said that they wanted to go see Charles R. Garry about my being gagged, and Hoffman knew he had gotten out of hand in gagging me. Then he tried to say there was a precedent for gagging me, but Hoffman was a stone liar because I had gotten hold of legal information on the other cats who had been gagged

in court and these cats had picked up chairs and thrown
them at people. I had never picked up chairs and thrown
them. I had never run up into the jury box, and shaken the
jurors' shoulders. I never did things like that.

The only thing I ever said to the jury after those threatening letters was, "Good morning, ladies and gentlemen of
the jury. I hope you don't blame me for anything." Hoffman
was rushing the jury out, and trying to talk over my voice.
"Because threatening letters that were purported to be sent
by the Black Panther Party, were *not* sent by the Black
Panther Party, and Judge Hoffman, you know it, and this
whole court knows it."

Hoffman was talking at the same time I was. I don't think
the court recorder got it all. I don't think the court recorder
was against me. I don't think she was on my side, but I got a
message from someone folded up in a piece of paper saying
that the court recorder said, "When you speak out, please
talk slower, so I can get it all on the record; it's in your
defense."

I began to feel that people were really getting on the
judge, because I even found out that a couple of the marshals didn't dig what Hoffman was doing. Behind the
scenes, in the lock-up, man, they'd shake their heads.

They had some deputy marshals in the court who were
actually guards over at the Cook County Jail and who
worked the late shift at night. When they got off in the
morning, they'd come over and get in their civilian clothes,
and work a day shift as special deputy marshals. Most of the
cats I saw in Cook County Jail in the morning before I'd
come over to court were marshals at the trial. The guards
turned out and got on my side because of the way Hoffman
was treating me. The guards—everybody—asked questions. "I just don't see *how* that judge can do that." And
some would just shake their heads.

One morning they attempted to remove members of my
family from the courtroom. I got up and I protested about
that, and I called the judge a racist again. It was actually

an old court matron who seemed to be the cause of it all. Every time I looked around at her she'd almost be breathing down their necks, breathing down the necks of every Black Panther Party member and black person in the courtroom. They had put them all in one little section and she was looking at each one of them, at every little move they made. All of a sudden, she told some chick to get out, and another cat to get out. They weren't being noisy, but she was getting them out of the courtroom. Kunstler got up and said, "Why are they removing black people from the courtroom?"

"It looks like a little bit of racism to me," I said, because the black people weren't carrying on at all.

Then one morning one of the marshals came back into the lock-up before court had started, and says, "Bobby, you've got a lot of Black Panthers, a lot of black people out there that's on your side today. I hope nothing happens."

"Well, nothing's going to happen," I said. "They're here to observe. They've got a right to observe. They've got a right to be in here."

"Well, the judge told us to go over and sit you down, and I just don't want any of them to start anything."

"They're not going to start anything," I replied. "When you guys are pushing me down in chairs and stuff like that, you're carying out a racist judge's orders. He's making you act in a racist manner."

"Well, I'm not really a racist."

I said, "Yeah, you say you aren't. But I'll talk to them."

Five minutes later, they came back and got me. Court still hadn't started. All the defendants were scattered around the defense table. Schultz and Foran were around the prosecution's table. I said, "Brothers and sisters in the audience, I want to say a few things to you. You've been noticing for the past few weeks in this courtroom that I've been threatened by the judge and they're talking about gagging me and all this kind of crap, but I have a right to speak out in my own behalf."

(A few days before, I had gotten into an argument with

Judge Hoffman, and I asked him—and this is in the court record—"Do I have a right or do I not have a right to stand up and make requests and motions and speak in behalf of myself on those requests and motions?" Give or take a few words, I said just that. Hoffman never answered me as to whether I did or did not have that right. That's very important, because he should have said, "No, you don't have a right to stand up and speak out in behalf of yourself." All he said was, "You have a lawyer."

"I'm contending that I don't have a lawyer," I said to Hoffman, pointing out that I had fired Kunstler. "And you can't appoint him for me," I said. "Do I or do I not have a right to speak out in behalf of myself, in making a request or a motion, and in fact arguing that motion?" Then I said, "This is a request and a motion." Just like that, but Hoffman wouldn't answer me on it.)

So I was speaking to the cats in the audience and I was telling them that I had a right to speak out in behalf of myself, and wanted to defend myself. "But I don't want you cats out there to get upset and get emotional and start doing anything that's out of the ordinary," I said. "You've got a right to be participants here. You've got a right to observe this trial and see what's going on. If anything happens, don't do anything unnecessary.

"If anybody attacks us, we defend ourselves. That's the principle of the Party. Whether they have a gun or not, if they attack us, we defend ourselves. If they make us leave the courtroom, they just make us leave the courtroom. We leave. But don't anybody do anything; keep your cool. We're human beings and we've got a right to defend ourselves. But don't do anything. Just be cool, because I still have a right to speak out in behalf of myself."

The court convened, and Schultz got up and said very nasty-like, "If the Court please, before you came into this courtroom, if the Court please, Bobby Seale stood up and addressed this group." Schultz tried to make it sound real bad.

He was up there talking, and I jumped up and walked to the lectern and said, "I can speak on behalf of my constitutional rights, too." Then I went back to my seat and went to sit down. Marshals were moving all around the room about to charge me. They were really coming in on me, man. Schultz still tried to say that I had spoken about attacking people. I stood up again.

The marshals ran over to me, grabbed me, and the big one hit me. He grabbed me and pushed me at the same time. He pushed me back in the seat when I stood up. When I hit the seat the whole seat went back over and I hit the floor. The chair didn't go all the way to the floor, but I was sitting right in front of some of the audience and spectators. The chair had wheels on it and rolled back at the same time I was being pushed. When the chair went back, my leg came up. When the marshal pushed me down, my leg came up and it hit the bottom of the defense table.

At the same time another cat, a big tall cat we called Slim, came up, pulled my arm, and put it in a hammer-lock.

"Hey, man, you're hurting me," I said. Now this was Slim, trying to do his job, but at the same time trying not to mess up with me. He pulled my arm back down and held it there. He said, "Hey, man, be cool."

"No, man," I said, and I was really yelling out. I started yelling out then.

"You're lying. Dirty liar. I told them to defend themselves. You are a rotten racist pig, fascist liar, that's what you are. You're a rotten liar. You're a rotten liar. You are a fascist pig liar."

Schultz continued at this point, telling the judge that I was trying to disrupt the court.

"Schultz, why don't you tell the truth?" I shouted. "Why don't you tell the truth about exactly what I said?"

By this time the marshals had let me go.

"Why don't you tell the truth about exactly what I said? What I said was, 'Be cool and don't do anything; we have a right to defend ourselves if attacked.' I didn't say anything like what you're trying to insinuate. Isn't that right? Tell the truth!" I hollered at him.

And you know what Schultz did? He says, "Yes, your honor, I'm sorry; Your honor will understand, I'm sure." And Schultz went and sat down. I had caught him in a cold, bold-faced lie.

The same day, Schultz passed around a photograph of a black cat wearing a T-shirt with a clenched fist on it—the Power to the People salute. Schultz said, 'I want to enter this photograph in evidence; it's a picture of a black man in a sweatshirt and on that sweatshirt there is a clenched fist, Black Power salute." I stood up at that point and said, "I object to the characterization of the evidence; it's not correct. The salute is directly related to the Black Panther Party, which started it. It really means 'Power to the People!' To characterize it and isolate it that way only as part of the Black Power movement is very racist."

Schultz jumped out of his chair. He was turning red, man —mad. "Your honor," he says in a very loud voice and trying to make it sound derogatory, "Mr. Seale has called me a racist, your honor. And he has called *you* a racist."

"That's right," I said, "that's exactly what you are if you're going to characterize evidence like that. You are a racist. Your honor," I repeated, "it's a mischaracterization; it's the 'Power to the People' salute, and is not just isolated to Black Power. Black people in the Black Panther Party initiated it, but what we mean by it is power to *all* the people." That was another form of defending myself. Schultz finally had to sit down.

They really had gotten to a point where they didn't want to have anything else to do with me. When they started trying to misconstrue things that pointed directly at me, I had no other alternative but to speak out on behalf of myself, or at least to object, because I had a right to defend myself, although Hoffman continued to deny me that right.

Some of these things the jury was able to see, although most times Hoffman rushed the jury out of the room.

GAGGED, SHACKLED, AND BOUND

■ The day I had to call Schultz a liar for trying to misquote me, was the day I was gagged. I had demanded my rights. I told them, "I demand my constitutional rights." I even banged on the table while I was talking. "And, Judge Hoffman, you know it," I said, "I have a constitutional right to defend myself." They recessed the court, then came back, and Hoffman said, "Mr. Seale, are you going to disrupt this court any more?"

"I'm not disrupting the court," I replied. "I am going to make my request and demand that I have a right to defend myself, because I know I have that right."

Then Hoffman told the marshals, "Take the defendant and appropriately deal with him." That's the way Hoffman said it—in that very shitty manner. They took me back to the lock-up right outside the courtroom. They got some tape and put it across my mouth. They handcuffed my hands down close to the legs of a metal folding chair and put the irons on my legs. They looped the chain through one of the rods running across the front of the folding part of the chair and brought it out and clasped it to my right leg.

The jury came back in, and Judge Hoffman says some kind of crazy crap, "Disregard this and disregard that." I shook my head from left to right at the jury and said, "Uh uh, uh uh." Some tears started rolling down one of the jurors' cheeks, and I looked at the jury again—"Uh uh."

Hoffman said stuff like, "Mr. Seale is trying to disrupt the court."

I shook my head at the jury, "Uh uhh, uh uh," to indicate I wasn't trying to disrupt.

I sat there and something else came up. Hoffman said something else about me, so I rattled the handcuffs against the metal chair—clang, clang, clang, clang—as a means of objecting, still trying to defend myself. A little later they brought a witness on to testify, and my name was mentioned.

Through the tape I hollered, "I object," in a muffled sound, but it could be heard. "I object." The tape wasn't holding too well because of my beard. So I said again, "I object, I object. I have a right to defend myself."

So they took me out again. Two or three marshals lifted the chair up and just took me back into the lock-up. They put the tape back on me, put a rag around my mouth, tied the thing, and took me back into the courtroom.

Later, Hoffman asked me if I would promise not to "disrupt" the court. He loved to use the words "disrupt" and "outburst" so the press could print "disrupt" and "outburst" and people wouldn't see what was really going on. What was involved was really an issue of constitutional rights. Hoffman said I should indicate my answer by shaking my head up and down for yes, or left to right for no.

I didn't shake my head up and down, nor did I shake it to the left or right. I said, right through that gag, "I have a right"—my voice was muffled but everybody could hear me —"I have a right to defend myself; you know I have a right to defend myself and you have no right to be gagging me and shackling me. I want to defend myself and that's all I'm going for."

People way in the back of the audience probably couldn't hear me at all, but the judge, the marshals, the press, and the audience close to me could hear.

The next day they strapped me to a wooden armchair, put a lot of padding in front of my mouth and tied a big large rag around it. Another rag came up under my chin.

The marshals tied a knot on the top of my head. The rag came across my mouth and went around the back of my neck. The first day I was shackled and gagged, a big black marshal put the iron around my leg real tight, so that the blood circulation had actually stopped in my right leg. The second time they shackled me I motioned to the girl law student sitting at the defense table, to give me a piece of paper, and I wrote a note that the blood circulation was being stopped in my arms because of the way they had the handcuffs around my wrists. The only way I could get some relief was if I slouched way down in the chair. Somebody in the court said that my circulation was being stopped, and another marshal came and loosened the handcuffs.

Next day they had some big straps instead of the handcuffs. "Sit down in the chair," one of the marshals said. I sat down in the chair and said to myself, "Hoffman looks like a damn fool, sitting up there gagging me and carrying on. He knows that I've got a right to defend myself; he knows I should have a lawyer here, a lawyer of my choice, and he's foolish." So this cat started wrapping straps around my arm.

"Say, man, they're kinda tight," I said.

"That's just the way it's gonna have to be."

"Aw, shit," I said.

He wrapped one strap down my leg, and he said, "Is that tight?"

"No," I said, "they're not tight down there." Then he tightened them up some more. Later another marshal came by and I said, "Say, man, these things are too tight," so he loosened them. After that he put the gag over my mouth.

After I was gagged and everything, they went out and this same big nigger punk pig, tightened them right back up again around my arms, just tightened them right back up again. Then he opened the door and said, "Come on," to one of the other marshals who was standing outside the door, and they picked me up, and took me to the table.

I was trying to wiggle my hands to circulate the blood in my left arm. I was sitting there and court was going on. I was listening, and every once in a while I was trying to wiggle my hands. I sat there for a while and I noticed that the circulation in my arms literally stopped unless I wiggled my hands. Then this one pig, sitting right beside me, tightened the straps right back up again, real tight.

I kept trying to wiggle my hands, but wiggling them wasn't getting any blood circulating this time, so I started pushing the thing and pulling it, pushing and pulling, trying to get some blood circulation. I beckoned to the law student with my head. She was my means of communication with Garry. "What do you want?" she asked me. She'd say, "Do you want a pencil?" and I'd shake my head to indicate, "Yeah." In fact I tried to talk through the gag.

While she was standing there, trying to help me, Schultz interrupted and said something about, "Your honor, I'd like the Court to know that the young lady touched Mr. Seale's hand in a very motherly way when he left the courtroom yesterday." He said that for the jury to hear hoping to discredit her for trying to help me out.

Anyway, I wrote a little note that said my blood circulation was being stopped and I told her to give it to Weinglass and tell Weinglass to tell the court. They were still doing some kind of cross-examining up there. I tried to move the straps. Those wooden chairs are kind of smooth and varnished. My arm was sitting on top of the arm of the chair, and I tried to slip my arm over to the side. The straps were going around the arm of the chair, and by moving my arm off of the chair, that kind of loosened it, and I said, "Ah." So I just pushed my arm back and forth, the straps were quite loose, and then started wriggling my hands to get some blood circulation. A big pig looked down and saw that I had loosened the straps and was wiggling my hand. He reached over and grabbed the strap, trying to tighten the strap up. Man. That hurt the hell out of my arm. When he pulled the strap, he pulled my arm tight against the chair again, and I was shaking my head, "Uh uh."

I started to mumble, but I couldn't half be heard, "I want

my blood circulation, I want to get my blood circulating."
At the same time he was reaching over me and jerking the
chair, two more marshals came up and grabbed at it. I bent
forward and said, "Uh uh," and the first pig stuck an elbow
in my chest. His elbow knocked me back against the back of
the chair. He hit me again. One marshal was trying to pick
up the chair, and one was trying to sit the chair down, and I
was pushing at the back of the chair, trying to get out of the
way of this cat hitting me in the chest.

But I also learned that even though my legs were
strapped to the bottom of the legs of the chair, my feet were
firmly on the floor, so that when he was elbowing me and I
was pushing back with my feet, the chair would move. Then
three more marshals attacked me, all at the same time with
the other two still trying to pick up the chair. The whole
chair went up in the air and fell all the way back into the
press section. The press was sitting directly behind the
defense table and I fell on top of them. They were frantically trying to get out of the way. All of the marshals ran
up to me at once. This one cat was still elbowing me,
tightening this strap up on my left hand. Another marshal
came rushing in, and the chair rose halfway in the air again
and fell over at an angle. Another pig rushed in and his
elbow hit me right in the balls. It hurt the hell out of me.

At that point I bent to my right, I turned my hand
around inside the straps, and finally got the tip of my fingers
up near by my moustache and yanked and pulled my head
back, yanking the gag off my mouth. I hollered out:

"You son-of-a-bitch. You hit me in the balls. Don't hit
me in my balls. I'm trying to get my blood circulation."

I said it three or four times. I cussed him out, and I
called him a fascist and everything. At the same time the
judge was hollering, "The court is adjourned, the court is
adjourned." The jury was running out; it looked like all ten
or twelve marshals were beating me over there, and killing
me.

Jerry Rubin, who was sitting next to me, got up and

hollered out, "Look what you're doing. Elbowing that man. You hit him in the mouth."

The judge said something; he was adjourning the court; it was just chaotic. This all happened because Judge Hoffman had gagged me, and then this rotten pig tried to treat me brutally, while I was gagged and bound and shackled to this chair. It was a scene and a half, man. Finally they got this other guy and they picked the chair up. Court was adjourned.

While they were taking me out, I hollered out, "Cruel and unusual punishment." I don't even think they got that on the record, but I hollered it out, "Cruel and unusual punishment." And I said, "You're a bunch of fascists; you're a fascist dog, judge."

I'd just got hit in the testes, and had been elbowed in the chest, and my blood circulation was gone. It was something else. They shut the door, and then this big marshal said, "You're just making this hard on yourself." "I ain't making nothing hard on myself," I said, "you're just in cahoots with the damn judge. You're working with him."

The next morning, when they tried to gag me, I thought I was going to die; I mean, really die, because of the way they were doing things. I was in the lock-up before court convened, and they said, "Sit in the chair."

"Don't tighten those things too tight on me," I said. This one marshal said, "We're not going to tighten them too tight." So they strapped me down, and after they strapped me down, this one cat who said he wasn't going to tighten the things too tight said, "Bobby, we're going to put something in your mouth."

"No, you're not putting a damn thing in my mouth," I said. "Not in my mouth."

"Well, we have to put something inside your mouth. The judge has ordered it, and that's what we're going to do."

"Uh uh. No sir. You're not putting anything in my mouth." I'd already made up my mind that if he so much as

got his fingers near my mouth, I was going to bit his motherfucking fingers off, because I wasn't going to let him put
anything in my mouth.

"You'd better not try to put it in my mouth, because I
have tonsilitis, and it's going to exhaust me along with this
other infection I'm being treated for. With all this penicillin
in me, my temperature goes up a degree-and-a-half, sometimes two degrees, and I have to go to sleep to get my
temperature down. So don't you be putting anything in my
mouth. I'm not letting you put it in my mouth no way."

"Grab his head," the marshal said. I was shackled down.
One of the marshals put the palms of his hands on top of my
head. He stepped up to me—he had rubber gloves on and
was holding a wad of rag that was rolled up. It was about an
inch or an inch-and-a-half long, and an inch in diameter. He
was going to jam this junk down my mouth. I was shackled
down, legs, arms, everything. He grabbed my nose and held
the wad of rag about three or four inches from my mouth. I
figured he was going to try to wait until I ran out of breath
by holding my nose, knowing I wanted to keep my mouth
shut. He was going to wait until I needed some breath, and
when I opened my mouth, he would move real fast and jam
the rag into it.

"But it ain't going to work," I thought to myself. "It ain't
going to work."

So I sat there. After a while I began to need some breath.
I held and held my breath as long as I could. He was getting
ready to jam the rag into my mouth, but before I opened my
mouth, I jerked my head to the left and then to the right
real fast, and got loose from the grip the other marshal had
on my head and the grip that this marshal had on my nose. I
put my head down and started catching my breath.

I looked up. They had stepped back. The next time they
tried it, the cat put his arm around my head as if he were
wrestling with somebody, only I was sitting shackled in the
chair and he was standing up. He put his arm around my
head, so that the back of my head was sitting against his

chest. His arm headed downwards, coming across my right ear. The cat grabbed my nose again. I was mad, man. I was mad as a motherfucker.

"You sons-of-bitches," I said. "You rotten dogs." They held me again and held my nose. When it began to look like I needed breath, he set the wad of rags right up against my lips and began to press real hard with the palm of his hand. He pressed so hard that I could even feel the blood seeping out of my gums and I could feel the inside of my lips busting, because I was holding out, I was holding out as hard as I could. Then I began thinking, "I'm going to pass out. I'm going to pass out." I didn't want to pass out. Then I got scared. I knew I wasn't going to let those cats put that rag in my mouth.

I thought a whole lot of things. Things flashed off in my head. I became aware of my feet being on the floor and wanting to push back and go to the left, but the cat holding my head could feel the tension in my body and he held tighter and harder. I was feeling like I was going to pass out and I didn't want to pass out. I didn't want to be forced to pass out. And this cat was pushing, pushing, pushing against my mouth.

So I pushed with my feet, and somehow I began to use my weight with the chair. My legs were attached to the legs of the chair. I pushed real hard. I was about to pass out. I thought about Eldridge and I thought about the struggle and everybody in the Party, and I was thinking about Nat Turner even—all kinds of crazy things. I even had the notion that I wouldn't open my mouth, even if I passed out. Although I knew that when you pass out, your mouth automatically opens, before you die.

All of a sudden, I pushed with all of my weight, and next thing I knew, I had this cat pinned up against the wall. He was in back of the chair, holding my head and I had him pinned between the wooden chair and the wall. I had pushed all the way back, almost two-and-a-half feet, and he had let go of my head. His body was between the wall and the chair, and I was pushing and yanking, and he was trying to push the chair away from the wall, and I was jamming him back against the wall. I was loose. I felt free, and I started breathing.

This other cat said, "We can't put this in this cat's mouth. That damn judge. Why did he order us to do this shit anyway?" They decided not to put anything in my mouth. But that was some battle that I fought with them.

The marshal holding my head was a white cat and the marshal trying to jam the rag in my mouth was a black cat. They were working together. They're both pigs. It doesn't make any difference what color they are. The black marshal said, "Well, we're not going to do it. We can't do it. We did what we could."

Then they got some bandage. It was a roll of the type that football players and basketball players use to wrap around their legs. You wrap it around your legs, and as you move it becomes tighter. They had a piece about three inches wide. First they put some tape and some heavy padding all across my mouth, and they began to wrap. They wrapped all the way around. They wrapped it tight, very tight. Then they brought it under my chin, and wrapped it above my head and under my chin—actually it was covering my throat, too. They got it real tight. I started losing my breath again. I was getting choked by the bandage. I started shaking my head from left to right, and the cat says, "I think he's losing his breath." So they unwrapped it real quick.

They started again and made it a point to come right under my chin and keep it away from my throat. They still wrapped it too tight, because when I came out in the courtroom and looked to the left and looked to the right, that thing got tighter and tighter.

The blood began to stop coming up to my head. That was too much. I started shaking my head, shaking my head, and Jerry Rubin and a couple of other people stood up.

"He's passing out! That thing is too tight on him!"

I started shaking my head and got my arm slightly loosened. I pushed my head down, and with the tip of my finger got hold of the gag and pulled it off. I called Judge Hoffman every kind of thing I could call him. "Fascist, sanctioning cruel and unusual punishment, and breaking the Eighth Amendment of the Constitution of the United States." The marshal snatched up the chair and was trying to rush me back to the lock-up. Court was adjourning and there was all this commotion, because the shit was getting to the point where I was about to pass out. That stuff was wrapped around me too damned tight.

I was calling Hoffman a fascist and constantly referring to the Eighth Amendment of the Constitution of the United States where it says there shall be no cruel and unusual punishment inflicted, and this big, old, pig marshal put his hand around my mouth and nose and started pulling. The other marshals grabbed the chair and started dragging it, but when they got to the door there was a little rise caused by the carpet molding between the door and the concrete floor, and the chair stopped. I was still calling them about everything I could think of and the marshals were jumping all around me, trying to get the chair out. This big pig grabbed me around my face and covered my mouth so I couldn't say anything, but I wiggled away from him. He grabbed me again and covered my nose *and* my mouth until I couldn't even breathe. He let go and I started hollering out again. The door was still open. He tried to reach to close it, but before he could, I was hollering so loud he reached back, grabbed my mouth and nose again so I couldn't breathe, and just held me there. Then he hollered to one of the other marshals.

Everybody in the courtroom seemed to be filing out. The jury was going out while all this was happening. Judge Hoffman was ordering them out. It wasn't an outburst, and it wasn't an attempt to disrupt the court. What it was, was a man trying to gain his constitutional right to defend himself or to have his lawyer there. It is his choice according to the

United States Supreme Court. I was pretty sure the United States Supreme Court had said that you can have a lawyer of your choice who is effective, and if this is not possible, the defendant has a right to defend himself.

Hoffman didn't see it that way and they re-gagged me, but real loose. They loosened the straps. When they brought me back in in the chair, Weinglass and Tom Hayden made a motion that the court take notice of the fact that Charles R. Garry was my lawyer. They said they were going to see Garry over the weekend. Hoffman adjourned court early that Friday so Hayden and Weinglass could go see Garry in San Francisco.

Anyone can read the court record and see that I wasn't trying to sabotage the trial, but that I was only trying to get my constitutional right—to either defend myself, or to have my lawyer present—recognized, but Judge Hoffman wouldn't recognize it.

The following Monday, they didn't gag me. I didn't say anything all day, because my name never came up. Nobody said anything about Kunstler being my lawyer that day, so I just sat there. That morning before the jury came in, Hoffman said he wouldn't gag me if I would act right. He put it in his little old, jive way. I said I was going to demand my constitutional rights and that I would continue to demand my constitutional rights. I tried to explain to him that I had been subjected to cruel and unusual punishment so that another of my constitutional rights, the Eighth Amendment, had been violated. I sat down and didn't have anything else to say. Nobody said anything against me.

Then they brought a witness to the stand who was testifying against me. He mentioned my name, so I stood up and said that I objected to this witness testifying against me because my lawyer was not there. That was late Monday afternoon. I said that I had requested and deserved the right to cross-examine the witness myself.

"Mr. Seale," Hoffman says, in his little, sarcastic, dramatized, puny, racist manner, "I remind you that you have a lawyer."

"I do not have a lawyer at all and I have something to say on behalf of myself," I told him. "You keep telling me that I have a lawyer but I don't have a lawyer." I went on to tell the court that Kunstler was not my lawyer. I made it clear with every piece of emotion and feeling that I could get forth that Kunstler was not my lawyer. The jury saw it and everybody saw it. The jury was well aware by this time that I didn't have a lawyer. They were well aware that Hoffman was messing over me. And Hoffman knew the jury knew. I saw a woman juror cry. I was always hoping that none of those jurors had been bought off by the government. When I said after being *gagged* that I had no lawyer, I think the jury must have seen even more what the situation was.

Tuesday morning court convened, and I made up my mind that I was going to demonstrate to Judge Hoffman that I could adequately act in my own defense. This was another way of arguing for my right to defend myself. After the jury came in, Hoffman asked Kunstler and Weinglass if they wanted to cross-examine the witness. They both said, "No, the witness isn't testifying against our clients and we do not represent Mr. Seale."

I got up and I said, "I would like to approach the lectern and ask the witness (a San Francisco sheriff) some questions." I asked him if he had ever killed a Black Panther Party member or participated in any raids on a Black Panther Party offices or on a Black Panther Party member's home. I asked him why he goes around following people in airports when they're travelling and when they're buying tickets.

"Sit down," Hoffman said.

"I'm going to ask another question," I said. Hoffman told me to sit down again. I was just getting ready to sit down, so I said, "This is a fascist operation," and turned and sat down. Hoffman cooled his marshals off. He didn't have them attack me as they had done previously.

Hoffman adjourned the court, and that afternoon he came back and read off a bunch of crap. He just took everything out of context and didn't report things as they really happened. He just read the court record and said, *this* was contempt of court, and *this* was contempt of court, and *this* was contempt of court. In every last one of those instances I was talking about my right to defend myself, my constitutional rights. He sat up and asked me if I wanted to defend myself, or if I wanted to speak in behalf of myself, after he got through reading off all those so-called contempts. I told him that I didn't want to speak to him because he wouldn't let me speak before, on behalf of myself. "I'm not going to beg you for no time," I told him. "How long have you been putting black people in jail and prisons, and railroading people, and denying them their constitutional rights?" I asked him. Then I sat down.

He gave me four years in prison. He sentenced me unjustly. He sentenced me to four years in prison because I had *demanded* my constitutional rights. He declared a mistrial, only for me, because the jury never would have gone along with him. That's the real reason. He tried to obscure it and say that it was something else, but four or five people on that jury were really mad. Those people didn't like Judge Hoffman. I was looking at them when I was gagged. Hoffman was observing that jury too. He knew what he was doing. So in essence, that is how the Chicago Eight trial turned into the Chicago Seven trial.

YIPPIES, CONVICTS, AND COPS

■ A lot of times when we were taken over to the Federal Building in Chicago, Jerry Rubin and I were isolated in a cell by ourselves. This went on for most of the remaining twenty-five days that Jerry had to serve in jail.

We always felt that they were putting us in an isolated tank because that tank was being bugged, and they were trying to find out what we were saying, or trying to get something so they could misconstrue it and use it against us. They hoped we'd talk about the legal strategy those other lawyers were using for the defense of their seven clients. Of course, we didn't.

I talked to Jerry a lot about the Party. I felt that Jerry Rubin had come to have a more political perspective about the situation. We talked a lot about the Yippie-hippie movement. I asked him the difference in the names "Yippie" and "hippie." He said Yippie is the political aspect of the hippie movement, and the hippie is the part of a group that hasn't necessarily become political yet. "They mostly prefer to be stoned," he said, "but most of them want peace, and they want an end to this stuff." Jerry ran down a lot about the discrimination that goes on with respect to Yippies, hippies, what have you, in the same manner it's brought down on black people or brown people or red people or other peoples. And I asked him, "Why really do you wear long hair?"

"It's a rejection, and a way of identifying yourself," he said. "When you're wearing long hair, and rejecting the system, it causes people to ask questions. What you do is, you become a walking, visible part of the revolution if you walk down the street wearing long hair. If I walk down the street and I've got real long hair, I know that people are asking questions and they're saying things. The middle-class world doesn't really understand what is wrong in the system, and the corruptness in the system. That is, not the way the history books put it." I found out that Jerry Rubin had been a top newspaper reporter for five years in Cincinnati. That really got off of me. I really had to think about that!

Jerry came to oppose the oppression, the poverty, the fascist tactics that the cops used, and the over-all system. He knew that the system needed an overhauling. He knew that some form of socialistic system was going to have to be implemented to really begin to remove the oppressive social obstacles and social evils in the system. Jerry told me he respected Jimmy Hoffa because Hoffa really fought for the workers to have a better life. Hoffa did a lot of things for the workers. I asked him if he thought Jimmy Hoffa was political enough to understand the need for a socialistic system. He said he didn't think that Hoffa was yet, but it would be very good if Hoffa would come around to the side of the masses of people and get the workers to understand that it is necessary to implement some kind of basic socialistic system here in America—for all the workers, both unemployed and employed. He really respected Hoffa's past work.

I talked to him a lot about black people being a nation within a nation. Setting forth to black people that they're a nation within a nation can be misconstrued and shouldn't be misconstrued; not only in words but in terms of deeds and practice. This shouldn't be confused with black racism, and I explained how Chicano and Latino people were a nation within a nation and how Chinese people were a nation within a nation, and that this is maintained because the exploiting system, which is racist, and the capitalistic system, which perpetuates racism, are really one and the same. As long as it exists, that in itself really defined black people as a nation within a nation, or any other group of people who were subjected to exploitation and racist tactics as a nation within a nation. When I told him that we wouldn't be defining ourselves as a nation within a nation based on color alone, that we would be defining ourselves as a nation within a nation based on the existing economic status of black America, Jerry understood this. Our geographical location here in America, that we are in fact second-class citizens, and that we are scattered in wretched ghettoes and rural areas in the thousands and millions, cooped up in these places, here in America; also the language of the black community as it is directly related to the colonialized situation that black people live in, the oppressive conditions that we are subjected to; all of this, from history to now, is the foundation for our psychological makeup. Our language is interconnected with our environment and expresses certain psychological understanding and attitudes in terms of our attempts to survive.

I think Jerry understood the psychology, the language, the economic status, and the geographical locations of Afro-Americans here in America: that in fact black brothers in Africa were our brothers in oppression, but their language is not the same as ours; that we live in a highly technical society here in America, whereas a large portion of Africans live in rural areas and underdeveloped areas in undeveloped countries; that since language and the environment are different, race doesn't necessarily constitute an over-all world-nation. He seemed to really understand it when I showed him how we were made into a nation within a nation—having been brought here from Africa, and after exploitation and segregation, becoming Afro-Americans. I explained the language to him, showing him some surviving African words and idiomatic expressions, which are directly related to our present situation here. I told him we were directly relating to the fact that racism existing in Africa is quite parallel to the racism that exists here in America. And Marxism-Leninism has to be stretched, and some more progressive ideas have to be set forth in relation to the need to change the system here in Amrica, to show people that black people have a right to our freedom as human beings.

Jerry, of all the cats I talked to among the left radicals and revolutionary white brothers, is one cat who I think understood it better than most people. In our general conversation, he was the most political in his understanding.

I had never known Jerry Rubin before. I had never met any of the other seven defendants in Chicago, before that Democratic National Convention, either. I never even talked to any of them before I came to make that speaking engagement during the convention. In fact, I didn't say any more than "Hi, hello!" to Jerry when I went to the park to make that speech.

That's the speech that they said was supposed to incite a riot. We have a transcript of that speech and it was a very typical speech. I certainly never told anybody to go and riot. First, I told everybody they had a right to defend themselves; second, I told the cats to put the guns in their homes, because they had a right to have guns in their homes, and that we had a right to defend ourselves in the black community if we were unjustly attacked. Those were the kinds of things in that speech. At one point the D.A.'s, Shultz and Foran, thought that they were going to railroad me on the basis of that speech, by saying that I incited a riot and told people to go out and riot. I oppose spontaneous rioting and the Party has always opposed spontaneous rioting. A spontaneous riot is generally without leadership of any kind. It's just a lot of black people who are ready to resist the system but who are totally unorganized, and they're only hurting themselves. I told people in that speech that we should *organize* in small groups, twos and threes and fours, and then went on to the fact that we had a right to defend ourselves when the cops come down into our community and occupy it like a foreign troop. That speech didn't incite anybody to riot. But in spite of these facts, here I was in the Cook County Jail, going to court every day on such an accusation.

Every morning at 5:00 they'd get me up and take me to the tank where I'd wait for three hours with whatever federal prisoners were facing court that day. And every day they'd turn court out and take me back, shackled, with handcuffs on and a chain around my waist. Sometimes they'd handcuff me to another cat. There would be an escort from the Federal Building to the Cook County Jail. It's about seven miles between the two places. Sirens would be flashing on the escort cars. We'd be riding in a big paddy wagon, a United States government truck, and they'd go

around all other traffic. Sometimes they'd have cats in there
who had federal charges and had to appear in other courts.
When there were escapees, they'd really put heavy security
down—three or four cars and shotguns.

One guard was about five-feet-eight, and he was a
fascist-minded fool. We named this deputy marshal James
Bond, because he carried knives in his boots. He always
carried two guns, a shotgun, and a .357 Magnum, in the
escort car, and you just knew he was going to trip over his
guns. You could tell he was really a psychopathic pig.
When they were transferring us he would always grab one
of those machine guns they have and take this ready-to-fire
stance. He was actually a foolish, stupid-looking pig, nowhere near the superficial, untrue movie character James
Bond, but you could see this cat must have related to that
stupid crap. Sometimes, when they closed the door to the
paddy wagon, you could look out the window and he'd take
his stance with his shotgun and his .357 Magnum, or his
shotgun and his machine gun, and you'd see him trying to
get into his car, and sure enough, stumbling over his own
guns. He almost dropped one one time, trying to get back
into the escort car.

We discovered that he kept knives in his boots, because
when they come into the prison area with us, the marshals
have to give up their guns to the jail sheriff and lock them
up. One day we watched from the paddy wagon's window
as the cats reclaimed their weapons. James Bond put his
foot up on a chair and pulled up his pants leg and stuck a
knife into his boot. Then he put his other leg up and stuck
another knife into his other boot. He wore a kind of desert
boot that came up about eight inches above his ankles and
he stuck his knives down into them like he had sewed in
scabbards down there.

A couple of those marshals were fanatics. You should
have heard us in prison—we talked about those cats like
they were crazy. James Bond was absurd. He was a fanatic
with a gun, just waiting for somebody to stumble, so he

could shoot. Sometimes a cat is shackled. What if he stumbles? This kind of fanatic would think he was trying to escape or something. If anyone stumbled, that kind of fool would shoot up marshals and everybody. That's why we didn't like James Bond. We didn't like that guy at all.

A lot of the cats who shared the Federal Building tank with me after Jerry had finished his twenty-five days and left, were some real out of sight guys. They understood in so much detail the corruption in Chicago, from the mayor all the way down, and the corrupt government operations. They told me about some of the slick moves Mayor Daley pulls, such as having two houses, one being near or about a black neighborhood so that people would see him on television going into that particular house, while actually he lived in another mansion someplace else. And the criminal activity in the city was directly interconnected with the government operations on a very large scale, from the way the prisoners put it.

The prisoners put forth this kind of information without any hostility, just very factually. It was obvious that they were aware of their own particular predicament and the predicament of many other people that were being charged. Most of the cats there were very well aware of the things that were happening although they weren't allowed the city newspapers in jail.

There was corruption in Chicago with the judges. A number of judges were forced to resign because of corruption and taking money behind the scenes. Most of the prisoners knew that if you had so much money, you could buy your way out of certain trials and certain kinds of cases, for two and three and five thousand dollars. And prisoners would explain these kinds of things quite often, when you were getting in a general kind of conversation about what was going on or when we'd get in a conversation about Judge Hoffman.

Hoffman is known to own some large businesses there or

have stock or ownership of some kind in businesses that actually produce war materials that are being used in Vietnam, which automatically shows his interest in prosecuting and having a biased point of view, completely negative to the eight defendants, and wanting more than likely to see them convicted. Of course, he would sit up and deny this. This is his public-relations front. But he's not much on public relations with his ignorance and his trampling tyrannically over people's constitutional rights.

When I was being put in the tank with other prisoners, they noticed something. When the three or four marshals would come and get me and take me downstairs to court, one of the prisoners was taken out and he never did return to the tank until I came back after the noon recess, to eat a sandwich and the stuff they give you in jail there. This prisoner would be returned, just before I got there. Some of the prisoners told me that they could smell a cop a mile away. So when we were talking they would say, "Be quiet, Bobby. Be cool." They'd pull me over in a corner and say, "This cat may try to misconstrue something."

Then I would say, "They can't misconstrue anything because all I'm talking about is Party philosophy and what have you."

Then they said, "Yes, but you know what these cats do. They'll jack up one of these prisoners in here, and he'll take some of the things you actually said and then twist them and add some lies on the stand and make it look like you were saying something else. Then they'll have a regular agent who's infiltrating, who'll take the stand and repeat these things, and exaggerate even more and tell all kinds of lies. Just because of what you said about your Party's philosophy, by their cooperating in lies they could trick a jury into believing them. They operate that way, so you have to be aware of that." I appreciated this very much from a number of prisoners there.

These were all federal prisoners. Many of them were getting big time. One cat there, his name was Bob, he seemed to have beaten some twenty-five cases in the last seven, eight years. And it tickled me that, although he wasn't political, he always knew what the hell I was talking about. He understood the talk about a basic socialistic system, and other things. He got convicted and got twenty-five years. And they hit him with another charge and tried to give him another twenty-five years.

They say in the federal system, the parole system's just all goofed up, in the sense that if you get ten years you're going to do six and three months. And if you get fifty years, you're going to do every bit of possibly thirty-five years. These are the kinds of things prisoners didn't dig at all, naturally, because the federal government has a tendency to snap a whole lot of time to a cat. Another thing that most of the prisoners said was that it seemed like cats were getting picked up everywhere, more so than in the past. People being railroaded. A number of cats, you could just hear their stories and their situations, and know they really weren't guilty. Some of them were obviously guilty, and showed that they knew this. On the other hand, there's a lot of cats just getting messed over.

Criminal activity is so rampant in Chicago on the upper levels, on the political levels, that smaller cats were getting used as patsies and run over. They were being used to save some big-time politician, someone who was connected to the politicians, or the businessmen who were running things and controlling the politics of the city of Chicago. I think that people could learn a heck of a lot from those prisoners who are getting railroaded.

There was even a case where both a father and his son were being railroaded on some jive murder beef. People were being used as stool pigeons, being charged with a crime and then offered freedom by the government, if they'd help convict another cat, by getting on the witness stand to lie and say that they saw this person here and this person there, when the person was actually someone that these cats had never seen in their whole lives.

It seemed like the prisoners knew quite a bit about when our constitutional rights were being violated. It amazed me, the insight they had. It was an experience for me to be able to really communicate with so many cats who were being railroaded in a very blatant way.

In that county jail, the brothers need to know a lot. They've got to understand that the power structure is what's messing them up.

A few cats who are guards tried to understand me. I gave those cats a lot of respect, the guards who did not try to fuck over me. Black guards did not try to mess me over, and I didn't try to mess over them. A lot of them were interested in the Black Panther Party and the philosophy. I tried to get 2,000 Panther papers into the jail, but I couldn't. They let the Muslim paper in, and they let the Catholics in to show movies and bring in all their little papers, with all the other kinds of religious groups. There was even a school in there, for some of the brothers. If they want to go to school at night, they can go to school, which is a positive thing. I felt the cats should also have the Black Panther paper and *Soul On Ice*. A lot of brothers could get a lot of correct concepts if they had the opportunity and took the time to read the Panther paper and *Soul On Ice*. Being in jail, they can see themselves as revolutionary politicians, changing the decadent conditions that we are subjected to, that caused them to be in jail in the first place, and caused the brothers and sisters to be murdered in the first place. But we shall consider them pigs in one form or another unless they are working and relating to end fascist, social injustices.

Those black guards learned from me and I learned from them. Cook County Jail is a good place to learn about what it's really like in Chicago. To me, Chicago is a big town with corruption pervading the whole situation, from Mayor

Daley all the way down to the pig on the street murdering people. That's the way I describe Chicago. And all the other towns in America where black people live are Chicagos.

In one month, the police in Chicago killed eighty black people, and that's genocide. Little girls just sitting on the steps doing nothing. Just shot down. Eighty black people were murdered in the streets.

While I was in the hospital in the Cook County Jail, they turned on the television and I saw this cat who was the president of the Afro-American Patrolman's League. This was right around the time that the Soto brothers were killed. What happened there was, one brother was murdered by a cop while he was walking down the street. It came out as a clear case of a cop just shooting the cat and killing him. His brother came home from the army, from fighting for his so-called country, for his brother's funeral. It wasn't three or four days later when he was shot in the back of the head by a cop. The people witnessed the fact that he was just walking down the street and the cop pulled his gun out and shot and killed him. Another of the brothers was there in the Cook County Jail. I never got a chance to see him, but they told me he didn't get emotional; he didn't crack up or anything. He went about his business. But everybody said they could tell that this brother isn't going to let that go, the way they killed his two brothers.

So I was watching this cat on TV, the president of the Afro-American Patrolman's League. There was another member with him, and they were running down how the racist aspect of the Chicago police department had accused them of having membership in the Black Panther Party. This patrolman didn't defend himself by *denouncing* the Party, but instead he definitely went forth to denounce the racist brutality and murder of black people in the black community. He set forth an understanding of the social evils and the social conditions that we are subjected to.

Prior to that, the only contact that I had had with the Afro-American Patrolman's League was when the cats

called up the office, a long time ago, when we were getting
ready to implement the community control of police. We
had already begun to move the community control of police
petition, where registered voters would sign a petition stat-
ing the fact that they wanted to have community control of
police with neighborhood councils who would do the hiring
and firing, and where also this kind of law would be voted
on as a yes or no proposition by all the citizens of the city,
and where all the policemen would be hired from the community that they lived in. And the Afro-American Patrolman's League was interested. They were not against this
kind of thing.

These cats I couldn't, and wouldn't, call pigs. The Party
wouldn't call them pigs, because in fact they are concerned
with the people in the community. And that's very significant. Some of the black cops right here in San Francisco,
call themselves the Officers for Justice. They even have
some white cats in their organization. We wouldn't call
those cats pigs either.

In Los Angeles, there was even one white policeman who
quit the police force a couple years back. He was going to
run for D.A. of Los Angeles County, because he was so
incensed about operations that were being used in railroading nearly half of all the black cats who were being put in
jail. They were actually being railroaded into jail with gross
violations of their constitutional rights. But as he put it, the
harassment by the racist police and the racist department
itself on black people in the black community was worse. I
thought of this, and the Officers for Justice, as I was listening to these cats from the Afro-American Patrolman's
League on the television in Cook County Jail.

It's very significant that black policemen would come
together like that. I see the necessity of even the black cats
who are deputies in the sheriff's department out there, regardless of what the sheriff says, or the superintendent—I
think they should get in the Afro-American Patrolman's

League and be a part of it and be really concerned with their community.

Most of the black cats in police departments really know that they're just there for a job. But I think that it's necessary that they raise their political consciousness and that of their fellow officers to a higher level, as the Black Panther Party's been trying to raise some gang members' consciousness to a higher political level. It's very necessary, because a lot of the cats who are committing crimes are really committing jive crimes against their own people and they don't have any basic political consciousness. And that's one thing the Black Panther Party's been trying to give to a lot of the cats in the black community, real revolutionary political consciousness, so they won't be running around committing petty crimes. They'll start defending themselves, and they'll find out they're defending something worthwhile. In this way, the black community, the black policemen, and those white policemen who are opposed to racism and oppression should move to expose the racism in the police departments. We really have to give the Afro-American Patrolman's League a lot of respect for taking that stand.

PIGS,
PROBLEMS,
POLITICS,
AND
PANTHERS

DO-NOTHING TERRORISTS AND OTHER PROBLEMS

■ From its very beginning, the Black Panther Party has had problems with a lot of people who come in and use the Party as a base for criminal activity which the Party never endorsed or had anything to do with. In the early days of the Party, we had to try a number of times to show brothers that they were breaking rules, and eventually tell them that they were no longer members of the Party and that they didn't represent the Party anymore.

Some brothers would come into the Party, and see us with guns, and they related *only* to the gun. But one of the things that the Party did from the very beginning was to sit brothers down and politically educate them. We assigned books and materials like *The Autobiography of Malcolm X, The Wretched of the Earth,* and helped them understand their constitutional rights and some basic points of law.

The ten-point platform and program was essential because through it the brothers would understand that we had guns, not for foolish criminal activity against their people, but for self-defense since there's so much brutality and murder unjustly committed on the part of cops against black people. We constantly tried to teach the brothers this from the very beginnings of the Party and many, many have learned well and understood the scope of the Party. But in the process and development of the Party, many have had to drop away, were expelled, or were told to get out of the Party.

There are some people who go around and say they are Black Panther Party members, when in fact they aren't. If they had been arrested or possibly had done something, or if the cops were just trumping something up on them, the police department would announce to the press that they'd just arrested some Black Panther Party members. Naturally the demagogic politicians and the police, who are the armed bodies of the state and protect the state and the greedy riches of the avaricious businessman, would lie and try to mislead the people. They didn't want people to understand the real philosophy of the Black Panther Party, the real ten-point platform and program, and the real community programs we were implementing on a very practical level to try to educate the people to end their oppression.

Violations of the rules of the Party were primarily due to previous conditioning and the oppression that we live in. The Party has the principle that only the worthy, those who are really dedicated to serving the people, those who are able to grasp the meaning of the rules and philosophy of the Black Panther Party, should be members. We have a rule that no one can be drunk while doing Party work. It doesn't mean that a Party member can't ever drink, but if he's drunk he can't do political work. You can't drink around the offices of the Black Panther Party. At one time brothers would bring around something to drink, but then we told them that they had to go into the back and they'd better not get drunk. Then we stopped that too. Brothers who were drunk would come around and say they wanted to get into the Party. We'd tell them they couldn't become members of the Black Panther Party.

If a member got sloppy drunk and became non-functional, then he would be put on a worker suspension. If he violated the rules again, we would expel him and put his name and picture in the Party paper, and explain that this person's selfish desires and needs seemed to be above the Party's principle of serving the people in the community.

Some people joined the Party for status reasons. The Party was well known in the community, and was written up in the papers a lot. These cats would put on a complete Panther uniform—black beret, black slacks, black shoes, black pimp socks or regular socks, shined shoes, blue shirt, and a black turtleneck. They were clean-shaven, or if they had a goatee or beard it was neatly trimmed. They'd stand up in front of the office with a mean face on, their chests stuck out, and their arms folded, watching people walk by. They were psychologically surviving off the incorrect sensationalism that had been put forth in the newspapers. We began to call them the "do-nothing terrorists." The only thing they did was rap to the sisters. There were some sisters who wanted brothers who would stand up, talk bad and loud, sell wolf tickets, and carry on. They never did any work at all or faked work, so we had to suspend and expel many of these brothers and sisters.

A bunch of them would stand around the office, and we'd ask them to do some work and pass out leaflets. They'd lie and say they had passed out the leaflets already. Half the time these cats would throw the leaflets away. We began to find stacks of leaflets thrown off in a lot or sitting in one of those Keep the City Clean wastepaper baskets. This really teed a lot of us off. All they wanted to do was front off being in the Panther Party and rap to the sisters. Some were just plain cultural nationalists, black racists. It was just a bunch of jive that we had to get rid of.

Sometimes white friends in the Peace and Freedom Party would come down to our office to drop off some money for transportation or some reams of paper. These fool, do-nothing terrorists would say, "You white people can't come into our office." There were a number of black racists around

also who *would* do some work but who would propagate
black racist attitudes, which was directly counter to the
Party's revolutionary line. We tried to tell the cats over and
over again that we had a working coalition for a specific
purpose with the Peace and Freedom Party. Some people
tried to take it out of context and tried to say that we trusted
white people, and we said, "No, we don't just 'trust' white
people. We just trust what white people *do*. Those whites
who do things that are positive, we respect. And those who
do things that are negative, we don't respect." That's the
way you have to see it. They would use this sometimes to try
and cover up their lack of work, so we cricitized them and
told them that they were just jiving and not working and
that they weren't doing anything positive for the Party.

Finally we told Huey about it, so Huey ordered all Black
Panther Party members not to wear their black berets anymore unless we were at a public function of some kind,
where the Party wanted to be conspicuous about the fact
that we had a uniform, and were a political party who had
members that were of service to the community.

Man, you should have seen the reaction. The do-nothing
cats were saying, "Man, what you talkin' 'bout! Baby,
you're ruinin' my game."

"That's just the point," we said, "so don't be wearing no
beret. This is going to identify who's doing work and who
isn't doing work. Don't be running around here fronting on
some kind of status in the Party."

Another problem at that time was that the brothers identified *only* with the gun. When we started the Party, Huey
and I didn't have any intention of having them identify only
with the gun. We knew that we had to teach them that the
gun was only a tool and it must be used by a mind that
thinks. When we first started out, the very first members had
to go to political education classes. Included was one hour
of field stripping of weapons, safety and cleaning of weapons in the home, etc. Then we had one or two hours of

righteous political education and study. The third area was work, coordinating various activities, and understanding the political significance of various actions we took, like when we went to the police department with our guns, when we had to go help out the brothers and sisters in Richmond, and when we went to the sheriffs' office and tried to enter armed with guns, along with community people, to protest murder and police brutality.

We also did the work in the community of patroling the police, actually trying to implement Point Seven of the ten-point platform and program. In all of these actions, we tried to teach the brothers the importance of politically educating the people. The correct political education among members was necessary to break up all these hassles that we were having trying to organize the Party. At the same time we wanted as many members as we could possibly get, so that the Party would spread and the members would carry the message. We also needed a really hard core of working people to get things off the ground. Huey finally sent a message out of jail that those who were not doing any work should be expelled from the Party, because he'd rather work with 100 smart people than 3,000 foolish people.

WHY THEY RAID OUR OFFICES

■ The raids on almost every Black Panther Party headquarters in the United States during 1969 were partially related to a move of the Party: Eldridge Cleaver made contact with members of the North Vietnamese government, and asked them to allow him to announce their proposal that if the United States government would release political prisoners in America, starting with Huey P. Newton and myself, then the North Vietnamese government would release the American prisoners of war they are holding.

Right after this was announced, while I was in Chicago at the trial, they readily cut it out of the newspapers and stopped the mass media from printing further information about this. The power structure did this and it is very related to the recent raids that came down and to the murder of Fred Hampton.

The raids upon the Black Panther Party were directly related to the purge that the Party had. The raids people heard about hit practically every Black Panther Party office in the country. The Black Panther Party began to purge in January 1969, by announcing that we weren't going to be taking any more members in. We worked and found out about a lot of fools, expelled them, and printed their names and pictures in *The Black Panther,* and explained to the people that they weren't representatives of the Pary anymore. This in itself stopped the CIA-FBI infiltration operation into the Panther Party. So the raids were also related to the fact that the Party had purged itself and stopped people from being able to come into it, infiltrate it, and work for the pig power structure to help distort the real objectives and goals of the Black Panther Party.

A technique typical of the power structure and their fascist pigs were those used in Los Angeles, from mid-1969 to the point where they attacked the Los Angeles Black Panther Party office in December of 1969.

Prior to the December raid, some 300 arrests were made upon the key leaders and organizers and coordinators of the Party throughout Los Angeles. About fifty members, the key ones, the ones who were leading and organizing other groups of people in the community, were arrested over and over again. Ninety percent of the charges on all those arrests were dropped after we bailed the people out. Those kinds of bails and exorbitant ransoms which they put on the brothers were a means they continuously used to deplete our funds.

There was consistent harassment. We have complete documentation of all the arrests that occurred and how the charges were dropped. This was a means by which the fascist, racist police in L.A. and the power structure were trying to wipe out the Black Panther Party.

This has been a national operation with a consistent pattern to it. It became more and more exposed when they murdered brothers Fred Hampton and Mark Clark in Chicago and shot up other Panther Party members.

Across the country in 1969, with their Mission Impossible-Mission Imperialist operation, it appears that they in fact murdered brother Alex Rackley in New Haven, Connecticut or used a lackey informer to do so.

Fourteen Party members were arrested in raids in which they supposedly were looking for Rackley's killers. The pigs raided the Detroit office, the Boston office, the New York office, the Chicago office, and the Denver office. They had previously raided the New Haven office and the Indianapolis office. They also raided the Sacramento office and shot it up. The San Diego office was raided but the Panther Party members weren't in it at the time. A lot of our offices around the country have been attacked and shot up two or three times, and Panther Party members have been shot up. The raids and the attacks upon the Black Panther Party are interlocked with the whole operation to kill as many Party members as possible.

That's one of the reasons we started the Black Panther Party newspaper: so the black person in New York could read what was happening in Los Angeles, Atlanta, or Chicago, or anywhere else in the nation. All the people who get the Black Panther Party newspaper can read about what is really happening, about the thousands of black brothers and sisters who are murdered, shot, and brutalized in the black communities and the wretched ghettoes throughout the country. Circulation for the Black Panther Party's paper has gone up in the thousands. It's gotten to the point where *The Black Panther* is out-circulating any other underground-type newspaper.

The power structure is trying to stop and smash the Black Panther Party, because the Party is ready to show and expose the racist power structure for what it is; to expose what Eldridge Cleaver identifies as the three levels of oppression: the avaricious businessmen, the demagogic politicians, and the fascist pig police forces that have been doubled, tripled, and quadrupled in every major city and wherever there are black people or brown people, people who are protesting or progressive white people. This is a fascist state that's breeding, and the power structure has to get rid of the Black Panther Party because the Party is setting forth ideology and teaching the people correct methods. We talk not only about the fact that we defend ourselves against oppression but we begin to expose the power structure with our Breakfast for Children, free health clinics, and free clothing programs. We've been arrested on the streets for selling the paper, and charged with loitering and blocking the sidewalk.

There have been underground, agent provocateur operations, and lies about Party members killing former Panthers. It's all an attempt to mislead the people about the real philosophy and program of the Party, so the cops can justify making raids on our offices. Agent provocateur operations were headlined in the papers and blown up. Some of the agents were black racists working with the pigs.

The McClellan Committee and people like them allow the pigs to raid us and they try to justify their actions in raiding our offices and shooting up offices. I hope the people can see the pattern forming. The pattern becomes set when the FBI and the local police department in Connecticut arrest fourteen members of the Black Panther Party and charge them with conspiracy to commit murder, conspiracy to kidnap, and also with murder and kidnap—fourteen people. Half of the people are leaders, righteous leaders of the Black Panther Party like sister Erica Huggins, who was the Deputy Chairman in Connecticut. At the time they were arrested they were ready to set up the Breakfast for Children Program. The brothers in New York were beginning to move with the Breakfast Program when they got busted on trumped-up charges. These operations and the way the power structure is moving make it clear and evident to me that it's a pattern. It's an attempt on their part to give us a lot of trouble and problems in trying to set up programs. This kind of attack is another part of the pattern. Complete information on all the arrests and all the charges that have been dropped against Party members will show how the power structure has been using these arrest tactics to deplete the funds of the Black Panther Party.

Nearly every Panther office in the country has been raided. In Des Moines, Iowa, they blew up the office, literally bombed it. There had been a big rally with people in the community who were ready to support the Breakfast for Children Program, white and black people were ready to support that program and get that program off the ground. And the pigs just bombed the office.

The year 1969 was the year of the pigs raiding Panther Party offices, trying to wipe the Party out, and trying to wipe out the community programs.

RENEGADES, JACKANAPES, AND AGENTS PROVACATEURS

■ When Huey found out I had been arrested on the shotgun charge, he immediately tried to get bail money. He got the brothers together and told them to get the Black Panther Party newspapers, take their cars, go out to Richmond, and sell the papers. He'd already scraped up some $60, but the bail against me was $1,400. We needed another $80 for my bond. Huey told the brothers we had to raise the money with the papers at twenty-five cents per copy.

There were about 4,000 copies left of the second issue of the Black Panther Party newspaper. The brothers took off with them, but instead of going out and selling the papers, they got to jiving around with some chicks in North Richmond. When they got back some three or four hours later, they had only sold about twenty-five papers, and used up a lot of gas. "You mean you haven't sold any more papers than this?" Huey asked them. One of the brothers admitted, after some debate, that they really hadn't been selling papers.

"To hell with selling these papers right now, man! I'm gonna jive with these chicks," one of the brothers had said. They had brought some of the chicks with them and Huey didn't want to embarrass the cats. He took the brothers to the side and said, "Take the girls back. You can get with them later. Go sell the papers!"

They went back out to Richmond, but they messed around again and didn't sell the papers. So Huey kicked every last one of them out of the Party.

"When you guys were all up in jail in Sacramento," he said, "Bobby got bailed out, and the first thing he did was go to work to get you out. He was really worried about you guys getting bailed out, and tried to get lawyers and everything. Now you guys are jiving around and the brother's in jail, and you won't do the same thing for him. That's not unity between brothers.

"You aren't captains anymore. Nobody is nothing. If you want to work for the Party, you're going to sell papers. Take off your guns. You don't know how to be responsible to the community and the people. You don't know how to be responsible to your leaders in the Party. So all of you are out of the Party. You're busted."

I had been out of jail three days but I still didn't know about this. I noticed a kind of depression around the office, and said to myself, "What's wrong with these guys?" They were still hanging around. They wouldn't leave because deep down inside they really liked the Party. It's just that they went astray and violated some basic rules.

Three days later they pulled me off to the side and said, "The other day brother Huey busted us all. The reason for it was because we goofed off, man. We should have been working to help get bail money to help get you out. Bobby, we're sorry, man."

I went and told Huey, "The brothers told me what they did, and the fact that you busted all of them." Huey said, "They're going to have to learn how to get themselves together." I said, "It's important that we stick together and not be jiving around with each other, or we won't have an organization. They asked me to forgive them for it, and I did." Huey agreed, and we let them back in the Party.

Problems like this kept arising though. About a week later we heard that some brothers had bags of weed in their possession. We called them all together, discussed the problem, told them that there was a rule in the Party that said we couldn't have any weed on us, because the cops were always watching us and it was dangerous for any Party member to have grass on him. We sat down and wrote some explicit rules. They were written out in an ordered form for the first time. We got the brothers to help us make the rules. We said that when someone breaks the rules, then it's the responsibility of all the other members of the Party to see to it that that person is put on suspension or kicked out of the Party. Some of the other rules that we made were that a Party member couldn't point or fire a weapon at anyone other than an attacking enemy, that members shouldn't steal anything, not even a needle or a piece of thread from the people, and that members weren't supposed to swear and cuss at the people because that's not serving them.

Today, we have twenty-six rules. About half of them are primarily for individual members of the Black Panther Party. The others are for office and Party functions as a whole, and for carrying out political duties in the community.

Since the early days, a lot of incidents have happened where cats have broken the rules. Some of this was because agents provocateurs have come into the Party, and have deliberately stirred up problems and done things in violation of the Party's principles and rules.

One of the things I remember very clearly was when J—— jumped out of a Black Panther Party truck and held up a diner. The big white van had BLACK PANTHER NEWS-PAPER written right on its side in big black letters, and was primarily used for hauling newspapers and distributing them around the community. David Hilliard and I had told J—— and S—— to take the truck across the Bay to San Francisco and pick up the eight or ten brothers who had been working most of the night over there putting out the paper. From what we found out through our investigations, S—— apparently drove the truck up to a diner and went to the restroom. They had already picked up the eight other brothers. J—— was in the front of the truck. The other eight cats were in the back of the truck and didn't know about anything that had happened. When S—— walked back to the truck, he saw J—— walking away from the diner with a money box and a gun in his hand. "Man, what's going on?" S—— asked. "Ain't nothin', man. It's cool," J—— said. S—— decided to drive the truck and get out of there. They were picked up by the pigs five minutes later. J—— shot and seriously wounded one cop.

What S—— should have done—he was a captain and a coordinator of the Party—was to have taken the gun away from J——, given the $80 back to the cashier, and then brought J—— to the Party Central Committee for disciplining. But he said he made the mistake of driving away from the diner, which is why at one point we suspected him of possibly being an agent provocateur. We didn't know for sure about J—— either, but our suspicions were high.

I was down in Santa Barbara for a speaking engagement at the time. I was sitting there when I read the papers about the shoot-out and robbery in San Francisco. I couldn't believe it; I thought it was some kind of trumped-up operation. When I got back to the office late that night I saw that David had written on the blackboard that no guns are to be carried unless authorized by the Central Committee. The next day we publicly put J—— out of the Party. We got all the other brothers out of jail finally, except J——.

About a month later J—— got out of jail and came to us. He said, "I was carrying out the Minister of Defense's program." "You're a damn liar," we said. "You weren't carrying out any Minister of Defense's program, not by pulling a petty jive robbery."

Then J—— asked me, "Well, Bobby, what do you think about it?" He was trying to divide me from David and Bunchy. David said, "What do you mean, what does Bobby think about it? It's what me, Bobby, the Central Committee, Huey, Eldridge Cleaver, everybody, thinks about it. It's all of us together." I said, "That's right, man. You weren't carrying out the Minister of Defense's program. Not like that you weren't. You must be crazy, man. I'm sorry, you just gotta get out of the Party."

Bunchy later saw that J—— was trying to put on some kind of front of still being a revolutionary. So Bunchy told him, "If you are a good man, if you just made a mistake, nobody can hold a good man down. If you're a true revolutionary, you'll serve the people. But you're still not in the Party. You can't explain that stuff to us, not by saying that you think that you were carrying out the Minister's program."

When that thing happened, we got phone calls from all over the place. We had a lot of support: it's some cops, some agents messing over you all, people said. They knew that petty robbery wasn't what the Party was about. If you get involved in that stuff then the older people in the community misunderstand the Party. You also mislead the young lumpen proletarian cat, who probably has got the guts enough to commit a robbery, but who we want in the Party so we can politically educate him that robbery isn't the way to go about solving the social problems that put him in the situation in the first place.

So we saw that somehow or another, this kind of activity was agent provacateur-type activity. We couldn't prove anything right away against J——. We thought that either he had flipped his lid or he was an agent provacateur.

We didn't kick S—— out of the Party, but after we helped bail him out, he came around trying to support J——'s position. I began to suspect him and decided to just watch his actions. A lot of times we actually bailed cats out even though they'd done wrong, to try to find out what the heck was wrong with them, to try to find out who was doing what and who was leading what and who was causing this stuff to happen.

Finally it got so bad that the next bunch of jackanapes who got busted—some cats riding around in a Panther car with broken lights, no registration, and carrying guns—we decided we weren't going to bail them out. David said, "We're not going to be putting out no more bail money for cats who're gonna violate the rules of the Party. When this stuff hits the papers, it looks like we're just a bunch of hoodlums and thugs, just because a couple of individuals start acting the fool."

About six brothers and sisters in the Party disagreed, and said we should bail them out anyway. When we asked why, they said, "Because they're black." We said, "No, we're not gonna bail them out just because they are black. They're not serving the people. In fact they're destroying the Party. We got to let people know that these type of individuals are not running the Party. We should kick them out." This small group of five or six cats didn't like that, so we told them to go raise the bail money themselves.

That was the start of a little black racist jackanape faction in the Party. As it turned out, this faction had an agent provacateur in it and we didn't know it. P—— was a righteous agent provacateur who came into the Party in 1968. This little faction of cats was hanging on more to black racism than to a progressive revolutionary program of serving the people. This little faction didn't understand that it was a class struggle we were in, and not a race struggle.

The agents provacateurs used the cats who refused to be politically educated and to follow the Party's revolutionary principles and rules. Half of the cats who didn't follow the program were being led astray by agent provacateur activity. We didn't know it at first, but we felt and knew that something was definitely going wrong.

A little crew of about ten or twelve cats had been meeting and getting together in a certain little corner around town at night. P—— was the leader of this crap, and behind the scenes was talking really negatively about the Party. These cats didn't understand that revolution doesn't only mean that you mass the people and teach them that they have the right to defend themselves against unjust police attacks. What they didn't understand is that revolution also means that you have to implement basic community programs, like Breakfast for Children, Liberation Schools, and free health clinics, and really work on these programs every day. They didn't understand how this educates the masses of the people to put more revolutionary political pressure on the power structure to implement similar programs. They didn't understand that you have to work hard at this, and P—— was consistently leading them away from working on these things.

These cats were what the Party calls jackanapes. A jackanape is a fool. He's foolish, but he's not scared of the police. He's foolish in that he'll get himself killed quicker. If you don't straighten him out, and try to politically educate him, he will definitely bring the Party down. If there's an agent provocateur around, the agent will hinder your attempts to politically educate these cats, and will lead them to do crazy things based on emotions rather than work based on understanding of social change. For example, a jackanape will come walking down the street with a gun in his hand, talking about, "Fuck the pigs. To hell with the pigs. I ain't going to jail." Then he'll be surrounded by twenty-five cops with shotguns pointed at his head and he'll go to jail. Deep down inside he really doesn't have anything to defend, because he doesn't know what he's defending. Real revolutionaries are like the brothers in the L.A. shoot-out, where the pigs attacked the office and pulled a pre-dawn raid on them. Those brothers defended that office because they were really defending the community programs that we were trying to set up. They defended themselves because they realized that the power structure wanted to rip them off and systematically exterminate them, that it wanted to prevent the organizing and uniting of the people around revolutionary programs.

A true revolutionary will get up early in the morning and he'll go serve the Free Breakfast for Children. Then when that's done he'll go and he'll organize a boycott around a specific issue, to support Breakfast for Children or support any other kind of program. He'll do revolutionary work in the community. He'll propagandize the community, he'll pass out leaflets. As a citizen in the community and a member of the Black Panther Party, he'll go to the firing range and take firing practice, but he'll follow all the gun laws and he won't conceal his weapon, or other jive stuff. He'll follow the rules and be very dedicated. He is constantly trying to politically educate himself about the revolutionary principles and how they function, to get a broad perspective. He'll also defend himself and his people when we're unjustly attacked by racist pigs.

Whereas a jackanape generally works from an opportunistic position. He centers things only around himself; he's still selfish. He thinks his pot and his wine are above the

Party. He thinks his gun is something that he can use at will, to rip off stuff for himself.

He can be politically educated, that's definite. But if you've got agents provocateurs running around sent in by the CIA and the FBI, black guys running around talking one thing and doing another thing, then it makes it much harder, because they mislead the jackanapes into doing all kinds of jive things to destroy the Party. You have to expose the informers and the agents provocateurs to the people.

The cats in the black racist faction, and some other cats who had come into the Party a long time before, were cats who had pulled robberies. We told them that if they were going to be in the Party, they'd better not do that kind of stuff, because that's not the Party's program and the Party doesn't endorse it. We even told all those cats that they didn't have to worry about rent and food as long as the Party had some funds. We said that five or six members could rent a house together, and the rent would be cheaper, and they wouldn't have to worry about a place to stay and their other needs. As long as people were dedicated revolutionaries, and worked around the clock, the Party would take care of them. We never pay anybody a salary. We just take care of the basic necessities of the Party members. These cats knew that they shouldn't be pulling robberies.

One day, just before David and I went to New York, A——, one of the cats relating to that little jackanape group, walked up to us and said, "Hey, man, I need to rip off some money." We said, "Say, man, before you came into the Party maybe that's what you were doing, but you don't do that anymore because the Party doesn't endorse that crap. You cats don't have to worry about rent and food." So he said, "OK, man," and we thought everything was cool. David and I had to go out of town that evening.

We went to New York, and the next day David called the National Headquarters to check in and he turned to me, real disgusted. "Bobby," he said, "We can't leave that damn place twenty-four hours before some jackanape or some

fool is messing up. K——'s old lady is on the phone talking
about some jive robbery that A—— and K—— were in."
I said, "A—— knows better than that, we were just telling
him yesterday that we don't go for that shit." David said,
"Man, we'd better hurry up and finish our business here and
get on back because these jackanapes and fools are going to
try to destroy this Party, if we don't watch them."

When we got back Deputy Chief of Staff June Hilliard
gave us the report and gave us some newspapers to read. It
really was a damn shame. They tried to rob a grocer for
$200 on a main street in broad daylight at 2:00 in the
afternoon. Six of them did it, with shotguns, M-1's, .45's,
etc.—they were Party guns too. We were really disgusted.
They could have walked up and asked me, or whoever was
handling the funds, for money for rent or whatever they
needed it for. We get $500 to $1,000 for each speaking
engagement we do, and I was doing ten or twelve a month
myself. They didn't have to rob that place.

We blasted them in the press. We said that they were
provocateurs, fools, and jackanapes, and that they only
wanted to use the Party as a base for some petty criminal
operation which the Party does not have anything to do
with, and does not endorse whatsoever. The Party's Central
Committee and the rules are completely opposed to this. We
ran this all through the Panther paper too.

K—— and A—— were in jail. Supposedly some of the
others got away. We had put the word out through the
grapevine, "Don't even come around the Party" to everyone who was supposed to have participated in that so-
called robbery because, "You're out of the Party. You're
no longer members of the Party, you don't represent the
Party." Two days later, the house where A——, K——,
and P—— had been staying was raided by the police. A
couple more brothers who were staying over there, and who
weren't necessarily in the little jive faction, were all busted.
We went down and got P—— out, because we thought he
was a good cat, who'd got busted just on this bullshit raid.

We also got a couple more out of jail, because we knew that they weren't in the hold-up. We trusted those cats and we just got them out of jail because they were getting rail-roaded.

Well, surer than shit, about a month later we got some information that P—— knew that the robbery was going to be pulled while David and I were in New York. We called him to a Central Committee meeting, and said, "Hey, man, look, we found out that you knew about this robbery, and that you didn't report it to the Deputy Chief of Staff. You were even the officer of the day then and you were supposed to report it in."

"Well," he said, "I didn't know nothing about it, man, I didn't know nothing about it." Then he sold us this story, that he just didn't have enough time to get back and report it—that he was being negligent. We put him on working suspension for one month.

Meanwhile, K—— and A—— were still in jail, and we refused to bail them out. The faction (some of them were still hanging around inside the Party) said, "You should bail them out." They didn't like it at all when we refused. We told K——'s wife that she didn't have to worry about anything, as long as she was working in the Party, but that if she wanted K—— out, she'd have to hustle the money herself.

The next thing that P—— was involved in was around that coloring book situation. It's very important because there was testimony at the McClellan Committee hearing against the Party about this. The coloring book situation started way back in November 1968.

That coloring book was drawn by a cat in Sacramento, an artist, who had black racist ideas. We tried to educate the brothers who had real narrow-minded cultural national-ist ideas which breed black racist thoughts, so we told him to start trying to do some kind of art that depicts the true revolutionary program. He went to Sacramento and did some drawings that he wanted to make up into a coloring book. He periodically brought back what he'd finished to the Party office. I would tell him, "Look, brother, you're showing a Black Panther with all muscles, every picture you draw. The Black Panthers all look like supermen, all muscle-bound and everything. We're not supermen, we don't profess to be supermen. We're just human beings and people like everybody else. Some of us are short. Some of the chicks are fine, but all of us are not what we call pretty. Some of us are skinny, and some of us are fat. Some of us do have muscles, but we're not all that way." I told him, "This coloring book you drew—it's got too many racist overtones. Another thing. You show a Panther shooting a cop. What you're showing is something without the political context, the reason why the Panther would shoot a cop. You've got to show the Panther defending himself from the unjust attacks by the cop. Now, if you show a black man being brutalized and unjustly attacked, and a Panther coming out of his door with a gun to help defend that black brother from that unlawful attack by that cop or something like that, then you're showing the political context and showing the right of black men to defend themselves. That's what you have to do. You know what I mean?"

I ran all this stuff down, and this cat took it back to work on it. In November, he finished and brought it down to the Central Committee meeting one Sunday. But it was still all wrong, and I told him, "No, man. This book doesn't show enough political content, man. It's got too much of the black racist overtones. You have to learn the Party's revolutionary principles and once you see the principles, you'll be able to draw like Emory, because Emory can give political content and meaning to the way he draws."

Well, I guess he loved his art, and liked the book the way it was. He had twenty-five of those books printed up in Sacramento and had brought them down to the office. Then he got someone working in the mimeograph room to print more of them up. We stopped him, and said, "No, man, don't print any more of these books, man. The books aren't right. You know what I mean. Let's make another coloring book, that shows more the revolutionary political content."

Sometime around January of 1969—after K——— was kicked out of the Party—he went and printed up a thousand more of those books. The little factionalizing schism group that P——— was running took the books and distributed them behind the scenes, against the orders of Central Committee. We didn't even suspect till a month after the robbery that something was wrong with P———. We heard, after we wouldn't bail out K——— and A———, that the factionalizing group was talking about, "The Party ain't right. The Party ain't doing right." We just thought they were a little group of dudes, acting the fool, and we said, "Man, later for them dudes." Then we found out from one person that P——— seemed to be the leader of it. His function was to be the advocate among this little group of cats who related more to black racism than to the Party's program.

During the month that P——— was on suspension he came down every day and worked in the office steadily for about three weeks. Then one day he walked into the office with somebody that no one had ever seen before. Now, we've got a little sign posted—NOBODY BUT AUTHORIZED PERSONNEL BEYOND THIS POINT. You can come into the front section of the National Headquarters office, but you can't go roaming all through the back unless you're a member of the Party. We figured that the cops would send agents provocateurs in to plant weed or something on us in the back room, or we figured that they might come in and plant a bomb in a briefcase, and leave it there to blow us up. That's why we don't let everybody walk back through the offices. Unauthorized people stay in the front section of the office, where the officer of the day, and all the brothers and sisters working in there can watch them.

P——— brought this cat all through the back. June

and David happened to spot him. David told me later on that evening, "Man, P—— brought some dude I ain't never seen, showing him our machines and stuff." There's a $2,500 machine, an electric stencil machine, a $450 mimeograph machine, our tape recorders, and other equipment back there. David said, "June stopped him and asked him, who in the heck did he think he was bringing strangers all in the back, showing the Party's equipment and carrying on." And P—— said, "Well, man, this brother here wanted to get in the Party, and I was just showing him around the place here." "Wait a minute, man, wait a minute," June said. "You can't bring anybody back here. The man isn't in the Party, and don't be doing that. You know you're wrong. Furthermore, I'm going to report you to the Central Committee."

At the Central Committee meeting, David told P——, "I heard about you over there, running around with this old bunch of jackanapes and cats who're relating to that black racism and perpetuating that crap. So, the best thing you can do is get on away from this Party. Get on away and don't even come around the Party office anymore, because it seems to me that maybe you're the one who's been getting people to steal other stuff out of our office when we're not here at night. Two .357 Magnums have been stolen and a couple more machines and tape recorders are missing." David ran it down.

"So, you come around here showing people that stuff. I've been on the block long enough to know a hood and a thug when I see one, and if a fool like you who was in the Party is going to run around and deal with cats like that, and isn't gonna send him through the proper channels of the Party, it seems to me that you're the one that's pulling all this stuff. You also got that factionalizing group over there. Get away from this Party and stay away and don't even come back here no more." That's the way it was.

The next thing we heard was that some chick in that group tried to hold up a Wells Fargo Bank with an M-1 rifle. She went in the Wells Fargo Bank, the cops were waiting for her, and she got arrested. The job was set up by P——. Well, we still weren't sure that P—— was a righteous CIA agent provocateur. But we knew he was doing something wrong, and all suspicion was pointed toward him.

Next, a brother dropped around after he got out of jail and said, "Man, I wasn't in that stuff." He heard K—— and A—— talking while he was in jail and he found out that P—— was the one who *planned* the robbery that the others were involved in. So we said, "Well, I'll be damned." We began to see what was happening. That's the way the stuff began to get exposed.

Then P—— got four or five other ex-Panthers and went up north to Seattle to try to sway the Seattle branch against the National Headquarters. They got up there and it came out in the papers that they had been busted for possession of hashish. Then they all got cut loose. We didn't dig the fact that they got busted up there, and then were automatically let off. There's something sneaky about it and it's tied into the fact that they were trying to split the Seattle branch (the Seattle branch told us that they were up there trying to do that).

Well, with all this information, and knowing that P—— was leading this stuff, we went back and figured out a few things. For instance, there was an article he got into the Party newspaper accusing Mark Comfort of working with the police in Oakland. The article said that the police department downtown had given them permission to carry guns, but we found out later that Mark Comfort had organized a program where some of his boys were to protect the black businessmen in the black community and guard their places. Apparently owners of stores who hire people to guard them can authorize these persons to have guns. P—— wanted us to publicize the fact that Comfort was working with the cops in the paper, but we said, "No, not till we get all the facts."

But in the next issue of the paper the article appeared,

under the pseudonym "Sip." Nobody gave authorization to put that article in the paper. We found out that P——rushed over to the layout room right before the deadline and said that we told him to put the article in there, which we hadn't.

After the article appeared, Mark Comfort and his group got so many phone calls and the people were so down on them, talking about how they were pigs, that it really destroyed them. It was a means by which P—— was actually moving to try to get an organization in another part of town fighting and bickering with the Party to cause disunity. So this was the next thing that pointed out P—— to be an agent provocateur in the Black Panther Party.

The clear exposure of P—— involved a black cat who was never really in the Party but who for months came around and hung around the front office. He floated around town. Well, three doors down from the Party's office he got into an argument with someone inside the little barber shop. Somebody shot this cat right there in front of the barber shop. Killed him dead. Sunday morning, the next day, P—— called a press conference with a small group of other jackanapes and renegades, and he sounded just like J. Edgar Hoover. He said that this dead guy was his brother, that they had both been kicked out of the Black Panther Party, and that the Party had killed this guy and were going to kill him. All this was an out-right bold-faced lie.

Now what this did was to spread all over the country the lie that we shoot and kill Black Panther Party members. From all my speculation, this stuff is all connected to that frame-up on me and the other brothers in New Haven, Connecticut.

The final thing that really showed P—— to be an agent provocateur was when the Grand Jury investigations came down. Who do you suppose comes walking in to testify, escorted by the FBI through the back doors? P——, who was still trying to pose like he's just somebody, trying to cover up the fact that he's an agent provocateur. He sat there saying that he'd been in the Party, and told them a bunch of lies about the Party. The pigs then used this in the press to try to distort the people's understanding about the Party.

Stuff about the coloring book came up in testimony at the McClellan Committee hearings. The national press really used this testimony to try to destroy the Party. They said, "The Black Panther Party has now kicked the book out of the Breakfast for Children Program," and tried to say that it was because of the Senate investigation. They hardly mentioned the real facts which we ran down in a press conference. The jackanapes, led by P—— on the side, were running around spreading the coloring books. What P—— had them do, is when the kids would leave Breakfast for Children, they would find the kids, give them a book and say, "I'm a Black Panther." So they staged all this stuff to move to try to destroy the Party politically, and to try to destroy the Party's Breakfast for Children Program.

Right around the time of the Senate investigations A—— sent a letter to Charlie Garry. In this letter he said that he had gotten mixed up with the wrong group, and that agents provocateurs and other cats were the ones who were doing wrong to the Party, and lying about it. He said that he'd been asked to testify before the McClellan Committee and had refused. A—— got five to life in jail.

The purge that we started in the Party came after all these provocateur operations by P—— and others that we didn't know about. After this happened we stopped letting members into the Party. This enabled us to spot the agents provocateurs better, because we could see who was doing work, who wasn't doing work, and who was messing things up. By not letting anybody else in, we cut down on the confusion caused by the constant influx of people. Over a thousand people from around the country have been expelled from the Party. These people are opportunists, jackanapes, renegades, agents, and other kinds who just refuse to understand that we subordinate ourselves to the people by serving the people.

We print the pictures of people we expel from the Party in the Black Panther paper. We also print the reasons why they were expelled, so as to explain things to the people. A lot of people will run around and say they're Panther Party members, when they're not. These people will do all kinds of crazy things like intimidating people, romping and running in the streets, and acting like fools. They give the Party a bad name.

If someone who is actually a Black Panther Party member is cussing people out or intimidating people or something like that, then we hope those people are reported to the Black Panther Party. They won't be in the Party long, because we'll expel them, and expose them for exactly what they are. Generally we keep the Party very well disciplined. Party members respect the people in the community, and work to serve the people in the community. At the same time they stand ready to defend the Party and the community from the cops who attack us.

The key thing to holding the Party together has been real political education and respect for the people. This is something for which brother David deserves a lot of credit. Brother Ray "Masai" Hewitt has been able to give Party members a broad perspective. The work on the part of the Party members can't be matched by the average organization in the black community. The dedication that the Party members have, is something that's above opportunism, above selfishness, and above sloth, and not caring about people. This is because Party members care about the survival of black people, even at the risk of being made political prisoners, or getting killed and murdered by the fascist cops, or being forced into exile.

Here are the rules as they appear each week in the Black Panther newspaper.

RULES OF THE BLACK PANTHER PARTY

National Headquarters
Berkeley, California

Every member of the Black Panther Party throughout this country of racist America must abide by these rules as functional members of this Party. Central Committee members, central staffs, and local staffs, including all captains subordinate to either national, state, or local leadership of the Black Panther Party will enforce these rules. Length of suspension or other disciplinary action necessary for violation of these rules will depend on national decisions by national, state or state area, and local committees and staffs where said rule or rules of the Black Panther Party were violated.

Every member of the Party must know these verbatim by heart. And apply them daily. Each member must report any violation of these rules to their leadership or they are counter-revolutionary and are also subjected to suspension by the Black Panther Party.

The Rules Are:

1. No Party member can have narcotics or weed in his possession while doing Party work.

2. Any Party member found shooting narcotics will be expelled from this Party.

3. No Party member can be DRUNK while doing daily Party work.

4. No Party member will violate rules relating to office work, general meetings of the BLACK PANTHER PARTY, and meetings of the BLACK PANTHER PARTY ANYWHERE.

5. No Party member will USE, POINT, or FIRE a weapon of any kind unnecessarily or accidentally at anyone.

6. No Party member can join any other army force other than the BLACK LIBERATION ARMY.

7. No Party member can have a weapon in his possession while drunk or loaded off narcotics or weed.

8. No Party member will commit any crimes against other Party members or BLACK people at all, and cannot steal or take from the people, not even a needle or a piece of thread.

9. When arrested, BLACK PANTHER MEMBERS will give only name, address, and will sign nothing. Legal first aid must be understood by all Party members.

10. The ten-point program and platform of the BLACK PANTHER PARTY must be known and understood by each Party member.

11. Party Communications must be National and Local.

12. The 10-10-10-program should be known by all members and also understood by all members.

13. All Finance officers will operate under the jurisdiction of the Ministry of Finance.

14. Each person will submit a report of daily work.

15. Each Sub-Section Leader, Section Leader, Lieutenant, and Captain must submit daily reports of work.

16. All Panthers must learn to operate and service weapons correctly.

17. All Leadership personnel who expel a member must submit this information to the Editor of the newspaper, so that it will be published in the paper and will be known by all chapters and branches.

18. Political Education Classes are mandatory for general membership.

19. Only office personnel assigned to respective offices each day should be there. All others are to sell papers and do Political work out in the community, including Captains, Section Leaders, etc.

20. COMMUNICATIONS—all chapters must submit weekly reports in writing to the National Headquarters.

21. All Branches must implement First Aid and/or Medical Cadres.

22. All Chapters, Branches, and components of the BLACK PANTHER PARTY must submit a monthly Financial Report to the Ministry of Finance, and also the Central Committee.

23. Everyone in a leadership position must read no less than

two hours per day to keep abreast of the changing political situation.

24. No chapter or branch shall accept grants, poverty funds, money, or any other aid from any government agency without contacting the National Headquarters.

25. All chapters must adhere to the policy and the ideology laid down by the CENTRAL COMMITTEE of the BLACK PANTHER PARTY.

26. All Branches must submit weekly reports in writing to their respective Chapters.

WOMEN AND THE BLACK PANTHER PARTY

In the Black Panther Party, we understand that male chauvinism is directly related to the class society. In order to explain how the Party deals with male chauvinism, I want to point out how the Party thinks and how the Party understands things.

The ideology of the Party is the whole historical experience of black people in America, the experience of all the social evils that have trampled on our heads and caused us to be oppressed. This historical experience of black people, translated through Marxism-Leninism, is really the ideology of the Black Panther Party. The history of the Party is a process of putting into practice the basic revolutionary principles that we've acquired. And these principles not only relate to the economic and social evils, but they're also *caught up* in the economic and social evils in this system that oppress black people. These social evils are created and maintained by this capitalistic government which is infested with a lot of ruling-class elite, greedy businessmen, and demagogic politicians. In the Party itself there has always been, on the part of Party members, the same kind of progressive, changing experience, in terms of being one with the people.

We need to establish a system based on the goal of absolute equality, of all people, and this must be established on the principle of *from* each and every person, both male and female, according to their ability, and *to* each and every person, both male and female, according to their needs. We see establishing socialism in the society as a means by which we begin to remove the oppressive social obstacles, and hope to build a society where someday a man and a woman can relate to each other totally on the basis of natural attraction.

When we study other societies (and you must to understand the society that you live in, to talk about any aspect of the groups which live in poverty within that society), we see that there is a consistently changing culture that exists among these people in poverty, and their economic, political, and social situation is directly related to our everyday lives.

When Eldridge and Huey and the Party as a whole move to get rid of male chauvinism, we're moving on that principle of absolute equality between male and female: because male chauvinism is related to the very class nature of this society as it exists today. And even in the Party there are relationships between male and female that have to be ironed out to a level where it makes some sense. The Party is working very hard and fast to break down male chauvinism: at the same time that we are moving on this matter in relation to the community, we are also moving and changing in relation to ourselves.

There are some fine sisters in the Party, Kathy, Marsha, and some others, who were walking in front of a little barber shop, two doors down from the National Headquarters in Berkeley. It's a shop where a lot of brothers, many of whom have just recently come out of the joint, go to get processes on their heads. Some of these brothers call themselves pimps, and you can figure that some of them, at one point or another, are pushing weed or something—the type of activities that black men are driven to, trying to live. These brothers are playing their old game, saying to each other, "Man, I know I can rap to one of the Panther sisters and take all of those chicks away from all of the cats over there in the Panther office."

Now this is an old game that's related to male chauvinism, to the brother dominating the sister. What that's related to—as Malcolm X put it one time—is that the President is the biggest pimp in the country. And this pimping the sister on the block is related to the continued existence of a class system. It's cross-related to the economic problems in the black community where the male is put into a position where he can't really be the breadwinner for the home.

So when the sisters walked in front of the little barber shop, I noticed some brothers were huddled among each other, speculating on the Panther sisters. They tried to rap to Marsha and a couple of other sisters, and Marsha set them straight.

She said, "Look, brother, you're getting none of this! You don't use this on the streets, either. The only way you can get close to me is to get hip to some of the real ideology of the Black Panther Party."

Then another sister said, "Yeah. If you want to get next to us, why don't you check out the Red Book?"

Well, those brothers were a little shocked. Then the other brothers inside the place started laughing at the brothers outside. Well, this got off with the brothers. It seemed like the whole barber shop got upset, not in an antagonistic manner, but wanting to know what it was that didn't allow these sisters to go for that old pimp game. Naturally their speculation was that the sisters made love to us, and therefore they agreed with our rap. What they didn't understand, is that you can't define it in terms of what kind of rap is going down, that it was the ideology of the Party that was helping to bring us out of that very same kind of thinking.

So their curiosity was aroused, and the brothers tried rapping with some of the other sisters, and got the same answers. The next thing I knew, all those brothers had come over to the Party headquarters, twenty-five or thirty of them, to buy some Panther literature and some Red Books. They stopped talking and started listening. And the sisters laid the revolutionary ideology right on them.

We had tried for a long time, in a lot of ways, to get these brothers motivated, but it took some sisters with a new and respectful way of looking at themselves, to bring these brothers in!

Down in L.A., over a year ago, brother Bunchy Carter had put up six offices in the black community, which attracted hundreds and hundreds of members. Now not all of them, but some, were coming around the Party office with wine in their heads. When Bunchy went down to one of the offices, he'd catch them walking up to the door. They were supposed to have been there at ten, but were coming along at noon or later. Bunchy used to call them the "drunk-for-lunch bunch."

Bunchy would say, "Who do you think you are? Don't you know that these fascist pigs are here to murder us and don't you know that we are surrounded by imperialistic wolves who murder and kill and commit genocide against black people? And here you fools come up late and drunk for lunch! What's wrong with you?"

So Bunchy, trying to cross-relate our principles on the level of our everyday lives, asked all the sisters to turn a cold shoulder to all these fools who came around late, and the ones who didn't do any work. "The Minister of Defense," Bunchy explained, "is going to start kicking them all out, and I'm going to start kicking them out right now. Will you sisters help the Party?

"These cats aren't doing any revolutionary work, but are wanting to go to bed with you, talking about how much they love you. But they must not love you very much at all, because they aren't doing revolutionary work so you can be free."

Well, the sisters dug that. Bunchy had to expel a few of the sisters and brothers who were lazy and just didn't want to do the work in the office and the community that is necessary to run a chapter of the Black Panther Party. But mostly, they straightened up and got down to work.

Originally, we had established rank in the Black Panther Party, according to the political work and political duties of each member. A captain was generally a coordinator, that was his political duty. We judged a person on whether or not he took responsibility, because one of the Party's principles is that you can delegate authority but you cannot delegate responsibility. Lieutenants were security people and sergeants were section leaders. Corporals were subsection leaders. A regular Panther with no special rank was one who was out of training, and a buck private was a Panther in training. Privates were Panthers who had completed the training, which was six weeks of Party political education classes. We had originally structured this, all the way up to the assistant central staff, with the chief of staff. But very soon we discovered that we were running into some problems with this system. For instance, in some office back East, a brother had been made the deputy minister of health, and didn't even know how to put on a bandage. We had to straighten that out right away, and show chapters they shouldn't give people a certain rank just to fill out a spot. Finally we just dropped this system, and stopped relating to rank altogether. But these problems are related to how some brothers, not all but some, had a tendency to misuse the rank concept, in relation to the sisters.

We found that, every once in a while, you'd get a brother calling a sister counter-revolutionary. And the sisters were getting mad about that because it seemed to be related only to the fact that the sisters didn't want to sleep with the brother. In other words, a brother would try to get next to a sister, and when the sister didn't dig him, he'd run around saying she was "counter-revolutionary." Some of the brothers said erroneous things, like, "I'm in the streets and I have to defend you." Some would say, "I'm a captain, so it's your duty to give in to me."

We broke this stuff up right away, and placed it forth that brothers who were captains or any other rank couldn't be using their rank just to go to bed with a sister. At the same time, it didn't go just one way. A few of the sisters had a tendency to go along with this. Finally one or two of them began to speak out, and we definitely got rid of this particular kind of male chauvinism. The main thing the brothers had to understand was that no one had any right to speak of a sister as counter-revolutionary on any personal basis, or to say that he had to defend her. The way we see it, the sister is also a revolutionary, and she has to be able to defend herself, just like we do. She has to learn to shoot, just like we do. Because the pigs in the system don't care that she's a sister; they brutalize her just the same. I think that since the pig structure has been trying to kill Erica Huggins, brothers have begun to see that the sisters can get arrested, too, just the same as the brothers. I know that the community can see this in the recent shoot-out in L.A., where the sisters were in there too, battling, defending just as hard as the brothers.

A lot of the brothers in the black community who only think of the sisters as secondary—brothers who are pimping sisters and think that this is the way life has to be—have begun to see that the examples that are being set by the Black Panther Party are more progressive. They see us winning on a higher level and treating the sisters on an equal level. The brothers in the community see that sisters don't want to oppress us; what they really want is equality. They want to be treated like human beings. And we've found that the sisters work better in the Party when they're treated in this way. If a sister's in charge and taking responsibility to do something, the brothers follow her orders. They don't say, "I ain't going to listen to no woman."

We did have problems of that sort until we politically educated some of them, and we finally all had to purge our hearts, and, as Eldridge says, purge our souls and purge our minds in relation to the old environmental conditioning. So with this attitude, the sisters related to the brothers even more, not on the basis of who's the cutest and who's the handsomest. Personal relations now are based more on knowing people personally and humanly, on people coming and working together and functioning in the Party. Now when men and women meet each other, their relation comes out of common interests, common goals, to function in the Party as revolutionaries.

There was an incident that happened when this kind of change was just beginning to take place. My wife and I had just moved to one of the Panther houses in Berkeley. There were three other bedrooms in the house and some Party members from out of town were staying there. One of these brothers had been working closely with a particular sister for several days, living and working there at the house. He really liked the sister and she kind of dug him too.

So one night, after my wife and I had gone to bed, there came a knock on our door. "Chairman Bobby?" the sister called.

I said, "Yes?"

"Can I ask you a question?"

"Sure," I said. I got up, put on my pants, and walked out. "What is it?" I asked her.

She said, "If a brother doesn't know the ten-point platform and program, I shouldn't give him any, should I?"

I said, "Well, wait a minute, now. Do you like the cat?"

"Yeah," she said, "I dig him, but I'm not going to give him any unless he knows the ten-point platform and program."

"What are you trying to do?"

"We got in bed, you see, and I asked him if he knew the

ten-point platform and program. He said he did, so I sat there drilling him, and he missed about ten words. He didn't say it exactly."

I didn't smile. This was serious to the sister, and because of that it was serious to me too. So, without making any male chauvinistic statements, I just said, "Not all the brothers are going to be able to know it exactly, word for word. But they might be able to know in a general sense what they're about. Maybe the brother explains it in his own words."

She said, "Well, I thought that everybody in the Party should know the ten-point platform and program by heart."

"No," I explained, "not necessarily. What we meant when we said that every Party member had to know the ten-point platform and program by heart was, that we put high responsibility on you to really study it and understand it. But what if you knew all the words just right, and still didn't understand the meaning of it? Would that do any good?" She shook her head. "Well," I went on, "if you could say the platform and the program in your own words, and what it was all about, each one of the ten points, of what we want and believe, why that's even better. Your own words are more related to your everyday life, and would have more meaning to you. So if the brother doesn't know the words just exactly, that doesn't mean he doesn't know the platform. But don't you *like* the cat?" I asked her.

"Sure," she said. "I like him lots, and I really want to make love to him. But I'm not going to trump over the Party's ideology."

"Well," I explained, "some of the brothers learn slowly, you know. And they know making love a lot better than anything else."

Now while I was explaining this to the sister, the brother had grabbed up a pillow and blanket to go downstairs. He said, "I'm going to find a sister in the Party I dig who doesn't know the program any better than I do, and we're going to have some real equality." In a way, of course, this was all funny to me, but the sister was very serious. She didn't want him to just run on over her and not pay attention to the things that were important to her.

But the sister that night called the brother back upstairs and told him she understood things a little differently and she really did care about him. This is one example of the kinds of things that happened between people in the Party when we began to deal with the issue of male chauvinism.

There was another incident that took place during the conference last summer that was important.

People came from all over the country to attend the National Committee to Combat Fascism conference, and every Panther house in the Bay Area was crowded way past capacity. People were sleeping on the floors on pallets, in sleeping bags, on couches and beds, and even in the hallways. Over at Eldridge Cleaver's house, all the bedrooms were occupied, and people were sleeping down on the living room and dining room floors.

One of the sisters sent in a complaint to Party headquarters, saying that a brother had attempted to rape her.

As we investigated this, it turned out that the brother had come into the room and had gotten into the bed where she was sleeping in her clothes. It wasn't uncommon when it was as crowded as that, for a brother and sister to sleep next to each other. And she had told him it was OK to sleep there. Well, it seems that he got sexually aroused from sleeping so close to her, and tried to get a little *too* close. But she pushed him away from her, and he simply quit trying. So we pointed out that since she had been able to just push him away, this wasn't really attempted rape. And she realized that it wasn't.

These are the kind of problems we came up with, and still do. We try to get rid of these petty problems. We try to teach the brothers and sisters the basic Party principles, and how to use these principles to relate to each other.

The problems between the brothers and sisters relate to

past conditioning. In a situation where a brother and sister are lying beside each other, past social conditioning has taught that brother that he can use force on the sister, and take her without caring about her feelings in the matter. Now the brother must learn that he has no right to use any kind of force on that sister, and she must watch herself for her own attitude, and not see everything he's doing as force, because that's the kind of conditioning she's had.

We had to make more rules in the Party because a number of similar incidents came up. One of those rules was that the brothers had better not use any force on any sister in the Party. It hasn't been all smooth and easy, getting these rules across. A year and a half ago, when this started, it even got to the point where a sister was hit by a brother. She fell back and her heel was cut by a piece of glass that broke when she fell on it. It was a struggle to stop this kind of thing.

Where the sister was previously regulated to typing and cooking and stuff like this, we broke up those roles in the Party. That was a struggle, too. We even had to deal with the way brothers talked to sisters, because every once in a while we'd catch a brother talking to a sister in such a harsh manner that it really scared her, enough so she'd do anything he said. The sisters brought these complaints up, and we told the brothers, "We're tired of that. We're not going to have that in the Party. We're not going to have any kind of messing over these sisters." I think that the sisters began to respect the Party much more for these things, seeing that the brothers wanted to treat them as human beings, and not as necessarily subordinate to us.

All these incidents and problems are cross-related to the economic system in our society, the fact that a black man can't get a job. These oppressive obstacles have to be removed, or they'll perpetuate themselves. Economic obstacles cause black men to commit crimes, especially around Christmas time. Many a black man who doesn't ordinarily commit crimes will go out and rob a gas station or a bus to get the money to buy his family the things the rest of the society has taught them to want. Many of the brothers just give up and leave their families. Because of this rotten system, a lot of young brothers grow up not wanting to get married. They want to be pimps and subordinate the sister.

In our Party, the sister is not told to stay home. If she's got a job, they take all the babies over to one house and one person, male or female, takes care of them all. We do that quite often, for the sisters who have children. Then of course there's the Liberation School, which brothers and sisters run; and sisters have to learn to shoot just as well as brothers. It works both ways, too. For instance, one sister didn't want to teach Charles Bursey shorthand and typing, because she felt that it was improper. Well, she learned brothers can be secretaries, too.

These principles come from Huey. Huey has always talked about the fact that he believed in equality for men and women. You'll find some women's organizations that are working strictly in the capitalist system, and talking about equality under the capitalist system. But the very nature of the capitalistic system is to exploit and enslave people, all people. So we have to progress to a level of socialism to solve these problems. We have to *live* socialism.

So where there's a Panther house, we try to live it. When there's cooking to be done, both brothers and sisters cook. Both wash the dishes. The sisters don't just serve and wait on the brothers. A lot of black nationalist organizations have the idea of regulating women to the role of serving their men, and they relate this to black manhood. But a real manhood is based on humanism, and it's not based on *any* form of oppression.

"OFF THE PIG," "MOTHERFUCKER," AND OTHER TERMS

■ *Off the Pig* means to kill the slave master. It doesn't mean commit murder. Some of the brothers in the Party made up a song: "There's a pig upon the hill/If you don't get 'im, the Panthers will."

But first one must understand what a pig is—police, bigots, and fascists. The Black Panther Party started the term.

A pig is an ill-natured beast who has no respect for law and order, a foul traducer who's usually found masquerading as a victim of an unprovoked attack.

This definition was printed in the second issue of the Black Panther Party's newspaper in May of 1967. If you read it closely, you'll see what is really meant by "pig." The police are generally referred to as such. But racist bigots and sadistic fascists who help maintain the oppression of any people are considered pigs. It is best understood when we look at the history of the KKK and Hitler's Gestapo.

Huey said, just before we went to press with the second issue of the newspaper, "We have to have some terms that adequately define the police and fascist bigots who commit murder, brutalize, and violate people's constitutional rights." I told him he already called those who actually do this "fascists" and "swine." Huey said, "Yeah, but black people aren't picking it up. It's not simple enough so they'll understand it. Children, teenagers, and older people, everybody." Then Huey, walking around the room thinking, said, "Swine . . . pig . . . swine" and Eldridge sat down at the typewriter and typed out the definition. He gave it to Huey. Huey said, "Yeah." Emory had a drawing of a pig. We put it on the front page and wrote under it "Support Your Local Police," a Birchite slogan which is also supported by "white citizen," white racist, so-called "patriotic" organizations.

Numerous reports at this time in 1967 had appeared on how the police department had been hiring Birchites, KKK members, and other white racists. It was later taken out of the news. But police departments had doubled and tripled across this country, especially where black and other poor oppressed peoples live in large numbers. Murder and police brutality had been going on for hundreds of years, but unjust treatment and slaughter of black people by racists and police which weren't reported by the press much at all, had taken on a new high in the last ten years.

We knew that this was the working and organizing of a more overt fascist police state right here in America and now, today, three years since the Party was organized, in many cities, especially Los Angeles, San Francisco, Chicago, New York, and other places, police departments have been quadrupled by the hiring of many sadistic, warped-minded blacks.

There are a few good policemen, black and white. But the majority are sadistic and racist and do not respect the constitutional rights of the people whatsoever. They actually believe in brutality, terrorizing, intimidating, and outright murder, and too many times come up acting and masquerading like a victim of an unprovoked attack.

Huey said, "This defining of the police as pigs will hopefully make some of them think, and oppose what the racists in the police departments are unjustly doing. It will spread to millions and millions of people who know that the cops are 'pigs' and will hopefully generate some political movement for real community control of the police. The police departments are acting like the old German Gestapo who the world called 'swine,' which is the same as 'pig.' The racists in this country are exactly that by the definition you have typed out, Eldridge.

"Pigs, pigs, pigs," Huey said. "If the people go forth using their constitutional rights to vote them out and make a real people's police force, and then, if the rotten politicians don't respect the right of the people's vote and use their guns like Hitler did, then they are officializing themselves as Gestapo and are oinking in the face of the people. Guerrilla warfare will have to be used then by the masses of the people. But we have to defend ourselves now. So when and if the police officialize themselves as Gestapo, 'off the pig.' Right now, if they unjustly attack us, 'off the pig' because we have a human right to defend ourselves and the people must learn now that they must also defend themselves against unjust, brutal, murderous 'pig' attacks."

Eldridge, Huey, and I checked out Emory's layout of the pig for the front cover and said, "Right on, Emory. That's together."

"A low-life pig, a foul traducer," Eldridge said, "who's usually found masquerading as a victim of unprovoked attack."

We were very enthusiastic about getting the paper off the press and into the streets.

"This will begin to let the people know how the black community sees the police who occupy our communities like a foreign troop and violate the people's constitutional rights," Huey said.

Eldridge said, "Man, these pigs are going to shoot us down on sight when this paper hits the street and they see this."

"But it's the right to freedom of the press and free speech that we're exercising to educate the people as to what's really happening and what must be changed," Huey said. "So if they attack us or try to kill us for this we'll defend ourselves. We'll off any pig who attacks us."

Eldridge said, "Emory, you've got to do some art to show the people what to do in defending themselves with guns and what to do in the future because I believe from here on in it's going to be nothing but a fascist police state, even more so than it is now."

"Also," Huey said, "The people have got to know that we don't believe in murder but only in self-defense in the future and in the present. They must understand that self-defense

goes beyond just defending ourselves with guns, but that
political organizing and implementing the ten-point platform and program are the real political, economic, and
social means of defending ourselves. So the people have got
to see some things that relate concretely to their problems
and the gun has got to be seen as a proper tool in defending
ourselves when we, the masses, organize revolutionary programs for self-determination and survival."

I said, "Yeah, you know Malcolm X said we had to deal
with the basic political and economic necessities for our
people, also."

Huey said, "And the gun, Malcolm said, was for self-defense since the government won't do its job. We stand on
Malcolm X's principle."

Malcolm had said:

We should be peaceful, law-abiding—but the time has come
to fight back in self-defense whenever and wherever [the black
man] is being unjustly and unlawfully attacked. If the government thinks I am wrong for saying this, then let the government
start doing its job.

Malcolm's many speeches clearly told Americans that we
must make up for past inequities. And people must understand in the language of the ghetto what "off the pig"
means.

"Off the Pig" started being used widely when the people,
black and white, were all demonstrating at the trial of
brother Huey P. Newton. It meant essentially "don't exe-
cute Huey," don't try to put him in the gas chamber. Put the
"pig" in the gas chamber for murdering black people. We
also wanted community control of police. "We'll patrol
ourselves," we said. So at the demonstrations during Huey's
trial there was a song, "No more pigs in our community/Off
the Pig/It's time to pick up the gun."

Motherfucker and Mothafucka': Motherfucker is a very
common expression nowadays. Eldridge ran it down to me

once after a number of people got upset over this vernacular of the ghetto. Eldridge said: "I've seen and heard brothers use the word four and five times in one sentence and each time the word had a *different* meaning and expression."

Motherfucker actually comes from the old slave system and was a reference to the slave master who raped our mothers which society today doesn't want to face as a fact. But today, check the following sentence:

"Man, let me tell you. This motherfucker here went down there with his motherfucking gun, knocked down the motherfucking door and blew this motherfucker's brains out. This shit is getting to be a motherfucker."

With the rising consciousness of black people learning about Black History in general, many black youth have a tendency to say in reference to a person they may dislike, "The dirty mother . . ." dropping the fucker part. But historically black men know black women have been oppressed and when we use the word we don't mean that a man has had sexual relations with his mother. This never enters into a black brother's mind. But it can be said in anger to mean just that, and the sayer knows it is completely from the truth, referring to the white exploiters and slavers in history.

Today, one can use the word refer to a friend or someone he respects for doing things he never thought could be done by a black man. In the past, the white man has always been the one who has done fantastic things. Raping our mothers was fantastically derogatory. Well, it's kind of a real complimentary statement to a brother or even a sister when one vicariously relates to someone who's black and pulls a fantastic feat. We will joyfully say, "Man, he's a motherfucker."

The racism and oppression of black people, from history to this very day, has caused this word "motherfucker" to be part of the vernacular of the ghetto. White boys have picked it up from black people, but without the different meanings as they have developed up to the day. It so happens that the lumpen proletarian, the brother off the block who comes into the Party, speaks this vernacular. But Huey was one not to use it much at all. He says people, especially the older people, won't listen to the real program of the Party if we use street language. Eldridge says that if we have to use it, use it in reference to the avaricious and demagogic politicians who oppress us, because when they murder a brother or sister, then it makes us mad at the racist. And use it in reference to sadistic pigs who at least need cursing out for what they are: oppressors, murderers, rapers of justice and peace in our society.

I say that we shouldn't curse at all, although after I went in to the U.S. Air Force for four years and was cursed out by instructors in basic training, I picked it up by being around G.I.'s so much. I left the service cursing the military, and my mother resents it today. So, it's a tough habit to get rid of, being still oppressed, but a habit we must get rid of. Huey says that even when one of us gets murdered by the pigs, we must restrain and educate the people to the correct methods. I've been well criticized, as have Eldridge, David, and many other brothers. So, for the respect of the people, and our mothers, we're working to break the habit.

Signifying: Lying or putting someone down. Telling him lies about his friends or old lady. Trying to get him in trouble. "Joe said you were a punk," but Joe never actually said anything.

Vamp on: When a large group of police attack you and/or your friends and close associates. In the Party it directly refers to an unjust vicious attack, fascist in nature. It can also mean, on a lesser level, just being busted (arrested). But I've received many phone calls or messages such as the following: "The pigs vamped on the L.A. office."

Nigger: This term is not generally used derogatorily by black people to each other. There are a very few sensitive black people with self-hate still imbedded in them, who resent it when brothers and sisters are in a general conversation and in a very laughing atmosphere and say,

"Ha, ha, man. You niggers is crazy" or "Say, man, this nigger is outa sight." When we are disgusted with each other, we might say, "What's wrong with you niggers" but we aren't offended by another brother's use in this context because the use is in the context of some criticism and the criticism specifically is what we'll focus upon. College people and intellectuals have more self-hate, and they resent it most.

White people use it to mean that we are backwards, stupid, innately lazy—all the derogatory connotations that can be associated with the term. Webster's Dictionary never has given this term full meaning as it's colloquially used by both black and white people.

Bull: Prison guard or jail guard. In jail when the guards come around, the prisoners say, "Here come the police." Or a brother will also say "Police" real loud, in jail. This is subtle irony. When someone in jail and calls for the "police" he links the prison guards, the bailiffs, and the police together. But "bull" most specifically refers to the guard in prison who is circulating among the "chickens," he thinks. The men resent the guard acting like he is the head rooster on the farm trying to fuck everybody.

But we refer to them all as "pigs" when we become revolutionary. If the guard isn't trying to violate the prisoners' rights, he may be called "police." If he's trying to violate your rights like he does a lot of prisoners', he's a bull.

Field Nigger: As opposed to House Nigger. The slave in the field working was a good, hard-working black, a field nigger, and the slave in the master's house, a house nigger, was a no-good bastard or an Uncle Tom, and usually was more docile. He had an easy deal to lose if he didn't shuffle enough.

Fire on: In a fight, someone strikes you or you strike them with your fist, you "fire on" them.

Throwin' Iron: Lifting weights.

Knobs: Shoes that are considered sharp. They're usually soft, alligator, and expensive.

Pimp Socks: Thin men's dress nylon socks, with vertical patterns on them.

Right on: Right on time. Black people used to say "right on time" a long time ago. It is a shortened form of identifying something that's said or done as really true and really right. Relates to something that's really correct and not negative.

Deal with: Take time to think about and work with a situation. To attempt to resolve a situation that's bad, or negative, or just to go forth and complete something that needs to be done.

Kill: Kill in the language of black community does not mean murder, but always comes as a reaction to someone or something that is about to unjustly attack the person or threatens to unjustly attack them. You always find the word "kill" in very defensive language on the part of blacks.

Motherfucker, I'll kick your motherfucking ass *or* I'll beat your motherfucking brains in means more in terms of murder. "Kill" doesn't carry the same weight as "kick your ass" or "beat your brains in." But I've said, "kill" is generally used among blacks in a defensive manner, when a black person thinks that something wrong or unjust is going to be done to him or her.

Jackanape: A fool who is busted for smoking pot while selling *The Black Panther* or who pulls holdups while he is a member of the Black Panther Party. He is not looked upon as malicious or as a traitor to the Party. He is seen as someone who doesn't have enough discipline or brains to be in the Party, although he means well.

PARTY PROGRAMS—SERVING THE PEOPLE

■ In 1969, the Black Panther Party tried to reach millions of people, both to organize resistance to fascism and to find out about, and receive service from, the basic community programs that we have already set up and will be setting up in the future. This is what we call a broad, massive, people's type of political machinery. It developed out of the rising tide of fascism in America, the rapid attempt on the part of the power structure to try to wipe out the Black Panther Party and other progressive organizations, and the use of more troops and more police forces to occupy our communities.

The cops in Los Angeles and several other places have walked in on the Free Breakfast for Children Program to try to intimidate the children and the Party. They come down there with their guns, they draw a gun or two, say a few words and walk all over the place, with shotguns in their hands. Then the little kids go home and say, "Mama, the police came into the Breakfast for Children Program." This is the power structure's technique to try to destroy the program. It's an attempt to scare the people away from sending their children to the Breakfast Program and at the same time, trying to intimidate the Black Panther Party.

Meanwhile, through the politicians and the media they try to mislead the people about the value of such a program and the political nature of such a program. We say that we want that program, not just right now for some political purpose—we say that the program should survive right into the future for years and years. The Party's community programs are the peoples' programs that we define as revolutionary, community, socialistic programs.

A lot of people misunderstand the politics of these programs; some people have a tendency to call them reform programs. They're not reform programs; they're actually revolutionary community programs. A revolutionary program is one set forth by revolutionaries, by those who want to change the existing system to a better system. A reform program is set up by the existing exploitative system as an appeasing handout, to fool the people and to keep them quiet. Examples of these programs are poverty programs, youth work programs, and things like that which are set up by the present demagogic government. Generally they're set up to appease the people for a short period of time, and then are phased out and forgotten about.

The objective of programs set forth by revolutionaries like the Black Panther Party is to educate the masses of the people to the politics of changing the system. The politics are related to people's needs, to a hungry stomach, or to getting rid of the vicious pigs with their revolvers and clubs. The revolutionary struggle becomes bloody when the pig power structure attacks organizations or groups of people who go forth with these programs.

We started the Free Breakfast for Children Program by asking businessmen in the black community and outside of it, to donate food and money. We also moved to get as many other people in the community as possible to work on these programs and take over running them. The programs are generally started off in churches. In one case we actually got a Free Breakfast for Children going in the school itself, which was very, very good, because the school cafeteria facilities and everything were used; this was over in Marin County, north of San Francisco. We generally work out of churches because the churches all have facilities, like a large hall, a kitchen, tables and chairs, etc. Members of the Party get up early in the morning, at 6:00 A.M. to get down and begin preparing the food so when the kids start coming at 7:00 and 7:30, everything is ready. We also try to get as many people from the community to schedule themselves,

for one or two days out of the week to come in and work on
the Breakfast for Children Program. It has to be a very
organized thing so that it's speedy and at the same time the
children get good, wholesome breakfasts.

There are millions of people in this country who are
living below subsistence; welfare mothers, poor white people, Mexican-Americans, Chicano peoples, Latinos, and
black people. This type of program, if spread out, should
readily relate to the needs of the people. Donations of food
and money can be gotten from churches, stores, and companies. When the stores and milk companies don't donate,
people should leaflet the community. Any particular chain
foodstores that can't donate a small, small percentage of its
profits or one penny from every dollar it makes from the
community, to Breakfast for Children and other community
programs, should be boycotted. We don't ever threaten or
anything like that, but we tell the people in the community
that the businessman exploits them and makes thousands
and thousands of dollars, and that he won't donate to a
Breakfast for Children Program that's actually tax deducti-
ble. This is exposing the power structure for what it is, the
robbery of poor oppressed people by avaricious businessmen. Black, brown, and red people, and poor whites can all
have the same basic program, and that means we're breaking down racism and focusing in on the power structure.

Another program that we're setting up is free medicine
and free medical care. We'll be setting those up in community centers. If we start off with nothing more than a doctor
and his bag, and some aspirin, this is the beginning of a free
health clinic, the beginning of free medicine for the people
in the communities. We work to serve the people in the
communities on a very practical level.

Right in the Bay Area we have some twenty-five doctors
and medical students who've pledged their time to be scheduled in different community centers that we're putting up
and this will be free of charge. We have free health clinics

all over the country and we are putting more up, just as fast as the people can work with NCCF.

In addition, Charles R. Garry is contacting a lot of lawyers who are opening their eyes and beginning to see that the black community needs more legal aid. So we're putting together free legal services, which will also be set up in the community centers. The poverty programs that have free legal service are always told that they can't get funds if they're at all political. That's done so they won't expose the power structure and the injustices of the system. They only handle civil cases. Our legal aid will handle both civil and criminal cases.

Another thing we'll be doing is heavy voter registration. The purpose of this registration will be to get more black and poor people on the juries so we can really be tried in courts by juries of our peers. The D.A.'s will try to get all white racist juries or maybe to put one jive Uncle Tom on them, but it'll be much harder if a lot of blacks are registered and are on the jury panel that they pick from. Black people have to understand the experience of serving on juries because black people are railroaded in these courts. Poor oppressed people are railroaded in courts because they don't have funds to obtain lawyers. A lot of the older people are frightened or allow themselves to be frightened away from being jury members, and a lot of black people move around so much that they don't bother to re-register. It's a real problem, but we've got to educate the people to the fact that they should be on the rolls for jury duty. Then we can begin to get some revolutionary justice. Right now the type of so-called justice that's being meted out to a majority of the poor oppressed people is the "injustice" of racism and capitalistic exploitation.

The Black Panther Party has black caucuses, Black Panther caucuses in a number of unions, and we definitely are working with the union people. We're not putting in

Black Panther caucuses as racist groups. We're talking about a caucus that works in conjunction with the union to help educate the rest of the members of the union to the fact that they can have a better life, too. We want the workers to understand that they must control the means of production, and that they should begin to use their power to control the means of production to serve all the people.

Workers have high taxes taken away from their wages, but they should begin to understand that they have to move not only for a 15 or 20 percent wage raise, because taxes have gone up, and not only for better working conditions, but also because they have to realize the need to use their working power for the benefit of all the other poor oppressed people.

They should use their union power to create employment for more of the poor people throughout the country. We're advocating that workers begin to move to control the means of production by first demanding thirty-hour work weeks with the same forty-hour pay. By doing this, they will automatically open up more jobs. These jobs can be filled by poor, unemployed people. This would be part of the program of educating the masses of the workers to be a political force against the three levels of oppression—the avaricious, big-time, greedy businessmen, the demagogic politicians who lie and use the unions, and also the facist pig cops who have been used in the past and are used today to break up the workers' constitutional rights to strike and redress their grievances.

Employed or unemployed, workers must unite with each other and with the community. They should be registered voters, too, and serve on jury panels and circulate the community control of police petition, too.

Another Black Panther Party program is the Liberation Schools. These schools are held in the afternoons, along with the free breakfasts and free lunches. They're held in churches and the community centers. We see the Liberation Schools as a supplement to the existing institutions, which still teach racism to children, both white and black. The youth have to understand that the revolutionary struggle in this country that's now being waged is not a race struggle but a class struggle. This is what the Liberation Schools are all about.

We are working to show children that a person's skin color is not important, but in fact it's a class struggle against the avaricious businessman and the small ruling class who exploit us and perpetuate the racism that's rampant in our communities. When we teach Black American History, we teach it in terms of the class struggle, not in terms of a race struggle.

In New York we also started a free clothing program. Black Panther Party members went out and asked businessmen to donate sets of clothes, for school children on up to teenagers. We tried to get brand new clothing, because black people are tired of hand-me-downs. Some of the clothing was very good clothing that people never came back and picked up from dry cleaners. We got all kinds of clothing together, but our primary objective was to get free clothing for the people by asking the businessmen to donate two complete changes of clothes for children. This is especially important before school begins in September and in mid-term around January. When this free clothing program got kicked off, some five or six hundred black people in Harlem, mothers and welfare people, came down and got the clothing for their kids.

It takes a lot of work, and a lot of people donating time and funds to run these programs. The programs are not run by the fascist government at all. Naturally, these programs spread and as they begin to reach more and more people, the Party is moving closer and closer to implementing the ten-point platform and program of the Black Panther Party.

When we have community socialistic programs such as these, and move them to a real level where people actually begin to receive help from them, it shows the people that by unity, by working and unifying around such programs, we can begin to end the oppressive conditions.

The Black Panther Party is not stupid at all in understanding the politics of the situation. We understand that the avaricious, demagogic, ruling class will use racist police departments and mass media to distort the real objectives of the Black Panther Party. The more we're successful with the programs, the more we'll be attacked. We don't take guns with us to implement these programs, but we understand and know from our own history that we're going to be attacked, and that we have to be able to defend ourselves. They're going to attack us viciously and fascisticly and try to say it was all justifiable homicide, in the same manner they've always attacked black people in the black communities.

We also go forth to advocate the right to self-defense from unjust attacks by racist, fascist pigs. Even when the policemen come into our communities with guns and tanks and the National Guard, we have the right to self-defense. Brothers and sisters shouldn't riot in large numbers. They should work in small groups of three, four, and five, to fight back when they attack our communities with tanks and start blasting buildings away and killing people. When they come and occupy our community and start killing people, those brothers running in threes, fours, and fives are going to have to know how to stop those tanks and those guardsmen from brutalizing and killing and murdering us.

We aren't hungry for violence; we don't want violence. Violence is ugly, guns are ugly. But we understand that there are two kinds of violence: the violence that is perpetrated against our people by the fascist aggression of the power structure; and self-defense—a form of violence used to defend ourselves from the unjust violence that's inflicted upon us. The power structure metes this violence upon the Black Panther Party because we've implemented programs that are actually exposing the government, and they're being implemented and put together by a revolutionary political party.

The freeing of political prisoners is also on the program of the Black Panther Party, because we have now, at this writing, over 300 Black Panthers who have court cases that are pending. In addition there have been hundreds of arrests, unjust arrests of Party members, who were exercising their constitutional rights. We believe in exercising our constitutional rights of freedom of assembly, of freedom of the press (the Black Panther Party newspaper), our constitutional right to bear arms, to be able to defend ourselves when attacked, and all the others. So we've been arrested.

What has to be understood is that they intend to destroy our basic programs. This is very important to understand. The fact that they murder Black Panther Party members, conduct attacks and raids on our offices, arrest us and lie about us, is all an attempt to stop these basic programs that we're putting together in the community. The people learn from these programs because they're clear examples, and the power structure wants to stop that learning.

We do not believe in the power structure controlling these programs, but we do believe in making the power structure admit that it has to change the system, because we, the people, united and together, can begin to change our conditions ourselves. We have to move with the power of the people, with the workers and the laboring masses of the people, to have control of the means of production and make the power structure step back. We're going to have to defend ourselves with guns because we know we're going to be attacked and we know they're going to attempt to make more political prisoners.

Community control of police is the key. We've got to have community control of the police in every city where there exists police brutality, in every metropolis in America

where black people, Latino people, and Chinese people live
in large numbers. In all these cities, and where there are
progressive and liberal white people who are protesting,
police forces have been doubled, tripled, and quadrupled,
and fascist oppression has been meted out upon the heads of
all of us. The workers too are attacked and threatened by
police when they strike and protest over their conditions.

Our community control of the police campaign is a petition drive. Registered voters will sign the petition and will
vote into their city charters a new legal structure for the
police department. The people will be voting in a law that
says that all policemen who patrol the community, must live
in the community. They will be voting in a decentralized
police department.

We will have neighborhood divisions with neighborhood
councils, who are duly elected in the particular neighborhoods. We'll have two, three, four, and five police departments that work in conjunction together through the commissioners of particular neighborhood divisions, so there
will not be a single police chief. These commissioners can
be removed by the duly elected neighborhood councils. The
fifteen-man neighborhood councils will be able to appoint
and fire a commissioner, will be able to discipline police
officers who are unjust, or who get out of hand, and will be
able to set salaries and pay the police officers. The people
throughout the city will control the police, rather than the
power structure, the avaricious businessmen, and demagogic politicians who presently control them. The point of
community control of police is that those people living in
those neighborhoods will actually do the hiring and firing of
the policemen who patrol that area, and those policemen
will be people from those neighborhoods—black police for
a black neighborhood, Chinese for a Chinese neighborhood,
white for a white neighborhood, etc. The tax money which
used to be given to the central police department will be
divided up among the neighborhood divisions. All the facil-

ities, all the cars, all the equipment for the police that the city now owns, will be in the hands and in the control of the people in the community.

Now when this begins to move, the pig power structure is gonna say, "OK, you can have civilian review boards." But all that does is allow the same old fascist power structure to keep control of the police while you have a front civilian review board, and this is not what we're talking about at all. What we're talking about is righteous community control, where the people who control the police are elected by the people of the community. Those people who are elected have to live in the community. They can be removed by circulating petitions for re-elections if they go wrong. We know that such a program is very positive and necessary in order for the people to have power in this country and to stop the avaricious businessman from ruling us with guns and violating our constitutional rights.

Everybody knows that they lied about the way they murdered brother Fred Hampton, and then tried to justify it. Mitchell, Agnew, and Nixon are running an operation to wipe out the Black Panther Party behind the scenes, when they send the Civil Rights Division of the Justice Department in to investigate the slaying of brothers Fred Hampton and Mark Clark. We don't want them to investigate anything. We want the civilian and people's investigation to come forth. Thousands of people went in to the brother's apartment and investigated, and found out that it was outright murder; that there was no shoot-out, but the brothers in fact, were shot in their bedrooms while they slept. This is outright murder, this is outright fascism. The next attack was on the Los Angeles office, a few days later. Community control of police is where it's at. The only other choice is guerilla warfare.

Guerilla warfare is going to exist if the power structure is not stopped with community control of the police. One of the reasons the people have to work on the community control of police campaign is to curtail civil war in America, because it's at that point right now. Community control of police is one of the most functional and most necessary programs to make all the other basic community programs work.

SEIZE
THE TIME

■ The philosophy of the Black Panther Party is just beginning to be understood. In the future, the Party will continue to be a political party and a revolutionary organization. The Party's philosophy will be better understood when people see our objectives and the practical programs that we are setting forth and actually implementing.

People who think that the Black Panther Party is now destroyed have an erroneous view. The question always seems to arise because newsmen constantly ask, "Isn't the Party destroyed now?" As though some of them—not all of them—were wishing that this was so. This is the impression that the newspaper headlines have tried to convey. People have seen or read about attacks on us, about people getting arrested, and brothers and sisters getting killed and murdered by the fascist cops and criminal agents working for the avaricious, demagogic, oppressive, capitalistic, exploiting, racist elite.

From the very beginning, from May 2, 1967 when we went to the California State Capitol in Sacramento, people have read many outright lies and false statements in the media about our Party. The Establishment press has said that we were "hoodlums," "thugs," and "criminals." They have tried to gear people into thinking that sooner or later the Black Panther Party will be destroyed. But this is not

the case at all. The truth is just the opposite. From the time
we were erroneously arrested in Sacramento, the Party's
ideology has been constantly growing.

The sufferings of the older generations, our mothers and
fathers, and the historical experience of black people is
being translated into a practicing, on-going ideology for the
Black Panther Party. Our ideology is to be constantly moving, doing, solving, and attacking the real problems and the
oppressive conditions we live under, while educating the
masses of the people. This is what we try to do, and this is
how we move to make the basic political desires and needs
of the people realized.

In a *Playboy* interview in the fall of 1968, Eldridge
Cleaver very profoundly and very concretely spoke about
the kind of society we'd like to live in one day. Eldridge's
concept of the future is very relevant to our lives today, as
relevant as it will be in the future. It relates to what the
economic situation is today, what oppression is, and to what
the existence of fascism will mean if it is not stopped by the
masses of the people, and by the rising up of youth—Afro-
American youth, Chicano and Latino youth, poor white
youth, American Indians and Asian-American youth, and
by progressive, liberal, and revolutionary white youth.

The youth of America are the new. I'm thirty-three years
old now, and Eldridge Cleaver is going on thirty-five. You
might have heard us say at one time that everybody over
thirty was out of it. We knew at that time, of course, that
Malcolm X was not out of it even though he was close to
forty years old. Malcolm was really into it. His ideas didn't
freeze up on him at an early age, but unfortunately he was
murdered.

Huey P. Newton, the leader and Minister of Defense of
the Black Panther Party was only twenty-four years old
when we formed the Party, and Huey was only nineteen
when I first met him. Some of the things I spoke about in
Huey's past happened to him before he was nineteen. We
realize that the world will be changed and molded by the

youth, because we know that today over half of the American people are under twenty-five, and a larger percentage is under thirty.

The greatest danger facing young people right now is the coming of a fascist state, like the one described by George Orwell in *1984,* where Big Brother is always watching you. In a few years, that book might be history. We must look into history and see it as being concretely related to the problems of today. In turn, we will find a lamp of truth by which we can guide our feet to oppose the fascist *1984*-type state that's rapidly coming into power in this country. That is why the racists and the narrow-minded chauvinists do not want black people, Chicano people, Puerto Rican, Asian, and poor white people to study and know their own true history—because their history will tell the truth about America today.

This is why our free health clinics, Liberation Schools, and our Breakfast for Children programs are so significant. They are a means to serve, educate, unify, and organize our people, to organize the youth, and let them know that in this time, in our time, we must seize our right to live, and we must seize our right to survive.

The youth are a vast reservoir of revolutionary potential. The lumpen proletarian brothers on the block, the sisters, and everybody in the streets who are trying to make it, are part of this reservoir which one day will overflow and come forth like a wild, rushing stream. The desire and the need for a revolutionary movement is manifested in the people. The future of the Black Panther Party is the future of the people, and the youth is the future of the Black Panther Party.

When Huey P. Newton put the Black Panther Party together and began to do something about the problems that existed, he was seizing the time. The Young Patriots, the Young Lords, Los Siete de la Raza, and many other radical and revolutionary groups are now beginning to seize the time and do something about the wretched conditions that exist, the poverty that exists, and the unjust wars that are waged in the world. The whole future must be directly related to what we, the people, want, not to the way the old fools, the backward ignoramuses want things to be. We must all start seeing ourselves beginning to seize the time. We must start coming forth with our energies, our thoughts, our intellects, and our abilities to begin to see what is right and what must be done, so the suffering will stop, and the phrase "life, liberty, and the pursuit of happiness" begins to make some human sense.

The Nixon-Agnew-Mitchell administration—hand in hand with the Reagans, the Daleys, the Hoffmans, the Carswells, Rockefellers, DuPonts, the Bank of America, and other exploiters—moves closer and closer to open fascism. The future of the Black Panther Party will be directly related to the smashing of the fascist state, and the smashing of the fascist regime. Every time the avaricious, demagogic ruling class gets down wrong on the people, violating their constitutional human rights, it's necessary for the youth of America, the revolutionaries, to move forth and jump on their asses. Every time we see a young child in the black community shot down by some racist pig policeman, it's necessary to use some kind of organized force against the pigs in a way that teaches them that the people are tired of that crap. Every time we see the power structure moving in a way which we know is wrong and against the progress of humanity, we must move to let them know that we're not going for any more of their shit.

We always prefer to move in a non-antagonistic fashion, but when the power structure moves against people in an antagonistic manner, and unjustly attacks them—whether they attack them in Alabama, Mississippi, New York, Chicago, San Francisco, Los Angeles, Oakland, Berkeley, or anywhere else in the country—it's necessary for the youth of America to resist them, and move things from a lower to a higher level, bust the Nixon-Agnew-Mitchell regime in their asses, and let them know the struggle is here.

At the same time, it is necessary for young people to know that we must use organized and practical techniques. We cannot let ourselves continue to be oppressed on a massive scale. We are not trying to be supermen, because we are not supermen. We are fighting for the preservation of life. We refuse to be brainwashed by comic-book notions that distort the real situation. The only way that the world is ever going to be free is when the youth of this country *moves* with every principle of human respect and with every soft spot we have in our hearts for human life, in a fashion that lets the pig power structure know that when people are racistly and fascistically attacked, the youth will put a foot in their butts and make their blood chill.

We look around in the world today, and we look around at home right now, and we see that oppression exists. We know that the workers are exploited, and that most of the people in this country are exploited, in one way or another. We know that as a people, we must seize our time.

Huey P. Newton seized the time when he moved and put the Black Panther Party into motion. Other brothers and sisters in the Party are continually seizing the time. The time is *now* to wage relentless revolutionary struggle against the fascist, avaricious, demagogic ruling class and their low-life, sadistic pigs. Power to the People! Seize the Time!

March 5, 1970

Publisher's Note

This book derives from tape recordings made by Bobby Seale
in the early fall of 1968 and the fall and winter of 1969–1970.
The first series was made with the cooperation of the editors
of *Ramparts* magazine. The second series was made in the San
Francisco County Jail. Art Goldberg, formerly an editor of
Ramparts, was responsible for the editing of the transcribed
tapes; however, Mr. Seale supervised the preparation of the final
manuscript and every word is his.

Eldridge Cleaver, David Hilliard, Robert Scheer, Charles R.
Garry, general counsel to the Black Panther Party, Laura Fur-
man, and John Simon were of assistance at various stages. The
editors of *Ramparts* provided the initial stimulus and encourage-
ment for this book. They have been cooperative throughout the
entire process of its writing and publishing. To them the author
and publisher wish to express their gratitude.

The author and publisher also wish to thank Carole Jones,
Vicky Arbas, Candy Yockey, Rose Mary Gross, Sheila Hill,
Luise Vorsatz, Kathy Bailey, Carole Kurtz, Sally Greenawalt,
Joy Schneider, Phineas Israeli, John Jacobsen, Karen Horo-
witz, Hilary Maddux, Larry Bensky, Susanne English Conley,
Big Man, and Linda Morse for typing and for editorial assistance
with the manuscript.